"THE BEST MEN"

"The Best Men"

Liberal Reformers in the Gilded Age

JOHN G. SPROAT

OXFORD UNIVERSITY PRESS
LONDON   OXFORD   NEW YORK

OXFORD UNIVERSITY PRESS

Oxford London New York
Glasgow Toronto Melbourne Wellington
Cape Town Salisbury Ibadan Nairobi Lusaka Addis Ababa
Bombay Calcutta Madras Karachi Lahore Dacca
Kuala Lumpur Hong Kong Tokyo

For my Mother
Grace Elwell Sproat

Preface

Historians of post-Civil War America once had some difficulty in fitting liberal reformers into narratives dominated by slippery politicians and vulgar entrepreneurs, or by bedeviled farmers and workers. Often the "best men"—the intellectuals, the men of substance and breeding, the voters of independent political disposition—seemed almost to be exiles in their own land, watching in impotent dismay as their countrymen gorged themselves at the "great barbecue." Scholarship of more recent vintage has by now persuaded us that the Gilded Age, with all its glaring faults, was not simply an orgy of self-indulgence, that it was also an era of profound and fascinating change in every area of American life. The politicians and tycoons—even the gamblers and the vulgarians —emerge today as figures we can accept and understand, if not admire, within the context of their times.

The recent surge of interest in the Gilded Age has taught us much about liberal reformers, too. Geoffrey Blodgett, Alexander B. Callow, Jr., Vincent P. De Santis, Ari Hoogenboom, James M. McPherson, David Montgomery, Robert P. Sharkey, Irwin Unger, and Kermit Vanderbilt, in particular, have looked critically at reformers and at issues in need of reform, and they have provided new insights into the changes and dislocations within late-nineteenth-century society. My footnotes, I trust, suggest the extent of my debt to their scholarship; certainly their work made my own investigation far easier than would otherwise have been the case.

My purpose in this book is to examine in some detail the liberal reformers as a distinct group, as a social and political movement in American life, from the uncertain days of Reconstruction to the decisive decade of the 1890's. If the story ultimately is one of frustration and failure, if it occasionally shows an ugly side of men who were basically decent, hopefully it also tells something about the limited nature of reform in America and about the difficulty of maintaining standards of moral conduct in a society enchanted by "progress." Perhaps, too, it reminds us that our own restless time of change and social upheaval is not really very far removed from the Gilded Age and its problems.

A traveling fellowship from the University of California enabled me to lay the groundwork of research for this study. Later, President Emeritus James Phinney Baxter, III, and the Trustees of Williams College provided me with several generous grants for research and writing. Major General U. S. Grant, III, kindly permitted me to examine certain of his grandfather's papers in the Library of Congress. Among the librarians whose assistance greatly facilitated my work, I am especially grateful to those at the University of California at Berkeley, the Massachusetts Historical Society, Harvard University, the Boston Public Library, the Staten Island Institute of Arts and Sciences, the New York Public Library, the manuscripts and newspapers divisions of the Library of Congress, the Rutherford B. Hayes Memorial Library, the State Historical Society of Wisconsin, the Stetson Library at Williams College, and the Donnelley Library at Lake Forest College.

While I naturally assume responsibility for the accuracy and validity of the material in this book, I am deeply grateful to the many friends and colleagues whose criticisms and suggestions helped to shape and reshape my thinking about the "best men." As a wise mentor and warm friend, Kenneth M. Stampp gave me advice and encouragement at every step in the preparation of this study. His intellectual integrity has been an inspiration to me; his apparently limitless patience has awed me. For her help and encouragement, I am profoundly grateful to Jeanne Nichols

Marengo. On a memorable cross-country trip, Henry F. May gave me the benefit of his informed views on liberalism and reform in American history. John Hope Franklin graciously read some of my early work with his usual percipience. Two uncommonly wise and kind scholars, Carl Bridenbaugh and Henry Nash Smith, gave me good, sharp criticism in matters of content and style, while providing me also with the kind of rare intellectual stimulation that stays with one for life. The late Stanley Pargellis, then director of the Newberry Library, talked with me at length about the nature of liberalism and directed me to useful sources. I am grateful to Sheldon Meyer and Caroline Taylor of Oxford University Press for their intelligent and considerate editing. A fruitful conversation with Herbert and Judith Gutman produced a long-sought title. At Williams College, Robert C. L. Scott was unfailingly generous with good advice and help. For encouragement, scholarly and otherwise, I am grateful to my good friend Leon F. Litwack—and to his Rhoda. My colleague at Lake Forest College, Arthur Zilversmit, cordially endured the ordeal of reading raw manuscript and never allowed our friendship to blunt his sharpness as a discerning critic.

Barbara literally grew up with this book, sharing her father's unpredictable moods with a devoted child's wonderfully encouraging assumption that things will come out right in the end. Finally, for her loving confidence, her gentle and necessary prodding, and her fine critical sense, I offer my heartfelt thanks to Ruth, my rare "best woman."

J. G. S.

Lake Forest, Illinois
August 1968

Contents

Contents

"THE BEST MEN"

I

The Nature of Liberal Reform

Nevertheless we shall go ahead and you need not be surprised to hear that we have covered ourselves with eternal ridicule by some new absurd failure, or have subsided into nothing for sheer feebleness, or have actually effected a brilliant coup, *brought our man in as President, and are the rulers of forty million people. Such is the chaotic condition of our politics that any of these results is possible. Of course it indicates that our whole political fabric is out of joint and running wild, but so it is. My scheme is to organize a party of the centre and to support the party which accepts our influence most completely. But I doubt whether we can absolutely overthrow both parties as many of our ardent friends seem almost inclined to try doing.*

HENRY ADAMS, 1875

BEFORE THE LIBERALISM OF OUR TIME AMERICA KNEW another form of liberalism. Historians refer to the earlier version as classical liberalism, and some have argued that it was really conservatism and should not be called liberalism at all. But during the Gilded Age, classical liberalism was still pre-eminently the liberalism of the intellectuals and leading opinion-makers, and its precepts were still the commandments in political economy for most middle-class Americans. If these commandments were often ignored or disobeyed, it was less because people found satisfactory substitutes for them than because the rules became increasingly difficult to apply in a society undergoing an industrial revolution. Even as its doctrines became outmoded and discredited, classical liberalism remained for most people the ideal explanation of the Nature of Things. Not until well into the twentieth century, when the middle class shifted its loyalties to doctrines of a different sort, did classical liberalism become part of a nostalgic, essentially conservative outlook.

To be sure, men of conservative temper and tastes in the late 1860's and 1870's often thought of themselves as classical liberals, doubtless because they found orthodox political economy congenial to their interests and because traditional conservatism had little to offer them at the time. Burkean conservatism, as Russell Kirk notes, went down with the Old South and suffered a long eclipse;

and certainly the blunt pragmatism of the business community in general, until the 1890's at least, was a far thing from traditional conservatism. Unless one chose to preach one's cause to a select few in a secluded drawing room, it was difficult to be a traditional conservative in those years—difficult, that is, if one wished to play a meaningful role in society and politics. Almost by default, classical liberalism had to occupy both the "center" and the "right" in the political-economic spectrum, serving somewhat awkwardly as a conservative link with the past and an inadequate guide to the future. Because the line between conservatism and liberalism was thinly drawn in America, the position was not an altogether incongruous one, although it did create moral and intellectual problems for men who thought of themselves as liberals.[1]

As for the "left" on the spectrum, neither the idealistic radicalism of the Social Gospel and the ethical reformers, nor the social science of the new academicians, nor the more earthy populism of the farmers and labor had sufficient appeal during the Gilded Age to displace traditional liberalism among members of the middle class. Notwithstanding its growing infatuation with democracy, America still displayed certain characteristics of a deferential society; and any new liberalism, to bring about a displacement of the old, would first have to gain acceptance among the intellectuals and moralists who instructed the average American in the matter of which opinions were "respectable" and which were not. Classical liberalism, to be sure, lost its hold on the people by the decade of the 1890's; but it is significant that not until late in the Progressive Era did politicians and reformers restore the term "liberal" to general usage.[2] By then, of course, liberalism had become a different creed from that championed in the nineteenth century by E. L. Godkin and Carl Schurz.

For dedicated liberals in the Gilded Age the task of representing both the "center" and the "right" was a difficult one. With almost all other Americans, they shared a sweeping optimism, stemming from the national infatuation with progress and the perfectibility of man. Who in America could reject the future or deny the inevitability of national greatness? At the same time, the spokesmen for liberalism had a deep and abiding respect for tradition and the achievements of the past.

Early in the Gilded Age most liberals were optimists, confident that the Civil War had been a creative national experience rather than a sterile national disaster. Through some strange alchemy, the conflict had given Americans at last a sense of purpose, uniting them behind principles of equality and individual freedom, imbuing them with high moral principles, ennobling them with a patriotism that only trial by battle could engender. The war had seemed to Charles Francis Adams, for one, a sublime spectacle of "the popular will acting energetically and unitedly in execution of a specific purpose." [3] Adams and his friends were sure that a period of greatness would follow the bloody struggle to achieve unity and equality.

But the nation that emerged from the war disappointed many liberals with its "hollowness at heart," as Whitman put it, and its contempt for the kind of patriotism liberals were sure had justified the conflict. Liberalism postulated a harmonious society of free individuals; but postwar America seemed to be a society rent with factionalism that threatened to become anarchy. Liberalism taught that scientific truths and democratic politics could be reconciled; but few Gilded Age politicians seemed interested in learning any truth at all, much less in squaring it with their behavior. Somehow, somewhere, things had gone wrong, the equilibrium had been upset; and only by restoring the liberal ideal of a natural balance in society could the political and economic system itself be saved. It was to this task that liberal reformers dedicated themselves.

As temperate critics they looked to moderate, well-considered reforms as solutions to the problem. They had little sympathy for labor's grievances, or the farmers' predicament. Their special fears concerned corruption in politics and business, extravagant government, excessive taxation, and the general breakdown of order and morality in society. For the abuses that offended them they proposed the simple remedies of "good government," economic orthodoxy, and moral rejuvenation. Put "good men" into positions of responsibility and power, they urged. Revive the Jeffersonian regard for limited government; respect and defend the tested Christian moral precepts and apply them to everyday affairs, as well as to government; trust in the "natural laws" of political economy to right the economic wrongs of the day. Only through dedication to a program of such liberal reforms, they insisted, could Americans preserve their nation's reputation as a stronghold of opportunity and individual freedom, a bulwark against despotism.

2

Liberal reform was pre-eminently the instrument of the "best men" in American society after the Civil War—the men of breeding and intelligence, of taste and substance. As Henry Adams told his brother during the war, "We want a national set of young men like ourselves or better, to start new influences not only in politics, but in literature, in law, in society, and throughout the whole social organism of the country—a national school of our own generation." [4] Although Adams's "school" never emerged in a formal sense, an aristocracy of brains, education, and talent—of which all the Adamses were obviously members—did offer its services to society. Liberal reform enjoyed the support of leading academicians and professional men, influential journalists, several important politicians, and a sizable number of businessmen whose self-interests often coincided with their reformist ideals. Although not all liberal reformers were intellectuals, they were intellectually oriented as a group and shared a social outlook that set them off from other reformers of the day. Certainly no other group of men had better intellectual and moral equipment to deal with the problems of the Gilded Age.

Among political leaders who worked for liberal reform were Carl Schurz, Abram Hewitt, Lyman Trumbull, Samuel J. Tilden, George F. Edmunds, and George W. Julian. Presidents Hayes and Garfield often supported liberal reform, and Grover Cleveland ultimately became its national champion. As ambitious young men, Theodore Roosevelt and Henry Cabot Lodge for a time flirted seriously with liberal reform, before moving on to a more pragmatic political position in the twentieth century. Charles Eliot Norton, William Dean Howells, Thomas Wentworth Higginson, and, in a half-tutored way, Mark Twain, were among the distinguished men of letters who spoke out for liberal reform at one time or another. At Williams College, isolated in the mountains of western Massachusetts, Mark Hopkins and Arthur Latham Perry taught and preached its tenets so effectively that at least two dozen Williams men later became prominent spokesmen for liberal reform.[5] Simon Newcomb and David A. Wells, both nominal natural scientists, worked energetically to promote orthodoxy in political economy, as did such successful businessmen as Edward Atkinson, John Murray Forbes, Henry Villard, and A. T. Stewart. Moreover, liberal reform claimed the sympathy of many businessmen and other citizens who did not take part in the everyday work of reform.

A handful of gifted journalists and publicists doubtless gave liberal reform its vitality as a factor in public affairs. George William Curtis, Edwin L. Godkin, Samuel Bowles, Horace White, Wendell P. Garrison, and Joseph Medill, among others, kept the demands of the reformers constantly before the public, and used their talents as commentators and polemicists to strike at the enemies of the "best men." Godkin's magazine, *The Nation,* spoke for more liberal reformers than any other journal of the time, although probably *The North American Review* and *Harper's Weekly* reached more readers. All three journals were "house organs" for the "party of the centre," with *The Nation,* especially, providing liberals with a clearing house for their views and a forum for their demands. Reviewing his many years as Godkin's assistant, Wendell P. Garrison once noted that *The Nation* drew its "intellectual and moral support" from a great body of "enlightened and humane men and women." Indeed, over the years, readers of the journal came to think of themselves as distinct *"Nation* men," linked by bonds of intellectual and moral congeniality. Above all else, as Garrison noted, the *"Nation* man" stood for "something definite in the social order." Indeed, *The Nation* was a periodical made to order for the "best men." [6]

Aside from their confidence that they were truly the "best men," liberal reformers shared other characteristics that gave them recognizable identity among dissenters in the Gilded Age. Their political economy was orthodox liberalism, idealistic and sternly inflexible. It had roots in England, where economic thinkers had identified, to their own satisfaction, a body of "natural laws" that regulated man's behavior in the market. Based on laissez-faire, English liberalism had a strong appeal among American businessmen and intellectuals, because it seemed to complement this country's traditions of property rights and individual freedom. Moreover, like most reformers, nineteenth-century American liberals were philosophical determinists. With Marx—although they naturally detested and feared him—they believed economic interests determined man's actions and that the science of economics was composed simply of a body of immutable laws. Unlike Marx, they made no provision in their economic philosophy for historical evolution. No dialectical process cluttered their thinking, for they viewed the "natural laws" of political economy as fixed precepts beyond the reach of either man or history. They had their stern prophets—Smith, Ricardo, Mill, Bastiat; but they had, too, the American's belief in the inherent goodness of man, and that, for a time at least, tempered their rigid economic determinism.

Their moral code, grounded firmly in the Protestant tradition, gave them the criteria by which they judged public questions and political candidates. Liberal reformers typically sought to convince businessmen that respect for traditional moral values produced material rewards as well as spiritual satisfaction. Only through moral rejuvenation, they insisted, could the United States fulfill its destiny.

Liberal reformers glorified the independent man in politics, the man who refused to permit the base spirit of party to corrupt his individual judgment. Political independence, their favorite weapon for attacking abuses, enabled them to shift their support from one party to another without submitting to the demands of party discipline or experiencing the qualms of disloyalty to any party. As Henry Adams proposed, they acted as an informal "party of the centre" in postwar politics, working to play off the two major parties against each other and to force one or the other to accept their demands as part of its program.[7]

Finally, the liberals' entire approach to reform was one of moderation; or, as Grover Cleveland observed, of "safe, careful, and deliberate reform." [8] They wished to reform only in the sense of restoring certain conditions of the past or of mildly amending certain new and disturbing developments. There was nothing remotely revolutionary about them, for they had no quarrel with capitalism or the industrial revolution, and they were uncompromising defenders of private property. They wanted no fundamental changes in the nature of American government, beyond enjoining the "irresponsible" elements in society from exercising an undue or dominant influence in legislative affairs. As a group, they possessed the broad, beneficent view of human affairs common to all liberals—at least until human affairs seemed to them to be falling into the hands of demagogues and miscreants. Early in the Gilded Age their favorite targets were irresponsible men of wealth whose ruthless pursuit of money impressed them as a threat to the fundamental moral bases of society. Later in the period, their enemies were the irresponsible men of "communistic" inclinations, whose wild-eyed schemes to interfere in the Nature of Things seemed to threaten the fundamental economic bases of society. Caught between two extremes in American society, they deplored all extremism. In all their attacks they sought to avoid precipitate action or surrender to base passion; both, they believed, would engender nothing but further threats to the nation's economic and political stability.

Reform was a tedious, irksome business, but it was the responsibility, the public duty of all right-thinking men. Without the active participation of the "best men," liberal reformers warned, reform would fail and the abuses in society would become stepping-stones to power for demagogues, time-serving politicians, and radical agitators of all sorts. "Most reformers prefer mounting a little mule," Godkin once observed, "arming themselves with some not generally accepted weapon, called a 'new idea,' and starting off on their own hook, spying out the land, exchanging shots and epithets with the enemy, and shouting out from every rising ground glorious accounts of what they see ahead." Well-founded reform, he noted, summarizing his own reform ideals, resulted only from the dedicated actions of the public-spirited man "who keeps his place in line on the day of battle, takes his turn of outpost duty, and is ready for all the obscure and inglorious duties of the service." [9]

Involving themselves in every major issue from Reconstruction to the economic crisis of the 1890's, liberal reformers tried hard to live up to their own lofty concepts of the reformer's role in a democratic society. How well they succeeded is the question explored here.

2

Retreat to Reform

If we were to remove our troops today, the Southern States would swim in blood tomorrow. I am expressing convictions based on experience when I say, that the only high light in this dark picture is the conduct of the negro.

CARL SCHURZ, 1865

Look a moment at the South. By the sudden emancipation and enfranchisement of 4,000,000 slaves a social revolution was thrust upon the South. . . . "Negro supremacy" became the horror, the nightmare, of the Southern people, and, naturally, justly so.

CARL SCHURZ, 1890

It is the opinion of the wisest Republicans in Mississippi of both races that it is best for the State that the Negroes should not vote, and outsiders may well accept their judgment as to the matter.

The Nation, 1892

TWENTY YEARS AFTER THE CIVIL WAR, GEORGE W. JULIAN of Indiana recalled bitterly the turn of politics that, during the era of Reconstruction, had lost him his seat in Congress. "While the issues of the war were retreating into the past," he charged, "the mercenary element of Republicanism had gradually secured the ascendancy, and completely appropriated the President." [1]

Julian had reason to complain. By the time General Grant took up residence in the White House, the Republican party's roster of leaders included few names of antislavery lineage. Thaddeus Stevens was gone, dead after losing his historic battle against Andrew Johnson. Although Charles Sumner still sat in the Senate, the new party leaders had remorselessly stripped him of his power. Julian lost his seat in the House of Representatives in 1870, and most of the other old abolitionist and Radical Republican politicians were dead, dying, or defeated. But Julian was wrong when he wrote in 1884 that his enemies, the "mercenary Republicans," had come to power gradually. "Mercenary Republicanism" had shown its teeth and flexed its muscles many times in the economic legislation passed during the war—legislation to which most abolitionists and liberal Union men had given their support, albeit often reluctantly.

Antislavery Radicals had long underestimated the political

strength of those Republican politicians who, even during the war, symbolized the influence of big business in the party. Like Julian, many failed to realize what had happened until Grant took office. By then, Grant's Stalwart supporters were demonstrating, with deeds as well as with words, that they considered themselves the managers of the Republican party. Roscoe Conkling, Zachariah Chandler, Simon Cameron, Oliver P. Morton, George S. Boutwell: these men were representative of the forces now in control of Congress. On occasion, they still referred to themselves as Radical Republicans; but with Grant in office their Radicalism more and more became a convenient toga to don only during election campaigns. Once a vital, commanding force in American politics, capable of driving Presidents to distraction and Southern whites to fears of a social revolution, the Radical Republican coalition disintegrated rapidly after the failure of its boldest thrust, the impeachment of Andrew Johnson.

2

Perhaps the coalition's heterogeneous nature and the conditional commitment of certain of its elements foredoomed it to ultimate failure. Agrarians and industrialists, liberal idealists and economic opportunists, artful politicians and political reformers—all somehow found a place in the faction during the war and early years of Reconstruction. Some Radicals called themselves free-traders and loathed the protectionists in the coalition. Others were inflationists, diametrically opposed to the "sound money" views of most Republicans. Many Radicals, committed to the economic orthodoxy of Manchester liberalism, feared the trend toward centralized government and concentration of power implicit in the Republican party's wartime program. Yet, the specter of a "Southern menace" held the coalition together far longer than logic would have dictated. From the gloomy early months of the war, when Radicals taught the compelling good sense of transforming slavery into a weapon in the Union arsenal, to the muddled years of the Johnson administration, when presidential ineptitude combined with Southern defiance to make a "thorough" program of Reconstruction acceptable even to men of studied moderation, the coalition clustered around a single standard, its Southern policy. As it turned out, the Reconstruction issue was much too complex and divisive to allow the "Southern menace" to serve as a base from which the coalition could mature into a permanent political entity.

Ironically, the first signs of serious dissension within Radical ranks appeared among the abolitionists. William Lloyd Garrison, by 1865 grown old and cautious, looked upon the Thirteenth Amendment as signaling the end of antislavery as well as of slavery. Earlier he had indicated his reluctance to extend the abolitionist crusade into a fight for Negro suffrage. Universal suffrage might come to pass, he thought, but only after a generation or two; during that time Negroes would prepare themselves to use the vote intelligently and Southern whites would accustom themselves to the idea. Garrison actually had never been more than a lukewarm Radical. Disdaining political action as a vehicle for moral reform, he had remained aloof from the Radical Republican efforts on behalf of Negroes during the war. By 1864 he stood in direct opposition to his friend and co-worker Wendell Phillips. The war had taught Phillips the value of political action and had made him a militant member of the Republican party. Emancipation was for him but the first battle in the struggle for equal rights, a struggle that would end only when Negroes were assured of absolute equality and freedom of opportunity.

Throughout the last year of the war the two great reformers battled for control of the Massachusetts Antislavery Society, with Phillips slowly but inexorably emerging as the stronger of the two. An open breach finally occurred at the meeting of the American Antislavery Society in May 1865. Garrison was ready to dissolve the organization; Phillips was not. After a bitter debate that shattered the friendship of the two men, the Society voted against Garrison. Some months later the last issue of the *Liberator* appeared, but the *National Anti-Slavery Standard,* under Phillips's hand, continued to circulate as an organ of Radical Reconstruction and reform.[2]

Many of Garrison's contemporaries shared his libertarian approach to the postwar problems of the Negro. Antebellum reformers had considered Emancipation a legitimate goal, because slavery mocked the natural laws in which they believed so firmly. Slavery interfered with freedom of the individual, slaveholder as well as slave, and negated the principle of equality. Few had been prepared to go as far as Garrison (and, for a time, Phillips) in condemning the Union of North with South as an agreement with hell, but some reformers had been willing to let the South secede in peace in order to rid the nation of slavery's scourge. Once they gained the great victory of Emancipation, many abolitionists were chary of further efforts on behalf of the Negro—efforts which surely would involve special legislation and the use of police power to benefit a special group. Actions of this sort, too, would interfere with the freedom of the individual.

Essentially, the battle against slavery had been one of good against evil. Garrison's son said that his father spoke always as a moralist, never as an abolitionist. Entering the crusade actively in 1856, George William Curtis denounced slavery as "against nature, against reason, against the human instinct, against the divine law," and cursed it as an institution "the most dreadful that philosophy contemplates or the imagination conceives." After Emancipation the choice was between the evil of Southern subversion of Negro freedom and the evil of government interference. Moral reformers were loath to choose between the two. Indeed, their fear of paternalism and government intrusion in matters of individual conscience was a heavy drag on Radical Reconstruction, and, in the 1870's, this fear made it easier for some Radicals to abandon the undertaking completely. Garrison expressed their doubts well: "While I am solicitous to maintain, uncompromisingly, all the principles I have advocated for the last thirty years, I am equally anxious to be entirely just to all men and all parties, in connection with the new order of things." [3]

Richard Hofstadter has observed that most Garrisonian abolitionists were so circumscribed by rigid moral imperatives that they were "driven inward intellectually," isolating themselves from the economic and political currents of mid-century America.[4] Emancipation and the end of the war left them dry of new ideas. It was not merely that they were intolerant of new approaches to postwar problems; more often, they were quite unconscious of the changed conditions around them.

Wendell Phillips was an exception. A product of the same moral ferment that produced Garrison, this Boston aristocrat emerged from the abolitionist crusade with a deeper understanding of the transformations wrought by the war. No sooner had Emancipation been proclaimed than Phillips was speaking out for Negro suffrage and economic equality for the freedmen. Often his demands for displacing the old Southern ruling class seemed to coincide with the interests of the representatives of industrialism in the Radical coalition. But Phillips was never a conscious spokesman for the new capitalism, to whose ramifications he later turned his reformer's zeal. He envisioned a reconstructed South in which the Negroes and poor whites would achieve economic as well as political independence. One of the few Radical Republicans who remained true to his radicalism, he came closest to attaining his goals for the South during the years of congressional Reconstruction. Southern contrariness then seemed to vindicate his demand for strong measures. That his proposal for redistributing the land in the South did not survive the attacks of economic conservatives was not due to any reluctance of his to publicize it. Indeed, it is more likely that he alienated much of the meager support confiscation could claim by his candor in discussing the subject. Restraint was not one of Wendell Phillips's talents.

Standing somewhere between the passive Garrison and the militant Phillips were other reformers who classified themselves, sometimes reluctantly, as Radicals. Cautious in politics and orthodox in their economic views, they were libertarians in their espousal of the rights of individuals. Some had been abolitionists; all welcomed Emancipation. Like Phillips, they favored equal rights and legal security for the freedmen. Unlike Phillips, they were not prepared to insist upon a vigorous, uncompromising approach to the issue. At first they were hopeful that Andrew Johnson's policy might effect a reunion of the states with full justice to the freedmen. As the results of presidential Reconstruction in the South became evident, however, they admitted the necessity for a more forceful line of action. If they often disliked the brand of politics Radical leaders practiced at Washington, they nonetheless found it expedient to support congressional Reconstruction.

As centrists in the Radical coalition, these moderate men exercised a restraining influence on the application of the congressional program as it evolved in the late 1860's. Probably most of them accepted the recommendations of the American Freedmen's Inquiry Commission for reconstructing the South. Reflecting the humanitarian, philanthropic outlook of the antebellum reform movement, the Commission was a wartime agency that antislavery men in the Republican leadership had persuaded the War Department to establish. After an extensive investigation, the Commission offered a plan for reconstruction that projected the enthusiasm of the antislavery crusade into the postwar period and carried abolitionism to a logical conclusion by insisting the emancipated Negroes needed legal, political, and economic guarantees. Doubtless, the Commission's suggestion that plantation lands in the South be confiscated and redistributed among freedmen and poor whites as an act of economic reconstruction did not set well with orthodox liberals; but, aside from this "extreme" proposal, the Commission's blueprint envisaged few measures that libertarians and reformers of all stripes could not have approved.[5] Insofar as moderates in the Radical coalition accepted the more far-reaching proposals of the Commission and of advocates like Phillips, they were to a great extent responsible for whatever success Radical Reconstruction enjoyed. But their early abandonment of Radicalism contributed fundamentally to the ultimate failure of the entire program. It was these men who became the leading political independents and liberal reformers in postwar America.

Perhaps typical of these circumspect Radicals was Charles Eliot Norton, the distinguished scholar and editor of *The North American Review*. Representative of old New England culture and dignity, patrician in heritage, yet not really exclusive in temperament, Norton was something of an oracle to such influential publicists as George William Curtis and Edwin L. Godkin. With a number of his fellow Brahmins, Norton had for a time seen the Civil War in almost apocalyptic terms as a struggle to discipline the nation through universal suffering and as an opportunity to purge American politics of weaklings and sentimentalists. It was a queer point of view, and as the war came to a close it gave way, in Norton's case, to a more orthodox estimate of the war's purpose. In 1866, Norton wrote of his disappointment in the South's response to President Johnson's leniency. "If the South showed that it understood what was meant by equal rights, that it had faith in free labor, free speech, and impartial justice," he conjectured, "we might say let us not quarrel as to the steps by which they come back to the Union, but . . . welcome them at once by whatever path they come." But the South had shown its contempt for the principles of the Declaration of Independence; and, although Norton had little faith in the efficacy of constitutional amendments as instruments of moral persuasion, he thought such formalities were necessary in the present situation. "To secure external acquiescence and formal recognition of principles, is the first step toward securing a hearty, true adoption of them hereafter." [6]

Norton represented the New England intellectuals. Edward Atkinson, another circumspect Radical, spoke for the Yankee businessmen whose fortunes had flowed from antebellum enterprises. Atkinson considered himself superior in conduct and intellect to the "shoddy" new industrialists and financiers, although he too could spot a good speculative venture. Like Norton, he agreed with Radical Republican leaders that equal rights must be guaranteed before the South could be readmitted to the Union. But Atkinson, whose business was milling cotton and whose hobby was the study of political economy, thought Southerners *might* be readmitted in the winter of 1866—if by then the price of cotton had risen. Money in their pockets would make them "safe men" looking to the future and forgetting the past. [7]

Several journals were organs of the "restrained Radicals" (notably *The North American Review* under Norton and James Russell Lowell, and *Harper's Weekly* under Curtis), but the New York *Nation* best epitomized their sentiments. Making its debut on July 6, 1865, *The Nation* was the creation of Edwin Lawrence Godkin, an immigrant journalist from the north of Ireland. More English than Irish in temperament, Godkin found it easy to cultivate friends among the Boston and New York intellectuals and men of affairs after his arrival in the United States in 1856. For some years he studied law in New York and tried some free-lance writing. He worked briefly as a reporter for *The New York Times;* and had he accepted Henry J. Raymond's offer, he could have become a partner in that paper. But Godkin had ideas of his own about journalism. He believed there was a vacuum in American publishing which could be filled only by a periodical similar to the English weekly, nonpartisan reviews.[8] Encouraged by Norton, he sought financial backing for his idea. Norton raised some of the necessary funds in Boston; but most of the capital came to Godkin from a small group of wealthy Philadelphia abolitionists. Led by James Miller McKim, these Quaker capitalists backed *The Nation* on the understanding that the new journal would champion the cause of the freedmen in the South.[9]

Well received from the beginning, *The Nation* quickly became one of the most influential journals in the country, not so much because a great many people read it as because those who did read it were the moulders of American public opinion. No question of the times escaped its attention or influence, and almost every article it published bore the imprint of Godkin's pen or of his authority. For the first thirty-five years of the journal's existence, *The Nation* and Edwin L. Godkin were synonymous. His assistant and editorial successor, Wendell Phillips Garrison, contributed some estimable literary criticism; but as a commentator on political and economic affairs he was distinctly mediocre. An obsequious disciple of his chief, during the years of Reconstruction the younger Garrison seemed most concerned with ostracizing the man whose name he bore, Wendell Phillips.[10]

Godkin's pen was sharp and often tipped with his own peculiar brand of vitriol. The counselor of patience and forbearance in others, he himself could be the most intolerant of men. He professed disdain for moralists; yet he never hesitated to invoke morality on his side of an argument. (Young Garrison thought in the same attenuated moral vein as his father.) Although Godkin insisted he detested violence, his writing could bristle with intemperance, even malignity. Yet if his mordant style often contravened his attempts at accurate, dispassionate discussion, it gave his writing force and provided the distinctive quality which accounts for Godkin's great influence on his contemporaries. When he wrote on the high, reasoned plane to which he always aspired, his articles were models of journalistic brilliance. When he engaged in name-calling and petulant phillipics, readers of *The Nation*—the editorialists, the intellectuals, the reformers—forgave him his excesses and praised his genius. They attended him faithfully, for Godkin wrote for them as well as to them.[11]

A herald of nationalism, *The Nation* made its appearance at the moment when American union was consummated. The very name of the journal was selected to emphasize the spirit of the new age. Godkin's nationalism, however, was considerably more limited in its implications than the rampant economic nationalism of American business after the war. "Sovereignty without centralization, consolidation without despotism, nationality under democratic forms" was Godkin's definition.[12]

But in 1865, *The Nation* advocated a broad national view on the issue of Reconstruction. Southern problems were national problems, Godkin wrote, and it behooved the North to eschew policies which would intensify and perpetuate sectional animosities. Reconstruction should be approached in a spirit of justice, not revenge. "What we have to do with the South," he argued, "is to let by-gones be as far as possible by-gones, but to see that justice is done within her borders, that she does it and receives it." [13] He opposed Radical demands that Confederate leaders be disfranchised. In time, *The Nation* would condemn disfranchisement for discriminating against the "better classes" in the South. In 1866, it argued only that restrictions on white suffrage would perpetuate class distinctions and sectional hatreds. In advocating equal rights for the freedmen, Godkin doubtless was sincere, but considering the abolitionist sentiments of his financial backers he had little choice in the matter: McKim and his associates expected the journal to crusade for equal rights. By late 1866, they had become so dissatisfied with Godkin's halfhearted adherence to this principle that they were more than willing to wash their hands of *The Nation*. Godkin bought them out and thus freed himself of dependence on the more extreme Radical influence.

Just prior to the appearance of *The Nation* in 1865, Godkin promised the journal would give "earnest and persistent consideration of the condition of the colored race at the South" as a matter of vital concern to the whole country. Godkin believed that the Negroes should be given educational opportunities lest the nation be endangered by the presence of "a large degraded and ignorant class" within its borders. He warned Southern whites that for their own good they must leave the Negro alone in freedom. Granting for the sake of argument that it might be "a natural and even excusable thing" to hang and harry the freedmen, he advised Southerners to ask themselves, "Will it pay? Is it expedient?" [14]

As the Reconstruction crisis dragged on, more and more frequently *The Nation* preached expediency as the correct approach to the problem. It advised Congress to disavow the moral attack on Southern questions, to declare the crusade against that section finished, and to consider now only measures absolutely necessary for uniting the nation on a sound political and economic basis. Late in 1865, while Senator Sumner was charging President Johnson with "whitewashing" the Southern situation, Godkin was accusing Sumner of engaging in "slapdash" moral phillipics.[15] The South would only be goaded to further resistance if these tactics continued, Godkin reasoned. His alternative was to appeal to the Southerner's pocketbook, to what he assumed was a universal desire to share in the blessings of Northern progress. In a rare flight of fancy, Godkin pictured a bright new day for the South—a day when Northern capital would revamp Southern agriculture and create a thrifty labor force of native whites, freedmen, and European immigrants; when villages would become great cities; when Baltimore, Norfolk, and Port Royal would challenge the commercial supremacy of New York, Philadelphia, and Boston. "But to think upon the future of the South is to become bewildered before the possibility of development such as even the West has not yet given us in her onward course." This great transformation would occur when Southerners created a political and moral climate that would be attractive to Northern capital, when they learned to accept progress as inevitable, when they deigned to labor with their hands at productive enterprises. Godkin saw no reason to upset or modify the basic socio-economic class structure of the South. His idea of land reform was to bring in enterprising Northern farmers to buy up the farms and provide employment for poor whites and Negroes.[16]

He was grievously disappointed when Southern whites interrupted this castle-building by indicating that they preferred a society more closely approximating the one they had defended in the war. Black Codes and Southern hostility to outside benefaction disgusted Godkin. He believed himself to be a reasonable man, and he could not understand how Southerners could be so unwise as to reject the minimal demands imposed by Johnson's policy and supported by most Northerners. Had Andrew Johnson and his friends in the South given some consideration to the freedmen's rights, they might have retained the good will of *The Nation*. Unwilling to compromise with even the more reasonable Radicals, they forced Godkin and men who believed as he did to support congressional Reconstruction. By 1867, *The Nation* was calling the Johnson state governments "totally unconstitutional" and was asserting that they could be removed "only by a vigorous exercise of the same military power which set them up." Thereafter, the journal lent its support to the Radical program, though Godkin frequently condemned the "vengeful, partisan spirit" of Radical leadership.[17]

Other cautious Radicals were obliged to support Congress as events in 1865 and 1866 revealed the weaknesses of presidential Reconstruction. Much as he regretted bowing to "party necessity," Samuel Bowles brought his *Springfield Republican* in line with Radicalism. From Cambridge, Norton bestowed his blessing on congressional policy and counseled his friends to allay their fears of the Radical politicians—the Butlers, the Stevenses, the Wades. "These men are not leaders in any true sense," he assured Frederick Law Olmsted. "The party leads itself." [18] Of course there were other reformers, generally prudent on political and economic questions, who were outspoken Radicals on the Reconstruction issue. The youthful Moorfield Storey, getting his first glimpse of political affairs as Sumner's private secretary in Washington, faithfully echoed his mentor's views on matters pertaining to the South.[19] And Carl Schurz, one day to become the champion of leniency, was an enthusiastic Radical Republican during the 1860's. An immigrant journalist like Godkin, this leader of German-American opinion had distinguished himself as a politician before the war and as a soldier in the fighting. Commissioned by President Johnson to make a tour of inspection through the defeated states in 1865, Schurz sent back such adverse reports of conditions in the South that the President quietly ignored him on his return to the capital. "This is the most shiftless, most demoralized people I have ever seen," Schurz wrote about the Southern whites. The only people he found willing to work were the Negroes, whose lives were not deemed "worth a wisp of straw" by the whites. "If we were to remove our troops today, the Southern States would swim in blood tomorrow," he concluded. A master of "bloody-shirt" oratory, Schurz stanchly defended Radicalism in the presidential campaign of 1868. A year later, he was elected to the United States Senate by the border state of Missouri.[20]

Until the summer of 1867, the Radical coalition managed to retain an appearance of internal harmony and seemed to be in a commanding political position. The moderate Radicals had acceded to the demands of their more aggressive colleagues and had approved military Reconstruction. Presidential policies had been rejected by the voters in the elections of 1866. Congress controlled Reconstruction, and the Radicals controlled Congress. But it was also apparent that many members of the coalition were distinctly unhappy about the prospect of any further association with the group. Radicals of temperate nature had always been less than enthusiastic about some of their leaders in Congress. Men such as Benjamin F. Butler and "Bluff Ben" Wade were crude, unprincipled, professional politicians in the eyes of gentlemen from Beacon Street and the editorial offices of *The Nation* and *The North American Review*. When these uncultivated party leaders made it known that they intended to secure absolute control of the government by impeaching the President, genuine alarm spread among the reluctant Radicals. They had no particular liking or respect for Johnson, to be sure; but they were apprehensive about the motives of the impeachers. Like the elder Pitt, they feared that unlimited power would corrupt the minds of its possessors.

3

Radical leaders never viewed impeachment as anything more than a political proceeding. Andrew Johnson was simply to be ousted as punishment for his past opposition to congressional Reconstruction and as insurance against future resistance to that program. Talk of impeachment started, in and out of Congress, as early as 1866, and the Johnson faction's overwhelming defeat in the congressional elections of that year did little to quiet those who were demanding the executive scalp. By the fall of 1866, Radicals of all shades were in general agreement as to Johnson's incompetence. But the more moderate supporters of congressional Reconstruction advised the Republicans to move slowly, to rely upon their two-thirds majority in Congress which would enable them to enact their program without referring to Johnson at all. "It ought not to be forgotten," *The Nation* reminded its readers, "that we are all, Congress and public together, in some degree morally responsible for the President's misdeeds. We knew what his antecedents were and what his character was when we elected him Vice-President." Expediency had triumphed over good sense in the election of 1864; now the nation must pay for its unwisdom. Although Johnson had failed miserably, the world ought to be spared "the paltry and degrading spectacle of a whole nation trying him judicially for having been presumptuous, conceited, obstinate, uneducated, and for having passed the flower of his years as a little village politician in a slave State." [21]

Advice of this nature could command the grudging respect of Radical leaders in 1866 only because neither the public nor a majority of Republican legislators were ready to resort to impeachment. By 1868, the President's persistent and tactless refusal to compromise with Congress created a situation made to order for the extremists. When Johnson removed Secretary of War Stanton, in seeming violation of the artful Tenure of Office Act, Radical leaders in the House of Representatives successfully pushed through a resolution of impeachment. On March 5 the Senate organized formally as a court to consider the charges against the President.[22]

In 1866 Charles Eliot Norton had advised his friends to discount the power of the Radical leaders. Eighteen months later he admitted his error. "The time for a moral hurrah has gone by," he lamented. Three months of Wade (who, as president *pro tempore* of the Senate, would become chief executive if the President were convicted) would be worse than two years of Johnson. If the impeachers succeeded in their impolitic scheme, Norton predicted that Sumner would become Secretary of State, Ben Butler Secretary of the Treasury, and Wendell Phillips Secretary of the Interior. Godkin agreed with his Cambridge friend, though he pointed out that Johnson had invited the treatment he was receiving by not tempering his own opposition to Congress. Moreover he thought impeachment would fail; there was too much division of opinion among the lawmakers on the nature of the impeachment process. Most Republican legislators were well aware that impeachment was a step of such political delicacy as to involve directly the future of the party. The failure of impeachment could mean the death of Republicanism, Godkin noted, with consequences "so tremendous, so disastrous to all good causes, that it is impossible to expect senators to be entirely indifferent to them." Norton, too, could not believe that the party would really take such a gamble. "If the party palters with honesty, consents to be doublefaced, and shrinks from plain and consistent assertion of the public faith and honor, it will be irretrievably lost." [23]

These dissenters underestimated the determination of the party leaders, who assumed that the Radical triumph had to be complete or it would be no triumph at all. "Do what you will," Godkin charged, as the Radicals prepared to try the President, "you cannot give the proceeding much moral effect." For three years *The Nation* had been preaching the doctrine of expediency to the politicians; perhaps the editor regretted this in 1868. Radical leaders did not hesitate to admit that the impeachment affair was a maneuver of expediency. As Moorfield Storey told his father, on the grounds of expediency there could be no doubt about the propriety of impeachment. Why should anyone in Boston be surprised? But Storey, who already considered himself a liberal reformer and political independent, was in a definite minority among his fellows in his enthusiasm for this aspect of the Radical program. To most liberals, impeachment somehow was an immoral act. Looking back on the crisis, George William Curtis condemned the trial as an insidiously shameful attempt to grab power, "an awful stain upon the public moral sense in our party." Whatever the offenses of President Johnson may have been, he reflected, they were nothing in comparison with "the party spirit which declared that it was tired of the intolerable cant of honesty." [24]

If most liberals viewed impeachment with feelings ranging from misgivings to disgust, they summoned up their moral wrath to condemn the Republican party's treatment of the seven "apostate" Senators who voted to acquit the President. To party leaders the apostasy of the seven amounted to political treason, and the dissenters were promptly drummed out of the party and into political oblivion. To liberal reformers, the Republican party acted in an unconscionable manner when it punished such faithful servants as Senators Fessenden, Grimes, and Trumbull. "I have little confidence in the stability or permanent success of a party which submits to the leadership in the House of B. F. Butler and attempts to cast out Fessenden," Edward Atkinson wrote indignantly to Sumner, condemning him for his part in persecuting the dissenters. Curtis printed the "dissenting opinions" of the seven in *Harper's Weekly* and described the writers as men of "distinct credit" to the party and the nation. To Moorfield Storey, the votes of the seven dissenters represented an abject surrender to "petty ambitions and measures"; yet the impeachment crisis also revealed to him the petty ambitions of the more vociferous Radicals. The young liberal came away from the fracas convinced more than ever that his own politics should be those of an independent. "I can see how small the prizes they struggle for are, how disgusting they make themselves to disinterested spectators," he remarked of all the principals in the trial.[25]

Genuinely concerned about the assault on independent judgment which the party discipline involved, liberals were disturbed as well by the political implications. They feared the power of the party whip, wielded by men unscrupulous of method and ruthlessly partisan in purpose. Partisanship, or "the party spirit," always disturbed mid-century American liberals, particularly when upstart and brash politicians controlled the machinery of politics. Even more disturbing, public reaction tended to support the tactics of the Radical leaders. "These people are afraid of Butler," mourned Richard Henry Dana, Jr., noting the submissiveness of the party faithful in Massachusetts.[26] The entire impeachment affair was of conspicuous importance in bringing on the defection of many liberals from the cause of Radicalism.

4

Radical solidarity, as well as the whole structure of congressional Reconstruction, received its most crippling blow in the controversy over economic measures for the defeated South. A few doctrinaire Radicals called for a truly radical solution to the economic problems of the area by the adoption and augmentation of the land reform proposals of the American Freedmen's Inquiry Commission. In Congress, Charles Sumner, Thaddeus Stevens, and George W. Julian attempted to include land confiscation and redistribution in the Radical legislative program.

Stevens, perhaps the most discerning Radical in Congress, and certainly the most audacious, proposed to confiscate all property held by rebels, then to divide the land among the freedmen on the basis of forty acres to a family. Julian foresaw a new South of Jeffersonian proportions—a land of thrifty, prosperous farmers working small, productive holdings. Linking confiscation with an aversion to land monopolies, Julian asked that the Federal government seize Southern property and hold it in trust for the people. Otherwise, he feared, "grasping monopolies" from the North would replace Southern planters as tyrants over the poor. Outside of Congress, the loudest voice in favor of confiscation was that of Wendell Phillips, who pronounced the redistribution of Southern land essential to the welfare of the freedmen. In the Senate, Charles Sumner echoed his views, though with considerably less force.[27]

Opposition by the Republican majority to any form of confiscation was uncompromising. A few mildly confiscatory measures slipped through Congress in the heat of war, but desultory enforcement rendered them ineffective. After the war, they were set aside and forgotten. All efforts to link confiscation with Reconstruction were easily thwarted. It would be difficult to imagine conservative former Whigs in the Republican party acquiescing in schemes to tamper with the institution of private property. Outside of Congress, those opposed to land reform argued that confiscation would only corrupt the freedmen. Land so acquired, *The Nation* contended, would prove a curse to its holder. It would "kill the soul" of the recipient and "render all labor irksome to him, all gains slowly acquired seem not worth having, and patience and scrupulousness seem marks of imbecility." Stevens's proposal, to some alarmed liberals, signified a decline in public morality to the point of possible revolution. Others feared its effect on the public credit—indeed, on the national honor itself. Clearly, if confiscation was dreaded for its iniquitous effect on the morale of the freedmen and poor whites, it was feared as much for the precedents it might establish in other areas of the national economy.[28]

Had the Radical Republicans embraced confiscation or some comparable method of land reform as part of their program, the story of the economic Reconstruction (and hence the political and social reorganization) of the South in the nineteenth century doubtless would have been altered. But proposals to confiscate land and other private property made no headway against the economic canons of the day. It was enough that slaves had been emancipated without compensation to their owners. Conservatives and liberals alike would consent to no further experimentation along such lines. Moreover, a system of moral values which equated governmental paternalism with corruption and demoralization of the individual tolerated no such equalitarian proposals as those made by Phillips and Stevens.

Although most Radicals rejected confiscation and redistribution of the land, they did recognize the need to secure economic independence for the freedmen. Their objections to land reform suggest the solution they offered. Cultivate the moral attributes of honesty, hard work, and frugality, they told the freedmen; for "every deposit in a savings-bank" was worth more than all the illusory schemes of idealists and demagogues.[29] Here was the time-honored American formula for success. Former slaves were not told how they could accumulate the funds needed to feed themselves, much less a surplus to deposit in a bank, or how they were to establish a just employer-employee rapport with Southern whites. The inexorable operation of natural economic laws would insure the triumph of thrifty, industrious freedmen over adversity.

In rehabilitating the Southern economy, the Republican leaders followed a simple program which retained intact the social structure of the area and virtually ignored the predicament of the freedmen. Political stability would be maintained sufficiently to facilitate the influx of Northern capital freely and with slight risk. The South then would be integrated into the nation's economy to serve the manufacturing North both as a source of raw materials and as a market for finished goods. In time, the South would be allotted a small share of the manufacturing. Political stability, to the Republican helmsmen, meant that Southerners must defer to the national leadership of Northern politicians and their allies in the business community. It meant that Southern whites had to adjust themselves to living with the freed Negroes. Radicals at first hoped to establish a Republican party of the South that would maintain political peace. When this failed, they left the matter to be solved by Southern whites. By then, most Northerners were indifferent to the problem and few were dissatisfied with the South's solution. On occasion Northern liberals protested against the more predatory methods used in exploiting the South; generally they accepted this program of economic Reconstruction.[30]

5

Doubtless, the most disturbing questions for liberals in the Radical coalition concerned the freedmen. How were the former slaves to be integrated into free society? What measures would best protect them and guarantee their rights in a hostile environment? To what extent, if any, should the Federal government involve itself in the problem? Were the blacks to be enfranchised and allowed to hold office immediately—or ever? Radicals had been united in demanding Emancipation, and somehow they had resolved the difficult problem of economic Reconstruction without alienating any but the "extremists" in their ranks. As they considered the social and political problems of the freedmen, however, the fissures in their ranks widened to canyons.

Like most white Americans, liberals viewed the Negro in stereotypical, but oddly ambivalent, terms.[31] On the one hand, they saw the Negro as an alien element in a white civilization. Whatever imperfections the individual black man displayed became the property of all black men; whatever admirable qualities the individual boasted were aberrations, not to be taken as typical of the race. Northerners accepted a Frederick Douglass as the exceptional Negro; generally, they thought it self-evident that Negroes were innately inferior to whites in intelligence, ability, and moral capacity. "After all," Charles Francis Adams, Jr., observed to his father during the war, "the negro is not the equal of the white man." It was as simple as that. *Harper's Weekly* reflected the popular view perfectly when it caricatured the Negro as a ridiculous, scrawny

"Rastus" or monstrously fat "mammy," fawning and shuffling before white superiors. Only at election times—at least as long as Republicans needed victories in the Southern states—did the magazine picture him arm in arm with his white neighbor, resisting Bourbon tyranny.[32]

On the other hand, the problem of the freedmen touched the Puritan conscience of American liberals. Inevitably, the humanitarian temper of the abolitionist crusade had limned in the minds of many reformers a picture of the Negro as the white man's equal. A labor system that violated every honorable American principle had victimized him, and now the white men had a duty to relieve him of his burdens and raise him in fact to the station he held in theory—that of a free and equal human being. Occasionally a writer of the time reflected this awareness of the Negro's feelings; probably Aunt Rachel in Mark Twain's "A True Story" was the most sympathetic and realistic portrayal of the black American in Gilded Age fiction. But the crude caricatures in the press may have blunted the sensibilities and eased the consciences of white liberals, especially when they began deserting the Negro in the 1870's. It was easier—and more convenient—to accept Rastus than Aunt Rachel.[33]

Lord Bryce understood the ambivalent attitudes of white Americans toward the Negro, and his comments reflected accurately the views of liberal reformers in the North, with whom he had close association. Bryce described the Negro as "by nature affectionate, docile, pliable, submissive," proud, and possessed of "a certain dogged inflexibility." Although shrewd, the black man showed "the childishness as well as the lack of self-control which belongs to the primitive peoples." He was incapable of "abstract thinking" and "scientific inquiry." But what he lacked most, Bryce thought, was a capacity for will and action: "Having neither foresight nor 'roundsight,' he is heedless and unthrifty, easily elated and depressed, with little tenacity of purpose, and but a feeble wish to better his conditions." Published in 1888, the views of the English observer coincided neatly with the Darwinian determinism just then becoming popular among American businessmen and intellectuals.[34]

Godkin anticipated by two decades Bryce's sentiments. Shortly

after the war, *The Nation* noted the plight of Negroes in struggling for security and equality in the South. Rejecting the notion
that the Federal government should do everything it could to protect the freedmen, the editor insisted that "No government can put
a policeman behind every man's chair or at the head of his bed."
Negroes ought to get tough with their white tormentors, he advised; they might consider adopting a little of the Indian's ferocity.
White Americans did not dislike the Negro because of his race or
color alone, he insisted; rather it was race and color combined with
the Negro's "apparent want of mental, moral, and physical vigor"
that caused friction between the races. "People whom an Anglo-
Saxon can 'lick' easily he never respects, and cannot readily be got
to respect." [35] These were strange words, coming from an advocate
of reason and responsibility in politics, but Godkin prided himself
on his ability to cut through moral trappings and get at the harsh
truth in public questions. Moreover, he thought he was reflecting
accurately the views of most Americans on the problem of the
black man in their midst.

Godkin was apparently an accurate reporter. Most Northerners,
reformers included, showed an inordinate, premature impatience
with the freedmen. Naturally, the freed Negroes encountered
baffling difficulties in overcoming the habits and regimen of slavery. Many Northerners who came in contact with them found their
loose moral behavior and apparent laziness intolerable. Even observers motivated by the highest humanitarian considerations came
away bewildered and frustrated from experiences with the ex-
slaves. "As for the blacks," Henry Lee Higginson wrote from the
South in 1866, "their future is a mystery as dark as their own
skins." They were bright enough and clever enough, he conceded,
"But their moral perceptions are deficient, either from nature or
from habit or from ignorance. They know it is wrong to steal and
lie, but they do it continually." Higginson had left the comforts of
Boston to operate a cotton plantation in Georgia after the war,
from concern both for his own financial welfare and for the well-
being of the displaced Negroes. Apparently he got on well with his
hired hands, but he never understood their attitude toward freedom. Charles Francis Adams, Jr., who commanded Negro troops
during the war, returned from the conflict persuaded that his

charges had "animal tendencies" greater than those of the whites. "Of the courage in action of these men, at any rate when acting in mass," he observed, "there can no doubt exist; of their physical and mental and moral energy and stamina I entertain grave doubts." Both Adams and Higginson obviously expected the freedman to adapt readily to conditions of freedom; yet, despite their impatience, they at least understood that slavery had warped the Negro's sense of values and given him a unique outlook on life. Most Northerners were not so discerning.[36]

Northern liberals, including Godkin himself, would have been horrified if the freedmen had actually taken the editor's advice to emulate the Indians, if they had taken up arms against the whites and fought for their rights. Over and above this bit of antic by-play, Godkin's more earnest remedy for easing the plight of the freedmen was a restrained one indeed. Education would infuse them with the moral vigor they so desperately needed, he thought. But even in advocating education, Godkin was less concerned with the humanity of the Negro than with the debasement of society if ignorant freedmen were permitted to participate in politics. Demagogues after the spoils of office or enemies of financial honesty might beguile the uneducated blacks into supporting their nefarious schemes. Responsible men would have to keep the enfranchised Negroes within reach of their influence and guidance.[37]

To be sure, liberal reluctance to enfranchise the freedmen reflected their determination to exclude ignorance of any sort from politics, as well as their fragile confidence in the Negroes themselves. Most liberal reformers advocated a national literacy test for all voters, particularly for the Irish immigrants whom they feared, in a strict political sense, even more than the ignorant freedmen. But liberals inclined to ask something more of Negroes, too—some evidence of "moral rectitude," in effect a "morality test" to accompany a literacy requirement for enfranchisement. Others would have granted educated Negroes the vote only if proposals to disfranchise white leaders in the South were abandoned. Why deprive the "best element" in the South of a right that was to be granted to the most unstable and unreliable element? they asked. Few were as patient as George William Curtis, who counseled that only time and sympathy would enable Emancipation to work the miracles Northerners expected of it.[38]

The longer the problem of the freedmen rankled, the more discouraged liberals became. Many of their worst fears seemed near to realization, as Radical leaders pressed for more and more Federal aid to the ex-slaves. Had they known the lengths to which some Radicals were willing to go in protecting Negroes, they might well have abandoned Reconstruction altogether as early as 1866. "Let confusion endure," Wendell Phillips advised Sumner in the spring of that year. "The nation was never so wise as today and never growing wise at such a rapid rate. We shall have everything only by being in no haste to settle anything." Sectional harmony was the last thing Phillips wanted until Negroes won their full rights. Beyond that, he had a vague notion of using the confused state of political affairs to launch an attack on industrialism on behalf of all laboring men, white and black.[39] Phillips was the kind of "incendiary" whose radicalism became abhorrent to many of his old associates. Yet his contributions to the antislavery crusade restrained them from condemning him too bitterly. Most of them concluded simply that he had lost his mind.

As early as 1867 Godkin was fed to the teeth with the problem. "The negro, I think, is safe," he wrote. "I would insist on equality for him at any cost, but do not let us ruin the country in order to set him up in business." Reformers had other things to do, and it was time for the Negro to strike out for himself. Other Radicals became cynical about the whole affair. "We need a strong, short, stirring address to the colored rabble of the South, setting forth *why* they should vote the Republican ticket," Greeley wrote privately during the campaign of 1868. No longer interested in aiding the freedmen, the erratic editor of the *Tribune* now wanted only to use them. Ironically, the only virtue Horatio Seymour, New York's Democratic party leader, could find in Greeley as a presidential candidate four years later was that *he* could be used in driving Negroes out of public office.[40]

Increasingly, liberals convinced themselves that Negroes never would be capable of joining "civilized society." Why pass further legislation on their behalf? For five years they had enjoyed the

fruits of freedom and had shown no propensity to elevate themselves intellectually or morally. To most liberal reformers even the
"Force Acts" of 1870 and 1871, designed to curb terrorist organizations in the South, were, as Samuel Bowles insisted, "unconstitutional, unrepublican, un-American." In *The Nation*'s view the
outrages of the Ku Klux Klan were deplorable, but the remedy lay
only in leaving the South to its own follies. Let the "trashy whites
and ignorant blacks" shift for themselves. Now representing Missouri in the Senate, even Carl Schurz opposed the "insane Ku Klux
legislation" and turned his back on the Negro. One prominent liberal, arguing in terms that have since become rote in America, denounced the Supplementary Civil Rights Bill in 1874 as a measure
designed to do the unnatural and impossible—force white children
to go to school with black children. By the early 1870's only a
handful of liberal spokesmen could agree with John Murray
Forbes that the freedmen deserved at least a few more years at the
business of working for themselves and adjusting to freedom before
being turned over to "the tender mercies of their old masters, under the plausible guise of 'local self government.' " [41]

With flabby impressionability, liberals were completely taken in
by the legend of "Black Reconstruction." Ignoring the constructive
achievements of the "carpetbag" governments, they were ready to
believe the worst that Southern whites had to say about the Negro
in politics. They professed great sympathy for Negroes who became demoralized at seeing the spectacle of their own people, "in a
state of grossest ignorance," thrust suddenly into positions of responsibility. Often they blamed Republican politicians in the
South for misleading the freedmen, and they urged the blacks to
join with their "white neighbors" to undo the damage.

Actually, the corruption, malfeasance, and extravagance the liberals saw in the Reconstruction governments disturbed them far
more than the "demoralization" of the Negroes. In plain language
they invited Southern whites to "take the bit in their teeth" if they
wished to rid themselves of Radicalism. Either that or "they must
suffer on," Godkin told them. Few protests came from liberal quarters in the North when the ex-Confederates took the advice and
removed the cause of their suffering. As Wendell P. Garrison
noted, it would do the Negroes no harm to "drop back" and stay

out of politics. What they really needed was to have a gospel of education, thrift, and chastity preached to them, and "if I were a single man not concerned with bread and butter I should feel tempted to be an apostle of this sort to them." Apparently *The Nation*'s editorial offices were too comfortable and his need for bread and butter too pressing for Garrison to embark upon this noble mission, for he remained in New York to help his editor and fellow journalists embroider an elaborate myth of Radical Reconstruction.[42]

No writer was more receptive to exaggerated accounts from the South than James S. Pike of the New York *Tribune*. Indeed, as Greeley's man in Washington, Pike contrived much of the Reconstruction myth himself. Before the war, he had been a blustering antislavery crusader, although the mainspring of his abolitionism was hatred of the South rather than concern for the enslaved Negroes. A Radical during the war, he quickly became contemptuous of the freedmen's efforts in the Southern governments during military Reconstruction. His reaction was all too typical of many liberal, onetime Radical, Republicans.

In 1872, without having set foot in the South since the war, Pike wrote a lengthy article for the *Tribune* in which he savagely attacked the Radical government of South Carolina as one of "ignorance and barbarism." Unscrupulous carpetbaggers and "pauper blacks, fresh from a state of slavery and ignorance the most dense," ran the state, he assured his readers. No self-respecting Northerner would for a month tolerate the fraud and immorality that plagued South Carolina. A year later, Pike journeyed south to see for himself the awful spectacle he had conjured up for his readers. As an extension of his article, he published in 1874 *The Prostrate State: South Carolina Under Negro Government,* a book accepted by historians for years as an accurate appraisal of Reconstruction. Few contemporary accounts were written with such impassioned bias and from such meager sources: the book was a mélange of preconceptions, hearsay, and information gathered from a few bitter Carolina whites. Above all, it was a feverish diatribe against the freedmen, particularly the "raw negro legislators" of South Carolina. The book had a warping influence on Pike's generation of liberals, who quoted and paraphrased from its pages extensively.

The Nation in particular drew heavily from Pike for its indictment of Radical Reconstruction.[43]

"The white South wanted the Negroes to fail as freedmen," Gunnar Myrdal concludes, "and saw in their failure a confirmation of their own wisdom and the Northerners' folly." [44] The tragedy of liberal reformers was that they uncritically accepted the Reconstruction myth as Pike, *The Nation,* and Southern white visitors to the North presented it to them. Perhaps the race problem frightened liberals, as they began to comprehend its magnitude. As libertarians, they could rationalize their failure to provide a solid economic and social base for Reconstruction by pointing to the assumed results of the "paternalism" the Federal government had already dispensed to the freedmen. Moreover, in a sense they reaped a whirlwind of their own making. Caught up in wartime hysteria, they had loudly demanded the unconditional surrender of the Confederacy. Impelled by high humanitarian motives, they had insisted upon absolute freedom for the slaves. The struggle became, as Norton proclaimed as early as 1861, "a war for the establishment of civilization in that immense portion of our country in which for many years barbarism has been rising." [45] Without much thought of the future, liberals aligned themselves in the Radical coalition with men who supported congressional Reconstruction from a variety of motives, some generous, some sordid: real concern that equality be granted the freedmen; determination to ensure the ascendancy of Republicanism in the South; ambition to reap personal benefits in the defeated section. An abstract desire to see justice done had attracted most liberals to the Radical cause. They saw only the abuse and the need for correction; and when the abuse failed to yield to their well-meaning but illusory ministrations, they veered away from the entire problem, frustrated and fearful.

6

As much as any man in the North, Carl Schurz made the liberal repudiation of Radical Reconstruction a settled fact. Capable yet unpredictable, Schurz retreated completely from his ultra-Radical stance just after the war to become the leading spokesman for reconciliation between the sections in the 1870's. There is little doubt that his political fortunes in Missouri had something to do with his shift from one extreme to the other on the issue. It appears he did his best to placate both the Radicals and the Southern sympathizers in his state. In doing so, he ended by siding with the former rebels. The irony of Schurz's political career is that the pro-South Missourians he restored to power repaid him by turning him out of the Senate at the first opportunity.

In 1868 Schurz had spoken ostentatiously about the meaning of Union victory in the war: "Ah, how contemptibly silly are those who dared to dream that the great American nation would be cowardly enough to throw away, with wanton levity, the great fruits of their grandest struggle for liberty and justice." Three years later, he was busily trying to unite the "liberal element" in both major parties to put an end to all Reconstruction. Chief architect of the Liberal Republican party in 1872, he viewed the nomination of Greeley and Brown by the new party as a near disaster. Yet, he dutifully supported his political brainchild and its bizarre ticket; for, as he saw it, the election presented the voters with a simple choice: was the Southern problem to be solved by "Ku-Klux laws or by moral influence?" Grant stood for the first alternative, Greeley for the second.[46]

Grant's triumphant victory in 1872 did nothing to daunt the champions of reconciliation. If anything, it strengthened their determination to resist all further Republican Reconstruction schemes. Godkin, who had refused to support Greeley only because he detested the man personally, kept *The Nation*'s editorial mortars firing away at Congress and the Radical governments. South Carolina was his favorite target: its government was a disgrace; its condition cried for any "reform" which might restore it to decency. Convinced that a national disease of corruption was spreading from South to North, rather than vice versa, he warned that the malaise of the "prostrate state" was contaminating the entire Union.[47]

When Republican and Democratic party managers arranged the compromise that settled the disputed election of 1876 and declared Hayes the winner over Tilden, liberal reformers in the North received the news with satisfaction. No longer need they fear the

Southern problem or feel compelled to divert their energies from more attractive tasks facing them at home. After twelve years of bungling the problem, they told themselves, the North at last had remanded it to the Southern whites. There it belonged and there, probably, it should have been returned long ago. Any qualms they had about the fate of the freedmen under the new dispensation were allayed by an eager willingness to trust in the honor and integrity of Southern white leaders. As honorable men, surely, they would treat the matter fairly. "As regards the South," Wendell P. Garrison noted comfortably, "you cannot explain the cessation of outrages since the overthrow of the carpetbaggers except by admitting that Hayes's course has proved itself best for the negroes." Immensely pleased with the outcome of the election, Edward Atkinson rejoiced that "we are enjoying a calm after a great politic⁻¹ storm and . . . gathering up our strength for an era of great prosperity." Godkin was happy to report that conciliation and confidence had triumphed over brute force. "Let us hear the last of it, and go forward in the nobler and more excellent way." All that remained to be done in the South was to convince Southern whites they had nothing to fear from Negro suffrage (a fact the conservatives who were "redeeming" the South from Radical rule already had discovered) and to use "all our influence with the negroes to prevent their abusing their newly-acquired powers." [48]

As for the Redeemers, they deserved the nation's gratitude for their "patriotic and conservative" restraint during the electoral crisis. All the fuss had been to no purpose, it seemed. The average Republican voter ought to feel much as did the Negro, who, sure that he was hearing the evangelist George Whitefield preach, "went into spasms accordingly, but admitted, on finding his mistake, that he had rolled himself in the dirt for nothing." [49]

Why did liberal reformers in the North acquiesce so readily in the bargain that put Hayes in the White House and completed the "redemption" of the South? Primarily because Reconstruction had become anathema to their relatively simple code of moral and political behavior—and because they became almost preposterously impatient with the Southern Negro. Ignorance, they convinced themselves, reigned supreme in Radical statehouses. The "best men" of the South—the intelligent, the propertied, the cultured men of the region—were prevented from assuming their natural positions as leaders. "Let whatever there is of intelligence resume its natural weight," Godkin counseled.[50]

Liberals rationalized their "new departure" by expressing special concern for the Negroes, who were learning their first lessons in civics from the worst of teachers. They feared that permanent damage would be done to sound principles of government in the South if the "carpetbaggers" continued to rule unimpeded. They felt real anxiety about the spread of corruption to the North, where reformers already were engaged in the crusade for good government. And the "fiscal irresponsibility" of the Radical governments genuinely appalled them. Taxes were ridiculously high, money was lavishly and foolishly squandered on needless, wasteful projects; and if proof of these iniquities was needed, Pike's graphic descriptions could always be cited. At times, disgust with the situation got the better of the "better element" in the North. Rarely did *The Nation* speak with such rancor as when it described the Radical government of South Carolina as a "queer aristocracy of color . . . with the rich Congo thief on top and the degraded Anglo-Saxon at the bottom." "Socialism" was rampant in the state, with the "blackest" members of the legislature clearly the worst offenders.[51]

Reformers argued, too, that all of the legitimate aims of Reconstruction had been gained with the adoption of the three amendments to the Constitution. Military government was an extreme that most of them supported only reluctantly. By 1876 the prospect of indefinite military rule in some states horrified them. The time had come to arrest the paternalism under which the freedmen were being restrained from finding their "free and natural" place in society. Everything the liberals saw in the Radical experiment convinced them that Reconstruction debased public morals and decent political principles. Worst of all, perhaps, it was diverting public attention from legitimate, pressing reforms elsewhere. The country needed a purified civil service, honest money, lower tariffs.[52]

Finally, the economic crises of the 1870's badly frightened liberal reformers. Labor unrest rose to a point where it became their personal nightmare. Already, they reasoned, the Molly Maguires in Pennsylvania had shown the extremes to which ignorance and irresponsibility could lead men. Liberals wanted no more of this Jacobinism. If they had any doubts about the propriety of the Hayes-Tilden decision of 1877, the railroad strikes and riots later that year put these finally to rest. A bargain between responsible propertied men in the North and their Southern counterparts seemed to accord with the orthodox economic canons of men like Schurz and Godkin and Atkinson. "Dogged Southern conservatives" were welcomed back into the fold and praised as men who had taken no part in the " 'advanced thinking' and general rage for social and political experimentation of the last twenty years." [53]

In abandoning Reconstruction, the liberal reformers were guilty of other inconsistencies, too. In effect, they stamped their approval on violence and deception as instruments of government. Far from condemning the first Mississippi Plan and similar conspiracies to disfranchise Negroes by force and intimidation and to promote "redemption," they encouraged Southern whites to rely on their own resources for regaining control of their state governments. George W. Julian, erstwhile Radical and Liberal Republican, went to Louisiana as a member of the Democratic "watchdog" committee in the electoral crisis of 1876–77. He totally ignored the corrupt practices of the Redeemers there. Although Republican campaigners who resorted to "bloody shirt" oratory were regularly condemned in respectable liberal circles, Redeemers who used the same tactics in reverse usually escaped censure.[54] In the light of the prevailing nineteenth-century racial concepts, the Northern abandonment of the freedmen can be much more readily understood than can this liberal retreat from professed standards of good government and moral conduct.

After 1877, Northern liberals accepted a simple method for disposing of the vexatious racial problem in the South: let the Southern states work out the matter by themselves. Southerners were not slow to accept the invitation to action. Now was the time to discard subterfuge and deception, to take the offensive openly in favor of white supremacy, to acknowledge frankly the economic superiority of the North, but to ask for a greater share of the nation's industrial wealth. Thus there began the Southern invasion of New York and Boston banquet halls. Henry W. Grady, the perceptive young editor of the *Atlanta Constitution,* set the new tone when he told the New England Society of New York that "conscience and common sense" would lead Southern whites along the path of righteousness in dealing with the Negroes. Have faith in the South, he said in effect, for the South had kept faith with the black man and would continue to do so in the future.[55]

These were reassuring words to Northern businessmen, anxious to prevent any reopening of sectional conflict which might interfere with commerce. Here was a prophet of a new South—a South politically stable, purged of its race problem, oriented to the doctrine of progress, anxious to do business with the North. Liberal reformers listened just as appreciatively. In 1890, members of the Massachusetts Reform Club sat down to a dinner in honor of Daniel H. Chamberlain, onetime Radical Republican governor of South Carolina. Not many years had elapsed since many of the diners had condemned Chamberlain as one of the worst "carpet-bag" offenders in the South, but time and reconciliation had mellowed both speaker and audience. Now, such respected reformers as Edward Atkinson, Moorfield Storey, Henry H. Edes, Thomas Wentworth Higginson, and Charles Francis Adams, listened attentively as Chamberlain recounted the history of the race problem in the South and blamed the troubles since the war on the North for having given Negroes the vote. Amid "tremendous cheering," he instructed his audience in its patriotic duty henceforth: *"let the negro alone!"* [56]

Perhaps their reaction to the Federal Elections Bill in 1890 showed how far liberal reformers had retreated, near the end of the century, from the Radical Republicanism and concern for the plight of the freedmen they had shown after the war. Introduced in the House by Henry Cabot Lodge, the measure proposed to ensure fair and free national elections, particularly in the South. Certainly Lodge and the Republican supporters of the bill acted as much from a determination to break the Democratic stranglehold on Southern votes in national elections as from a desire to free Federal elections from fraud and chicanery. But elections in the South *were* farcical after Negroes were disfranchised, and the Southern states *were* disproportionately represented in Congress, in violation of the Fourteenth Amendment. "We have clothed the negroes with the attributes of American citizenship," Lodge declared, in supporting the measure. "We have put in their hands

the emblem of American sovereignty." It no longer mattered
whether or not this action had been wisely taken. Having made the
black man a citizen, the government now was bound in honor to
protect his rights as a citizen, "and it is a cowardly Government if
it does not do it." [57]

Liberal leaders could not stomach this "Force Bill," as they
called the measure. It was time to call a halt to all the benefits
Negroes had been receiving, Godkin asserted. "Tens of thousands
of philanthropic and conscientious men at the North are beginning to ask themselves to-day whether the highest interests of the
American commonwealth do not call for a resolute and peremptory
resistance to any further political sacrifice for the negro's benefit."
Carl Schurz agreed. Before the Massachusetts Reform Club, he insisted that "no disturbing hand" should interfere in the South,
after all the "confusion and agony" that section had endured. Interference would only disturb the friendly relations the two races
had worked out with each other. Opposed as well by representatives of big business, the "Force Bill" met ignominious defeat in
the Senate. As Senator Don Cameron put it candidly, the bill deserved defeat in principle and in detail, solely on the ground that
its passage would disturb the quiet relations between sections.
With capital flowing into the South, with manufacturing and commercial interests everywhere working to obliterate sectional lines,
the near future would see "one homogeneous mass of people" in
America. Why jeopardize this happy development? [58]

"A bare and miserable business," Lodge commented bitterly.[59]
Perhaps so; but Northern liberals generally were quite satisfied
with the fate of the measure. As *The Nation* observed, in commenting on one Southern state's plan to ensure the continued disfranchisement of Negroes: "It is the opinion of the wisest Republicans in Mississippi of both races that it is best for the State that
the negroes should not vote, and outsiders may well accept their
judgment as to the matter." [60]

7

Reconstruction has been described as the "tragic era" in American
history. Until recently the term was used to stigmatize the Radical

Republican approach to the defeated South, to condemn the corruption in Radical state governments, to deplore the use of military force as a device for burdening the white people of the South with unreasonable peace terms and the use of that force in an attempt to effect a social revolution.[61] The real tragedy of the period, as Kenneth M. Stampp suggests, involved the manner in which Southern Negroes were rescued from legal slavery only to be thrown into virtual peonage. Responsibility for this ugly regression can be assigned, with finality, to no single group or party in North or South. Given the prevailing political and economic climate in mid-century America and the heterogeneous character of the Radical coalition, the failure of Radical Reconstruction and the abandonment of Southern Negroes by the North were probably inevitable developments.

Still, liberal reformers and men of independent political tendencies within the coalition gave up the struggle for equality and justice in the South with remarkable alacrity. Considering their collective background as humanitarian reformers and abolitionists, their enthusiasm for the struggle against the Confederacy, their determination to rescue the Southern Negro from tyranny, and their high concepts of individual duty and public morality, they displayed a timorous flaccidity in the face of pressures to deny their commitment to right the wrongs in Southern society. Had they accepted some policy of land reform for the South, they might have tilted the political scales in favor of a Reconstruction program that would have given some economic strength to the freedmen. Had they remained true to their humanitarianism and given the Negro some genuine support in his painful struggle to become a truly free man, they might well have kept alive, even among cynical Northern politicians, an appreciation of viable alternatives in dealing with the difficulties of Reconstruction. After all, liberals controlled influential organs of public opinion; many were eminent, respected national and local figures; and as a group they had the ears of many important politicians. But most liberals were committed to rigid political and economic dogmas, fashioned in an era of unhurried commercialism, and to moral principles even more inflexible.

Perhaps they refused to yield their principles on the issue precisely because the doctrines of laissez-faire and individualism were under such heavy attack in other quarters. But in struggling to maintain fixed principles in the Reconstruction crisis, they sanctioned a solution to the Southern problem which severely weakened these same principles while it strengthened the political and economic forces they feared and disliked. It was but the first of their many fruitless journeys to Canossa.

3

Reluctant Reformers

This modern cant about the corruption of politics is fatiguing in the extreme. It proceeds from the tea-custard and syllabub dillettanteism, the frivolous and desultory sentimentalism of epicenes.

SENATOR JOHN J. INGALLS, 1890

And he grew up and married, and raised a large family, and brained them all with an axe one night, and got wealthy by all manner of cheating and rascality; and now he is the infernalist wickedest scoundrel in his native village, and is universally respected, and belongs to the Legislature.

MARK TWAIN, "Story of a Bad Little Boy"

FEW SELF-MADE MEN OF THE GILDED AGE DID AS WELL FOR themselves as William Marcy Tweed. Like Rockefeller and Carnegie, Tweed took spectacular advantage of the opportunities America offered her poor but willing young men. In only fifteen years this son of immigrant parents rose from the ranks of New York's artisan class to become political boss of the city. With a bank account probably equal to that of the most affluent businessman, possessing power as yet unknown to the new generation of industrialists and financiers, Tweed plundered and ruled the first city of the land from 1866 to 1871.

Unfortunately for The Boss, certain aspects of his success story distinguished him from the other "rags to riches" specimens of his day. Instead of investing his skill and intelligence safely in railroading or banking or oil, he had been unwise enough to turn to the business of politics. Moreover, in pushing his way to the top he committed certain acts clearly defined as crimes by law. Probably Tweed saw politics as a perfectly legitimate business, and certainly it resembled many other enterprises of mid-century America. An ambitious man worked hard at his job and relied on ability, perseverance, and luck to move him to the top. He crippled his competitors, took what profits the market would yield, and entrenched himself in power with a tight, efficient organization. As in other businesses, too, certain obligations had to be met. In the political corporation, food, money, coal, and petty jobs were distributed as wages to workers and as dividends to "stockholders." Votes were stock certificates, to be bought, sold, and manipulated like railroad securities. When outside criticism became too pesky to ignore, one called in other businessmen (as Tweed summoned John Jacob Astor) to examine the books and attest to the firm's integrity and honesty. Indeed, the political firm of William M. Tweed & Co. bore a remarkable resemblance in many respects to "Commodore" Vanderbilt's transportation empire or J. P. Morgan's banking syndicate.[1]

But not in the eyes of certain gentlemen reformers. On the contrary, these men ("man milliners," Roscoe Conkling called them) considered politics not an ordinary business at all, but the serious responsibility of unselfish patriots. They viewed Tweed, Conkling, and others of the new political breed as downright scoundrels. As big business and politics became open allies after the Civil War, the idealists embarked upon a long, arduous campaign of correction and education, at all levels of government and in every segment of society. As Godkin of *The Nation* once noted, the duty of reformers went far beyond the mere electing of decent legislators and good Presidents. It included the conversion and education of "a large body of political heathen," who were the protagonists, with thoughtful men, in a great conflict between civilization and barbarism.[2]

2

It was a difficult task to arouse the patriotic spirit of the decent and thoughtful men, let alone to convert the "heathen." By 1865 politics was no longer an alluring profession to bright young Americans, as railroading, high finance, and manufacturing caught their interest and commanded their talents. To be sure, thoughtful men of affairs retained an interest in politics; but they recoiled from the disagreeable everyday activities of a political system that became more complex and seemingly more unmanageable every year. Almost by default, the direction of both major parties, and thus of government, became largely the prerogative of "inferior men"—politicians whose primary interests, so liberal reformers believed, were to enrich themselves and to attend the needs of their friends.

Politics thus became a source of bitter frustration to many responsible men, particularly in the Northeast. As party activities became more debauched, decent men became more reluctant to participate in party affairs. And as they withdrew or were driven from the inner circles of the parties, they were replaced by additional "irresponsible," "inferior" politicians. Many high-minded men became disgusted with politics in general. The political scene looked like one in "Alice through the looking-glass," one bitter observer grumbled, "the gutter governing the side-walk, the slums pouring out their vice and ignorance to masquerade in seats of honor, guilt taking refuge in 'dignified silence', the saloons posing as the temples of liberty, foreign adventurers pouring in to control us with more than autocratic insolence, everything just the opposite of what it ought to be." "Politician" and "political worker" became opprobrious terms to reformers who looked upon service in government as a patriotic duty. At the initial meeting of the New York Reform Club in 1882 the members resolved that no man should be eligible for membership who could be called a "political worker." A society of gentlemen reformers, the Reform Club was determined to protect itself from capture by the politicians.[3]

Reformers used many colorful adjectives to describe the unwholesome element in politics, but the epithet "Butlerism" most eloquently expressed their disdain. The term referred to Benjamin F. Butler of Massachusetts, a politician whom General Grant once remarked "it is fashionable to abuse."[4] Butler was a political adventurer who changed party allegiance at least six times in his remarkable career. A Democrat before the war, he became a controversial major general in the Union army and a Republican in politics during the conflict. In 1866 he was elected to Congress, where, as a confirmed Radical Republican, he became a leader in the effort to oust Andrew Johnson from the White House. Later, he served as a Greenback congressman and as a Democratic governor of Massachusetts. He was an accomplished politician, a ruthless opponent, an aggressive campaigner, and a genuine democrat. No mere surface examination of his career can suffice to gauge the extent of sincerity in his efforts on behalf of Radical Republicanism and postwar reform, for his was an exceedingly complex personality.[5] Doubtless he resembled many apparently corrupt and opportunistic politicians of the period.

To liberal reformers, however, Ben Butler was the epitome of political villainy. " 'Butlerism,' whether in Massachusetts, New York, or South Carolina," *The Nation* charged, "is simply a plan for the embodiment in political organization of the desire for the transfer of power to the ignorant and the poor, and the use of Government to carry out the poor and ignorant man's view of the nature of society." As interpreted by Godkin, its essential features were the characteristics of late-nineteenth-century politics that all liberal reformers detested: excessive taxation amounting to blackmail, bribery of legislators, government by bosses, denunciation of "all persons laying claim to education or professing much scrupulousness," dangerous extensions of the executive power, disregard of constitutional restrictions, and willingness to solve all questions by the "naked vote" of the majority.[6] If it was disgust with politics that drove some liberals into sulky isolation, it was fear of the Butlers that forced others to redouble their efforts on behalf of reform.[7]

Many well-intentioned liberals, potential recruits for reform campaigns, were plainly indifferent to political affairs. They conceded their obligation to vote, but they did not take easily to the everyday drudgery of politics. Lord Bryce noted this apathy among the "luxurious classes and fastidious minds," the "respectable, steady-going part of the population." According to this astute English observer, respectable voters were unwilling to interest themselves in "confessedly disagreeable work," for they found the world of politics a strange and uncongenial environment. Samuel J. Tilden, the Democratic reform politician who ultimately helped break Boss Tweed's power in New York, always encountered difficulty in rallying good men to reform. As early as 1867 he complained to a friend that the whole burden of reform fell on a small number of men forced to fight not only the entrenched corruptionists, but also the "indifference and discouragement" of bystanders.[8] In the campaign against Tweed, Tilden and his aides did manage to interest a number of influential New Yorkers; but most of these reluctant reformers retreated into indifference once The Boss was behind bars. New York City rid itself of Tweed in 1872, but not of Tweedism.

Some years later, young Theodore Roosevelt voiced Tilden's complaint in stronger terms: "The people of means in all great cities have in time past shamefully neglected their political duties, and have been contemptuously disregarded by the professional politicians in consequence." And only four years after its establishment, the New York Reform Club found itself unable to secure a quorum and was forced to suspend operations, "due to a lack of interest among the members." [9]

George William Curtis, an eloquent speaker and respected reform politician, often chastised his friends and fellow liberals for their indifference. To Curtis, politics was the public duty of educated men, and he made this principle the theme of his most important address. By public duty, he told an audience at Union College, he meant more than mere official duty. "I mean that personal attention—which, as it must be incessant, is often wearisome and even repulsive—to the details of politics." It meant attending meetings, serving on disputatious committees, enduring "rebuffs, chagrins, ridicules, disappointments, defeats." One ran the risk of being labeled a "mere politician;" but by constant, honorable, and vigilant performance, one would know the satisfaction of contributing to "that great temple of self-restrained liberty which all generous souls mean that our government should be." If good men sat at home, nursing their prejudices and persuading themselves that nothing could be done to rescue the republic from mob rule, then surely the result would be not a government mastered by ignorance, but a government betrayed by intelligence; not a victory for brave bad men, but a surrender by cowardly good men.[10]

3

Reformers were fond of contrasting the old days, when men were selected for public office because they were faithful statesmen rather than mere party managers, with the new era, which had elevated a new type of man to prominence. No longer the statesman of unbending integrity, "sturdy independence," and unimpeachable honesty, the postwar lawmaker or party manager was a slave to organizational tyranny and a pawn of special interests. He neither understood nor cared to learn the qualities that the founding fathers and antebellum giants had brought to the conduct of public affairs. Lord Bryce thought the typical American politician began as a saloon-keeper, "vulgar, sometimes brutal," or as a "lawyer of the lowest kind, or lodging-house keeper," or as a "failure in store-keeping." Ignoring the great issues of the day, these postwar practitioners of the statesman's art saw politics as little more than a scramble for jobs. Their most conspicuous virtues were "shrewdness, a sort of rough good-fellowship with one another, and loyalty to their chiefs, from whom they expect promotion in the ranks of the service." [11]

It was unfortunately true that postwar America had little use for the concept of the gentleman in politics. Charles J. Bonaparte of Maryland, for example, doubtless thought of himself as a gentleman, if not as a patrician gentleman. He also considered himself a democrat. What respect could Bonaparte command as a gentleman reformer or a democrat when the public read his blunt comments on education? Bonaparte had nothing but contempt for public schools and the idea of equal education for all children. Public schools ought to charge tuition, he argued, for there was really no difference between a "public soup-house and a public free-school." Bonaparte's appeal for civil service reform thereafter could not have impressed many voters, particularly inasmuch as his views on education earned him the nickname of "Souphouse Charlie." [12]

According to Charles Eliot Norton, the absence of gentlemen from politics contributed to the Liberal Republican debacle in 1872. Had gentlemen been in control of the Cincinnati convention of that nascent party, a candidate more acceptable than Greeley might have been nominated. Norton thought that a loss of respect for the gentlemanly qualities, a "loss of feeling, even among our women, for the fine nature of gentlemanliness," had long foretold the "decline in public morality" that marked the contest between Grant and Greeley.[13]

Twice during his career as editor of *The Nation*, Godkin believed he had found a resurgence of "gentlemanliness" in politics. In 1867 he described Curtis as one of the Republican party's most promising prospects for high office. Commenting on the tactics which a gentleman of Curtis's stature should use in campaigning, he noted that any man of culture and refinement should take care not to "carry his sense of his own superiority to the people" to the political platform. "He must treat the voters not as social equals, but as his fellow-citizens; he must in talking with them, take the air of a man advising, and not of a man instructing them . . . must, in a word, show in his manner that he is capable of sympathizing with them." [14] But Curtis was unable to compete successfully with the machine politicians, and Godkin despaired of ever electing gentlemen to office.

Then, in 1884, he noticed young Theodore Roosevelt in the New York legislature. Once again he became sanguine about the prospects for promoting gentlemen in politics. What did Roosevelt's success thus far disclose? It indicated, in a striking way, that the term "politics" was returning to its original meaning—"the management of public affairs, as distinguished from the working of the nominating machinery." Roosevelt, in Godkin's eye, resembled the old-fashioned leaders—statesmen like Silas Wright, Sumner, and Calhoun, who accepted the hardships of public office as the personal responsibility of intelligent men. All "young men of leisure" who wished to enter politics could learn a valuable lesson from Roosevelt's selfless devotion to duty. But during the presidential campaign later that year, Godkin completely reversed himself and withdrew his blessing from the young New Yorker. For Roosevelt refused to join the editor in the Mugwump ranks of Cleveland supporters and remained loyal to Blaine and the Republicans. Godkin concluded that his promising young statesman had decided to become a mere professional politician—an odious choice.[15] Thereafter, the two men became bitter personal enemies.

Commenting on the overthrow of Tweed in 1871, Samuel Bowles urged every "honest, God-fearing man" to make the performance of even the most trivial public duties a matter of conscience. Tweed and Tammany, to the editor of the *Springfield Republican*, were only ulcers on the body of the state. "The disease is in the blood," he argued, and only when "all hands fall to work to clean out and disinfect the national premises" would a remedy be found.

Let nothing stand in the way of political duty, George William Curtis counseled an audience at Wesleyan University. If duty clashes with a man's "ease, his retirement, his taste, his study, let it clash, but let him do his duty." Some young liberal reformers did not need to be reminded that their duty lay in public service. "It is well to fill any political office when you can," Henry Cabot Lodge wrote in 1874, "for honest men of moderate intelligence are not too common in office." [16]

No reformer was more forceful than Moorfield Storey in defining politics as the public responsibility of enlightened men. While secretary to Charles Sumner during the Reconstruction crisis, Storey resolved to make politics his vocation. He never fulfilled his ambition to hold high office, but throughout the remainder of his career as a prominent lawyer and reformer he referred often to the duty of the "better classes." "It is an evil day for a nation," he asserted, "when its best men fail in their duty, and cease to take an interest in its government." All great public questions should be of interest to every citizen, and particularly to men of leisure and means. Political decisions, Storey contended, "must be the result of cool and deliberate reflection," and only persons of intelligence and standing could devote their time to such matters. "We may refuse to do our duty," he warned, "but we cannot escape the consequences." [17]

Storey and most other liberals took it for granted that the "best men" were rich men, and they sometimes became obsessed with the problem of attracting wealthy men to the political arena. Terribly disturbed about the plight of the "unemployed rich," Godkin considered the problem worthy of an essay in *The Nation*. Europe had no such problem, he noted, for there gentility was commonly associated with idleness. But in America, the spectacle of a class of idle rich men tended to stimulate all sorts of delusions about capitalism and capitalists—delusions which gave rise both to "theoretical communism" and to "simple working-class discontent." Nor would a rush of the unemployed rich into charitable work solve the problem; indeed, it might cause positive harm. "Philanthropy needs in our day, in order not to be mischievous, to have a good deal of the hard and cold and incredulous countinghouse spirit infused into it, and needs, like commerce, to get the worth of its money." Inexperienced philanthropists might distribute their inherited wealth too indiscriminately among unworthy causes. It was best that businessmen control the dispensation of charitable gifts.

Where men of leisure might best be used, Godkin concluded, was in the public service. For the welfare of the country as well as for their own satisfaction, rich men ought to seek office and take seriously to politics. As it was, the legislative chambers of the land were infested with "veritable *chevaliers d'industrie,* or by venal politicians," intent only on pillaging the public. What was needed was to give some element of social prestige to public service, so that men of leisure and wealth would be tempted to offer their talents. "In the absence of this, the spectacle of their idleness must be treated as one of the severer tests of the regime of freedom." [18]

To Moorfield Storey's disgust, too many rich men refused to participate in disinterested reform politics; indeed, often they financed the very corrupt politicians who were his enemies. Who was responsible for the epidemic of official malfeasance in the country? Storey charged that the real culprits were the rich and respectable members of society, "who supply the money to accomplish a desired political result, who select unscrupulous men to spend it, and then shut their eyes." [19] Better than most liberals of his day, Storey understood that political corruption could be linked to exploitative, expanding capitalism. But his faith in moral persuasion was unshakable, and he could do no more than appeal to the integrity of those misguided rich men who financed evil politics.

With all the appeals to their sense of public duty, most politicians and reformers naturally professed great reluctance in asking for the voters' support. Politicians in democracies probably have always used the technique of disclaiming personal ambition when running for office; but the office-seekers in late-nineteenth-century America made a fetish of the practice. In the case of some liberal reformers the protests often bore a note of sincerity. After all, George William Curtis gave up a promising literary career to enter politics, and one can give credence to his description of the attraction of politics as "not a fascination, but a sense of duty—that terrible Conscience, the little domestic Chaplain, that makes me unwilling not to lend a hand as well as a hope and a prayer to the battle of the time." Knowing how introspection could rack the mind of any Adams, one can sympathize with Charles Francis Adams, Jr., in his complaint that being a reformer was "a most dispiriting task, which only a profound sense of obligation renders any man equal to." But Samuel J. Tilden, a shrewd and practical politician as well as an occasional reformer, also claimed that "only a sense of duty discharged to the state" kept him in politics. And surely, there was little candor in Grover Cleveland's lament in 1884, after a lifelong career as a professional politician, that he looked upon the coming four years as "a dreadful self-inflicted penance for the good of my country." [20]

4

Nor was it surprising, in view of their ambition to recruit gentlemen in politics, that reformers should have organized so many reform clubs during these years. Repelled by the coarse professionals, particularly in local politics, reformers naturally associated together in efforts to exert the pressure of decency and intelligence on government. After false starts and many disillusioning experiences a few of these reform clubs achieved considerable success.*

Hopefully, reform clubs would stimulate the interest of the "best people" in political affairs. Moorfield Storey commented in 1871 that the newly formed Massachusetts Reform Club clearly crystallized "the best political sentiment of the State." In New York, the Reform Club resolved to exercise great care in admitting to membership only "men on whose character dependence could be placed." Few reform organizations could have been more exclusive or more congenial for their members. As its directors modestly announced to the members, the club furnished the "usual facilities afforded by New York clubs" and aimed to develop a congenial circle of resident New Yorkers, while affording a "hospitable rendezvous for those of like tastes" visiting the city. Included in the club's "usual facilities" were parlors, dining halls, guest rooms, a library, a billiards room, and news and stock tickers. For the use of

---

* The organizations discussed below are representative of similar groups throughout the Northeast and West. Some specific organizations, such as the Civil Service Reform League and the Free Trade League, are considered in succeeding chapters.

these conveniences the club charged very modest fees. Bylaws, not dues, were relied upon to keep out undesirable members.[21]

Reflecting the primary interests of liberal reformers in the late nineteenth century, the New York Reform Club established committees on sound currency, tariff reform, city affairs, electoral and legislative reform, and civil service reform. Most of its activities, like those of its sister clubs throughout the country, consisted of publishing educational pamphlets on local and national issues, publicizing through friendly newspapers the iniquitous behavior of machine politicians, and endorsing candidates acceptable to the reform element in the community. Saloon watching, a chore often performed on election days, once raised a delicate question among members of the New York club. How much liquor ought to be drunk by "visiting members" in the saloons? After serious discussion, the point was resolved to the satisfaction of all: "At the suggestion of Mr. Opdyke it was thought best for each man to try to have some conversation soon after his day's work with some friends so as to enable the latter to testify in case of need that such work had not intoxicated the member, and that with this in view the matter might be safely left to individual discretion." [22]

Not all reform organizations were as worldly as the New York Reform Club. Some, like the venerable Radical Club of Chestnut Street in Boston, devoted their time to the discussion of popular and philosophical issues. Perhaps the most ambitious effort to organize liberal reformers nationally was undertaken by the Society for Political Education. Dedicated exclusively to the dissemination of educational material in the name of good government and reform, this body aimed to convert a million Americans to the cause of "free trade" and civil service reform. Promoted originally by David A. Wells, Charles Francis Adams, William Graham Sumner, and Horace White, the society published a weekly bulletin, *Million*, carrying the latest intelligence on civil service and tariff matters to a distinguished, exclusive membership. Apparently it was also a tightfisted membership, for the society perished within a few years, a victim of debts and lack of interest in its work.[23]

Troubles of a different sort beset the American Social Science Association, which many reformers helped to organize in 1865. Originally growing out of the efforts of Massachusetts to cope with the social headaches brought on by Irish and other immigration during the 1850's, the Social Science Association quickly involved itself in a bewildering mélange of issues and causes. Its interest in public charities, sewage disposal, life insurance, criminal law, Texas cattle diseases, music and art education, railroad libraries, kitchen improvements, the national census, infant mortality, teacher certification, public parks, and vaccination—as well as in civil service reform, free trade, sound currency, and honest politics—tended to diffuse its impact, both on the public and on reformers. With a zeal worthy of the antislavery crusade, the association once campaigned to introduce plaster heads of famous men into the schoolrooms of America and actually spent over $1,500 to so improve one school in Boston. To be sure, Curtis, Godkin, Atkinson, Wells, and a host of other gentlemen reformers belonged to the association and directed many of its activities during the 1860's and 1870's; but its roster included, as well, the names of such professional politicians as John Sherman and James G. Blaine. Moreover, as the historians of sociology in America note, it appeared at a time when the separate social sciences were beginning to mature as disciplines, so that a fusion of the several fields into one social science was impossible.[24]

Still, the association's *Journal of Social Science* became an important outlet for the views of liberal reformers and a pioneer scholarly journal in America. Although it professed to aim at harmonizing conflicting opinions on the great problems of the day, its approach to economic issues was distinctly orthodox. Doubtless, it contributed significantly to the crystallization, if not the ossification, of opinions among orthodox liberals about the direction and nature of reform.[25]

Reformers constantly faced the ridicule of the press. It was difficult for them to interest voters when their motives and actions were lampooned by clever newsmen. Under the headline "The Dudes Reform Club," the New York *World* once lashed out at the "fancy-pants" members of the Reform Club following a meeting of the group:

> At 8:15 the reporter of *The World* asked a young man attired in full evening dress when the meeting would be called to order: "I don't know," he answered with a drawl; "It is rahther hard to

get, ah, the members here before hahlf-past eight, you know, ah."
When the Chairman . . . rapped for order, those present, thirty-
eight in number, stopped eyeing each other in wonderful admiration and faced front. Fourteen were in full-dress suit, thirty-six
carried canes and twenty-two had their hair furrowed down the
centre.

Two Irishmen who walked into the room by mistake looked
around for a few moments and then went out, one of them
remarking: "If that's a Skirmishing Fund meeting, shure, it must
be a gathering of the treasurers of the branches."

"You are wrong, Mike," remarked his companion quietly;
"them's the sons of New York landowners, and they are going to
tell each other how their fathers collect the rent. It's a school in
hereditary economy, so it is."

According to the *World* account, the first speaker "made the political dudes—all Republicans—scowl when he referred to popular
uprisings to rebuke a party that becomes domineering." Theodore
Roosevelt, whom the reporter called "chief of the dudes," was introduced to the members as representing "the best quality in the
Legislature." The young assemblyman told his audience that there
was no such thing as class in politics, that "the vote of a bricklayer,
if honestly cast and cast with good intentions, should command as
much respect as the vote of a millionnaire." When Roosevelt finished, "the other dudes took the tops of their canes out of their
mouths and tapped the floor with the other end, and then they
lighted cigarettes." [26] Carrying canes and smoking cigarettes, apparently, were sure signs of "man millinery."

Such reports could not have made the work of reform groups any
easier and probably alienated whatever support they might have
received from the working class in New York and Boston. But the
reformers invited this kind of attack by advertising their ultra-
exclusiveness, their obvious class-consciousness, and their fastidious
approach to politics.[27] In seeking the support of masses of voters,
entrenched politicians could point to substantial, visible benefits,
which people in need actually received from the party organizations. More important, they could talk with the people in language
the common man understood. Reformers could only scold evil-
doers and predict the assumed results of their own corrective pro-

posals. What was needed was reformers who would go down into the wards of the cities and persuade voters that their best interests would be served by deserting the political machines.

Perhaps because it profited from the mistakes of earlier reform groups, the City Club of New York progressed a long way toward the objectives of liberal reform, at least in local politics. Founded in 1892, the City Club continued the work of the Reform Club in educating the voters to the issues. Like the Reform Club it maintained a club house with the "usual facilities" for its select membership. But the City Club did not stop at that point. Acknowledging that the present deplorable condition of the city government was not entirely the fault of the working class, the club endeavored to inform all classes of people on matters of concern to the community. Further, it went directly into the wards and helped workingmen organize their own clubs, "with club houses to take the place of the saloon to which they now resort." The advantages of this approach were obvious, the members thought. In the first place, it would give the club a large membership of rich and poor "on an absolutely democratic basis." At the same time, it would satisfy the needs of both groups by supplying the rich with a political meeting-place and the poor with a social club. Here was patrician reform allied with moral uplift.[28]

In practice, the City Club first established five subsidiary clubs known as "Good Government Clubs A, B, C, D, and E." Wealthy members of the parent organization paid for the rent of clubhouses, while the running expenses of each sponsored club were paid for by its own members, thus creating an ideal situation with "every member, rich and poor, paying exactly the same fees, and being put therefore on an absolutely equal and democratic footing." Eventually more than twenty of these Good Government clubs appeared, and, although Charles A. Dana of the *New York Sun* contemptuously labeled them as "Goo-Goos," they succeeded in rallying the voters of New York to the cause of municipal reform. Godkin, now editor of the *Evening Post* as well as of *The Nation*, was exuberant about the plan. "The main duty of the City Club," he advised its members, "will be . . . the duty of finding out who these creatures who reign over us are, how they get into city service, and in what manner they are earning their salaries, and of

explaining to the voters what they discover." The members themselves looked upon their task as twofold. First, the Club was to act as
a watchdog over the state legislature, helping to defeat bad legislation affecting New York City and securing the passage of beneficial
legislation. Second, it was to study carefully the work of the municipal government, correcting abuses where they existed and stimulating municipal officers to "progressive and constructive work." [29]

In 1894, the City Club and its Good Government offspring
achieved a spectacular victory in New York City politics. Acting
with other reformers, Democratic and Republican, the group nominated a "non-partisan" Republican candidate for mayor and succeeded in defeating the Tammany slate. This triumph was the first
significant success for reform in New York City since the overthrow
of Tweed. Godkin congratulated the reformers and the voters. His
Nation and his *Evening Post* had fought vigorously for the reform
ticket, and the reformers gave him credit for much of the victory.
Soon after the election, he warned his readers that Tammany
could be expected to rise again in about twenty years and that they
must remain alert. He was too optimistic. In 1897 the reformers
were swept out of office and Tammany was installed again at City
Hall.[30]

Nonetheless, the members of the City Club and reformers generally were encouraged by the attempts of the spoilsmen to campaign
as "non-partisans" in elections after 1894. More important, the enthusiasm for reform engendered among people of all classes in the
city augured well for the future.[31]

5

Liberal reformers also abhorred what they termed "party spirit."
The phrase was simply another name for intense partisanship or
devotion to political party. To reformers, it was a major cause of
debauchery in government.

Liberals did recognize the need for parties in the American political system. "Organization is the lens that draws the fiery rays of
conviction and enthusiasm to a focus and enables them to bury a
way through all obstacles," Curtis once told an audience. In 1870,
Carl Schurz assured his Senate colleagues that he recognized the

necessity for political parties; he even acknowledged that discipline was needed to make them function effectively. But "I have never been able to look up a party as a deity that has supernatural claims upon my veneration." It was the tendency to identify patriotism with loyalty to a political organization that liberals deplored in the American party system. Mark Twain, his interest in politics aroused enough in 1884 to make him a Mugwump, well expressed the opinion of most liberal reformers: "People seem to think they are citizens of the Republican Party and that that is patriotism and sufficiently good patriotism. I prefer to be a citizen of the United States." [32]

For many conscientious liberals the impeachment of Andrew Johnson and the aftermath of the trial dealt a murderous blow to political integrity. George William Curtis, a gentle person who rarely used strong language in his public addresses, castigated his party in caustic terms for its conduct during the crisis. Republican leaders were guilty of cant and hypocrisy; their ruthless treatment of the seven "apostate" senators reflected a party madness that was "treason not alone to the country, but to well-ordered human society." [33] Curtis believed that American elections should appeal to the intelligence of the people; but too often, he lamented, party spirit turned them into mere contests for success, "to be achieved by any means—by money, by forgery, by falsehood, by slander and venomous prejudice, and by the brute force of a military party discipline." Party loyalty ought always to be kept subordinate to patriotism, he argued; yet zealous partisans were always at hand to merge patriotism with party and to define "honest doubt and reasonable hesitation" as treason to the nation. To sophistry they added moral coercion. [34]

Mark Twain, in Washington in 1868, watched the impeachment crisis develop at first hand. Although he felt no sympathy for Johnson, the petty vindictiveness of Republicans in Congress toward the President shocked him. "Everybody is willing to see a fair stand-up fight between the President and his Congressional master," he observed, "but nobody is willing to see either of them descend to scratching and hairpulling." Some years later, when he had become better acquainted with politics and politicians, Mark Twain expressed his disgust at the idolatrous partisanship of most

Americans. Without a blush, he charged, the average citizen "will vote for an unclean boss if that boss is his party's Moses." Still later, as he reviewed a lifetime of political beliefs and experiences, he concluded that "we are all discreet sheep; we wait to see how the drove is going, and then go with the drove." In a mordant arraignment of "party spirit," he coupled political hypocrites of the postwar years with hypocrites of an earlier generation who had preached liberty and independence, while "closing their doors against the fugitive slave, beating his handful of humane defenders with Bible texts and billies, and pocketing the insults and licking the shoes of his Southern master." [35]

In opposition to "party spirit," liberal reformers exalted "true public spirit." The public-spirited individual ignored captious party arguments and considered each political question on its own merits. Although he might serve the party of his choice in promoting responsible measures and virtuous candidates, he would never hesitate to repudiate the organization for deviating from sound principles and respectable practices. Above all, he recognized at all times that popular government, like all government, was an expedient, not a panacea. Its abuses and evils must be exposed and resisted without thought of the consequences to parties or mere politicians. In the gospel of political reform, as one reformer preached it, true public spirit "suffereth long and is kind; envieth not; vaunteth not itself; is not puffed up; thinketh not evil; rejoiceth in the truth; beareth all things; hopeth all things; endureth all things." It was the foundation of all decency, the "perennial spring of liberty, of intellectual progress." Without true public spirit, human society would be a moral wasteland. [36]

Admirably complementing this interpretation of true public spirit was the concept of the independent man in politics. True independence in politics ultimately meant antagonism to the established party structure and was best reflected, perhaps, in the various agrarian and labor reform parties of the period. Few liberal reformers in the late nineteenth century were authentic independents. Rather, they asserted various degrees of conditional and usually temporary independence in their politics. George William Curtis exemplified the "conscience Republican," the reform politician who kept his roots deep in Republicanism, but who unstintingly censured and criticized his party when it erred. Basically, and despite his distaste for "party spirit," Curtis was a party man and an earnest worker whose contributions to Republicanism never were appreciated by the organization's leaders. His belief in the necessity for parties was strong, although always subject to the qualification that parties be instruments of responsible government and never implements for oppression in any form. He urged his audiences and his readers to join parties and to take an active part in party affairs. As he said in an oft-repeated speech, "Speculations about independent voters which imply that they should support neither party omit the cardinal fact that in politics as elsewhere a sensible man will do the best that the circumstances will allow without dishonor." [37] To be sure, Curtis deserted his party in 1884 to vote for Cleveland; but his defection was temporary and inspired by his conviction that the Republican party had deserted him.

Closer to the prototype of the true political independent was Moorfield Storey. To his last days, this leader in various reform movements of the nineteenth and twentieth centuries adhered to the principle that causes were better than parties. By the 1870's, Storey was convinced that the party system, having been tried faithfully, had proved a failure. Possibly the system was of value during periods of "strong excitement when some important question has stirred the people deeply," or when a party was young and its members were willing "to sink their personal preferences and ambitions for the good of the common cause." But during ordinary times it had been found absolutely ineffectual for securing so simple an objective as honest government.[38] Thus, the Republican party had been a worthy organization as the champion of Emancipation and Negro rights during the war and early Reconstruction years. In peacetime, however, it had failed miserably to sustain its idealism and to move ahead in pursuit of other needed reforms.

Storey left the Republican party, unofficially, in 1868, immediately after the impeachment crisis. Thereafter he considered himself a man without a party, yet a man of all parties. He associated himself with numerous organizations for municipal reform, lower tariffs, and civil service revision, and he always attracted appreciative audiences for his views on public questions. Storey was the minority man, the "congenital Mugwump" who raised the questions that embarrassed politicians and who became a nuisance at political gatherings. As his biographer observed, he was often a "remarkably uncomfortable fellow to have about," but he added a positive element of richness and strength to the community.[39]

Somewhere between Storey's conspicuous individualism and Curtis's more strategic independence most other liberal reformers stood. All of them preferred to think of themselves as "independent animals"; but before liberal Republican reformers could break out of their party's confining postwar structure they had to pass through a period of uncomfortable political soul-searching.[40] With them it was not a question of how to leave the Republican party, but of what to do once they had made the break.

Most liberals, of course, emerged from the Civil War as Republicans even if they had not been members of that party before the conflict. They had joined the party because it opposed slavery and championed human rights. As for the party's economic program, as written into law during the war, there were points in it to which many liberals objected. They supported the program chiefly because it seemed to strengthen the Union cause. Later, as the party's leaders demonstrated their determination not only to retain the program intact, but to strengthen it further and to extend it, liberals rebelled. With few exceptions liberals were advocates of reduced tariffs, and party leaders ignored their demands for financial reform. All liberal reformers insisted upon some degree of civil service reform, but Republican spokesmen too often scoffed at their arguments.

As the revelations of scandal in the Grant administration multiplied, liberal Republicans began to lose faith in their old organization as an instrument for good government. Godkin concluded that the party, after all, had "nothing ecclesiastical" about it, no "divine mission," no "personal consecration." On the contrary, the Grant scandals proved that it was "a common human organization," existing for the ordinary political purposes of keeping itself in power and extending its influence by using any device, any subterfuge. Under the leadership of the Chandlers and Conklings and Camerons, said Carl Schurz, the Republican party was "rapidly going to perdition." One reformer believed it would be better for the party if it lost an election rather than have it "die in the act of perpetuating a brutal one man power." [41]

But where were these liberals to turn for political expression if they left the Republican party? For years they had viewed the Democratic party as the political home of ignorant voters. They deplored the rush of Irish and other immigrants, particularly in the big cities, to the party of Tammany and Tweed. They accused the Democrats of contaminating the political atmosphere, of catering to the irresponsible whims of the working class, and of championing dangerous and immoral schemes to debase the currency. "The Democratic party was the first to treat character as if it were of no consequence," Godkin charged. A friend wrote to Charles Sumner of his fears that the Democrats, if they ever took control of the country again, "will never part with it save through revolution." [42]

As fraud and corruption mounted in their own party, liberal Republicans found it painful to consider giving the Democrats another chance to govern the nation. They hoped that the Republican party either would clean itself or allow itself to be purified by its reform-minded members. It was this type of thinking that inspired Carl Schurz and other reformers to launch the Liberal Republican party in 1872. Fundamentally, the new organization was designed to coerce the Grant Republicans into accepting some reforms. To be successful, however, a reform movement on so grand a scale required the support of thousands of Democratic voters. Liberal Republicans were forced to take a fresh look at the old "party of treason."

Godkin, for one, considered the problem carefully. Could Democrats possibly be used in a national party of reform? "If we remember with any gratitude the 500,000 soldiers who perished in the struggle," he reflected, "we can never consent that the party which was sneering, dabbling, and hindering while they were fighting shall in its old form and character again come to the front." Yet, he acknowledged, "we all of us know individual Democrats who are very nice people." Some Democrats were "good husbands and good fathers," some even paid their debts and went to church. Taken together, to be sure, they made up the "dreadful Democratic party," but perhaps they were not all beyond redemption.

The answer, then, was to exorcise the devil, to "eliminate from a respectable Democrat his democracy, separate him from his evil associations," and thus transform him into a useful citizen.[43]

Reconciliation between liberal Democrats and liberal Republicans first occurred with the Greeley candidacy in 1872, and it was placed on a more substantial basis following the Compromise of 1877. It was a *rapprochement* that reformers viewed with satisfaction, for it indicated to them that "party tyranny" was giving way to good sense in politics. No longer did reform-minded Republicans feel compelled to support their party when its leaders showed contempt for their suggestions. By endorsing the reform candidate Greeley and by accepting the election of Hayes, the Democratic party had proved that it contained some element, at least, of sense and respectability. Liberals of both parties could now unite on occasion to punish machine politicians and cynical office-holders. "The signs of sense and health are increasing," wrote Samuel Bowles after the election of 1876. "The people will yet speak out against the politicians; the moral forces will assert their supremacy."[44]

6

John J. Ingalls was the kind of politician the liberal reformers loathed. When he became a Republican senator from Kansas in 1869, Ingalls made no pretense to being a statesman. He was in politics for whatever he could get from it, and he served his party best as a specialist in the "bloody shirt" brand of political declamation. His talent for derisive rhetoric had first shown itself at Williams College, where, as a student, he had made life miserable for several of his teachers. As commencement orator in 1855, he had uncharitably characterized his four years at the other end of Mark Hopkins's log as "Mummy Life," and the faculty had very nearly denied him his diploma for his effrontery. As a professional politician he retained his outspoken habits and seemed to enjoy discomfiting reformers. "Government is force," he told them bluntly. "Politics is a battle for supremacy. Parties are the armies. The decalogue and the golden rule have no place in a political campaign. The object is success." [45] To many reformers, Ingalls was evil incarnate in the Senate chambers.

Ingalls's cynical approach to public service and his attitude of undisguised self-interest contrasted starkly with liberal concepts of public spirit and independent judgment. Many liberal reformers thought of themselves as practical men who approached politics with cold, shrewd objectivity. Indeed, they looked upon the intense partisans as impractical political theorists who attempted to let an organization take the place of a policy. "I believe politics to be an extremely practical kind of business," Godkin wrote, "and that the communities which succeed best in it are those which bring least enthusiasm to the conduct of their affairs." The editor of *The Nation* even recognized the need, in a reformed civil service, for paid party managers and political henchmen. He claimed that no one expected the "man inside politics" to disappear from the scene when civil service reform became a reality. "All that we ask is to improve him. We want to mend his morals and his manners; to give him a little better education, a little stronger sense of moral obligation. . . ." The author of a popular treatise on municipal reform urged reformers to apply strict business principles to their work, for "it is easier to appeal to men through their purse than by way of their conscience." [46]

Reformers doubtless learned much about practical politics from their disheartening experiences with the professionals. After the Liberal Republican defeat in 1872, Charles Francis Adams, Jr., concluded that future gatherings of reformers must be kept as private as possible. He and his friends wanted no more contact with the "political bummers" and misguided idealists who had ruined them at Cincinnati. To the organizers of New York's City Club, the first essential in starting any reform organization was to shun the advice and company of earlier, impractical reformers, such as those who let victory slip away so quickly after deposing Boss Tweed. Ever since the 1870's they had roamed about town sanctimoniously and dolorously offering their advice to anyone who would listen, and they were still "deadly in their ability to kick the common sense out of any plan that might be proposed." In the course of their political education, many reformers learned how to use the tricks of the professionals—how to "scratch" the ballot and how to confound the machines with separate "irregular" party lists, for example.[47]

But in the minds of most reformers, all of these pronouncements and devices were secondary as instruments of reform to the power of moral persuasion. At the base of all liberal reform were the traditional values of Protestant morality—values they considered essential to the operation of clean, responsible government. The virtues they most frequently emphasized were integrity, truthfulness, patriotism, fair-dealing, scrupulousness, simplicity, and manliness. "That government is not best which best secures mere life and property," Mark Twain moralized; "there is a more valuable thing—manhood." Seemingly, manliness or manhood implied courage, decency, and forthrightness. Godkin, who had difficulty discriminating in his own actions between the moral approach and the practical attack, believed that the American political system rested necessarily on a moral foundation. The great trouble of his day, as he saw it, was the drift away from the moral sense of the past. "One of the very valuable social features of Puritanism was the weight of its moral yoke," he contended. "It made right living so stern and hard, so full of self-denial, that the cheats fled from it, and sooner than assume the burden gave up all claim to the good opinion of their neighbors." In his own age there was a growing indulgence for "all kinds of immorality which may be covered by the term 'smart.'" One reason his journal was respected by liberals was because it aspired to a moral purpose.[48]

For many liberal reformers, the remedy for corruption and deceit in high places was very simple: resurrect the moral principles of the past and apply them to business, politics, and everyday life. No problem was so great that stern, simple morality would not solve it. "Make it noble enough, firm and absolute enough, and it will carry the country," one reformer said of civil service reform. All the better laws and institutions and all the refining influence of culture would not suffice to bring about municipal reform unless men developed "more Christian character." Legislation and social panaceas were vain "unless the heart be renewed." Wendell P. Garrison was convinced that the nation was in need of nothing so much as "further instruction in morality . . . the example of pure character." Even more emphatic than his friends, Carl Schurz suggested that dishonesty and corruption were treason to the nation and that offenders should be treated accordingly.[49]

Reformers tolerated few lapses by politicians from these stern moral requirements. Men in public office were expected to battle constantly for reform and to trust in the people for support when parties and "managers" inflicted punishment on them for performing "good deeds." The ideal politician, most reformers agreed, was the man willing to sacrifice himself for reform. He was a teacher who taught by example as well as by precept, and his lessons were always compounded of the noblest ideals of virtue and patriotism. He was a man like George William Curtis, "always fair, always candid, always honest, and always polished; never . . . misrepresents, distorts, or makes the worse appear the better reason." Or he might fit the description of David A. Wells given by one of his acquaintances: "an instance in a conspicuous way not merely of the crusading but of the proselytizing and preaching spirit." [50]

Few politicians, even those who were sympathetic to reform, could have met these exacting moral standards for political excellence. Late-nineteenth-century America produced only ordinary mortals, and liberal reformers wanted perfect human specimens in public office. Circumscribed as it was by rigid, yet chimerical idealism, the reformer's concept of public service was impossible to attain. Old-fashioned liberalism, which had lost its vitality long before the Civil War, became an anachronism in the Gilded Age. As it languished, its defenders sought to salvage and revive its moral content; but they failed to perceive that most Americans had become unreceptive to ethical discourses in the old vein. The post-Civil War period was an era of transition in which old values and settled ways inevitably were outraged. Liberal reformers stood almost alone in attempting to maintain standards of right and wrong at a time when other public figures spurned such standards. For their efforts, they deserve distinction; yet, in one respect, at least, liberals proved themselves to be as fallibly mortal as their antagonists. Their moral precepts and standards of conduct were always qualified by their own emotional responses to the specific issues of the period.

4

"Sadly Honest-Looking Gentlemen"

We have been terribly beaten. . . . I was assailed so bitterly that I hardly knew whether I was running for the Presidency or the Penitentiary.

HORACE GREELEY, 1872

I cannot help laughing to think how, after all our labor and after we had by main force created a party for Schurz to lead, he himself, without a word or a single effort to keep his party together, kicked us over in his haste to jump back to the Republicans.

HENRY ADAMS, 1876

"AN ILLEGIBLE CANDYDATE," SAID MR. DOOLEY TO MR. HEN-nessey, "is a candydate that can't be read out iv th' party. 'T is a joke I med up." For liberal reformers in the Gilded Age, the task of finding "illegible" candidates for high office was the farthest thing from a joke. On the contrary, it was an ordeal they suffered through every four years, as they sought a champion who could run for the presidency without being read out of his party for associating too closely with the "reform crowd." In each campaign they invited some aspiring politician to take up reform as a personal crusade and hold to it against the worst the opposition could throw at him. Early in the period they assumed their task would be a simple one, for they could not believe that voters would reject sound principles and good men. Offer the voters candidates they can trust and respect, they argued, and reform will come naturally. If neither major party responds to the demands of decent, responsible men for clean politics and sound economics, organize as a "party of the centre" to swing support for reform from one banner to another. Ultimately, liberals were sure, the regular parties would have to acknowledge the strength of the independent men in politics.

From the start, however, liberals suffered disheartening experiences. As Senator Ingalls told them bluntly, the only purpose of

national elections was "to defeat the antagonist and expel the
party in power." [1] Neither party wanted to take forthright stands
on the issues most dear to reformers, and party leaders seemed intent only on safeguarding their personal sinecures. Under the circumstances, the struggle for liberal reform at the national level put
the talents and determination of the "best men" to a severe test.
They looked to General Grant as a reformer, but their hero
quickly disappointed them. Horace Greeley almost turned their
crusade into a comedy; and Rutherford B. Hayes proved too weak
to carry out his own good intentions. When New York Democrats
trundled Grover Cleveland onto the national scene in the 1880's,
the "best men" wanted desperately to believe that, at last, they had
found their long-awaited advocate.

2

Prior to the election of 1872, liberals within the Republican
party worked chiefly to prevent the "dreadful Democrats" from assuming control of the national government. They supported Grant
in 1868, sure that the national hero would restore morality and
dignity to politics after the frenzied disorder of the impeachment
crisis. Republicans had an easy time in the 1868 election, for the
Radical coalition still functioned relatively intact and the Democrats still suffered from their wartime reputation as the "party of
treason." "Bloody shirt" oratory was the outstanding characteristic
of the campaign, for party leaders wanted the election to result in
an emphatic mandate to continue the policies they had pursued
since the war.

Liberal reformers waved the bloody shirt as frantically as any of
the Republican scaremongers. Southerners might "roar even more
gently than sucking doves," Carl Schurz told a Chicago audience,
but the rebel element had shown its hand again, and "we have
seen the dagger in the sleeve." Democrats would stir up old troubles, ruin national credit and prosperity, and jeopardize the peace
of the country. Samuel Bowles told his readers that "Vallandig-
ham, the Jonah of the Democratic party from '61 to '66, is still its
prophet, still its ruler, still its grave-digger." [2] Much of the fearful
ranting of many Republicans undoubtedly reflected their deter-

mination to exploit fully the timely Reconstruction issue. But most liberals sincerely feared the Democratic platform's heretical "Ohio idea" for redeeming government bonds with Greenbacks rather than with gold. Orthodox liberals had opposed currency inflation during the war, and they looked upon the Democratic party's "surrender" to financial schemers as an unforgivable blunder. No matter that the party largely nullified its currency plank by nominating the "sound money" New York politician Horatio Seymour. It was clear that the Democratic party contained a dangerously large number of reckless men.[3]

Republican liberals did not all admire Grant, although generally they accepted him as the logical candidate. Several years before the election, Godkin had warned of the danger in placing military men in civil offices, and he advised Grant to stay out of politics and confine himself to a "judicious silence" on public issues.[4] In 1867 Moorfield Storey viewed the general as an "ordinary rowdy officer" and thought him quite unfit for the presidency. But other liberals expected great things from their hero. "Let them that can, pronounce a name more dear or more renowned," Samuel Bowles challenged. Grant was the man who would secure the "full and final reconstruction of the South," bring about a "thorough and searching retrenchment in the expenses of government," and introduce into the civil service "the same high standards with which his military selections have ever been made." Above all, Grant would be a President free from the usual party ties and indifferent to re-election. In Cambridge, Charles Eliot Norton expressed confidence in Grant's strong will and character, although he wished the general had "less of the habit of command and more responsive popular sympathies."[5]

The reformers not only had an aversion to the Democratic party in 1868, but they sincerely believed that the Republican party was still the stronghold of morality and responsibility. To be sure, the extremism of some Republicans on the question of Reconstruction had frightened liberals, and the whole impeachment fiasco had shocked many of them. But the party was stronger than its loud leaders, they believed, and with Grant in the White House it would reassert its essential integrity. As Norton saw it, the election afforded reformers a great opportunity to purge the party and free it from "the burden of the sins of the extremists" who were trying to dominate it.[6] There was no other party the "best men" could support, nor did they have any real inclination to look elsewhere. They voted straight Republican in 1868 as a matter of course.

3

Several days after Grant's inauguration, George William Curtis expressed "profound disappointment" at the new President's announcement of his cabinet selections. The worthy editor of *Harper's Weekly* saw no reason to lose faith in Grant, however. "I only see that if he loosens his hold upon the party he loses his chance for real reform, and I shall be grievously disappointed if he does not see it more plainly than anybody." [7] Although Curtis later came to know Grant as a man of many weaknesses, he retained his faith in the President during the next four years. Other liberal reformers became disillusioned with the hero-President, quickly and decisively.

As President, Grant accomplished little to win him the support, much less the respect, of liberal reformers. He proved to be a man of ignorance where important national issues were concerned; worse, he showed no desire to be informed by competent men. His cabinet was indeed a "profound disappointment" to many of his early supporters; and Grant himself seemed to be completely in sympathy with the postwar leaders of American big business. Moreover, he consorted with such characters as Jim Fisk and Roscoe Conkling—men whom reformers considered utter scoundrels. Reformers who supported Grant in 1868 had been confident he would attack the spoils system and institute some measure of civil service reform, but during his first two years in office the President ignored reform and made full use of the patronage machinery.

Late in 1870, Grant and his Stalwart supporters seemingly made an important concession to the reformers by establishing a Civil Service Commission. George William Curtis, who had pleaded earnestly with the President for the creation of such a body, became its first chairman. The chances for substantial political reform looked bright to Curtis, for he believed Grant sincerely desired it. Long after the general left the White House, Curtis continued to defend his motives. But unfortunately for the reformers, the new Commission had little opportunity to function, for Grant gave it only perfunctory recognition, and Congress soon relieved his administration of the troublesome reformers by cutting off the Commission's funds. Most liberals never were as sanguine as Curtis about the Commission, and they gave the President little credit for his gesture as a reformer.[8]

Grant's ignorance of reform issues and his essential sympathy with the aims of big business contributed to a steady rise in tariff rates during his early years in office. True, in 1870 and again in 1872 Congress made minor reductions, but Grant's men tolerated no real deviation from the principle of protection. Tariff reformers were not deceived, and they blamed the President for not taking the initiative in pressing for reduced duties. Further, although Grant ostensibly was a "sound money" man, reformers felt he vacillated dangerously on the currency question. The second Legal Tender decision in 1871, probably dictated by Grant's appointees to the Supreme Court, upheld the constitutionality of paper money and badly frightened currency reformers.

The manner in which Grant and his advisers treated the few friends the reformers could claim in the administration offended liberals. In 1870 Grant squeezed Attorney General Ebenezer R. Hoar of Massachusetts out of the cabinet in a maneuver to gain Stalwart support for his impulsive scheme to annex Santo Domingo. The issue of expansion in the Caribbean also brought an end to the political career of Senator Charles Sumner, who was removed from the chairmanship of the Committee on Foreign Relations and stripped of his influence in the Senate as punishment for his outspoken opposition to the scheme. Sumner was an annoyance to the new leaders in the Senate, who struck a hard blow at the reform element in the Republican party by destroying his political power. David A. Wells, the President's Commissioner of Internal Revenue, also left the administration by request in 1870. Wells's removal was a particularly serious blow to reformers, for they had counted on the liberal economist to keep the President "responsible" on financial matters. His "free trade" views, however, made Wells an unwelcome participant in the administration.

Mounting grievances of this sort against the administration

sufficed to alienate scattered groups of liberal reformers; but it is doubtful that a full-blown revolt within the party would have ensued had it not been for the continued rankling of the Reconstruction issue. This irritant above all originally inspired reformers to start the Liberal Republican movement. Instead of pressing for a speedy and efficient end to the problem of the South, Grant allowed his leaders in Congress to continue what liberals termed the "oppressive treatment" of the defeated section. For several years liberal opinion had been moving steadily in the direction of reconciliation with the South, and it probably accepted fully the idea of final reunion when Grant approved the Force Acts of 1870 and 1871. These measures seemed to indicate that the administration was determined to continue military rule and to subject the "better elements" in the South to new indignities. With few exceptions, liberal reformers opposed the acts and began to call publicly for an end to Reconstruction. "The South ought now to be dropped by Congress," Godkin declared tersely in *The Nation*, and most liberals agreed with him.[9]

Liberal Republicanism essentially was a movement to rid the Republican party of Grantism, not to alter permanently the two-party system in America. But it was far from a pure reform effort, for many Liberal Republicans were interested chiefly in promoting their personal fortunes at the expense of Grant and his followers. Disgruntled Republican politicians, rivals of the Stalwart faction, looked to the movement as a weapon with which to strike at their political enemies. Some extreme protectionists saw the new party as an instrument for committing Republicanism firmly and irrevocably to a high tariff doctrine. Grant's failure as President was a "pitiful story, one of the most pitiful in political history," as Godkin observed; but there was no universal agreement among the delegates who gathered at Cincinnati in 1872 as to exactly where and how the President had failed. They all conceded only that he should be defeated in the coming election.[10]

Before the Cincinnati convention, many liberal reformers were convinced that the Republican party could be cleaned from within its existing structure. Republicans in the early 1870's naturally shied from admitting that their party, which so recently had saved the Union and emancipated the slaves, had become permanently demoralized by corruption. Regardless of any differences among its members about the currency or the tariff, Samuel Bowles insisted, the party would be successful as long as it was "the party of ideas and is not broken down by corruption." At the first sign of the movement for a new reform party, the Massachusetts editor claimed that the Republican organization had the vitality and flexibility needed to grapple with any problem. He advised "doctrinaires and reformers" to look to Republicanism as their instrument of progress and as the means for reforming even its own abuses. After all, he concluded, what hope was there of reforming the Democrats? [11]

Carl Schurz, first of the Liberal Republicans, as late as the spring of 1871 believed the parent body could be saved. Its corrupt leadership had to be routed and its "office-mongering" element had to be convinced that Grant's renomination was impracticable. By the next winter, he predicted confidently, the Stalwarts would be in a demoralized condition as a result of exposure to the "breeze of public opinion." Perhaps George William Curtis was more keenly sensitive to the shortcomings of Grant than many of his friends, for he was intimately associated with the Republican party in New York. But he was positive that the party could be reformed from within. Grant, with all his faults, stood as a bulwark against "every kind of Democratic, rebellious, Ku-Klux, disconcerted, hopeful, and unreasonable feeling." Another editor warned that any bolting from the Republican party would have to be done "in the name of extreme protection, and in the interest of abuse and not of reform." [12]

Some liberals feared that the Democrats would be the only beneficiaries of a split in Republican ranks. "Can you save Schurtz [sic]?" asked one of Sumner's friends. The Missouri senator already had declared himself a "Liberal" and was being pushed to a position from which he would be "forced at last to jump into the embrace of the enemy." Everyone agreed that reformers ought not to go over to the Democrats, Godkin asserted. Reform should be sought "inside the party lines," for a Democratic administration would create fearful confusion by reopening old questions and by experimenting with new schemes. [13]

Despite the confidence of many liberals that the Republican

party could save itself from destruction, insurgency rose steadily among party members all over the country. Probably the strongest impulse to revolt came from some of the Southern states, where the more conservative Whiggish spokesmen for reconciliation were engaged in a bitter struggle for power with Radical "carpetbagger" politicians. Insurgents in Missouri were particularly successful in their efforts to overthrow the Radicals, and the triumph of these self-styled "Liberals" there in 1870 led directly to the formation of the national Liberal Republican party two years later. Carl Schurz, senator from Missouri at the time, was the leading figure in his state's rebellion against Radicalism.[14]

Schurz was also instrumental the same year in bringing the American Free Trade League into alliance with insurgent Republicans. This organization's activities in the early 1870's furnish an excellent example of the effect political independence sometimes had on party politicians. Organized in 1869 by a group of tariff reformers, including David Ames Wells, Horace White, Edward Atkinson, and William Cullen Bryant, the Free Trade League was a temporary rallying point for all liberal reform forces. It furnished lecturers to interested audiences, published numerous tracts and pamphlets, and entered actively into the congressional elections of 1870. It was a successful organization, for the New York *Tribune* (Horace Greeley's strongly protectionist paper) credited it with responsibility for the defeat of a dozen Republican congressmen.[15]

Shortly after the elections of 1870, the Free Trade League called a conference on revenue and tariff reform at New York. An illustrious group of public figures attended the meeting, including Schurz, Godkin, Bowles, Wells, White, Bryant, and Charles Francis Adams. Styling themselves "Independents," these reformers forced the regular Republican leaders to give some attention to their gathering. Speaker of the House James G. Blaine, in particular, speculated that these irksome reformers might continue displacing loyal Republican congressmen and thus jeopardize his own powerful position in Congress. After the meeting adjourned, he promised Horace White that League-supported men would be given a majority on the House Ways and Means Committee at the next session of Congress. The wily Maine Republican later reneged on his pledge, thus adding to the dissatisfaction of reformers with regular

Republicanism.[16] In coping with the Liberal movement, regular party leaders always moved carefully, yet confidently. They realized that many insurgents were influential publicists, and they made concessions of a minor nature whenever concession seemed advisable. It is likely that this attitude of discretion prompted them to concede the trifling tariff reductions of 1870 and 1872.

By late 1871, it was clear that a definite Liberal Republican faction existed and that its sympathizers were in regular communication with each other.[17] Once under way, the Liberal Republicans had to decide where to go. Were they to remain within the Republican organization to act as the party's conscience? Or should they form a new party and move into competition with the two established organizations? Prominent editors, such as Samuel Bowles and Murat Halstead, were reluctant to leave the old party, although they continued to move steadily closer to the idea of an independent movement. No longer confident of the party's ability to purify itself, Bowles urged Republicans to seek a candidate in sympathy with the party's "moral and intellectual tone, its reforming and progressive traditions." In an editorial in the *Cincinnati Commercial,* the most influential Western newspaper at the time, Halstead pleaded with Grant to save the party by making some sincere concessions to the reform faction. In March 1871, Schurz thought the party still could save itself by jettisoning Grant. As he told Godkin, "Then the liberal and vigorous element in the Rep. party, who alone can save its future usefulness, will have a chance to assume control of the organization and shape its future policy." But Schurz already had publicly denounced the administration so scathingly that few observers doubted his desire for a new party. The Missouri leader made his position unmistakably clear in October, when he asked Ohio's Jacob D. Cox: "Would not the 'Central Republican Association' [a Liberal group in Cincinnati] be now prepared to open its ranks to progressive Democrats and to work in harmony with the movement commenced in the South?" Schurz's Liberal Republicanism would work closely with the Democrats and forsake the Grant Republicans entirely.[18]

Throughout the winter many liberal reformers consulted their consciences as they watched the administration continue on its "irresponsible" way. By April 1872, most of them were ready for a separate convention and a reform ticket for the coming election. Some thought this action would force the regular Republicans to drop Grant.[19] Others, more realistic in appraising the situation, realized that a new ticket would have to remain in the field for a showdown with the President. Charles Nordhoff, in California early in 1872, wrote Schurz urging him to "screw up the courage" of the Liberals and keep them in the campaign to the end. One old Radical, George W. Julian, studied the Liberal movement carefully and pronounced it "conscientious and patriotic, and profoundly in earnest." Once he had called for the confiscation of Southern land; but in 1872, bitter at the party which he felt had sacrificed him to expediency two years earlier, he had no difficulty in reconciling his recent radicalism with the new forces of reconciliation. And Horace White informed Sumner: "I, for one, am going to fight out the battle . . . not because *you* were made a victim of despotism . . . but because such a despotism exists." "Can you do any less?" he asked the mistreated senator.[20]

Among leading liberal reformers only Bryant, Godkin, and Curtis did not openly favor the formation of a new party as their friends convened at Cincinnati. Curtis was in sympathy with the aims of the insurgents; but, detesting the thought of working with the Democratic party, he remained loyal to Grant. Moreover, he saw through the reform façade of the Cincinnati movement. There were too many disappointed spoilsmen in the group, too many unreconstructed rebels, to suit him. No thoughtful Southerner, he reminded his friends, could truthfully say that the policy of the Republican party had ever been "a vindictive policy." Not a life had been taken, not a dollar confiscated. "Political and civil rights have been made equal, and all that has been required is that they shall be respected." [21]

Godkin and Bryant attended the convention and participated in some of its business. The octagenarian Bryant gave the Liberals only cautious sympathy, for he still thought the regular Republican organization sound. After the convention he campaigned with surprising energy against his old rival Greeley. As for Godkin, there was no doubt where he stood on the issues that brought the Liberal Republicans together. But he was skeptical that the motley gathering of tariff reformers and protectionists ever could work in harmony. He did not object to the idea of forming a new party; indeed, he believed a new reform party was an absolute necessity. But he preferred to see a party composed entirely of reformers who agreed with his views. Godkin actually believed that his kind of reform party would sweep Grant from office.[22]

As they gathered in the Ohio city for the opening session of the convention, the reform-minded delegates were enthusiastic and confident. They were about to smash Grant's machine and give the nation a slate and platform that would bring decency and responsibility back to government. "The gathering disgusts of three years," one journalist at the scene predicted, "are about to drive from office an administration elected with unanimity, tried patiently, and found incurably vicious." [23]

Yet the Liberal Republican convention was a melancholy disappointment to most liberal reformers. From the start they had difficulty persuading "good men" to attend the meeting. One great weakness was the gathering's heterogeneous composition: it was as motley a collection of politicians and reformers as ever tried to form a political party in the United States. Among the delegates were free traders and protectionists, conservative New England patricians and agrarian radicals, civil service reformers and unvarnished spoilsmen, advocates of Negro rights and Southern Redeemers. Reformers went into the convention strong and optimistic, to be sure, and Carl Schurz gave them their battle cries in his address as permanent chairman. Liberal Republicans would defiantly set their sense of duty against "the arrogance of power, like the bugle blast of doomsday," he told them. Out of their labors at Cincinnati would come "a Government which the best people of this country will be proud of." But the reformers were quickly scattered by a combination of bad luck, their own political bungling, and the resourcefulness of their opponents. In three days of hectic political lightheadedness, the delegates wrote a platform that called for an end to Reconstruction, denounced repudiation "in every form and guise," and referred the tariff issue to "the people in their Congressional districts." And they climaxed the crusade for reform by nominating Horace Greeley, whose claim to the title of reformer stemmed from his record of having lit briefly on virtually every new scheme he had encountered in a kaleidoscopic career.[24]

Long after the event, Godkin wrote of Greeley: "His stock of general knowledge was deplorably small; his great merit in my eyes was his sincerity, though his prejudice and self-conceit made him ridiculous." Had the Cincinnati delegates deliberately worked to select the candidate most unfit for the presidency and most perilously vulnerable to attack, they could have done no better. To be sure, the quixotic editor of the *Tribune* had a reputation as a reformer; but it was a reputation made in another age and on issues other than those confronting the nation in 1872. He understood little about the aspirations of postwar liberals, and his editorials had been frankly contemptuous of their efforts. Not the least of his weaknesses as a reformer were his ties with certain unsavory Republican politicians in New York. Above all, Greeley was a dedicated protectionist, completely intolerant of the Free Trade League and scornful of all reformers who advocated a low tariff.[25]

Many reform leaders and "independents" were shocked by the developments at Cincinnati. Norton, who had hoped to see Charles Francis Adams receive the nomination, groaned at the thought of Greeley's election. Godkin and his assistant, Wendell P. Garrison, described the convention's results as "dolorous or farcical, or both." "If it is Grant or Greeley, I remain at home on election day," Garrison vowed. Others made the best of an unfortunate situation. Julian was disappointed, but he decided to support the convention's choice. He had been impressed by the "determined moral purpose" of the gathering and by the fact that he had not seen "one drunk man in the convention or on the streets of the city." Nordhoff decided to "stick to Cincinnati" despite his regret that Lyman Trumbull had not been nominated. On the last day of the convention, Samuel Bowles telegraphed his paper the opinion that Greeley's election "will freshly illustrate and powerfully advance the cause of representative government." Reflecting editor Horace White's reconciliation to the results, the *Chicago Tribune* announced that "Greeley is the people's candidate and it is useless to oppose him." Probably many delegates consoled themselves, as White did, by arguing that Schurz would continue to be Liberal

Republicanism's "leader and the master mind of this great movement, no matter who is President." [26]

Certainly no liberal faced a more woeful dilemma as a result of the nominations than Carl Schurz. Liberal Republicanism had been his personal crusade, and now it had degenerated to a fiasco. "I cannot yet think of the results of the Cincinnati convention without a pang," he confided a few days after the meeting adjourned. Schurz's pang probably resulted, in part, from knowledge that his political foes in Missouri, led by B. Gratz Brown and Francis Preston Blair, had been instrumental in sabotaging his own candidate, Adams. Indeed, Brown had received the nomination for vice-president partly as a result of the Missouri delegation's maneuver. Yet, Schurz also sincerely distrusted Greeley, personally and politically; and he sought to persuade the editor to withdraw from the campaign on the grounds that trickery had been employed in securing the nomination and that the candidate's views on revenue reform would alienate the Free Trade League. In reply, Greeley accused the Missouri senator of worrying more about the German vote at home than about the success of the ticket. "Of course most of the Germans dislike me, not so much that I am a protectionist as that I am a Total Abstinence man," he charged. But Schurz was determined to test the opinion of other reformers before he announced publicly his support of the Greeley-Brown ticket. [27]

Late in May, a group of revenue reformers and other dissatisfied Liberal Republicans met in New York's Steinway Hall to discuss their plight. Some suggested a new convention be called to nominate Charles Francis Adams and write a platform faithful to reform. All that resulted from the meeting, however, was a decision to await the results of the regular Republican convention in June. If Grant was renominated, liberals then could take steps to name a new candidate. On June 20, after the President's easy victory, the reformers reassembled in New York. By this late date, most insurgents had persuaded themselves that Greeley was the lesser of two evils. Schurz made an effective plea for support of the Liberal ticket and rebuked the diehard anti-Greeley reformers for having failed to participate more actively in the Cincinnati convention. In effect, they could blame only themselves for their present unhappy

predicament. Moreover, he asserted, the most pressing of "public
considerations" was the deplorable condition of the South, and all
reformers ought to unite in resisting Grant's oppressive measures
there. Still chagrined, but reconciled, the reformers could do nothing more, and the meeting adjourned. "The Conference has doubt-
lessly convinced you that there was no escape from the Greeley-
Grant alternative," Schurz confided to Godkin. Any attempt to
create a new ticket would have increased the confusion and put the
new man in a ridiculous position. But Schurz's rationalizations did
not convince Godkin, for in the editor's opinion the lesser of the
two evils was Grant, not Greeley.[28]

In July the Democrats met at Baltimore to decide between
Greeley and one of their own. At the White House, the President
likened the convention to an incubation. What would the egg now
being hatched produce, he wondered, and how much care would
the parents give their offspring once it appeared? Grant predicted
the progeny would resemble "a full moon, with spectacles on the
man in it," but he doubted it would be "caressed as much after
hatching as during incubation. . . ." When the Democrats chose
Greeley and his platform, the President decided the election would
require no active campaigning on his part. As he told Conkling,
from a somewhat simplistic view of political history, only two previous presidential candidates had gone to the stump. "Both of
them were public speakers, and both were beaten. I am no public
speaker and don't want to be beaten." [29]

Orators for the regular Republicans could now "wave the bloody
shirt" at their old enemies, the Democrats, and at their new foes,
the reformers. The campaign was "nasty," as Curtis noted, but it
was also a one-sided affair from the start. Greeley was easy to ridicule, and Republican editors made the most of the opportunity to
strike at their old competitor. Godkin publicly announced his support of Grant, distasteful as the choice was for him. Greeley was
bad for reform, he wrote; defeat him now and insure the nomination of a *real* reformer four years hence. Sharply criticizing his old
friend Charles Sumner for supporting the Liberals, John Murray
Forbes insisted that all other issues in the campaign were incidental to the fate of Reconstruction—and with Greeley in the White
House, anything might happen. "I don't object to novelties in a

small way, but when the fate of millions is involved, I want steadiness and safety." Sumner, whose allegiance to the Greeley cause the Liberals viewed as a great advantage, was particularly biting in his attacks on reformers who remained loyal to the Republicans. "Sumner, you must learn that other men are as honest as you," Curtis admonished him gently, after the senator had attacked the editor's motives. In his *Springfield Republican,* Samuel Bowles did his best to portray Curtis as a political hypocrite. But old friendships among the "best men" were only strained, not broken. After Grant's easy triumph they forgot their differences and looked ahead to the next election.[30]

How important was the Liberal Republican movement in American political history? It contributed little of lasting significance, certainly, although probably it publicized the aims of liberal reformers in places where earlier efforts had gone unnoticed. Ironically, its chief importance was to demonstrate decisively the power of the new Republican alliance of politicians and industrialists. With a well-disciplined machine, backed by thousands of party workers and a huge campaign fund furnished by supporters in the business community, the regular party had little trouble dominating the campaign, even with the defection of the liberal reformers. The Liberal Republicans, by contrast, were disorganized, amateurish, and relatively unenthusiastic about their candidate. Grant was still a hero to most Americans, while Greeley's personality alone alienated many voters. Liberals cried that the nation was in the grasp of "party tyranny"; but Republican orators made them sound ridiculous by reminding voters that the country was enjoying peace and prosperity. As for the issues of intrigue and corruption, Republicans had only to remind their audiences of the manner in which Greeley's forces had taken control of the Cincinnati convention from the reformers. To be sure, as James M. McPherson notes, Greeley was a leading advocate of amnesty and reconciliation, and thus a natural possibility for leadership of the Liberal Republicans. But few of the "best men" could work up much excitement over his candidacy, and most of them believed, rightly or wrongly, that he and his cohorts had somehow "stolen" the nomination from such eminently qualified candidates as Lyman Trumbull and Charles Francis Adams. This matter of chicanery at the

convention, indeed, was the point on which Liberals themselves
recognized their vulnerability. As Lyman Trumbull had warned
before Cincinnati, "A reform movement cannot succeed which
starts off under the auspices of trading politicians." [31]

The rout of Liberal Republicanism disclosed how innocent of
political reality reformers could be. Having convinced themselves
the country was on the verge of ruin, they assumed a majority of
Americans were equally apprehensive about the future. The reformers plunged into a campaign with a platform and a candidate
that made a joke of reform. Having helped stir up popular emo-
tions about the treason of the South four years earlier, they now
expected the public to reverse itself. But "bloody shirt" oratory
still made sense to many voters in this election, for the Ku Klux
outrages in the South seemed to justify Radical claims that military control should be continued.

Reformers in the Liberal Republican movement probably would
have gained only temporary and slight ascendancy in politics had
the new party succeeded in electing Greeley. A Liberal Republican
President would have been dependent almost entirely upon the
Democratic hierarchy for support and, in fact, would have been a
Democratic President in all but name. And the Democratic party
of the early 1870's was no more a vehicle for reform than the Republican party. Perhaps some measure of civil service reform could
have been effected by a Liberal Republican administration, but
the temptation to use patronage as a means of remaining in power
would have been great. Realistic Democratic politicians could
hardly have been expected to abstain from seizing the spoils of
high office. Reconstruction would probably have been abandoned
sooner under Liberal leadership than under Grant; but reconciliation between the sections was all but concluded by 1872. No administration could have prolonged the process for more than a few
years. As for tariff reform, it was no more a party issue in the contest between Grant and Greeley than it was in most other elections
in the late nineteenth century. Perhaps the principle of protection
claimed more adherents among orthodox Republicans than among
Democrats; but even liberal reformers were far from united in
their attitude toward the revenue problem, many nominal free-
traders in reality being advocates only of mild, dilatory reform.

More important, Greeley and a substantial number of Liberal Republicans repudiated the whole concept of tariff reduction.

Thus, the Liberal Republican party was relatively unimportant as a force in American party politics and was singularly unsuccessful as a reform movement. It had repercussions, however, that were important for both major political parties as well as for the cause of liberal reform. The events in 1872 marked the end of the old Republican coalition of the Civil War years.[32] Having tasted insurgency in the Liberal Republican movement, many erstwhile Republicans remained out of the old party and either became nominal Democrats or joined the various agrarian reform parties of the period. In the 1870's party lines were not sharply drawn and few vital issues separated the two major parties, despite the lingering emotional partisanship that was a legacy of the war. A dedicated revenue reformer such as David A. Wells, for example, found it easy to consider himself a Democrat after 1872, not so much because he expected real tariff reform from the Democrats, as because he hoped to see the Republicans punished politically for their uncompromising high tariff stand. Other liberal reformers also took advantage of weakened party barriers to assert their political independence. After 1872, former Liberal Republicans in the West often joined with insurgent Democrats in coalition parties that enjoyed considerable success in state and local politics. Lyman Trumbull and George W. Julian were among the prominent onetime Republicans who, after Greeley's defeat, became Democrats and agrarian radicals of a sort.

Liberals in the East likewise considered themselves political independents, although party lines in the Northeast were not as weak as in the agrarian states. Eastern liberals, moreover, learned less from the debacle of 1872 about the changing nature of American society than did their counterparts in the West. Most of the reformers who joined the Liberal Republican movement did so in protest against shifting economic and social patterns they did not understand and therefore feared. When the regular Republican coalition of politicians and protectionist businessmen thrashed them at the polls, Western liberals at least learned that a more vigorous kind of insurgency would be needed to combat the abuses of industrialism. But most liberal reformers in the Northeast returned to the Republican party, more alarmed by the rising radicalism of Westerners than by the implications of their own defeat in the election. Such frightening heresies as the demand for government regulation of railroad rates and various schemes for "tampering" with the currency convinced many liberals that the Republican party, for all its faults, was their most reliable safeguard against radicalism.

4

Four years later, in the election of 1876, liberals in the Republican party demonstrated clearly the contingent nature of their political independence. By all political logic, that election should have resulted in victory for the Democratic party. Sufficient scandal in the Grant regime had been uncovered and enough factionalism had arisen within the party to increase the prospects for a successful revolt among Republicans which could have benefited only the Democrats. Moreover, the Panic of 1873 and the ensuing depression, the virtual collapse of Radical Reconstruction, and the return to "respectability" of at least part of the Democratic party added to the difficulties facing the Republican leaders. Long before the parties assembled for their conventions in 1876 it was decided that the Democrats would name their "new Jefferson," Samuel J. Tilden, the reform governor of New York. Tilden was a formidable threat, and the wisest Republican leaders realized that they would have to choose their own candidate with great care.

Although Grant probably retained much of his popularity with the mass of voters, his inept conduct of the presidency had alienated many party leaders and all liberal reformers. Republican troubles became serious early in 1873 when congressional investigators bared the Credit Mobilier scandals, implicating such supposed friends of reform as James A. Garfield and Schuyler Colfax, as well as many Stalwart politicians. A month later, the "Salary Grab" Act passed Congress. Although this measure provided legitimate pay raises for legislators and government officers, an unfriendly press labeled it a raid on the Treasury and forced Congress to repeal it in 1874. Democratic victories in the congressional elections of that year indicated the effect these revelations had on public opinion. Moreover, when New York voters swept in Tilden as governor, Republicans knew they were in for a fight in the next presidential contest.

Still the scandals mounted. In 1875, Treasury Department investigators exposed the "Whiskey Ring" as a conspiracy to defraud the government of revenue from the tax on liquor sales. Secretary of the Treasury Benjamin H. Bristow, who pressed for indictment of the offenders, emerged from the affair as a hero to reformers. Fearful that he would leave the administration prematurely, they rallied to his support and urged him to "hold the fort which seems the only one left to the people" in Washington. Many liberals began to think of Bristow as their choice for the Republican nomination in 1876.[33] Another scandal broke several months before the Republican convention, this time in the War Department, where Secretary Belknap had been involved in granting fraudulent concessions in the Indian Territory. Reformers were shocked by all of these developments, and even many regular Republican leaders decided that the party must nominate a man of unquestioned purity.

To many liberals, the Supplementary Civil Rights Act of 1875 was almost as deplorable as the scandals. Aimed at eliminating racial discrimination in public places, particularly in the South, this measure was Charles Sumner's last significant contribution in his long career as a statesman. But to some of Sumner's erstwhile friends, the Civil Rights Act signified the intention of administration supporters and diehard Radicals to continue paternalistic control over Southern state governments. During debate on the bill, Schurz challenged the measure's constitutionality and urged Southern Negroes to stop relying on the Republican party for protection. "Instead of exercising over one another a system of terrorism in order to enforce party discipline," he argued, "they should encourage among themselves individual independence."[34] Clearly liberal Republicans were determined to be done with even the bedraggled remnants of Radical Reconstruction.

After 1872, reform-minded Republicans frequently discussed the strategy they should follow in the centennial year election. Liberal Republicanism's failure showed the futility of forming a strict "reform party," but reformers remained convinced that the mere

threat of a third party would force Republicans to adopt their proposals and their candidates. Charles Francis Adams, Jr., urged his
friends to gather occasionally for consultation. "Once met," he asserted, "we must lay down the future faith boldly and loudly,—
show the country in fact that we yet live." Like other liberals,
Adams viewed Carl Schurz as the natural leader of liberal reform
and thought it essential to support him with a strong organization.[35]

Another Adams remained active in liberal reform. Appalled by
the corruption in Grant's administration, Henry Adams took time
from his professorial duties at Harvard to encourage the formation
of a "party of the centre."[36] In 1874, a congenial coterie of old
friends, including three of the Adams brothers, Moorfield Storey,
and Henry Cabot Lodge, gathered in Boston to discuss the idea.
From their informal meetings the Commonwealth Club emerged as
an organization to stimulate an "intelligent interest in politics"
among New England intellectuals. The group first entered active
politics in 1875, when it supported Charles Francis Adams, Sr., for
the Senate seat left vacant by Sumner's death. The young liberals
worked hard for their candidate; but Henry L. Dawes, whom reformers suspected of being tainted by ties with Ben Butler, easily
defeated the "cold-blooded old Adams" at the Republican state
convention.[37]

Henry Adams's "party of the centre" was the beginning of the
"Independent" movement to force a reform platform and candidate on the Republican convention of 1876. Once again Carl
Schurz assumed leadership of the group. For young Henry Cabot
Lodge the movement was an enlightening initiation into the mys-
teries of politics. "Were I to quote the [Independent Movement]
as a stock I should say it was dull and flat," he wrote in his diary
in the summer of 1875, then added optimistically, "*Mais—Es-
perons.*" Reassuring reports from his friends throughout the East
soon persuaded him that the chances were good for getting a reform ticket. By early 1876 he could report that in Massachusetts, as
elsewhere, the independent vote was increasing daily. Lodge played
an important role in the independent group, for Schurz used him
as a liaison man between the reformers and some of the party regulars.[38]

Schurz and other liberals had hoped to carry the name of Adams into the Republican convention, but the defeat of Charles Francis, Sr., in the Massachusetts Senate race blocked their plans. Instead, they began to estimate the extent of Bristow's interest in reform. Bristow's reputation as a reformer rested solely on his handling of the "Whiskey Ring" investigation. Doubtless, he had honorable intentions about the need for some reform; but he was also a loyal Republican who probably wanted nothing from the insurgents so much as that they not ruin his career by supporting him. Many liberals, nevertheless, convinced themselves that he was the man to lead them in 1876. In *The Nation,* Godkin repeatedly warned the friends of reform that they might be risking their cause with Bristow. The editor was alarmed by the readiness of many liberals to accept a candidate whom he considered a "professional politician" and whose views on most public issues were unknown or, at best, vaguely expressed.[39]

The climax of the "Independent Movement" came in May 1876, when several hundred gentlemen reformers gathered for a conference at the Fifth Avenue Hotel in New York. Six leading liberal Republicans issued the call for the meeting, but Schurz was the real instigator. Widespread corruption in the public service threatened to "poison the vitality of our institutions," the invitation declared; it was imperative that reformers gather and exert a decisive influence on the election. Schurz appealed to the patriotism of the nation by noting that 1876 was the centennial year of the republic, and by asking that the election be made more than a "mere choice of evils." The honor of the American name was at stake; no effort should be spared to gratify the people's desire for "genuine reform." [40]

An illustrious group convened on May 15 for three days of discussion. Among them were Horace White, Parke Godwin, the Adamses, Mark Hopkins, Henry Cabot Lodge, David A. Wells, Dorman B. Eaton, Peter Cooper, William Graham Sumner, Francis A. Walker, Thomas Wentworth Higginson, Godkin, and Schurz. But once assembled, the well-intentioned reformers actually did not know what to do. They made no definite decisions about the coming contest, although the sentiment seemed to favor Bristow's candidacy. One of the group's journalistic enemies, mixing its metaphors in grand style, attacked the meeting as a "show" put on by

"ancient mariners on the sea of politics." Schurz had learned the
"tricks of politics" from the "sharpest and most unscrupulous politicians" in the West; the meeting's organizers were "showmen who
exhibit the distinguished actors performing a short engagement at
the Fifth Avenue." [41] The account was not entirely inaccurate, for
the reformers wanted the meeting to be a show—a demonstration
to both parties that important men expected them to nominate reform candidates.

Before adjourning, the group issued an "Address to the People,"
written by Schurz. Intended as a warning to the approaching conventions, the message also stipulated the conditions under which
reformers, purportedly, would support either presidential ticket. Its
wording was ambiguous, however, and some liberals later became
confused as to its precise meaning. Essentially, the address asked
the voters to make the centennial anniversary of the Declaration of
Independence an occasion of "sincerest pride and rejoicing" by
cleaning out the scoundrels in government. "Never was there cause
for keener mortification, and keenly does it strike every patriotic
heart." The duty of all Americans was plain and immediate, for
the "worn-out clap-traps of fair promises in party platforms will
not satisfy." To guide voters in the coming election, the conference
laid down standards by which all candidates could be judged. No
candidate who carried the slightest taint of corruption deserved
support. No candidate, however conspicuous in position or brilliant in ability, deserved support unless he clearly demonstrated
that he was a reformer, not a mere party man. No candidate deserved the votes of right-thinking men unless he was publicly
known to possess "those qualities of mind and character which the
stern task of genuine reform requires." For all decent citizens, the
pressing duty was to "re-establish the moral character of the government." [42]

Thus forewarned by the "Independents," the Republican party
held its convention at Cincinnati in June—and promptly proceeded to ignore the demands of the Fifth Avenue Conference.
Two factions of the regular party organization struggled for power.
The Stalwarts, friends of Grant, sought to perpetuate the President's policies. To the complete disgust of reformers, the leading
Stalwart candidates were Roscoe Conkling and Oliver P. Morton,

both notorious machine politicians and Senate spokesmen for Grant. The Half-Breeds, discontented politicians whose candidate was James G. Blaine, opposed the Grant faction. A man of great ability, the powerful congressman from Maine was no "plumed knight," despite the elegant appellative his friend Robert G. Ingersoll gave him. Indeed, Blaine was suspected of having been involved in a scheme to defraud investors in certain railroad stocks and, although the charges never were proved, liberals generally assumed his guilt. No fundamental issues divided the Stalwarts and Half-Breeds; their only disagreement was on the question of who should dispense the spoils of office during the coming four years.

Bristow's name went before the convention, but the favorite of the reformers never was a serious contender for the nomination. In the end, the Stalwarts wrecked Blaine's candidacy by throwing their support to the dark horse from Ohio, Governor Rutherford B. Hayes. The nomination was engineered by the professional party managers, and the reformers at the convention had very little effect on the outcome. The most Schurz's men could claim was the inclusion in the platform of mild and ambiguous statements in favor of civil service reform and sound money. Godkin watched the proceedings with dismay. "Looking at them," he wrote of the liberals, "and seeing the thoroughly 'visionary' way in which they tried to push the fortunes of their candidate by appeals to the desire of the convention for honest government . . . it was impossible for the most genuine reformer not to regret that they were too moral to use other arguments." Just what other approach they might have used the editor did not specify. He could only conclude that the liberals were a "sadly honest-looking" group, the only "gentlemen, in a strict sense of the word," at the convention.

Rutherford B. Hayes had played the role of a dutiful party politician since the Civil War. Radical during the early Reconstruction period and untinged by the Liberal Republican heresy, he was accepted by the Stalwarts in a gesture of compromise with reformers in the party. Harvard educated and moderate in all things, Hayes was the epitome of respectability. Although his background and temperament were such that the "Independents" viewed him as an immense improvement over Grant, he did not have an outstanding record as a reformer. Probably the most conspicuous aspects of his "liberalism" were his adamant stand against currency inflation and his desire to see Reconstruction finally abandoned. As an old Whig, the Ohio governor recognized the persistence of strong Whiggish principles in Southern politics, and in 1876 his approach to the Southern problem was simple: reorganize the Republican party there by replacing its base of Negro voters with Southern Whigs and remove the barrier between North and South by allying the propertied classes of both sections in defense of their common interests.

Personally Hayes was a mild-mannered man whose speeches were uninspired and innocuous; but he had no compunctions about allowing his supporters to engage in political demagoguery on his behalf. In 1875 his campaign for governor of Ohio was marked by anti-Catholicism against the inflationist Democrat William D. Allen. And in the presidential campaign of 1876, Hayes countenanced the use of an inordinate amount of "bloody shirt" oratory.[44]

As expected, the Democrats nominated Samuel J. Tilden. Combining the shrewd skill of the practical politician with some of the idealism of the reformer, the governor of New York was an excellent choice. Not only had he been instrumental in breaking Tweed's hold on New York City politics, but in addition, as governor, he had exposed and destroyed the "Canal Ring" which for years had squeezed tribute money out of state public works contracts. Tilden represented in the Democratic party an element comparable to the liberals in the Republican fold, for his reform objectives were mild, safe, and unconcerned with fundamental causes of corruption. Among his closest advisers were Abram Hewitt, an ironmaster turned politician-reformer; Daniel Manning, an Albany newspaper publisher and financier; and John Kelly, a Tammany chief who recognized the expedience of reform politics. Hewitt's call for reform on a national scale was identical in tone with the pronouncements of leading Republican liberals. "The spirit abroad is the spirit of reformation," he declared. "The people are determined to bring back that better era of the republic in which, when men consecrated themselves to the public service, they utterly abnegated all selfish purposes." Tilden, in short, was presented as a candidate who had fought corruption successfully and who was publicly known to possess, as the Fifth Avenue Conference had demanded, "those qualities of mind and character which the stern task of genuine reform requires." Moreover, he was nominated on a platform that did not differ markedly from that of the Republicans. "Independents" had asked the two parties to nominate reform candidates, and the Democrats had responded by naming their best man.[45]

On his record alone, Tilden deserved the support of liberal reformers. His views on the South coincided entirely with theirs. Many participants in the Fifth Avenue Conference had praised the New Yorker for several years and had supported his attacks on corruption. Indeed, some liberals had criticized George William Curtis sharply for his "partisanship" in working to defeat Tilden in the state election of 1874.[46] A genuine coalition of reformers in both parties might have put Tilden in the White House; and, although all of the stern demands of liberal Republicans would not have been met, some degree of reform would have been achieved. With few exceptions, however, liberal Republicans cast their votes for Hayes in 1876.

Curtis, at least, was consistent in his opposition to Tilden. Still an active worker for the Republican cause, he belittled the "new Jefferson's" record and described him as a "most adroit politician" whose attempt to pass himself off as a reformer was confounded by the fact that he was "before all and above all, a *Democratic* politician." Correctly assessing Tilden's part in the Tweed affair, Curtis noted that the candidate had openly attacked the Tammany machine only when it was safe to expose The Boss. "That Mr. Tilden despised Tweed we do not doubt, but he was a politician, and he thought the necessities of his party required him not to break openly." During the 1876 campaign Curtis advised Hayes on various issues and was instrumental in persuading the Republican to issue a relatively bold statement in favor of civil service reform. To the editor of *Harper's Weekly*, as well as to many other loyal Republicans, the Hayes candidacy was an undisguised blessing. For years decent Republicans had attempted to defend an indefensible administration that brazenly condoned corruption and ignored "sound principles" of government. Now, at last, the party had nominated a respectable man to whom they could "point with pride." The long years of bitter embarrassment had ended.[47]

Curtis's old friend, Charles Eliot Norton, also supported Hayes from the beginning of the campaign, although he feared that the candidate would be too much influenced by the Blaines and Conklings. Samuel Bowles gave Tilden full credit for his past career; but the editorial page of the *Springfield Republican* really never wavered from support of Hayes. Seemingly, Bowles would not have been greatly disappointed by a Tilden victory, for he noted that the Democratic candidate had surrounded himself with "the best influences and the best elements." Indeed, indifference to the outcome of the election prevailed throughout much of the electorate. Bryant's *Evening Post* endorsed Hayes, but the editor hinted that the nation would not suffer from the election of either candidate. Oddly enough, Moorfield Storey, the self-proclaimed professional "independent man in politics," also accepted Hayes and would not even consider Tilden.[48]

In Boston, the talented new editor of the *Atlantic Monthly,* William Dean Howells, wrote a eulogistic campaign biography for his distant relative and fellow Ohioan, Hayes. He was encouraged to do so by his friend Mark Twain, who advised him to "get your book out quick, for this is a momentous time." If the election should go to Tilden, Twain feared, "I think the entire country will go pretty straight to—Mrs. Howells's bad place." At the time, the impressionable Twain was enjoying his first taste of New England culture and society at the little intellectual community of Nook Farm in Hartford. His companions there—the Stowes and the Beechers, Joseph H. Twitchell and Charles Dudley Warner—had been antebellum reformers; but time had run away from most of them, and by 1876 they were living in a political fantasy land in which the Republican party still was the symbol of humanitarianism and reform. At Nook Farm Mark Twain did little thinking for himself on politics, and he followed the lead of his friends there without question. His Boston friend and literary mentor, Howells, was associated closely with New England liberal reformers. That fact, plus his personal relationship with Hayes, led Howells naturally to support the Republican candidate. "The man fascinates me!" he wrote exuberantly during the campaign. Not until the next decade did Howells emerge as a reformer with a skeptical political eye and an awareness of the new conditions created by industrialism in America.[49]

For E. L. Godkin and *The Nation,* the choice between Hayes and Tilden really was not a very difficult one, although the editor made it seem so in his columns. Soon after the conventions he wrote an auspiciously favorable estimate of Tilden, in which he discounted the fears of liberals that the candidate was surrounded by the "worst element" in the Democratic party. "Of his ability to fight the prevailing forms of corruption," Godkin noted, "of his courage and determination in doing it, even when the offenders are men of his own political faith, he has given an excellent example in the governorship of New York." Tilden had mastered the currency question, clearly understood the needs of business, was a lawyer of considerable talent, and had done much to raise the general level of politics. Moreover, he had wiped out, "so far as it can be wiped out by mere utterance," the taint of mischief and obstructionism in the Democratic party. Not only was Tilden the better candidate of the two, but the Democratic platform was a "more creditable and plain-spoken document" than that of the Republicans. Still, it would be difficult for decent Republicans to cast their votes for *any* Democrat. Or, as Godkin explained to Norton early in the campaign, "I suppose we must support [Hayes] in the *Nation,* but I confess I do it with great misgivings."[50]

Whatever misgivings Godkin had in July disappeared within a month. Perhaps Carl Schurz changed the editor's mind; for, after he accepted Hayes as his own candidate, the German-American leader worked diligently at persuading his friends to support the Republican ticket. By mid-August, Godkin was doubting Tilden's ability as a reformer and announcing that Hayes's background made him a better candidate than the New Yorker. With a prodigious twist of logic, *The Nation* decided that the doleful experiences reformers had endured with the Republican party's chiefs made it wise for good men to vote for Hayes. Tilden had "grown old in the business of party management," whereas Hayes's training made him the more likely of the two to "put his foot down vigorously and say No firmly."[51] Apparently, Rutherford B.

Hayes, who entered politics actively in 1858, still retained his amateur standing in the game eighteen years later.

Still, Godkin was determined to preserve his "independence" in the campaign. Shortly before the election he warned his readers not to look for campaign work in his columns. If anyone wished to see a journal "steadily 'throwing its influence' " to one candidate or the other, he should buy a paper other than *The Nation*. "He must not seek it here." [52]

Schurz's position in the campaign of 1876 was a crucial one. He had lead the "Independent" movement from its inception and had worked actively for Bristow at the Republican convention. Many members of the Fifth Avenue Conference, thus, looked to him for advice in choosing between Tilden and Hayes. They did not have lonk to wait. Within a week of the nomination, Schurz offered his support to Hayes. As he suggested to Charles Francis Adams, Jr., "unless I am very much mistaken, the Cincinnati Convention has nominated our man without knowing it." Tilden he described as a demagogue and "wirepuller," too much the machine politician to be trusted as a man of principle.[53]

Among German-American voters, Schurz's leadership was promptly challenged by Oswald Ottendorfer, editor of the influential New York *Staats-Zeitung* and as ardent a reformer as Schurz. Ottendorfer accused the liberal leader of turning his back on reform and of denying his own convictions. Schurz's present course was "absolutely irreconcilable" with all that reformers had advocated and commended in recent years. Stung by the charge and anxious to bring the German-American vote to Hayes, Schurz responded with a long, ponderous letter, in which he set forth his own comparison of the two candidates.

Of primary importance was the money question, he insisted, and here the Republicans were clearly "sounder" than the Democrats. By pairing Tilden with the notorious Western inflationist Thomas A. Hendricks, the Democrats had revealed an irresponsible, ambiguous stand on the question of finances. Should the ticket be elected, the party's inflationist element might easily come to dominate the government. How could Ottendorfer afford to take such a chance with the fortunes of the country?

As for corruption and the possibility of civil service reform, Hayes was every bit as reliable as Tilden and was a man of scrupulous integrity. Moreover, although Tilden had a commendable record as a reformer, he, Schurz, could never feel "quite easy and comfortable" with a man in the White House who had "grown old in the peculiar school of New York politicians." With Hayes, reformers would have a man who "throws down the gauntlet to the political machine managers, robs the Congressman of his patronage and, by decisive measures of reform, puts an end to the prevailing abuses." There was no conflict whatsoever, Schurz insisted, between his own leadership of the "Independents" and his support of Hayes.

Schurz was, of course, naturally attracted to Hayes's temperate personality, and he genuinely feared the inflationists in the Democratic party. At the same time, his response to Ottendorfer revealed that the condition of the South was still uppermost in his mind. A Democratic triumph would arouse false hopes among the "lawless element" in the South and perpetuate the "terrible excesses" of Reconstruction, in spite of the attempt by the "better part of the Southern people" to suppress disorder. A liberal, just, Republican government was necessary for the peace and welfare of the South. Schurz also insisted that he had never intended to unite himself with the Democrats, notwithstanding his past "separation" from the Republicans.[54]

Coming from a man who had been condemning Republican Reconstruction for six years and who had led two major revolts against his party, these were strange words. It is clear that his stand on the Southern question in 1876 resulted from the same Whiggish propensities that influenced Hayes.[55] Evidently the candidate persuaded Schurz, if indeed the liberal leader needed persuading, that an alliance of propertied and business-minded men in both sections, under Republican leadership, would provide an honorable and pragmatic solution to the Southern problem. Whatever moral compunctions Schurz and his "Independents" felt about withdrawing Federal protection from Southern Negroes were assuaged, in this approach to the problem, by a conviction that responsible men in both sections would assume positions of leadership. It was this spirit of roseate confidence that enabled most liberal reformers to accept the compromise which followed the disputed election as a just and honorable settlement.

Carl Schurz's reform sentiments, however sincerely motivated and honestly expressed, were rationalized easily to suit his political ambitions. He was convinced that Hayes was sympathetic to reform, and events later proved his judgment at least partially sound. But Hayes was no stranger to the liberal leader in 1876. Schurz had campaigned aggressively for the Ohio politician a year earlier, and it was due partly to his influence among German-American voters that Hayes had won the governorship. Before and during the Republican convention of 1876, Hayes's managers had quietly reminded Schurz of their candidate's qualifications. Thus, it was a simple matter for the leading "Independent" in the convention to shift his support to Hayes after it became obvious that Bristow would not gain the nomination.[56] Throughout the campaign Schurz worked energetically on behalf of Hayes. When the disputed election was settled in favor of the Republican candidate, Hayes rewarded his friend with a position in the cabinet as Secretary of the Interior. Schurz accepted the offer without hesitation.[57]

As a politician and statesman, Carl Schurz was an outstanding exception to the generalization that American politics produced only mediocre men in the late nineteenth century. He was an intelligent campaigner, an able senator, and a distinguished cabinet officer. While in the Interior Department he labored manfully for civil service reform and was largely responsible for Hayes's reputation as a reform President, however equivocal the reputation. Schurz's ambition for high office and public acclaim was undisguised, however, and sometimes it conflicted seriously with his concept of himself as a reformer. He did earn his appointment to the cabinet and he did merit the acclaim he received as a distinguished public servant. But he did not fully deserve the reputation given him by his contemporaries and by some later historians as the classic "disinterested independent" in post-Civil War politics.[58]

Not all the members of the Fifth Avenue Conference were as hasty as Schurz in declaring for a candidate. Early in the campaign Henry Cabot Lodge inclined to Hayes, probably because of Schurz's confidence in the candidate; but after he consulted with

Henry Adams, he quietly determined to vote for Tilden. Not that Tilden was an ideal candidate; but by voting Democratic, Lodge felt he would be punishing the Republican party for having nominated a mediocre politician. After a "devil of a lot of thinking," Charles Francis Adams, Jr., also concluded that Tilden could be used to strike at the Republicans, even though the man had "paddled in dirty water." [59]

As for Henry Adams, a man easily disillusioned by men and events under the best of circumstances, the campaign took on the appearance of a farce. Hayes was a "third rate nonentity," obnoxious to no one and therefore acceptable to most voters. "Politics have ceased to interest me," he wrote petulantly—and prematurely—in June. By August, he had concluded that the campaign was little more than a conventional struggle in which the same old forces "stand without pretence of reform and idiotically pound at each other." When Lodge complained that the Fifth Avenue Conference had deserted its high ideals, Adams advised him to console himself about politics. He agreed that Lodge had a right to complain, for both men had worked hard to form "that rope of sand, the Independent party." But the failure of the conference was not their fault. Rather it was Carl Schurz who had sabotaged the movement by speaking out so early for Hayes. "Well! We knew what he was!" Adams wrote peevishly. "I am not angry with him, but of course his leadership is at an end." By treating his friends badly, Schurz had become a "mere will-o'-the-wisp." Adams's indictment was harsh, but prophetic: "I hope he will get his Cabinet office." [60]

In October, the Adams brothers spoke out strongly for political independence in a biting commentary on American politics which marked Henry's farewell as editor of the *North American Review*.[61] All political campaigns, they asserted, were compounded of "rubbish, formalities, and essence," but this particular canvass was noted most for its rubbish. To date it was distinguished chiefly by rambling discussions of the candidates' war records, and charges and counter-charges about their "transactions in mules, their stealing railroads, plundering widows and orphans, 'dodging' taxes, issuing 'shin-plaster' currency, and the number of watches they own, and the date at which they may have purchased pianos." Despite such clap-trap, the authors noted, both candidates were "respectable gentlemen," although their two platforms resembled Swift's "big-endians" and "little-endians" more than statements of principle.

For the Adamses, the campaign resolved itself into a question of which party had nominated the candidate most experienced in government and boasting the best observable record. Hayes, they agreed, had been a gallant officer during the war, a "faithful though uninfluential" congressman, and a "respectable, though not brilliant" governor. He had good intentions, doubtless, and would work at the task of reforming the government if he was elected. "All this, however, ill supplies the place of long public service," they noted. Was not Hayes precisely one type of politician the members of the Fifth Avenue Conference had resolved to abjure? Citing Schurz's own words, they questioned whether the voters should risk the nation's future "in experiments on merely supposed virtues or rumored ability, to be trusted on the strength of private recommendations." [62]

Good or bad, the Democratic candidates were experienced men with observable records. The party had named its "most distinguished reformer," who was now appealing in the campaign "to facts, not to fancy; to the record, not to the imagination." Tilden clearly was a master of the issues, whereas Hayes's information filtered in from his advisers. Either candidate would probably give the country a satisfactory administration. But because the Republicans had failed to make even a decent pretense at nominating a tested reformer, the Adamses would support Tilden.

Thus, liberal reformers divided their strength in the election of 1876. Presented with a choice between a reform-minded Democrat and a reform-minded Republican, most of them supported the Republican without much hesitation. Many of them feared the very name "Democrat," and others found it difficult to believe that the party of "Tammany and Treason" could contain enough responsible men to offset its broad base of ignorant voters. They preferred a "respectable" Republican President who would promise them civil service and revenue reforms and, at the same time, be comfortably immune from the pernicious influences of the Irish vote and Western radicalism. Liberal Republicans feared particularly the inflationary element in the Democratic party. "The Ohio Communists have carried the Democratic State Convention," Godkin had declared bluntly in his journal after the inflationist Allen won the gubernatorial nomination in 1875.[63] "Independents" ignored the fact that Tilden was far more "sound" on the money question than many Republican leaders. And they conveniently overlooked the conservative fiscal views of the New York governor's financial supporters throughout the East.

Although liberal Republicans recoiled from the "bloody shirt" declamations of some party orators during the campaign, they were well satisfied with the Compromise of 1877 and with Hayes's Southern policy after the inauguration. The temperate reaction of Southern whites to the new administration pleasantly amazed them. The country had been through a terrible crisis, but most liberals agreed that the peaceful solution of the electoral dispute had effected a firm and final reconciliation between the sections.

As they watched the new President perform his duties in his mild, unspectacular way, liberal Republicans became convinced that Hayes's election over Tilden had been a great boon to the nation. Those who had lost faith in Carl Schurz quickly forgot his "apostasy" and became warm admirers of his conduct as Secretary of the Interior. If the President and his advisers failed to institute sweeping reforms in the civil service, at least they emerged from office untainted by corruption. If they were unable to prevent Congress from fixing Greenbacks as a permanent part of the currency, at least they made plainly evident the ability of the government to redeem the noxious paper in gold. If Hayes himself was neither brilliant nor magnetic, at least he was a man of unbending integrity, common sense, and "sturdy independence." In short, he was the type of man liberals preferred to see in the White House.

5

In accepting the Republican nomination in 1876, Hayes had pledged himself to a single term in the White House; and, true to his word four years later, he made no effort to seek the presidency again. His decision to retire, once pressed upon him by Carl Schurz and other liberal Republicans, meant that reformers once again

had to search out a candidate to carry their banner in 1880.[64]
Their problem was not without a certain irony. Reformers in 1876
had hoped Hayes's disclaimer would set a one-term precedent and
prevent the entrenchment in the future of personal political machines at Washington, as had occurred under Grant. Yet, Hayes
had proved to be a better President than expected and had become
something of a reformer. With his retirement, liberals would lose a
proven friend in the White House.

If liberal reformers shared any of the public's apathy about politics in 1880, the threat of a third term for General Grant startled
them out of their complacency. Stalwart Republicans, contemptuous of the "old-woman policy of Granny Hayes," [65] were determined to recapture complete control of the party by renominating
their old warrior. Buttressed by the political machines of Roscoe
Conkling in New York and Don Cameron in Pennsylvania, the
Grant boom got off to an early, formidable start. On the Democratic side, Tilden still controlled the party machinery, and most
observers expected him to run again for the office which had been
"stolen" from him four years earlier. A few liberal Republicans
still believed Tilden had been the victim of fraud and theft in
1876; none, however, wanted to see him elected in 1880. Since the
disputed election, newspapers and a committee of Congress had
unearthed the scandal of the "Cipher Dispatches," involving
fraudulent election practices and outright bribery among high-
ranking members of Tilden's entourage.[66] Although the affair did
not directly involve Tilden, it cast shadows on the New Yorker's
reputation for honesty and integrity. The mere possibility of a
choice between Grant and Tilden in 1880 prompted liberals to
resurrect the "party of the centre" and to scan the field for candidates strong enough to frustrate the plans of the regular party
leaders.

What the country needed most, announced the *Springfield Republican,* was another "moderate, safe, conservative, reforming administration." But what candidate would best satisfy that need?
President Hayes and some of his advisers within the administration
were inclined to support John Sherman of Ohio for the Republican nomination. Sherman deserved the honor as much as any
man in the party, for he had rendered long and distinguished ser-

vice in the Senate and as Secretary of the Treasury and was well known for his conservative economic and political views. To many reformers, however, Sherman was a mere professional politician, who had blighted career and character with tawdry compromises. "To my mind," Henry C. Lea observed, "the idea of Sherman as the Apostle of Civil Service Reformers is a contradiction in terms." Probably the strongest candidate, after Grant, was the perennial aspirant from Maine, James G. Blaine. But liberals and "independents" within the party were no more receptive to his candidacy in 1880 than they had been in 1876.[67]

Rather, they preferred Senator George F. Edmunds, a crusty old Vermonter with no popular appeal, no support within his party, and no reputation save as the most cantankerous member of the Senate. Probably he was in sympathy with the general aims of the reformers; but his contentious nature made him unfit for such a position of responsibility as the presidency, where compromise and conciliation were everyday requirements. Certainly he had no national political appeal, for he had contributed nothing of a particularly constructive nature while in politics. Liberals admired him for his "sturdy independence" and "dogged fidelity," however, and hoped that the Republican convention would turn to him after Grant and Blaine had eliminated each other from the running.[68]

First things first, Carl Schurz counseled as the liberals prepared for the convention. Obviously, the greatest threat to reform came from the Grant Stalwarts, and the threat had to be met forcefully. "There seems to me no reason," he told Lodge, "why the Edmunds, Sherman and Blaine delegates should not cooperate on all preliminary questions." It would be "fatal" not to unite against Grant, and when the general was out of the way the other elements could fight it out among themselves. Liberals, he believed, had little to fear from the Blaine forces; the odds against Blaine being nominated "are one hundred to one." In *The Nation,* Henry Adams and Henry Cabot Lodge tried to stir up interest in a new conference of liberal reformers. No such meeting took place, however, for most Republican liberals realized that Grant had to be checked from within the party ranks. Time enough to organize a new "independent" movement or consider supporting a Democrat if Grant (or Blaine, for that matter) should win the nomination.[69]

Liberals naturally claimed credit for the results of the Republican convention in 1880. Somehow they convinced themselves that their support of Edmunds kept either Grant or Blaine from receiving a majority of the votes, thus forcing the convention to turn to a "dark horse" compromise candidate. Actually the Edmunds forces had very little to do with the outcome; their candidate never mustered more than thirty-four votes. The two leading candidates simply battered themselves into a deadlock through thirty-five dreary ballots, and James A. Garfield won the prize only because the Blaine forces outwitted the Stalwarts by throwing their support to him on the thirty-sixth. Garfield's background as a Half-Breed and his reputation as a party regular had much more to do with his nomination than did his mild approval of the civil service and tariff reform demands of the liberals. Several other possible candidates (but not Sherman or Edmunds) might have welded together the anti-Grant forces at the convention; Garfield, simply, was the most available man at the time. As Hayes noted in his diary, "General Garfield's nomination . . . was the best that was possible." The Stalwarts held firm to the last, and even the sop thrown to them of a vice-presidential nomination for Chester A. Arthur failed to reconcile the "solid Grant phalanx" to the results of the convention. It was the last stand of the Stalwarts, although their ability to do mischief lingered on.[70]

At the Democratic convention, an ailing Tilden formally withdrew his name from consideration, and the nomination went to General Winfield Scott Hancock, a military man with no experience whatsoever in politics. But nothing that either party could do in 1880 aroused much enthusiasm among the voters. Except for degrees of invective, the two platforms were remarkably alike, and the election became a contest between Tweedledum and Tweedledee. Liberals reasoned that they had achieved a major victory by checking the political ambitions of Grant, Blaine, and Tilden; and the country, they knew, could expect moderation and conservatism from either Garfield or Hancock. Henry W. Bellows of Boston probably reflected the feelings of many voters when he wrote to congratulate the Democratic candidate on his nomination. He would not vote for him, Bellows told Hancock, but neither would he fear his election. A Democratic victory, indeed, might be a good thing, for "no dangerous change of policy is likely to ensue from a change in the administration into democratic hands." After all, he noted, despite the extravagances of party newspapers, no great issues really divided the country.[71]

Issues, other liberals noted, were swallowed up by "meaningless generalities" in the Republican platform. The party ignored revenue reform, favoring instead a tariff "for the purpose of revenue" which would "discriminate as to favor American labor." Even the mild plank blessing Hayes's attempts to reform the civil service was added at the last minute and then only over the violent protests of the Conkling crowd. When Garfield in his letter of acceptance adopted the platform intact, many liberal Republicans howled as though the candidate had betrayed them.[72]

Mainly, the controversy between Garfield and the liberals concerned civil service reform. Realizing that a President could do little in the way of cleaning up the public service without the whole-hearted co-operation of Congress, the candidate believed that reformers should put pressure on the legislators to enact a workable civil service reform measure. John Sherman surmised, however, that the liberals would be dissatisfied with anything less than an unequivocal promise of executive action, and he warned Garfield that the statement was too weak. Sherman knew his reformers. George William Curtis interpreted the letter as a surrender to Conkling and mourned that the candidate had not yet learned that "Conkling is of the kind that goeth not out but by kicking." Garfield's letter and Arthur's position on the ticket, he decided, indicated that reform was not an issue in the election.[73]

Carl Schurz, on the other hand, believed that reform very definitely was an issue—the only issue worth discussing. At first he was enthusiastic about the nomination. Garfield, he noted, was "incapable of a dishonest act" and the country "will soon be fully satisfied of the uprightness of his character." But when Garfield published his letter, Schurz immediately scolded him in the manner of a stern adult chastising a small boy caught cheating. The statement on civil service reform, he insisted, suggested a return to the worst of the old abuses. Considerably overestimating the power of the liberals in the party, Schurz referred to possible defections among the "independent elements" in the party. "Without them you can scarcely hope to win," he warned. Garfield must immediately take steps to impress reformers with his determination to continue Hayes's sound policies.[74]

Garfield thanked the Secretary of the Interior for his "frank and faithful criticism," and then proceeded to give Schurz a lesson in practical politics. After all, he reminded his friend, the letter of acceptance was only a brief campaign summary of Republican doctrine, not an inaugural address or an "exhaustive essay." He was completely "sound" on the money question, he pointed out, and he had surrendered on no essential point gained by the Hayes administration. As for civil service reform, "there is more room for difference of judgment, because there are real differences among Republicans." For several years past he had been urging reformers to put more pressure on Congress and less on the Executive if they desired to see any substantial reform. Those who now accused him of "surrender to the machine," he charged, "treat my letter as though I had never spoken before." [75] Schurz apparently was mollified by Garfield's pronouncements as the campaign progressed, for he actively supported the Republican candidate.

Godkin, too, supported Garfield, though not without seriously questioning the candidate's "professionalism." Dismissing the rumors of scandal in Garfield's past, the editor considered the nomination a qualified triumph for the cause of good government and decent politics. For years, *The Nation* had lauded Garfield as one of the soundest men in Congress on the currency question; and Godkin never let the slightest deviation by a politician from his own views on this question slip by without a wrathful denunciation of the offender. As for Hancock and the Democrats, Godkin accused them of practicing "Bonapartism" by nominating a military man and of having done "their utmost . . . to demonstrate the fact that the defeat of the Republican party does not mean reform." But when Garfield's letter of acceptance appeared, the editor immediately labeled it a "cruel disappointment" which would give encouragement to the Stalwarts. "The unworthy phrases in which Mr. Garfield's ideas are concealed betray a want of backbone," he charged. Obviously the man had been too long submerged in the mire of professional politics. Godkin's reaction to this mild attempt to conciliate all factions of the party was typical of his shallow grasp, as Garfield's biographer noted, of the underlying forces in American political life.[76]

Had he not chosen early in his career to switch from education to politics, James A. Garfield probably would have been a leading liberal reformer himself. A product of Mark Hopkins's course in moral and intellectual philosophy at Williams College, he displayed throughout his life a keen awareness of the ethical standards that liberals sought to preserve in American life after the Civil War. As a politician he was best known for oratorical eloquence and skill as a parliamentarian. But never did he ridicule the reformers, as did so many of his Republican colleagues. Rather, he saw them as a healthy influence in politics—naïve and intolerant of other opinions at times, perhaps, but nonetheless sincere and valuable to society. Under such attacks as Godkin leveled at him he reacted quietly and earnestly, hoping to convince the liberals that decent politics need not require a man to view each controversial question as all black or all white. To his friend Burke A. Hinsdale, president of Hiram College in Ohio, he candidly criticized the Schurz-Hayes approach to civil service reform. What good had it done the President to antagonize Congress? No meaningful reform was remotely possible without the support and acquiescence of the legislators. "While the Executive attempts, by mere regulation, to fight the battle alone," he asserted, "it will not only be a losing contest, but every new Administration will adopt its own regulations, and make the confusion more confounded." All he had attempted to do in his letter of acceptance was "to lift the movement for reform to a higher line" and force Congress to take some action in the matter.[77]

Better than many of his contemporaries, Garfield recognized several major weaknesses in the liberal reform movement. Liberals were impatient and intolerant of parliamentary procedures. They blandly ignored the necessity for "the steady performance of current public duties." Godkin of *The Nation*, for example, might be a learned authority on many European questions; but "I have for a long time felt that Godkin was becoming cynical, partisan and unjust in his treatment of American affairs." Above all, too often these reformers expected the successful politician to sacrifice all of his other interests to their own narrow demands.[78]

For the most part, this running debate between the candidate and his liberal critics was restrained in tone and privately conducted. "Garfield suits me thoroughly and exactly," Mark Twain said, and most liberals agreed with this estimate. The election was close, but Garfield became President-elect on November 2. "Your real troubles will now begin," Schurz notified him.[79]

And so they did, for Garfield had some political debts to pay. Schurz advised him to ignore political and geographical considerations in picking his cabinet, to make the cabinet *"your* Constitutional council, not an assemblage of agents of party leaders." But Garfield owed his victory at the convention to James G. Blaine, not to Carl Schurz. When Charles Eliot Norton learned that Blaine was to become Secretary of State in the new Administration, he concluded that "this single fact settles Garfield's character, and determines the limits of confidence in him." The man intended to try for harmony—"that is, for mixing the unmixable. It is a great pity." Reformers might have been even more disconcerted had they known that Garfield and Blaine were in general agreement as to the value of the "independents" in the party. "Unco goods," Blaine called them. "They are to be treated with respect, but they are the worst possible political advisers." Conceited and foolish, ignorant both of politics and of men, they spent their time "shouting a shibboleth which represents nothing of practical reform that you [Garfield] are not a thousand times pledged to!" His new chief thought this estimate correct, though he urged that "reasonable pains" be taken to keep them in the party. They were impracticable in their methods; still, "they embrace a class of people who ought to be with us." [80]

Unfortunately, Garfield never had an opportunity to demonstrate clearly whether or not he was a reformer at heart. Shortly after he took office he was assassinated by a demented Stalwart; and on September 20, 1881, Chester A. Arthur became Chief Executive. Arthur, spoilsman extraordinary, former autocrat of the New York Custom House, first lieutenant to Roscoe Conkling in the Stalwart faction of the Republican party—and now, President of the United States! It was enough to make the "best men" ponder the fate of the republic.

5

The Myopic Mugwumps

This country does not want brilliance nor magnetism nor a magnificent foreign policy. It asks for common sense, for unbending official integrity, for sturdy independence, which like a great, healthy heart, will send the pure life blood of honesty through all the veins and arteries of the Administration.

GEORGE WILLIAM CURTIS, 1884

Why should it be so suddenly wicked in me to run on the Blaine ticket after freely declaring my own independent views? If every man who votes the Republican ticket is to be branded, the Independent movement will die of narrowness and prejudice.

HENRY CABOT LODGE, 1884

IN 1884 THE REPUBLICAN PARTY NOMINATED FOR PRESIDENT the ablest politician in the country, James G. Blaine. Twice previously the durable New Englander had sought the nomination and twice his party had rejected him. Ironically, an incongruous alliance of Stalwarts and "independent" liberals in the party had blocked him both times. On the third try, with the Stalwarts badly weakened, the liberals alone were powerless to prevent him from receiving the nomination. But in the election, both the Stalwarts and the liberals deserted Blaine to support the phlegmatic governor of New York, Grover Cleveland. Never did liberal reformers display more explicitly their whimsical concept of the American party system.[1]

Why did James Gillespie Blaine excite so much fear and outright hatred among his liberal contemporaries? First, because he was an admitted professional politician; and liberals disliked and distrusted politicians who openly professed their trade. And second, because Blaine made at least one serious mistake in a generally commendable career of public service. In 1876 his political enemies accused him of having used his influence as Speaker of the House for personal advantage in a land-grant deal involving an Arkansas railroad. No doubt, the accusation was at least partially true. But incontrovertible proof never was uncovered, probably because Blaine himself somehow acquired many of the "Mulligan letters" in which the indictment against him purportedly was substantiated. In any event, the affair ruined Blaine's reputation with the liberals, who accepted the charges at face value and condemned the politician for his equivocal behavior. Thereafter, they considered it a "moral necessity" to prevent Blaine from reaching the highest office in the land.[2]

As a politician and statesman, Blaine clearly stood above his colleagues in Congress and in his party. An antislavery Whig before the Civil War, he became one of the Republican party's earliest members. He was intensely loyal to Lincoln during the war, and he joined the Radical faction of the party during the Reconstruction period. Yet, he was no more positively or irrevocably identified with the Radical wing than such liberal reformers as Curtis, Norton, and Godkin. On the Radical legislative program for Reconstruction, Blaine often shifted from one position to another; thus the Radical leaders did not consider him a reliable member of their coalition. Indeed, in 1874 he demonstrated clearly his proximity to the liberal position on Reconstruction by blocking passage in the House of the important Supplementary Civil Rights Bill. As an ambitious politician, however, Blaine understood the value of the "bloody shirt." A year later, during a debate on a bill to grant general amnesty to ex-Confederates, he leveled a furious verbal attack at Jefferson Davis. Most liberals blandly ignored his basically moderate stand on Reconstruction—a position that should have commended him to their attention as a potential instrument of liberal reform—and considered him entirely too radical on the Southern question.[3]

On the tariff issue, so important to liberal reformers in both parties, Blaine unquestionably supported the principle of protection. But he was somewhat less a doctrinaire protectionist than Horace Greeley, for example, and liberals could have found many men in their own ranks whose tariff views coincided perfectly with Blaine's. As a politician with strong support in the West, Blaine moved and spoke cautiously on the currency question; but his basic sympathies clearly lay with the advocates of a sound money policy, and his occasional flirtations with inflationists generally were innocuous and noncommittal in nature. Had liberals carefully studied his pronouncements and votes on these two key issues, they would have found as little to fear from him as from Garfield. Moreover, Blaine's views on civil service reform advanced consistently throughout the 1870's and 1880's to a position not far from that of many liberals. Certainly he was more sympathetic to reform than most Stalwarts in his party. Like Garfield, he believed that effective reform could come only through the positive action of Congress. As a practical politician, he knew by 1880 that political reform had to come; indeed, he welcomed it, although he demanded that it be effective reform achieved primarily through legislative procedures. No Executive dictate alone could possibly effect civil service reform unless it enjoyed the support of a substantial majority of legislators.[4]

Blaine's political record, though spotty and sometimes indicative of opportunism, should not have affronted any but the most dogmatic of the liberal reformers. The trouble with the man was that he had ambitions. He wanted to be President and he made no secret of his aspirations. This design alone was enough to arouse serious suspicion among liberals as to his fitness for the office. In seeking the presidency, moreover, Blaine sought to unite the various incongruous elements in his party. He knew, if the liberals did not, that no man could become Chief Executive by claiming to represent solely one faction or one point of view. To be successful, a presidential candidate had to present himself publicly, at least, as the representative of all Republicans or all Democrats, if not all Americans. Liberal reformers stubbornly refused to acknowledge this simple truth about politics.

But Blaine was not the only regular Republican whom liberal reformers might have supported for the nomination in 1884. Chester A. Arthur, far from endangering the "fate of the Republic," proved to be a Chief Executive surprisingly sympathetic to the demands of reformers. Handicapped by the accidental nature of his succession to the presidency and by his Stalwart connections, he was unable to carry out much of his program. Yet the Pendleton Act to reform the civil service became law by his signature and with his wholehearted approval. And Arthur, to the immense delight of the liberals, ousted Blaine from the administration soon after taking office. "No harm he can ever do," Henry Adams ex-

ulted after that happy development, "will equal the good of eject-
ing Blaine." [5]

Republican liberals would have preferred to see Arthur continue
in office rather than to allow Blaine to win the prize; but they
shrank from seriously considering him for a new term on his own
merits. One erstwhile liberal was astonished to learn that his old
friends were unwilling to stand by the President, and he concluded
that reform Republicans "are not sensible men in the main." [6]
But, after all, Arthur was a professional politician with a Stalwart
background; he had no chance of winning the blessing of the
purists who hoped to see a triumph for moral reform in 1884.

2

Mugwumpery, the revolt of the Independent Republicans in 1884,
was more an indication that the "party of the centre" was an anachronism in postwar politics than a triumph for reform. True, the
country was ready for reform—as both Arthur and Blaine acknowledged. But had not the path to reform been cleared more by
the excesses of the corruptionists in business and politics than by
the agitation of the Godkins and Schurzes? Many professional politicians argued that the professional reformers obscured the issues
and delayed the coming of reform by dogmatically insisting upon a
narrow approach to correction. Moreover, who was to decide precisely what reforms the country needed? Liberals and self-styled
"independents" continued to call for the old panaceas: sound
money, free trade, strict governmental economy, and general moral
and political regeneration. But in the West and the South, during
the 1880's, aggrieved farmers and small businessmen clamored for
relief from the constrictive financial policies of Eastern bankers and
middlemen. In the industrial cities, workers insisted bluntly that
they deserved better working conditions and a greater share of the
wealth they produced. And an odd assortment of critics and crusaders in the universities and churches throughout the nation issued demands for startling new legislation to curb the abuses of
business and to treat a wide variety of social ills.

With few exceptions, orthodox liberals viewed these unexpected,
unwanted byproducts of industrialism as dangerous threats to or-

der and property. Many liberal reformers became despondent early in the 1880's as they considered the political prognosis. Where could men of morality and discrimination turn in the next presidential election if the Republicans nominated a scoundrel and the Democrats heeded the siren calls of the economic heretics?

Two years before the national election, events in New York offered Republican liberals a hopeful solution to their dilemma. By winning a decisive victory in the state's gubernatorial election, Grover Cleveland gained national recognition and provided the "party of the centre" with a potential champion. Not that Cleveland was a political independent. On the contrary, he was a thoroughgoing Democrat whose managers included some of the party's ablest politicians. His record as mayor of Buffalo and his conduct as a gubernatorial candidate, however, convinced many liberals that he was a man safely orthodox on economic questions and unafraid of the machine politicians in his own party. His subsequent performance as governor reinforced their estimate. If the Democratic party had the good sense to nominate Cleveland in 1884, liberals reasoned, enough "independents" could safely bolt the Republicans to teach the professional politicians once and for all the importance of the "party of the centre" in national elections.

Very little in Grover Cleveland's personality and background hinted that he could be the champion of anything. Unimaginative, colorless, and ill-informed, he happened on the national political scene purely by chance at a time when a variety of mounting grievances made many voters receptive to new faces. As a young man he had shown little talent for his profession of law and had turned early to small-town politics in order to make a living. He served as an assistant district attorney and as sheriff of Erie County, performing his duties with stolid honesty. Because he defied a number of his political enemies, he quickly won a reputation as a man of "sturdy independence" and unbending integrity. Elected mayor of Buffalo in 1881, he practiced strict economy in the city's affairs and kept himself and his regime free from corruption and scandal. And the step up the political ladder from sheriff to mayor sharpened his ambition. Throughout his term in City Hall he engaged in a quiet but active campaign to win the Democratic nomination for governor.[7]

Disgruntled Republicans and "independents" helped put Cleveland in the mayor's chair and in the governor's mansion. But they were neither completely nor even primarily responsible for his spectacular statewide victory in 1882. Rather, such conservative Democratic managers as Daniel Manning and William C. Whitney decided privately that Cleveland was young enough, unknown enough, and safe enough to trust with the nomination.[8] The Republicans had named a known machine politician as their candidate and were suffering from the backlash of several state and national scandals. New York voters, the Democratic bosses decided, might welcome the opportunity to elect a newcomer untainted by the unsavory reputations which both parties had managed to acquire in state politics.

During the state campaign, Cleveland impressed "independents" throughout the country with his aloof and seemingly hostile attitude toward Tammany Hall. Indeed, he deliberately antagonized the Manhattan machine's leaders and publicly avoided committing himself to the support of any faction in the party. But behind the scenes his astute managers worked out mutually satisfactory compromises with the Tammany bosses, and Cleveland was elected governor as much by the support of Tammany as by the votes of rebellious Republicans. More significantly, although Cleveland refused to negotiate personally with the Tammany bosses, he did not hesitate to accept the support of an equally notorious machine— Irving Hall in Brooklyn. Blaine was a clever politician; but his adversary in 1884 was no bumbling amateur at the game. As his most recent biographer has noted, Grover Cleveland early found one important key to political success: be a politician without seeming to be one.[9]

As governor of New York, Cleveland displayed the same negative attitude toward the role of government that he had adopted as mayor of Buffalo. Public officials, he believed, were the trustees of the people—the tax-paying people. Their duties consisted almost exclusively of safeguarding the public treasury and scrupulously defending the rights of property. With monotonous regularity, Cleveland rejected all appeals for public assistance made in the name of charity or to relieve pressing social needs. His favorite weapon was the veto; and he used it remorselessly to cut down all acts of the state legislature which trespassed beyond his own narrowly conceived boundaries of government action. He believed that written law was the only law; thus, he interpreted the New York and Federal constitutions in the most narrow terms. Coupled with his usual refusal to act, his legalistic opinions and decisions effectively prevented the legislature from dealing with any of New York's many social and economic problems. With querulous deliberation, he scrutinized minute administrative details and legislative proposals. On one occasion he dumfounded Theodore Roosevelt by vetoing an important reform measure because the language of the bill was "slipshod." Because his attention seldom wavered from the papers which crossed his desk, Grover Cleveland failed utterly to comprehend the issues of the day or to realize that the affairs of the state of New York required considerably more positive action than the affairs of Buffalo did.[10]

Yet, in another sense, Cleveland reflected admirably the temper of the times. Many voters, whatever their other grievances, looked askance at the politicians who had been running the country since the Civil War. The same old figures had been on the scene too long; many had become cynics and had worn thin their welcomes as candidates and bosses. Cleveland appealed to many vaguely dissatisfied citizens if only because he appeared on the political scene as a new and relatively unknown personality. Moreover, his reputation—carefully nurtured—for frankness, honesty, and resolution impressed many voters. No visible ties bound him to the old bosses; before the general public he stood as a man independent of all influences save those of his own conscience. The average voter could not have known that Cleveland's ambitions were as intense as Blaine's, for the canny governor always publicly disavowed any fondness for politics.[11]

Liberal reformers applauded Cleveland's performance as governor, and as the New Yorker's chances of capturing the Democratic nomination in 1884 steadily increased, reform Republicans became more and more confident of their strength. In effect, they laid down a challenge and a threat to their own party's leaders: nominate Blaine, and we bolt the party.

First signs of open revolt came from Detroit, where the National Free Trade Conference met in the spring of 1883. Proclaiming their willingness to unite politically for "genuine revenue reform," the delegates warned the nation that they might enter into active, "independent" politics to achieve their goal. Later that year, at Boston, New England "independents" met and resolved to work for the adoption of measures and the nomination of men "fitted to command the hearty approval and support of the independent, thoughtful and discriminating voters" of the country. On Washington's Birthday, 1884, reform Republicans from all over the East met at New York and formally launched the Independent Republican Committee. They resolved unanimously to force the regular Republicans to nominate candidates whose "character, record, and associations" would guarantee a victory for liberal reform in the coming election. Later, the Committee circularized the delegates to the Republican convention, advising them of their clear duty to nominate respectable candidates on a reform platform.[12]

New York, the Independent Republicans decided, would be the chief battleground in the election. Without the state's thirty-six electoral votes, no Republican candidate could win. And New York, according to *The Nation,* possessed from 80,000 to 85,000 voters who would vote according to their principles rather than their party affiliations. Should the Republican party foolishly name Blaine as its candidate, Godkin predicted, these insurgent voters would take whatever action was necessary to ensure his defeat. And if the election became a choice between Blaine and Cleveland, neither Blaine nor the Republican party would escape disastrous consequences. Other liberals agreed with Godkin's estimate. Independent Republicans in New York, Curtis warned his readers, held the balance of power in national politics. Carl Schurz concluded that Blaine could not possibly carry New York, for the "independents" there were much too strong. *The New York Times,* referring to Blaine as an "utter scoundrel," predicted that the Republican party would destroy itself if it nominated the controversial New Englander.[13]

Some of the younger insurgents, notably in Massachusetts, asked for the formation of a third party. But older reformers, recalling the disaster of 1872, advised their ardent friends to await the results of both party conventions. Perhaps the Democrats would surprise the country by abandoning their old irresponsible ways and by naming their best man on a reform platform. Meanwhile, reform Republicans should attempt to defeat Blaine at the regular party convention.[14]

Not all liberal Republicans promised so early in the campaign to bolt the party unless it named a reform candidate. Theodore Roosevelt and Henry Cabot Lodge agreed to attend the Republican convention and do everything possible to block Blaine's nomination. But by 1884, both men had lost much of their taste for political insurgency. "Of course," Lodge told Godkin, "if we go to the convention and Blaine is nominated we shall have to support him." George William Curtis still distrusted the Democratic party. Early in 1884, he advised Moorfield Storey that he would have to support the Republican ticket, regardless of its candidates, if the Democrats nominated Tilden. Some Democrats, he admitted, were "earnest and efficient friends of reform." But "would any candid Democrat contend that his party can be trusted as securely as the Republican party with the future conduct of reform?" Do not take the Independent Republicans for granted, *The New York Times* warned the Democrats. The party would deserve the support of the Republican insurgents only if it nominated its best man on an "honest" platform.[15]

Liberals within the Democratic ranks understood well the doubts and fears of their Republican brethren. David A. Wells, for example, worked strenuously in the Democratic party on behalf of a reform ticket and platform. He looked upon Cleveland as the only logical candidate the party could offer the nation, and he deplored the reluctance of some prominent Democrats to rally around the New Yorker prior to the convention.[16]

At the Republican convention in June, the liberals suffered a crushing defeat. Blaine's forces, after losing an early minor skirmish in the selection of a convention officer, easily dominated the entire proceedings. The only real threat to his candidacy came from the supporters of Arthur. Had all of the anti-Blaine delegates united in a drive to nominate the incumbent President, they might have succeeded in defeating Blaine. But the liberals refused to make any "deals" and insisted that their own lackluster candidate, Senator George F. Edmunds, was the only contender worthy of the presidency. Seconding his man's nomination, Curtis denounced the

Democrats as "a party without a single definite principle," praised the Republicans in ebullient terms, and urged the convention to select a man of "unquestioned and unquestionable purity" in personal and public conduct. The speech was as much an attack on Blaine as an endorsement of Edmunds, but it contained no hint that Curtis planned to bolt the party. Nor did it aid his cause. Blaine received the nomination on the fourth ballot, and John A. Logan of Illinois became his running mate.[17]

Probably few of the party regulars at the convention took the liberal delegates seriously. One observer noted that the liberals "applauded with the tips of their fingers, held immediately in front of their noses." Another described Roosevelt as "a rather dudish-looking boy with eyeglasses and an Olympian scowlet-for-a-cent," who possessed "an inexhaustible supply of insufferable dudism and conceit." All of the liberal delegates, it seemed, "had their hair parted in the middle, banged in front, wore an eyeglass, rolled their r's and pronounced the word *either* with the *i* sound instead of the *e*."[18] Reports of this sort, though obviously exaggerations, suggested that too many of the liberals behaved as downright snobs in their relations with the other delegates. Indeed, Roosevelt confirmed the bad impression he and his friends made when he remarked that the Edmunds delegation included not only all the men of the "broadest culture and highest character" at the convention, but also those with the keenest sense of honesty and integrity as well. Little wonder that one reporter described the "gentlemen from the East" as the only delegates who "pouted and sulked like whipped school boys" when the convention finally made its choice.[19]

With the conspicuous exception of the tariff plank, the Republican platform repeated pledges that few liberal reformers could have condemned. In an attempt to make the tariff an issue in the campaign, the party openly avowed its adherence to the principle of protection and insisted that duties be maintained at a level to ensure labor its "full share in the national prosperity." But the party promised also a further extension of civil service reform and called for legislation to cope with railroad abuses and problems of interstate commerce.[20] Liberals in 1884, however, were more interested in candidates than in platforms. The ticket of Blaine and

Logan was evidence enough for them that the Republican party cared little for reform.

Blaine was the popular choice of the rank and file Republicans at the convention. The worst that liberals could say of his nomination was that he had been the only candidate willing to make bargains. They predicted, however, that he would go down to defeat and that the Republican party would suffer terrible consequences. On June 16, the Independent Republicans reconvened at New York and issued a manifesto. Charging that the Republicans had named their candidates "in utter disregard of the reform sentiment of the nation," they announced that they looked "with solicitude" to the coming convention of the Democrats. "They have the proper men; we hope they will put them before the people for election." George William Curtis, who left the Republican convention convinced that his party had deserted every principle he had struggled for, chaired the New York conference and delivered the keynote address. Before adjourning, the Independent Republicans appointed an executive committee to carry on a desperate campaign against Blaine.[21]

Carl Schurz, the inveterate political nomad, helped organize the Independent Republican Committee and became one of its most aggressive members. Bitterly disappointed by the choice of the Republican convention, he denounced Blaine in scathing terms. The candidate's election would mean "the planting of a seed which, if permitted to grow, will bear a crop of demoralization and corruption hitherto scarcely dreamt of." Not only would it mean "the poisoning of the ambition of our American youth," but it would cause as well the eventual destruction of republican government "by rot and disgrace." (Independent Republicans, one journal insisted, were not vindictive creatures; on the contrary, they were "temperate, intelligent, conscientious, and perfectly resolute.") [22]

Only by nominating Grover Cleveland, the editors of *The New York Times* contended, could the Democrats save the situation and bring honor to the nation. Some Republican liberals had little faith in the ability of their traditional opponents to rise to the occasion. "I must confess," President Charles W. Eliot of Harvard observed drily, "that it will be only by a dispensation of Providence that the Democratic Party will give us the candidate we want." Others, such as Moorfield Storey, were supremely optimistic. "We are united to rebuke corrupt men and corrupt methods in politics," he announced jubilantly.[23]

In July, the Democratic convention gave the Independent Republicans exactly what they wanted: Grover Cleveland and a cautious, conservative platform. Tammany Hall and Ben Butler did their best to prevent the party from making its choices. Speaking for the New York City machine, W. Bourke Cockran ridiculed the attempts of Cleveland's supporters to compare "that obscure man from Erie County" with Samuel J. Tilden. "Gentlemen," he cautioned the delegates, "when the mantle that fits the shoulders of a giant falls on those of a dwarf, the result is disastrous to the dwarf." Perhaps Cockran's audience had some difficulty in understanding the metaphor, for the portly governor scarcely resembled a dwarf. The Tammany delegate spoke plainly enough, however, when he remarked that "I am too warm a friend of his to desire his promotion to an office for which I do not believe he has the mental qualifications." Cleveland, he charged, far from being a self-made politician, was the puppet of a faction in the New York delegation. But Cleveland's managers smashed Tammany's attempt to divert the uncommitted delegates by insisting that their man would attract the "independent" vote in the East.[24] Convinced that Cleveland was a winner, the delegates nominated him on the second ballot.

More equivocal in all its planks than its Republican counterpart, the Democratic platform promised to "purify the Administration from corruption, to restore economy, to revive respect for law, and to reduce taxation." It demanded respect for the rights of the individual states and called for revision of the tariff "in a spirit of fairness to all interests." The problem of corporation abuses received only scant mention; but the platform affirmed that the welfare of society depended upon a scrupulous regard for the rights of property.[25] Clearly, the Democratic party had become by 1884 as strongly committed to the defense of the status quo as the Republican party.

Ben Butler's minority report on the platform echoed the rumbling voices of dissident Democrats in the agricultural West and South and in the industrial cities of the East. The unpredictable

Massachusetts politician denounced monopolies and demanded strict government regulation of corporations. He praised the high tariff and greenback currency as blessings to the common people. As for civil service reform, he condemned it outright and called for rotation in office to counteract the "growing aristocratic tendencies to a cast of life officers." Independent Republicans shuddered momentarily and reminded themselves that the Democratic party, after all, still contained a great many "irresponsible" and dangerous adventurers.[26] But the convention ignored Butler's report; and the Independents, happy that Cleveland had won the nomination, chose not to criticize the platform's failure to take forthright stands on the civil service and tariff reform issues. Butler, on the other hand, was so disgusted with the conservative triumph at the convention that he deserted the party and ran for President as the candidate of the National Greenback Labor party.

Cleveland immediately established himself as a reform candidate. Responding to the convention's committee of notification, he rang all the changes on the reform issue and appealed directly for the Independent Republican vote. His campaign would succeed, he predicted, because the "plain and independent voters of the land" would rebel against party tyranny and corruption. Asked to list the most important issues of the election, Cleveland gave first priority to "honest administration of public affairs." Public business, he asserted, could be reduced to the "simple common sense" of everyday life by subjecting it to the same principles that prevailed in private business. This involved ruthless elimination of needless extravagance and the employment of "the best men possible." Cleveland expressed amazement that anyone should think he might remove qualified Republican officeholders merely to make room for Democratic office seekers.[27]

In his letter of acceptance the Democratic candidate again appealed for Independent Republican support, promising a nonpartisan approach to public affairs. Government by the people, he contended, could be fully realized only when voters selected men to whom office was a public trust rather than a political end. To help achieve that goal, he advocated a constitutional amendment limiting the President to a single term in office. The allurements of power and the "temptations to retain public place," he noted, discouraged the calm, deliberate, intelligent political action which was so necessary for good government.[28] Four years and eight years later, Cleveland found the "temptations to retain public place" too strong to withstand. But the single term proposal, at the time he broached it, was an extremely effective campaign stratagem. Such selfless devotion to high principle, according to *The New York Times,* made the duty of reformers plainer than ever.[29]

Throughout the campaign, Cleveland's supporters contended that their man was free from the pernicious influence of political machines. Blaine and Butler were the only professionals in the race; Cleveland was a self-made politician. To be sure, a few disreputable characters somehow invaded the candidate's entourage; but Mugwump editors found ways to ignore or excuse the existence of these contaminating influences. Regrettably, the Democrats named Senator William H. Barnum as their national chairman. For years, Godkin had castigated Barnum as an incompetent, thoroughly pliable party hack; but during the campaign he dismissed the Connecticut boss as a mere incidental figure in Cleveland's camp. Second in command was Senator Arthur P. Gorman of Maryland, a spoilsman of long standing and the absolute boss of his state's politics. Closer to Cleveland, Daniel S. Manning and William C. Whitney controlled a state Democratic machine based upon such groups as Irving Hall in Brooklyn, the County Democracy in metropolitan New York, Albany's notoriously corrupt county committee, and various upstate county factions.[30]

Many liberal reformers were more impressed by the enmity between Cleveland and Tammany Hall than by any other factor in the campaign, for they believed their candidate could be depended upon to defy the grafters and office seekers within his own party. Confident of Cleveland's rugged independence, they failed to perceive that he simply did not need Tammany Hall. The Manhattan machine was an easy target for any politician like Cleveland, whose own machine could match it vote for vote. Moreover, Tammany still suffered in the 1880's from the scandal of the Tweed Ring; to attack the machine was good politics. Tammany continued to wield influence in city elections; but north of the Spuyten Duyvil and west of the Hudson, its support commonly was a liability to Democratic candidates.

Cleveland and his managers, on the other hand, did not indiscriminately alienate all city machines. Irving Hall, for example, enjoyed peculiar immunity from the governor's reforming zeal. Its boss, Sheriff Alexander V. Davidson of New York County, strongly defended Cleveland against Tammany's attacks at the Democratic nominating convention and continued to support him throughout the presidential campaign. According to the report of an Assembly investigating committee chaired by Theodore Roosevelt, Davidson was guilty of misconduct in office on six specifications. "So gross are these irregularities," Roosevelt informed Governor Cleveland, "so deficient does the Sheriff appear in even the lowest sense of responsibility . . . that the Committee deems it its duty to prefer against the Sheriff . . . specific charges of malversion and neglect of duty." Cleveland took no action on the charges, however, and Davidson retained his office and his influence. Several times during the campaign Roosevelt pointedly reminded his liberal friends of their candidate's collusion in a "miscarriage of justice." But the Independent Republican leaders ignored the reminders and neglected even to ask Cleveland for an explanation of the Davidson affair. Their candidate, they continued to assert, had never shown the "slightest indication" of an attempt or desire to build up a personal organization.[31]

3

Branded as Mugwumps by the *New York Sun,* the Independent Republicans moved quickly into action after the Democratic convention. On July 22 they issued a statement urging all Republicans and "independent voters" who could not stomach Blaine to vote for Cleveland. "Official integrity" was the only issue in the campaign. A victory for Cleveland would resolve the issue and, at the same time, save the Republican party from its own folly. Throughout the campaign the Independent Republican Committee worked strenuously for Cleveland—furnishing speakers, raising funds, issuing broadsides. In major cities of the East, such important newspapers as New York's *Times* and *Herald,* Boston's *Advertiser* and *Transcript,* and Philadelphia's *Record* and *Times,* deserted the Republicans to support Cleveland.[32]

Few other important political forces joined the Mugwump revolt. In June, a number of prominent party leaders had sided with the Independents in the Republican convention against Blaine and in support of Edmunds. A month later, Carl Schurz was the only professional politician of any importance left in the rebel ranks. Most of the Independent Republican leaders were the same purists and idealists who had supported liberal policies for twenty years—Godkin, Curtis, Atkinson, Storey, Higginson, Beecher, and Henry Adams. Their strongholds were New York and Boston, the two cities in which they expected to exert enough influence to swing the election to Cleveland.

Carried away by their own enthusiasm, the Mugwumps overestimated their strength and importance. Theodore Roosevelt concluded that no more than 5 per cent of the members of the New York Young Republican Club defected to the Independents. He noted that the insurgents compiled their lists of bolters by sending out circulars which stated, in effect, that the recipients would be considered bolters unless they sent word to the contrary.[33] Godkin's estimate of 80,000 "independents" in the city of New York alone rested entirely on his own optimistic count. But even his enthusiasm did not match that of the *Springfield Republican,* whose editor claimed that the Independent Republicans had been the dominant factor in politics since 1876. They had nominated and elected Hayes and Garfield and had passed the Pendleton Act. To climax their "noble work" for the health and well-being of the American people, they would now elect Grover Cleveland.[34]

Edward Atkinson rationalized his decision to desert the Republicans by arguing that the Democrats had changed. No longer the defender of slavery and enemy of progress, the party had become "truly Democratic" and now deserved the full consideration of reformers. "Philosophically speaking," Atkinson insisted, "I am a radical Democrat, and I therefore welcome the reconstruction of the Democratic party on right principles." A "radical Democrat," apparently, was a Democrat who advocated the "right principle" of tariff reduction. As in every campaign, Henry Adams underwent a time of troubled doubt about the health of American politics before deciding which candidate to support. In July he was certain that Massachusetts would go either to Blaine or to Butler. "Taxes will rise," he mourned. Later he resolved to vote for Cleveland as a "free-trade" Democrat.[35]

At Hartford's Nook Farm, most of the residents could not bring themselves to vote for a Democrat. But Mark Twain decided to support Cleveland and tried heroically to persuade his friends to join him. "We may fail to kill *this* fraud," he wrote of Blaine, "but I am betting that we Independents will be strong enough to kill the next one that ventures to hoist his nose out of the sty." Blaine had so discouraged him in the business of lying, that "I don't seem able to lie with any heart, lately." Mark Twain knew nothing about Cleveland and very little about Blaine; but he saw the Democratic candidate, in some vague way, as a symbol of resistance to artificial party labels. "I am persuaded," he said during the campaign, "that this idea of *consistency*—unchanging allegiance to *party*—has lowered the manhood of the whole *nation*—pulled it down and dragged it in the mud." He was amazed that newspapers which in May had condemned Blaine as a menace to decency could make quick about-faces in July and lavish praise on the "plumed knight." Moreover, his friend Howells grievously disappointed him by remaining "regular" throughout the campaign. "Somehow I can't seem to rest quiet under the idea of your voting for Blaine," Mark Twain wrote him. "I don't ask you to vote *at all*—I only urge you to not soil yourself by voting for Blaine." [36]

In some ways Mark Twain already had become a nonconformist—a rebel against the hypocrisy and cant he found in American society. But in 1884 he was still naïve enough, politically, to think that the Mugwumps were really nonconformists. He failed to see that Cleveland stood squarely on the same principles which the majority of Republicans advocated. During the campaign he extolled the Mugwumps for their "mighty ancestry." Every great and beneficent accomplishment in "the whole history of the race," he insisted, owed its birth and success to the Mugwumps of the past—Washington, Garrison, Galileo, Luther, Christ. "Loyalty to petrified opinions never yet broke a chain or freed a human soul in *this* world—and never will." If the analogy was somewhat bizarre, at least the theme of the address indicated that he was struggling to think for himself.[37]

No liberal reformers worked harder for Cleveland than Godkin and Curtis. *The Nation* viewed the candidate as a statesman comparable in integrity and stature to the greatest men in the nation's past. No candidate in half a century, "except Lincoln in his second term," Godkin told his readers, had offered reformers such solid guarantees that he would do his own thinking and be his own master. Godkin condemned Blaine as a thoroughly unscrupulous adventurer, the perfect product of corruption in America since the Civil War. During the campaign, *The Nation* and the *Evening Post* repeatedly printed excerpts from the "Mulligan letters" and excoriated Blaine for his scandalous behavior. "It is not pleasant reading any more than chloride of lime or carbolic acid is pleasant smelling," Godkin acknowledged, "but it will be found a powerful purifier." [38]

Somehow Godkin convinced himself that his candidate would not receive any support from the nation's big industrialists. Corporation presidents and railroad titans had no desire to see a man of "unbending and puritanical temper about public rights" in the presidency. Blaine was the candidate of the Goulds and Rockefellers, and "all the railroad magnates are supporting him with both voice and purse." Cleveland, a lawyer of the "stern, unbending, trustee type," could never be persuaded to take a "practical business view" of things. But Godkin must have known that his friend J. P. Morgan supported Cleveland; and, as a good newspaperman, he should have learned that James J. Hill generously delivered both money and votes to his champion. Moreover, Manning and Whitney did not hide the fact that Cleveland had the solid backing of New York's biggest bankers and industrialists. Doubtless the sober Cleveland appealed to many businessmen as a more reliable candidate than Blaine, whose known inclination to bid for popularity might cause him to surrender to "irresponsible" pressures. Godkin, like other liberals, was too impressed by Cleveland's reputation as a reformer to examine critically the candidate's rapid rise to political prominence.[39]

Unlike Godkin, who never considered himself a loyal Republican, George William Curtis bolted his party reluctantly, almost sorrowfully. The party had deserted him, he believed, and "fidelity to Republican principles" required "indifference to present Republican success." One of the party's original members, Curtis praised its past services and predicted that it would rise again, after the defeat of Blaine, to reassume its role as the champion of political morality and personal liberty. As for Cleveland, he deserved the votes of Independent Republicans, who could be confident that the Democrat's "commanding executive ability and independence" were precisely the qualities demanded by the political situation. Cleveland's financial views were in harmony with those of the "best men" in both parties. He would resist both "corporate monopoly" and "demagogue communism." [40]

Curtis took comfort in the knowledge that Cleveland's Democratic opponents denounced the candidate as a sham Democrat. Indeed, the "bitter and furious hostility of Tammany Hall and General Butler to Governor Cleveland is his passport to the confidence of good men." For once, Curtis concluded, the voters could make a clear-cut choice between good and evil. Untouched by dishonest politics, unaffiliated with rings and "party traders," Grover Cleveland symbolized political courage and honesty.[41]

Few liberal reformers allowed the scandal about Cleveland's youthful amours to influence their votes. Theodore Roosevelt professed to be shocked by the revelation that Cleveland had fathered an illegitimate child; but he opposed the Democrat, in any case, for more pertinent reasons. William Dean Howells told Mark Twain that he did not condemn Cleveland for past indiscretions; yet, "as an enemy of that contemptible, hypocritical, lop-sided morality which says that a woman shall suffer all the shame of unchastity and man none, I want to see him destroyed politically by his past." He suspected that the very men who defended Cleveland so indignantly during the campaign would not go near him if "he married his concubine—'made her an honest woman.'" Godkin labeled the moralistic bombast of Republican orators as "cant in its most loathsome form." The whole business of trying to besmirch the candidate's name on moral grounds infuriated him, and the low level of the entire campaign genuinely shocked him. "In no other country," he observed acidly, "has an appeal been made to the lewd, and vicious, and prurient to bring their crapulous minds and foul tongues to the decision of the great political controversy." [42] Yet, doubtless, Godkin was exactly the sort of person Howells suspected of moral hypocrisy.

4

From start to finish of the campaign, rancor and acrimony marred relations between the Mugwumps and the Independent Republicans who supported Blaine. Old friendships dissolved in the intense emotional heat generated by a steady flow of insults and recriminations; and in several instances the enmity long outlasted the campaign. Mugwumps argued that all liberal reformers ought to bolt the Republicans as a matter of loyalty to principle rather than to party. Liberals who supported Blaine contended that reformers must remain within the Republican ranks for the sake of future influence in the party. Considering the pharisaical tempers of the principals in the dispute, the clash between them was bound to produce bitterness and even hatred.

Why did so many of the "best men" support Blaine, despite their obvious sympathies with Independent Republican ideals? The question perplexed Mugwump leaders. All reform-minded Republicans had united behind Edmunds in the attempt to block Blaine's nomination. Yet, surprisingly few Edmunds men swung to the support of Cleveland after the conventions. Godkin was furious with these apostates. "We say deliberately," he wrote in *The Nation,* "that greater disgrace than these men are to-day inflicting on American Government and society has not been witnessed in modern times." These were harsh words to fling at old friends and associates in the twenty-year struggle for reform. But Godkin and his fellow Mugwumps believed earnestly that the battle was about to reach a climax, and they were stunned by the defection of so many liberals at such a crucial moment. As one politician, who never professed to be an "independent" of any sort, remarked of the Mugwumps:

> I have observed that most men who have distinguished them-
> selves in my time by loud profession of superior virtues and de-
> votion to reform, have been men who would violate every pre-
> cept they preached for the sake of forcing their views upon
> others, and then sulk and refuse to play if they could not have
> their way.[43]

Some Independent Republicans refused to support Cleveland because they genuinely feared the Democratic party. Cleveland was "too much like a Trojan horse," Andrew D. White noted, in explaining his own decision to vote for Blaine. A Democratic victory would bring too many men into power with Cleveland who would work to undo what he sought to accomplish. Cleveland's running mate, Thomas A. Hendricks of Indiana, frightened off other liberals. A known inflationist and machine politician, Hendricks was an excellent choice to balance the ticket. But Republican liberals had disliked him for his monetary views when he ran with Tilden in 1876, and many disliked him still in 1884. Not even the Mugwumps were happy about Hendricks, although they accepted him on the ticket as a necessary evil. Godkin, who in 1876 had called Hendricks a "ridiculous" candidate, simply ignored the Democratic vice-presidential selection eight years later.[44]

Mugwumps singled out a number of the original leaders of the Independent Republican movement for especially vindictive treatment. Senator George F. Edmunds, the erstwhile champion of the Republican reformers, particularly disappointed many of his old friends when he announced his intention, albeit "reluctantly," to support Blaine. But the Mugwump editors treated Edmunds with gentle consideration by comparison with the verbal punishment they meted out to Senator George F. Hoar. No man had fought more heartily for Edmunds at the Republican convention. For years he had been a responsive friend of reform in Congress. Yet, when Hoar spoke in favor of Blaine at a Harvard rally, Godkin accused him of standing "knee-deep in perversion, tergiversation, and sophistry." Almost overnight this liberal reformer of long standing became a "real whole-hog Republican, who opens his mouth and shuts his eyes whenever he hears the rattle of the fork in the party pot." Wendell P. Garrison rejoiced that his employer had used his "singular power of humor" against a man who had become a "political knave and charlatan." Understandably embittered by the attack, Hoar never again spoke charitably of the Mugwump movement. "When I think of the provocation which comes to me from these Mugwumps," he once remarked, "I am astonished at my own moderation." What would happen to him, he speculated, if they had the fires of the Inquisition at their command?[45]

Most Independent Republicans who supported Blaine did so, of course, because it was the politically expedient thing to do. Seasoned politicians and ambitious newcomers alike knew that a bolt from the party during the campaign meant consignment to political oblivion in the future. Hoar and Edmunds, for example, would have been exceptional politicians indeed had they sacrificed their seniority in the Senate merely to cast votes for Grover Cleveland. And Hoar, at least, thought the Mugwumps grossly exaggerated the danger from Blaine.[46] Ambitious younger men in the party also looked at the matter from the practical side. The country was still predominantly Republican in its political sympathies and the Democrats appeared to have little chance of holding the presidency (assuming they won it at all) for more than one term. Clearly, the most direct route to political success for young men of the "better sort" lay through Republican channels.

Theodore Roosevelt and Henry Cabot Lodge faced that fact in 1884. Both men were politically ambitious, both were leaders in the convention fight to nominate Edmunds, and both were highly displeased when Blaine won the prize. But they digested their indignation and remained within the party to support the convention's choice. Roosevelt had no immediate political goal in 1884, although he already had chosen politics as a career. He planned to announce quietly his support of the regular ticket and then to retire to his ranch in the Dakotas and "sit out" the campaign. Lodge, on the other hand, was chairman of the Republican state committee in Massachusetts and could not dodge his responsibilities as a relatively high party official. Moreover, he wanted to run for Congress in 1884; and neither he nor the Democratic bosses in the state, understandably, could conceive of his candidacy on the Cleveland ticket. The young Nahant aristocrat really had no choice: in order even to seek a seat in the Forty-ninth Congress he had to give his wholehearted support to his party's presidential nominee. Roosevelt fully endorsed his friend's plans.[47]

After Roosevelt and Lodge announced their intention to remain "regular," Mugwump leaders treated them as little better than political traitors. It was a trying experience for the two young politicians, both of whom were proud and sensitive men with quick tempers. They were convinced that their kind of intelligence and public spirit had a place in politics; and, indeed, George William Curtis could have found no more enthusiastic respondents to his plea that educated men enter politics as a public duty. But Roosevelt and Lodge also knew that the party system was entrenched deeply in American politics and that an aspiring politician could hope for very little success unless he attached himself to a regular party organization. Already they had thrown off many of the dogmas of the liberal reform movement and had learned that politics was a give-and-take proposition.

Insulted and reviled by their former friends, the two men responded in kind; and the resulting political brawl persisted for a quarter of a century. Early in the campaign Schurz gave Cabot Lodge a strong hint of the treatment the two "apostates" could expect from their old friends and associates. Any young man might commit an "impulsive indiscretion" with impunity, Schurz admitted; but a man who stifled his own best impulses only in order to get office as quickly as possible, would taint himself in the eyes of his friends forever. To remain in the esteem of the "best men," Lodge need only follow a "noble impulse" at the risk of temporarily compromising his standing in the party.[48]

Lodge bristled at the implication that he would "taint" himself by supporting Blaine. "If social ostracism is to be attempted in this business," he retorted testily, "I confess a feeling of revolt would master me completely." Doubtless, Lodge recalled Schurz's own unseemly haste in declaring for Hayes—haste which Henry Adams had attributed to Schurz's desire to "get quickly into place." But Lodge did not remind the old liberal leader that many "independents" then had mumbled such imprecations as "traitor" and "deserter" against him. He noted merely that, having considered the situation carefully, he had concluded that no party ever was founded on opposition to one man. "Whatever the result of the election the parties will remain." By staying in the Republican party, he could be of some use. By going out, he would destroy "all the influence and power for good I may possess." Schurz decided that his young friend was lost to the cause. Thereafter, he confined his advice to Cleveland and his censure to Blaine.[49]

Other Mugwumps took a less charitable view of the two alleged backsliders. Commenting on Lodge's decision to run for Congress as a regular Republican, *The New York Times* observed that he was "entitled to the sympathy which is naturally excited by a well-meaning man in a losing fight with temptation." Another Mugwump editor chided Roosevelt and Lodge for overindulging their favorite dish, "crow." As usual, Godkin leveled the most waspish and imperious attacks. Roosevelt, he charged, had tossed aside all principle and destroyed his reputation as a promising young reformer. By committing the unpardonable sin of seeking political advantage, the young New Yorker forfeited forever the respect of his equals. Roosevelt's opinions had not been worth much in the past, Godkin decided; they would be worth nothing in the future. As for Lodge, he defiled himself by retaining his high position in the state Republican organization. Moreover, Godkin accused him of disseminating "filth" in his campaign for Congress.[50]

For a brief interlude, Roosevelt applied his outrage to the grizzly bears and outlaws of the Dakota badlands. He wrote encouraging letters to shore up Lodge's confidence, advising his friend to ignore the Mugwumps and to keep on good terms with the party machine. Godkin's assaults seemed for a time to impress him as rather ridiculous banter, and he observed that his friends, after reading *The Nation*'s diatribes, were surprised to find that "I have not developed hoofs and horns." Perhaps Godkin was a sick man; at the moment, certainly, he seemed to suffer from "a species of moral myopia, complicated with intellectual strabismus." But as the Mugwump onslaught continued, Roosevelt weakened in his resolve to "sit out" the campaign. "I am glad I am not at home," he confided to Lodge in August. He was so angry with the Mugwumps that he feared he might soon be "betrayed into taking some step against them, and in favor of Blaine, much more decided than I really ought to take."[51]

In October, Roosevelt decided that Mugwumps in New York were more dangerous predators than grizzlies in the badlands. He returned to the city, confronted his tormentors, and matched them insult for insult during the remaining weeks of the campaign. He denounced them as liars, lunatics, and political hermaphrodites. He chided them for excusing Cleveland's shabby behavior in the Davidson-Irving Hall affair. Conforming completely to the role of a party stalwart, he defended the Republican record and challenged the Mugwumps to justify their support of the despised Democrats. "You apparently think that the Democrats have always been wrong, but that now, for some unknown reason, they really mean to do right," he admonished one Mugwump leader who criticized him for supporting Blaine; "your faith is touching, but your judgment seems to me bad." He even dragged out a badly rumpled "bloody shirt" and waved it at the Mugwumps for supporting Hendricks, who had been a Copperhead during the war. "Certainly I would prefer to go with a party that has a record of which it is proud," he declaimed before one audience, "than to act with a party which has a record of which all honest men must be ashamed." [52]

It was all good politics, and it put him firmly on the side of the professionals whose support he needed for his budding political career. But the acrimonious contest with the Mugwumps cost him many old friends and made him the lifelong enemy of several of his detractors. Godkin, for example, not content to forget the rancor of the campaign after his man had won, threw a few final gibes at his former friends. He described Roosevelt as a "ludicrous" loser. "What is disappointing people now," he remarked caustically, "is not that Mr. Roosevelt is not a great thinker or observer, but that he has not more faith in honesty." Lodge's defeat in Massachusetts impressed the editor as a "distinct discouragement" to political opportunists. These two young upstarts had thought to "show the theorists a wonderful 'wrinkle' in the way of practicalness." Now they were "out in the cold," and their former friends and allies had no sympathy for them. After all, both men had forgotten that "the path of duty is the way to glory." [53]

Either victim of this journalistic lashing probably would have relished meeting Godkin on the dueling field. For the rest of his life, Lodge made a fetish of collecting derogatory information about Godkin. He denounced the editor in the most insulting terms at every opportunity and upbraided anyone who spoke well of *The Nation* within his hearing. After he had disproved Godkin's rash prediction of his political demise, he informed his colleagues in the United States Senate that the editor belonged to "the class known as informers, whose business has always been to sell and lie." In 1903 he peevishly opposed the establishment of the

Godkin Lectures at Harvard, asserting that the college might just as well establish a fund in honor of Ben Butler.[54]

Roosevelt and Lodge both criticized James Ford Rhodes for writing sympathetically of Godkin and the Mugwumps in his history. After all, Roosevelt insisted, Godkin was a "brass rivetted liar" and Schurz was a "pinchbeck." He once referred to an article written about him by an unfriendly author as "marked by all the broad intelligence and good humor so preeminently characteristic" of a Mugwump. "In fact it was quite Godkinesque—two parts imbecility and one part bad temper." [55]

Much of the deep-seated hostility between the Mugwumps and the pro-Blaine Independent Republicans derived from the volcanic temperaments of the principals in the dispute. A clash between two such explosive protagonists as Godkin and Roosevelt over the delicate question of personal honor inevitably produced rancor. But antagonistic personalities did not account for all of the enmity. Liberal reformers were a contentious lot, but they had managed in the past to maintain reasonable accord on candidates and issues. Perhaps the Mugwumps in 1884 viewed the defection of so many experienced reformers and promising younger men as an indication that unity was crumbling just at the moment of triumph. Convinced that Cleveland was a real reformer, Mugwumps could not understand why all other reformers did not welcome his election. After twenty years of frustration and defeat, they became impatient and purblind. Afflicted with a bad case of political myopia, the typical Mugwump leader became a zealot who believed that anyone who disagreed with him was either an ignorant pawn of Blaine's managers or a shameless enemy of good government.

Independent Republicans who supported Blaine, on the other hand, believed that the contest had very little bearing on the issue of reform. Either candidate would succeed as a reform President only in direct proportion to the strength of the reform sentiment within his particular party's ranks. They saw no evidence that the Democratic bosses were more amenable to real political reform than the Republican bosses. Indeed, two decades of constant agitation for reform from within the Republican party already had produced positive, if meager, results during Arthur's term. Why dissipate the aggregate strength of the reform movement now, they asked, by dividing it between the two parties? And more to the point, why put such extraordinary faith in the ability of one particular individual to clean out the corruption and immorality which plagued American politics? Many Independent Republicans refused to concede that the contest between Cleveland and Blaine was as important to the success of reform as the continued solidarity of the reform phalanx within the Republican party.

Thus, the discord among the Independent Republicans basically concerned the question of unity. Each side charged the other with responsibility for destroying the solidarity of the reform movement. Short tempers and hot words intensified the debate and demonstrated clearly the incompatibility of the purists and the practical men within the movement. Pro-Blaine Independents resented bitterly the Mugwump accusation that they had surrendered to the forces of corruption. Those who once had been closely associated with the insurgents reacted violently to the epithet "professional politician" which Mugwumps flung at them so indiscriminately. Neither side ever completely forgave the other for its insulting behavior, and unity among the liberal reformers disappeared forever. The "party of the centre" really had nothing more to offer American politics after 1884.

5

Mugwump spokesmen hailed Cleveland's victory as the greatest triumph "since the fall of Richmond." They claimed full credit for the outcome and asserted that the results in New York, where Cleveland won a slim plurality, proved that the "independent" voters held the balance of political power. "That point is so clear in the result," Godkin announced, "that nobody questions it." The editor also spoke for most Mugwumps when he proclaimed that they had saved the country without making a compromise of any sort. As for the scoundrels on the other side, they were "cleared away forever with the other rubbish, and their influence as a disturbing element in Presidential elections is destroyed." Curtis thought the election demonstrated clearly that the good sense and patriotism of the "intelligent people" were surer guides to success than "subservience to mere party politicians." Other Mugwumps agreed with the two editors that the revolt had rescued the nation from a variety of disasters.[56]

But did the Mugwumps really swing the election to Cleveland? The victor won a national plurality of 62,683 popular votes, of which only 13,255 came from states north of Mason and Dixon's line. Outside the Solid South, only New York, New Jersey, Connecticut, and Indiana went Democratic. As expected, Cleveland carried every Southern state by a comfortable margin. Indeed, Texas gave him a plurality which was more than twice as large as his entire national plurality. But the country as a whole did not give the Democrats or their candidate a convincing endorsement; indeed, without his large pluralities in the South, Cleveland would have trailed badly in the popular voting. Moreover, the Republicans retained firm control of the Senate and recouped some of the losses they had incurred in the 1882 elections for the lower house. The Democratic margin of control in the House of Representatives was reduced from eighty-one seats to forty-five; and two-thirds of the party's total strength in Congress came from the Solid South representatives. Charles Eliot Norton found the results "disappointing, even discouraging" for liberals, although he attributed the strong showing of Blaine and the regular Republicans to a "low average of moral sense in the people." [57]

Yet, as the insurgents predicted months before the election, New York was the crucial state. It went to Cleveland by 1,149 votes—a slim margin, considering the pre-election forecasts of Mugwump strength. The shift of 575 votes from Cleveland to Blaine would have given the state and the election to the Republicans. Because he embarrassed the Blaine camp by referring to the Democrats as a party of "rum, Romanism, and rebellion," the Reverend Dr. Samuel Burchard received credit, in some accounts, for the results in New York. Others were sure it was the Mugwumps. Certainly the state's thirty-six electoral votes gave Cleveland the election, but a number of factors other than the supposed strength of the Mugwumps or the chance remark of an obscure preacher probably brought about the Democratic victory. The fact that Blaine polled several thousand more votes in New York City than had any pre-

vious Republican presidential candidate in history hints that the
Mugwump interpretation of the results cannot really be sustained.[58]

Blaine undoubtedly suffered from the effects of the depression
that afflicted the nation during the early 1880's. Poor business conditions and widespread unemployment already had contributed to
Republican defeats in the congressional and local elections of 1882
and 1883. Many stricken workers in the industrial states (especially
New York) probably voted for Cleveland simply because they
wanted a change—any kind of change. On election day, moreover,
heavy rains throughout New York state caused unusually light voting in a number of traditionally strong Republican districts. And
several prominent Republicans contended that corrupt Democratic
election officers in the precincts controlled by the Irving Hall machine gave Cleveland a large number of votes that had been cast
for Butler. The charges were never proved, and probably the ac-
cusers spoke with the bitterness of defeat. Yet Senator George F.
Hoar of Massachusetts remained convinced long after the election
that the Democrats had altered the results in the city to favor their
candidate.[59]

Blaine's most formidable obstacle in New York, however, was the
rankling hostility of his old Republican enemies, the Stalwarts.
From his home at Utica, Roscoe Conkling directed the remnants of
his Stalwart machine and effectively sabotaged the Republican
ticket in the state. Throughout the campaign, Blaine feared the
situation in New York. Mugwumps mistakenly thought he feared
the strength of the "independent" vote; but it was Conkling's lingering power that really troubled the wary New Englander. "Can
Conkling be induced to speak for us?" Blaine asked his managers
during the campaign. But when a Republican delegation approached Conkling with the question, the flamboyant old politician spurned their plea: "Gentlemen, you have been misinformed.
I have given up criminal law." Doubtless, Conkling controlled
more than enough votes to offset whatever strength the Independent Republicans could muster for Cleveland. On election day,
however, he and his followers either stayed away from the polls or
cast spite votes for the Democrat. Oneida County, the center of

Conkling's influence, went to Cleveland by nineteen votes. In 1880, Garfield had carried the county by over two thousand.[60]

Elsewhere in the country, the Western states provided the most significant development of the election. Blaine carried every agricultural state north of Mason and Dixon's line, with the single exception of Indiana. And Senator Hendricks's home state gave Cleveland a plurality of 6,512 votes—more than any other state outside the South. Democratic strength in Indiana stemmed from the power of the state Democratic machine and from Hendricks's appeal as an advocate of soft money. Ironically, then, the one Northern state to give Cleveland a decisive plurality went Democratic because of two influences which all good Mugwumps detested: machine politics and economic heresy.

6

The Nature of Things

Do not let builders work more than eight hours a day; then if many houses are not built, and house-rents rise, keep the rents down by law, and in this way a rush of capital into the building business will be caused that will be perfectly wonderful, and we shall all have houses for an old song, except the hateful, hardhearted political economists. It might be well to pass another act compelling all disciples of Adam Smith, Mill, and Ricardo to live in tents and do their own cooking.

E. L. GODKIN, 1866

Economics was regarded as a finished product. One could become an economist by reading a single volume. In fact, at Columbia we studied economics from one little book, Mrs. Fawcett's Political Economy for Beginners. *Mrs. Fawcett defined economics as the "science which investigates the nature of wealth and the laws which govern its production, exchange, and distribution." Man was not mentioned in this definition. . . .*

RICHARD T. ELY, *Ground Under Our Feet*

PERHAPS THE MOST FORMIDABLE OBSTACLE STANDING IN THE way of liberal attempts to support orthodox economic liberalism was the genius of American businessmen at promoting the nation's industrial expansion. Quickly mastering the art of economic planning, business leaders retained or cast aside at will the "natural laws" that lay at the heart of the liberal creed, in order to advance their own interests and facilitate industrial progress. Laissez-faire, liberals believed and businessmen affirmed, was a "natural law" governing men in their social and economic relations. Free and unlimited competition was another. But businessmen in the Gilded Age found unlimited competition a wasteful, inefficient system, and they made a mockery of laissez-faire with their demands for subsidies, high tariffs, and government suppression of organized labor. Reflecting a singularly pragmatic approach to business affairs, their economic philosophy was a hearty mixture of favored leftovers and tempting new ingredients, satisfying but not particularly exotic. For while the dish was spiced throughout with the rhetoric of democracy and sealed over with a thin pastry of orthodox textbook maxims, its meat and potatoes was economic nationalism.

For their times, American businessmen were genuine radicals. Conservatives distrust change and are generally content with the status quo; they look reverently to the past and cherish society's traditional values. The entrepreneurs who transformed the economy after the Civil War, whether they were robber barons or epic heroes, wrought more changes in American life than any group of men in the nation's history. To be sure, they spoke of traditional moral standards and liberal economic principles; but in everyday affairs, abstract matters of this sort received little attention. Old values and settled ways disappeared like so much underbrush in a forest fire, making room for new growth, innovation, and change in every aspect of American life.

At first glance, liberal reformers seemed to champion a blunt conservatism in opposition to the radicalism of big business. Antebellum America, they believed, had fostered values worth preserving; and few orthodox liberals were ever completely comfortable in the age of enterprise. Godkin thought of himself as very much a man of the present, but now and then he recalled the attractions of an older, agricultural America, when "stern, simple, enduring, self-reliant, self-respecting" men had formed the backbone of society. And Samuel J. Tilden, being groomed in 1873 by the Democrats for the next presidential contest, pleaded for a revival of Jeffersonian democracy, with the "high standards of political morality" established by the Revolution of 1800. Those salutary days would stand forever as the "golden age" of the republic, he was sure. Tilden, the urbane corporation lawyer about to become leader of the party of Jefferson! The Gilded Age was indeed an era of change.[1]

If liberal reformers seemed to be conservative, it was orthodox liberalism they sought to conserve. They saw themselves as the guardians of laissez-faire, unfettered competition, and the other "natural laws" of political economy. In an age when economic nihilism seemed to threaten, they appointed themselves custodians of morality and discretion in business affairs. Often the rampant radicalism of business stunned them and made them behave as conservatives. But few liberals had any real quarrel with progress, and they were as enthralled by the Industrial Revolution as any of their contemporaries. They even expected a certain amount of venality and foolish change to accompany the growth of an industrial society. What shocked them to the marrow was the cruel realization that many businessmen and politicians could blandly, even

willingly and eagerly, ignore the "natural order of things" in economic relations and make immorality a matter of everyday routine.

Throughout the postwar years most American liberals adhered
desperately to the view that the "natural order" could function
only when unhindered by outside factors. Still, in an age increasingly characterized by marketplace pragmatism and the ubiquitous
ethics of the parvenu, they encountered contradictions and dilem-
mas that strained their orthodoxy and forced them into a painful
ambivalence. For a few, the innocence of common sense opened a
way out of the predicament; for others, recanting their ideological
commitments proved to be a more intolerable ordeal than enduring the predicament itself.[2]

2

Dozens of professors taught orthodoxy in their classrooms, and
scores of ministers preached it in fashionable churches. But probably no individual in America subscribed more passionately to orthodox economic doctrine than E. L. Godkin. And, with the possible exception of Arthur Latham Perry at Williams and William
Graham Sumner at Yale, certainly no one influenced more budding intellectuals than the hardworking New York editor. More
rigidly orthodox than most of his fellow "best men," Godkin nonetheless epitomized their economic philosophy. He learned his liberalism at its sources in England and Ireland, and he remained
faithful to orthodoxy long after liberalism's English progenitors
had abandoned the original harsh prescriptions of their creed. Far
from advocating pure and undefiled laissez-faire, the leading English liberals acknowledged frankly what their observation of industrial society told them—that the government must intervene,
on occasion, to redress obvious imbalances in the social order. It
was an acknowledgment Godkin could never make with any real
conviction. John Stuart Mill was his prophet, he claimed; yet Mill
was never as zealous a liberal as Godkin. Of his undergraduate
days at Belfast's Queens College, the editor recalled that he had
studied political economy as a "real science," consisting simply of
"the knowledge of what man, as an exchanging, producing animal,
would do, if let alone." Unhappily, political economy since those

pristine days had become something entirely different. No longer
did it influence statesmen, as it had "when Pitt listened to Adam
Smith and Peel to Cobden." For all practical purposes, political
economy had become a mere "adviser, who teaches man to make
himself more comfortable through the help of his government."
Certainly, it had no more claim to be called a science than philanthropy or "what is called 'sociology.' " [3]

As taught by its English prophets, liberalism rested philosophically on the principle that men ought to rely on mutual free consent in all their relations, rather than on coercion either by the
state or by other individuals. If the state had any function at all, it
was to use coercion in a negative way—to prevent individuals from
coercing each other. For Godkin, the principle was a truism, admitting of no deviation. The best instructions any legislature could
receive from the people, he avowed, would be "let us alone." All
real growth and progress came from the people, never from government.[4] Actually, Godkin reduced liberalism to a few simple maxims about society and the economy: wages and prices seek their
natural levels when left alone; society and government can exert
no direct control over the individual; poverty and economic suffering result only from shortcomings in the individuals they afflict.
Doubtless, few other disciples of Smith and Bentham ever defined
the concept of laissez-faire in more explicit terms or put such narrow restrictions on even the negative function of the state.

Liberals believed nature had created a perfectly balanced economic order, governed by immutable laws. Left alone, the order
ideally served man's needs; any tampering with a single component
would destroy the entire system or radically alter it. Free to function naturally, the system worked in perfect harmony to provide
the greatest possible good to mankind. Free to function naturally,
the individual found his proper place within the system: either he
contributed to the good of the whole and of himself, or he proved
himself unfit and incapable of achieving economic well-being.

Anyone who meddled with such a delicately balanced order was
either a demagogue or a dangerous fool, Godkin insisted. Commenting on the operations of some speculators who succeeded in
momentarily "cornering" the gold market shortly after the war, he
admitted that the swindle would drive up the cost of living and

work a terrible hardship on the poor. But, "we can only 'grin and bear it.'" There was no remedy, "save the inexorable operation of the laws of trade," which must come into play sooner or later. To be sure, misguided legislators might attempt to punish the speculators by imposing state taxes on brokerage licenses and gold sales; but no such "vindictive legislation" would cure the evil. What recourse did the individual have in a situation of this sort, when others were injuring him and when the "natural order of things" was out of balance? Aside from patiently awaiting the play of the "natural laws," only the sure knowledge that gambling and fraud would prove a curse to the offender. Money acquired by dishonest or unscrupulous means, Godkin assured his generation, would "kill the soul" of its possessor.[5]

Almost as devoted to orthodoxy as Godkin, Edward Atkinson asserted that self-interest—enlightened or not—inevitably contributed to the moral and material welfare of mankind. During the period of economic readjustment following the war, Atkinson complained that workingmen were receiving "unnaturally high wages," while they showed a shameful reluctance to do a full day's work. Clearly, he concluded, this derangement of the "natural order" was causing high prices and low profits for businessmen. What remedy would restore the natural balance? Only a period during which production must cease for lack of profit, while commodity prices remained high and labor's wages were reduced sharply. "Hard on labor," he admitted, "but necessary and wholesome in the long run."[6] By recognizing their self-interest and acting on its behalf, businessmen could quickly put an end to a situation that legislation could only prolong. Little wonder that liberals enthusiastically accepted Grover Cleveland in the 1880's and thrust their reform banner into his hands; for Cleveland agreed entirely with their dogmas about the role of government in society.

3

As defenders of a faith and guardians of the right, liberal reformers recognized their duty to instruct the American businessman in matters of morality and political economy. Although they defended the business system assiduously, they could not condone all the activities of the postwar entrepreneurs and financiers. Some liberals, moreover, frankly resented the new capitalists who challenged their own positions in politics and the business world. "There is fast forming in this country an aristocracy of wealth," warned old Peter Cooper, whose own sizable fortune came from prewar manufacturing, "the worst form of aristocracy that can curse the prosperity of any country." William E. Dodge, who grew up in the old New York mercantile tradition, deplored the greed and immorality of the postwar businessman. Somehow things in the past had been better, businessmen had been honorable gentlemen, affairs of commerce had been conducted according to strict rules of morality.[7]

Perhaps it was natural for men of wealth and position to idealize the conditions under which they had won success. Yet, liberals who asserted after the war that business in the past had been conducted in a spirit of cordial decency and fairness forgot that the "age of rapacity" began with the railroad boom of the antebellum period. Moreover, they had short memories about the operations during the 1830's and 1840's of the Boston merchants and manufacturers who later became respectable patrons of culture and social leaders. Such tutelar leaders of the antebellum Brahmins as the Lawrences, the Lowells, and the Eliots, with other members of the fifteen Boston families known as the "Associates," by 1850 controlled most of the nation's industrial and banking facilities. As early as 1837, William Ellery Channing established a rhetoric of censure that liberal reformers after the war would adopt almost intact, when he warned that a "spirit of commercial gambling, or what is called by courtesy speculation" threatened to undermine the virtues of businessmen. "Money is not the supreme end of the social compact," he reminded the commercial community; businessmen must learn to strive for a "higher, wiser application of Christian truth" in their daily affairs.[8]

But the prewar entrepreneurs conducted their affairs quietly and with much less ostentation than their successors, and they avoided widespread criticism by remaining aloof from such tawdry practices as "cornering" gold or openly buying up entire state legislatures. Moreover, they had the good fortune to be few in number and first in the field. They prepared the way for the postwar rush of economic adventurers. Their own earlier exploits, less frantic, less spectacular than those of the new entrepreneurs, commended them to liberal reformers as examples of responsible men in commerce and industry.

"Who knows how to be rich in America?" Charles Eliot Norton asked gloomily shortly after the war. Plenty of people knew how to get money; but not many knew what to do with it. Already, the genteel Cambridge professor saw disturbing signs of a general deterioration in cultural and moral values resulting from widespread greed and waste. "We are young and fond of youthful follies, and shall get over them in time, no doubt," he observed; "but it is a pity that our good sense should be bullied by the vanity of 'shoddy' and 'petroleum.' " According to Godkin, the "aristocratic contempt for money as compared with station and honor" had completely vanished in America. No longer did people revere wisdom and simple virtue. The new national hero was the successful stock-gambler, who epitomized all the cheap and tawdry traits of the common marketplace.[9]

Liberals did not condemn wealth in itself. Indeed, they encouraged young men to enter business and acquire honest fortunes. But they insisted, too, that certain responsibilities to one's self and to society accrued as one amassed wealth. Theodore Roosevelt detested rich men who sacrificed everything to "mere money-getting." Society knew no more ignoble character, he insisted, than the man who sought only to amass a fortune and then put his money to such base uses as buying up titled foreigners for his daughters and allowing his sons to lead lives of idleness and debauchery. Such a scoundrel was even more contemptible, incidentally, if he occasionally founded a college or endowed a church, for his mendacious philanthropy caused "those good people who are also foolish" to forget his real iniquity. Perhaps the model businessman of the period, for many of the "best men," was Abram Hewitt, a good man who, according to his biographer, lived in the plainest way, worked harder than his employees, and forsook all luxuries to use his capital for employing men at wages "higher than he could really afford." Abram Hewitts, needless to say, were rare specimens in the Gilded Age.[10]

Although the myth of the self-made man eventually infiltrated the liberal creed in America, some liberal observers belittled the concept—less because they considered it a myth than because they thought it glorified mere money-grubbing. *"Self-made men,* indeed! why don't you tell me of a self-laid egg?" Francis Lieber scoffed when he heard the term. Others accepted uncritically the view that a man could become rich and powerful solely on his own initiative and through his own resourcefulness, though they disliked the motives that prompted such adventurers to seek their fortunes. As Godkin observed, "self-made men" were too often individuals of no education or intellectual refinement. Contemptuous of experience, eager in the pursuit of money, lacking in respect for learning, and profoundly confident of their own "natural qualities," such men were totally indifferent to the future and bleakly devoid of taste in letters and the arts. These disagreeable creatures, Godkin noted, were not exclusive to America; but wherever they appeared, they lowered the moral and cultural tone of society.[11]

A cardinal sin of many businessmen, it seemed, was their lack of social and cultural refinement. How could any man who had no appreciation of the arts, ignored books, took little or no interest in politics and civic affairs, and squandered his wealth on foolish luxuries, ever contribute anything of lasting value to America? Godkin complained that the Century Club, an exclusive sanctuary for select New York gentlemen, was in danger of being overrun by brokers, bankers, and merchants who seldom opened a book other than a ledger. They were all "excellent and agreeable men, whom I am glad enough to meet, but not properly Centurions." Too many businessmen, he complained, were no less ignorant, unread, and inarticulate than the average bricklayer or plumber.[12]

Reviewing Brooks Adam's melancholy analysis of social evolution, *The Law of Civilization and Decay,* Theodore Roosevelt praised the author for his scorn "of what is ignoble and base in our development, his impatient contempt of the deification of the stock-market, the trading-counter, and the factory." Another Adams observed that his own experiences in the world of commerce had convinced him that businessmen were the least interesting, least refined, least thoughtful persons he had ever encountered. "Suppose 'stocks' to be ruled out, where would the topics of conversation be found?" Godkin asked, ridiculing the illiteracy of businessmen. "Would there be much to talk about except the size of the host's fortune, and that of some other persons present?" [13]

Businessmen who flaunted their wealth were not only foolish, unworthy men; they were dangerous influences in society as well. Because the "common people" naturally emulated the successful men they saw on the streets or read about in the newspapers, they would surely be corrupted by examples of riotous living, extravagant display, and conspicuous idleness. An unwise display of great wealth had introduced to America that greatest of European curses, class hatred. Convinced that vast accumulations of money were debauching American society, Rutherford B. Hayes warned that, while in Europe the anarchist was the offspring of despotism and aristocracy, an unchecked plutocracy here would produce the same vile progeny. Godkin, too, thought the spectacle of a "growing idle class" lay behind the discontent of the masses. The "workers of the world," he observed, provided the rich with "police, with courts of justice, and means of travel—in short, every agency which makes their enjoyment possible, for sums in cash which they would hardly pay to a good club." Reasonably or unreasonably, the masses resented this situation—and so did Godkin, for it gave "mere envy" an air of respectability and rationality. For Roosevelt, the profligate businessman was a more pernicious influence in society than the average murderer, thief—or even professional labor leader.[14]

For all their dislike of the tawdry, predatory aspects of business, few liberals questioned the economic system itself. As long as businessmen respected the traditional "natural laws," capitalism would prove a blessing to mankind. At heart the problem was one of individual morality. If businessmen could be persuaded to tend their moral ledgers as carefully as they scrutinized their account books, most abuses would disappear and the dangerous designs of labor leaders and other misguided critics would be thwarted. The state, of course, could do nothing to remedy whatever defects afflicted the system. As Sumner emphasized, civil institutions were designed only to protect "the property of man and the honor of women" against the vices and passions of human nature. Liberals made some remarkable distinctions between the "vices and passions" of businessmen and those of farmers and workers. Even when the evidence was overwhelming that greed and fraud were poisoning certain areas of business life, they sanctioned no laws that might interfere with the "natural" accumulation of wealth. But they clamored indignantly to enjoin greedy "labor agitators" and "communistic agrarians" from exercising any political or economic influence. After all, as Godkin noted, the businessman had been appointed "by natural selection" to oversee the savings of the community and to use them to the best advantage. If money got into the wrong hands or was used perniciously, government was powerless to intervene.[15]

Here was political economy in its most purblind form. And here, too, was the dilemma that plagued the "best men" throughout the Gilded Age. Businessmen often behaved badly: some of them cheated and deceived; others terribly abused the laws of political economy; too many seemed interested only in making money and flaunting their wealth before the masses in a vulgar, totally reprehensible manner. Yet, more than any other group in America, businessmen represented property, and property represented order and stability. To undermine public confidence in the business community was to invite anarchy, liberals were sure. Moreover, some liberal reformers were businessmen themselves, and all had close ties with the business community. Naturally, they were loath to encourage any indiscriminate attacks on the integrity of that community and its leaders; and who could be sure that discriminate attacks on offensive businessmen would not inspire, among less "responsible" critics and the general public, feelings of distrust and hostility toward all businessmen? The risk was too great, liberals decided, as the years passed and protest rose from other quarters. Attacks on any part of the business community might well degenerate into an attack on the system itself.

Mark Twain, in many ways, typified the ambivalence of those Americans who disdained mere money-making, yet admired the businessmen who mastered the art. Fascinated by the Industrial Revolution, he never tired of wasting his money on dubious business ventures in the hope of getting rich quick. Indeed, he came very near to amassing a great fortune with the Paige typesetting ma-

chine. While at Nook Farm, he spent days hobnobbing with Hartford businessmen when he should have been writing. Perhaps he
aspired to become a captain of industry himself—a captain of the
literary industry. Certainly the daring deeds and commanding personalities of successful businessmen dazzled him, and he boasted
that he was the "principal intimate" of Henry H. Rogers, Rockefeller's associate in Standard Oil. Occasionally, Rogers allowed
Mark Twain to lounge on a couch in his office, the better to watch
the master manipulate millions of dollars and thousands of individuals. "His mind is a bewildering spectacle to me," the admiring
author confessed, "when I see it dealing with vast business com-
plexities like the affairs of the prodigious Standard Oil Trust, the
United States Steel, and the rest of the huge financial combinations
of our time—for he and his millions are in them all."

Although he ridiculed Andrew Carnegie's pretentiousness, Mark
Twain greatly admired the steel magnate's business achievements.
Often he insisted that high tariffs created the great monopolies
that hindered the growth of some industries to the advantage of
others. But he would not admit that his friend Rogers's Standard
Oil Trust was an undesirable monopoly, or that it undermined, by
its practices, the traditional moral and economic values Mark
Twain and his liberal friends respected. Rather, as one critic
noted, he found it easier to charge the offenses of industrial capitalism to some vague, partly anonymous influence: "Guggenheim
and Clark [who were] alleged to have bought legislatures, other
plutocrats who bought foreign titles, and Jay Gould who bought
everyone and everything that was for sale." Mark Twain understood simple human relationships and recognized the simple injus-
tices brought by man against man. Neither his admiration of successful businessmen nor his own rapid rise to fame and social emi-
nence destroyed his essential sympathy for mistreated people. Yet,
like other liberals, he put his trust in decency, honesty, and fair
play to solve the serious social and economic problems created by
the Industrial Revolution. Much less sophisticated in political
economy than most liberals of his day, he reflected in his own confusion about the business world the ambivalence that troubled
them all.[16]

4

A handful of liberal reformers took leave of orthodox political
economy during the period and kept pace with changes in the actual economic situation. After he left the White House, Rutherford B. Hayes became increasingly critical of a system which permitted the accumulation of huge personal fortunes. One day as he
sat in church, it occurred to him that the public should be told of
the great evils and danger that resulted when vast wealth fell into
the hands of only a few persons. "How would it answer to limit the
amount that could be left to any one person by will or otherwise?"
he asked himself; and the longer he considered the question, the
more convinced he became that Congress should enact laws to
guarantee a more equitable distribution of wealth in the United
States. Moreover, the government should subject corporations to
close regulation and overhaul the entire tax structure in the interest of equity for all.[17]

Doubtless, Hayes's ties with such reform groups as the National
Prison Association and the Slater Fund helped to direct his attention to other examples of social and economic injustice. Perhaps,
too, his old friend William Dean Howells taught him to question
the dogmas of orthodox liberalism. Certainly Howells introduced
him to Tolstoy's works and engaged him in long discussions on
topics ranging from anarchism to the eight-hour day. More and
more, Hayes found his literary friend a man of "wisdom and
heart." During the 1880's Howells underwent a striking change in
his attitudes toward liberalism and capitalism. Having watched the
state of Illinois rashly condemn the Haymarket "anarchists," he
began to question seriously the safety of traditional democratic
values in a capitalistic society. Awkwardly and slowly, he groped
his way out of the dismal reaches of orthodox political economy;
and by the end of the century he had become a passionate critic of
doctrines he had once supposed were sacred. "I'm not in very good
humor with 'America' myself," he told the expatriate Henry James
in 1888. "It seems to be the most grotesquely illogical thing under
the sun; and I suppose I love it less because it won't let me love it
more." Frankly, he admitted, he was afraid to divulge the "audac-

ity" of his social thinking. But he could say that he had come to abhor the civilization he had once so much admired. No civilization could come out right ultimately unless it was based on "real equality," and American civilization at the moment was based on inequality.[18]

That same year he published *Annie Kilburn,* a novel he described as "a cry for *justice,* not *alms.*" Hayes thought the book opened the "democratic side" of the great questions before the country. Its theme was "the doctrine of true equality of rights," which some critics called "nihilism, communism, socialism, and the like," but which the former President thought was synonymous with the Sermon on the Mount and the Declaration of Independence. Howells observed later that he had decided merely to join the "religion of humanity," to heed the call to do good for his fellow men. What good was liberty, he asked, if it was circumscribed by poverty? Liberalism meant nothing unless it was linked with charity and humanity. Howells praised the English liberals, the "inventors of *laissez-faire,*" for having had the good sense to recognize the inhumanity of their doctrine and to pass laws for the benefit of labor and society in general. "These things are the effect of a larger humanity than is yet active among us"; moreover, they indicated that business was not the supreme English ideal. "Is business, is money-making, the supreme American ideal?" he asked.[19]

Howell's first job as a reporter had been with *The Nation* in 1865. Fortunately, after a few months, long before the editor could imbue him with his own moral and political absolutism, he left the job and escaped Godkin's influence. In later years, Godkin seems to have overlooked Howells's apostasy, probably because a more ominous threat to orthodoxy appeared in the guise of the new social scientists. As early as 1870 Godkin began to flay the fledgling experimentalists, who were trying to find a less dismal economic philosophy than liberalism. Social science had but one legitimate purpose, he insisted: to teach the "right use" of reason. Equality, freedom, female suffrage, Prohibition, common schools, the ballot—all such devices for reforming the world were no better than patent medicines. The "right use" of reason, Godkin assumed, would lead any man inevitably to conclude that liberalism was

truth. Other liberals were as fiercely protective of the classical doctrine, especially against the attacks of Richard T. Ely.[20]

Ely was the leader of the new social scientists ("ethical economists," *The Nation* called them scornfully) who began to move
away from orthodox liberalism in the 1880's. When they formed
the American Economic Association in 1885, the new economists
and sociologists denounced laissez-faire as "unsafe in politics and
unsound in morals." More important, they declared boldly their
acceptance of traditional political economy only as a subject in the
first stages of development, not as a "final statement." Working together and exchanging views within the new organization, the social scientists hoped to subject the actual conditions of economic
life to impartial study and scientific evaluation. "We believe in a
progressive development of economic conditions which must be
met by corresponding changes of society," they announced.[21]

Frightened orthodox liberals viewed the newcomers as breeders
of socialism, if not of anarchism. Arthur Latham Perry accused Ely
of "tossing God's plan of providence and government" into the
"wilds of Australian barbarism." The astronomer Simon Newcomb
plunged into the controversy over the nature of economic man
with a spirited defense of the classical position. Nine-tenths of the
new social scientists, he charged, were "filling the bellies of the
poor with the east wind" of socialism and agitation. Ely's teachings
resembled "the ravings of an Anarchist or the dreams of a Socialist." Doubtless, many of the "best men" agreed with Newcomb
in pronouncing Ely unfit to hold a university chair.[22]

Perhaps the heretics could yet be saved, Edward Atkinson decided; accordingly, he joined the American Economic Association
and worked doggedly to promote faith in the natural harmony
views of Frederic Bastiat, his personal economic prophet. Abhorring
the views of his unorthodox fellow members, Atkinson at least argued with them without rancor and did not dismiss them as vicious
demagogues. Not so Godkin. The new economics, he insisted,
simply was not legitimate political economy. He scoffed at the
"young lions" of the historical school, with their predictions of the
"glorious future" that awaited mankind if only men would try a
new approach to economics. But he had his own notion of what
was in store for America, should economic heresy prevail, and it

was a bizarre prediction indeed. Rich men would be stripped of their riches, frugal men of their savings. People of ability and intelligence would be trampled under by the stupid and lazy. Children would be packed off to foundling homes. Even worse, smoking would be permitted at funerals and men and women would "mate in the streets." [23]

But the new economists did not call for startling economic changes. They proposed merely to broaden the scope of the government's police power. Although they objected to liberalism's rigid dogma of laissez-faire, they subscribed fully to the other basic assumptions of orthodox economics. Ely, for example, thought of economics as a moral matter as much as a science. But laissez-faire had become an excuse for "grinding the poor," whereas the new economics denoted a return to "the grand principle of common sense and Christian precept." Henry Demarest Lloyd, who became the foremost publicist of the new view, sought relief from traditional political economy chiefly to escape a doctrine permeated with "Calvinistic logic and cruelty." The new social scientists turned against orthodoxy because it adhered to "brute laws," which were supposed to govern everything, including the treatment of human beings. But many sponsors of the Association considered government interference in economic affairs no more desirable as the normal condition of human relations than laissez-faire. The great problem, as Henry Carter Adams of Cornell and Michigan asserted, was somehow to correlate public and private activity "so as to preserve harmony and proportion between the various parts of organic society." Moreover, the academic reformers enjoyed the enthusiastic support of clergymen and humanitarians who preached the "social gospel," a wholly moralistic approach to economic and social problems. In a sense, the new school advocated a "Christian liberalism" to replace the orthodox "mechanistic liberalism." [24]

Liberal reformers thought of themselves as tolerant men who would never resist change merely for the sake of resisting. But the kind of heresy advocated by the social scientists—direct intrusion of government into the delicately balanced economic order— frightened them and impressed them as subversion of liberalism's most elementary principles. By questioning the laissez-faire dogma, thus, the "ethical economists" forced liberal reformers to act more and more as dogged conservatives. Whether they wanted to or not (and probably the role became a congenial one for most of them as the years passed), they became the virtual paladins of the business ethos.

5

As disciples of laissez-faire, most liberal reformers rejected almost automatically all suggestions that the state restrict competition or impose "unnatural" fetters on the free play of commodity prices and transporation rates. Moreover, many liberals tended to view monopolies as inevitable and perhaps beneficial derivatives of the free competitive system. As moralists, on the other hand, they disliked the illiberal implications of monopoly capitalism, and they were haunted by a fear that irresponsible monopolists would so antagonize the public that agitators would press for punitive as well as regulatory laws. "Natural laws" forbade any artificial interference in the economy, but moral considerations suggested that monopolies might eventually undermine liberalism itself. Thus, post-Civil War liberals faced the dilemma confronted by all liberals in modern history: at what point does "natural freedom" require artificial protection to prevent it from destroying itself? Unlike their English counterparts, most American orthodox liberals of the nineteenth century fought desperately to uphold the letter as well as the spirit of their sacred canons.

Probably not many of the "best men" understood much about the problem of business consolidation. Like David Ames Wells, their foremost practicing economist, they supposed that great size necessarily meant greater efficiency; and they were unable to distinguish between mere size and monopoly. Almost to a man, liberals condemned the high tariff and other government aids to big business as the chief breeders of monopoly. Because politicians failed to adhere strictly to laissez-faire policies, they argued, favored industries grew "unnaturally" larger than others. Thus basing their approach to the monopoly question on the assumption that government already had interfered unduly in private economic matters, they rejected as a matter of course the remedy of more government interference. Perhaps, too, some liberals dimly perceived the dangerous implications in the monopoly problem. Left entirely alone, monopolies conceivably could destroy all competition and invalidate a "natural law" of political economy. For whatever reason, liberal spokesmen said and wrote surprisingly little on the subject. And most of those who did consider the question generally treated it as a matter of private and public morality.[25]

Not that liberal reformers were unaware of the phenomenal growth of large business empires. On the contrary, during the immediate postwar business boom they noted with some apprehension the tendency of money and business control to fall into the hands of a few men and corporations. Several influential liberals were ready then to impose effective artificial control on certain specific businesses, notably the railroads. Rutherford B. Hayes denounced business evils while serving as governor of Ohio, and he approved the state's first code of mining safety. As President, however, he ignored the monopoly question and generally followed a laissez-faire course. Not until his later years did Hayes favor strict government control over all corporations, and then he insisted that Standard Oil, in particular, required immediate effective regulation. That great trust, he charged, was a "menace to the people," for it antagonized the principle of personal liberty, the "very corner stone of republican government." Moreover Hayes scoffed at reports that Standard paid its employees good wages and treated them well. "The Roman people," he observed sardonically, "were fed and entertained while being robbed of their liberties." [26]

In *Harper's Weekly,* George William Curtis asked for strict government regulation of railroads to protect farmers, workers, and small businessmen from the "tyranny" of railroad rates and "money control" of politics. A great railroad trust, he warned, might well defy the government itself or seek to control it. Yet, Curtis considered the Interstate Commerce Act at best a partial remedy. It might correct some of the more immediate abuses, he noted, but it failed to get at the heart of the problem. Railroad abuses were due essentially to "the covetousness, want of good faith, and low moral tone" of the railroad managers! In the Midwest, Joseph Medill's *Chicago Tribune* put the blame squarely on state and Federal governments for having alienated much of the public domain in land grants and subsidies to railroads. As the leading liberal organ in the West, the *Tribune* called for a government postal telegraph system and effective regulation of commerce among the states. Clearly, Medill sacrificed some of his economic liberalism to represent the grievances of Mid-western farmers and small businessmen, but neither Medill nor Curtis broadened their criticism of monopolies to include businesses providing services other than transportation or communication.[27]

As for *The Nation*, its approach to the monopoly question was oddly equivocal. As early as 1871, one writer in Godkin's weekly intimated that Federal control over railroad rates might become an inevitable expedient if "the right of locomotion" came too much under the control of a few unscrupulous men. Not that such a radical expedient was desirable; on the contrary, the writer pointedly observed that unwise government interference—subsidies, preferential laws, indiscriminate charter grants—had created the abuse. Further abuses would bring on more legislation. The public would not tolerate forever the evils bred by despotic railroad officials, and eventually it would demand remedies restrictive in nature and interstate in application. Horace White, Godkin's associate on the *Evening Post,* also feared that the American people would not allow themselves to be "bound and strangled, like a blind Samson or an aged Laocoon" by these "new-fangled monopolies" called trusts. They might even resort to regulatory legislation, a most unwelcome possibility. Standard Oil, the financial expert noted, had "blazed the way" for all other trusts and had excited the investing public with "a vision of equally large profits to be derived from the magical name of trusts." But White could not bring himself to propose government action against Standard Oil. Somehow and sometime, the giant would be destroyed, most probably by its own insatiable ambition.[28]

In considering several other fields of private endeavor, *The Nation* did more than merely hint that government might take positive action. "Self-interest and humanity alike" compelled the Federal government to regulate the merchant marine. Although the government had no more concern in holding forest property than it had in "working the unoccupied wheat-fields," it had a clear duty to protect the great rivers of the nation. Insofar, then, as the forests affected the rivers, they should be subjected to some form of national attention. But Godkin warned that the less government mixed itself up in matters of this sort, the better for everyone.[29]

In 1870, Charles Sumner introduced in the Senate a bill to slow down and restrict the consolidation of cable companies. Although the measure failed to pass, it received the hearty endorsement of at least one outstanding liberal reformer. "Our government has been very generous toward these companies heretofore," Samuel Bowles observed; "in fact it has let them do whatever they choose." It was time for the government to inform the companies that the people had some rights. But Bowles, too, restricted his demands for interference to cases of industries engaged directly in providing communication and similar services to the public.[30]

Actually, the few liberal reformers who favored positive, comprehensive government regulation of railroads were only slightly less bold in their approach to the monopoly question than the academic social scientists or "ethical economists." Henry Carter Adams and Richard T. Ely, for example, differentiated sharply between "natural" and "artificial" monopolies and directed their attacks primarily against the former type. Public utilities, railroads, and communications companies were "natural" monopolies; and social scientists consistently pressed for government ownership or regulation of these industries. But they were wary in considering how to control such "artificial" monopolies as the Standard Oil and sugar trusts. Ely argued that Standard's oil monopoly stemmed directly from its control of transportation facilities. The way to attack the oil trust, thus, was to attack the railroad trust. Free competition would return to the oil industry, or at least be stimulated, and no further regulation would be necessary.[31]

Henry Demarest Lloyd agreed with Ely that Standard Oil originally had grown fat as a result of its railroad holdings. But the original muckraker insisted that the question of monopoly origins was interesting only historically, that monopolies had reached a stage where the "mere force of money" could create them. "If any one says these monopolies will all break down sometime—we have only to wait—I think the proper reply is to refuse to wait." Lloyd has been criticized for making rash and unsubstantiated charges against Standard Oil; but at least he understood better than the leading academic economist of his time the nature and power of industrial monopolies in general. Ely thought trusts were products only of special government privileges; the public should oppose them chiefly because they were devices contrary to "principles of Christian morality." Moreover, he disdained critics who denounced big business as such. Economists should teach people to distinguish between monopolies, which were fields for public activity, and competitive industries, which were fields for private enterprise only. Liberal reformers who expressed serious concern about the monopoly problem lacked Ely's knowledge of economics, but they agreed with him on solutions.[32]

Ironically, almost all the "best men" repudiated laissez-faire and petitioned the government to interfere directly in one aspect of the transportation industry. Railroads, they complained, were a menace to the safety of life and property. The Federal government had a clear obligation to enforce the use of safety devices. "I refer with effusion to our railway system, which consents to let us live," Mark Twain told an audience in England.

> It only destroyed three thousand and seventy lives last year by collisions, and twenty-seven thousand two hundred and sixty by running over heedless and unnecessary people at crossings. The companies seriously regretted the killing of these thirty thousand people, and went so far as to pay for some of them—voluntarily, of course, for the meanest of us would not claim that we possess a court treacherous enough to enforce a law against a railway company. But, thank Heaven, the railway companies are generally disposed to do the right and kindly thing without compulsion.[33]

Doubtless, he spoke for many nineteenth-century Americans. "We shall never travel safely till some pious, wealthy, and much beloved railroad director has been hanged for murder," one harassed traveler observed. A man could not ride from New York to Albany without imminent danger of being killed by "a certain railroad corporation under certain corporate franchises conferred by the state."[34]

Even Godkin lashed out at the irresponsible railroad managers whose reckless indifference to safety and comfort made travel a risk to life and limb. On one occasion he applauded a strike of New

York transit workers—not because he sympathized with their demands or approved their strike, but rather because the strike would focus public attention on the "evil effects" and unsafe practices of transportation monopolies. Yet Godkin concluded that railroad officials were not really depraved or inhuman men. They were simply victims, along with the public, of government largess in conferring special privileges on favored corporations. Railroad managers had come to resemble "a bad and very unscrupulous aristocracy." The problem was to prevent them from acquiring monopolies that might be injurious to the public comfort and safety. Here was an area in which government had the right—indeed, the duty—to intervene. In what appeared to be an amazing departure from economic orthodoxy, Godkin speculated that the day might come when the people would lay aside their "extraordinary fear" of government as an enemy of the individual and come to regard the state as "the organized co-operation of all for the benefit of each." But his ideas only verged on heresy, for he meant that the people and the government should act co-operatively, with each remaining strictly within its separate sphere. Privilege legislation, the root of most business abuses, thus would become a thing of the past.[35]

As for laws to curb other abuses in business affairs, most liberals adamantly resisted all but the most innocuous measures. Such matters as railroad rates, price-fixing, working conditions, and corporation finances, they insisted, were exempt by "the Nature of Things" from state interference. To Godkin, all attempts to regulate railroad rates in the interest of Western farmers was "spoliation as flagrant as any ever proposed by Karl Marx or Ben Butler." In effect, legislation of this sort amounted to "taxation without representation" all over again and reflected the influence in government of the worst elements in society. Any such meddling would have a baleful effect on business generally, Godkin was sure, for "nobody likes to hold property which it is in the power of a hotheaded, passionate man, against whom there is no appeal, to injure or destroy." [36]

Probably Godkin learned his railroad economics from Charles Francis Adams, Jr. During the millionaires' war for control of the Erie Railway, Adams studied the business tactics of Gould, Van-

derbilt, and Drew, and wrote several essays exposing the struggle as
a brutal contest among predatory business rivals. Chaotic conditions in the Erie, as Adams described them, pointed clearly to a
need for some form of state railroad regulation.[37] But Adams, who
was the best informed man of his day on railroad and transportation problems, proposed no government regulation of rates, profits,
and franchises. After all, the railroads were "fighting for their lives
and property." Why should ill-informed state legislators put them
at an unfair disadvantage by burdening them with such "singularly medieval machinery" as the Granger laws? Adams admitted
that the railroad problem resulted from a complete breakdown of
competition; and, at one time, he even urged the Commonwealth
of Massachusetts to take over a single railroad line and operate it
as a stimulus to competition among private lines. Not surprisingly,
the proposal came to nothing; and Adams, back in character after
one startling slip into economic heresy, thereafter relied chiefly
upon "natural laws" and the power of public opinion to police the
railroads. "Competition will regulate where it has free, full play,"
he asserted, "but where it has not such full, clear play, it must confound." Rather than enact such restrictive legislation as the
Granger laws, state governments should establish commissions to
investigate and publicize pertinent facts about railroad operations.
Adams thought publicity alone would force the railroads to mend
their arrant ways.[38]

Godkin called the Interstate Commerce Act "a piece of State socialism." During debates on the proposed law, he warned Congress
that the object of any legislation should be as little government interference as possible. Railroads must continue to attract the investments of prudent people. The government had no right to
tamper with rates or to harass private property, "a very sacred
thing." Horace White noted that Charles Francis Adams, Jr., Edward Atkinson, and Samuel Bowles all had testified before Congress that "the law of competition" would correct railroad abuses.
Hasty legislation demanded by popular passions would create more
evils than it would cure. Perhaps Henry Villard best described the
kind of Federal regulation envisioned by Godkin, White, and the
rest of *The Nation-Evening Post* crowd. A railroad president himself, as well as a publisher, liberal reformer, and intimate of God-

kin, Villard would have limited the government to the collection
and publication of statistics.[39]

Despairing of the country's future prosperity when the Interstate
Commerce Act became law, Edward Atkinson grumbled: "Alas!
Alas! with what foolishness we are said to be governed." But he
was not totally pessimistic, for he hoped the law would prove "so
ambiguous as to be inoperative." So did most businessmen. As Senator Nelson Aldrich of Rhode Island, one of their chief spokesmen
in Congress, noted, the Act was an "empty menace to great interests, made to answer the clamor of the ignorant and the unreasoning." His colleague from Kansas, Senator Ingalls, had not the
faintest idea of the meaning of the law; it was a measure which
practically nobody wanted and which everybody intended to vote
for. Perhaps because they observed the Interstate Commerce Act in
operation and concluded that it was an ineffective, harmless instance of government intervention, most liberals simply ignored the
Sherman Anti-Trust Act when it passed Congress several years later.
Not one word on the measure appeared in the pages of *The Nation*. Only two notable liberal reformers took any interest at all in
the anti-trust law. Senator Edmunds, during the congressional consideration of the measure, tried unsuccessfully to include labor
unions and farm organizations under its provisions. And Carl
Schurz condemned the Act as a violation of "natural laws" and accused the Republican party of creating it only as "a lightning-rod"
to attract public resentment to the trusts and away from the
tariff.[40]

6

Throughout the post-Civil War period, both major parties qua-
drennially condemned the "profligate waste of public lands" and
promised new efforts to check the growth of undesirable monopolies and trusts. But monopoly control and Federal interference in
business affairs (excepting the tariff) were relatively minor issues
between Republicans and Democrats until 1896. As Lord Bryce
noted, neither party had anything distinctive to say about regulatory legislation and neither was entitled to full credit for the Interstate Commerce Act or the Sherman Act. Both measures passed

Congress with strong bipartisan support, the legislators being divided more along sectional lines than by party labels.[41]

In 1884 the Democratic national convention announced that, while it favored a more equitable distribution of property and the protection of individual rights against corporate abuses, the welfare of society itself demanded a "scrupulous regard for the rights of property." The statement reflected perfectly the feelings of Independent Republicans and orthodox liberal reformers generally toward the monopoly problem. It committed the party to nothing and left Grover Cleveland free to interpret the "rights of property" and the "welfare of society" as he saw fit. His subsequent interpretations, as President, immensely pleased his Mugwump liberal supporters. He filled his cabinet with businessmen and corporation lawyers, instructed his subordinates to practice the strictest economy with the public's money, and committed the government to the business community's unique version of laissez-faire. Thus, in 1887 he vetoed the Texas Seed Bill with a message that castigated Congress for assuming that the Federal government should alleviate individual suffering which was "in no manner properly related to the public service or benefit." The general public as well as the drought-stricken Texas farmers had to be taught that "though the people support the Government the Government should not support the people." This was good orthodox liberal doctrine put into practice.[42]

In his second administration, Cleveland chose Richard Olney, a prominent Boston railroad lawyer, as his Attorney General. Olney viewed laissez-faire as a valuable asset to businessmen and had no use for the anti-trust and regulatory legislation on the statute books at the time he took office. But he was disposed not to tamper with the existing laws, for they "satisfied the popular clamor" for Federal regulation of business. To reopen the subject and attempt to repeal the laws, Olney correctly assumed, would probably provoke demands for new and stricter legislation. As for the Interstate Commerce Commission, he observed that the older such an agency got to be, the more it would tend to reflect the business and railroad view of things. He advised his friends in railroads and industry not to destroy the Commission, but to use it.[43]

During Cleveland's second term, the United States prosecuted ten cases under the Sherman Anti-Trust Law. Five of the ten concerned alleged violations of the law by labor union leaders; two charged monopolistic practices against specific industries; one accused a man in Salt Lake City of restraining commerce in the delivery of coal; and two proceeded against railroad combinations. Only in the labor cases did the Attorney General mark up an impressive record of zealous anti-monopolism for the administration: he won four of the five cases. Of the other five, he successfully prosecuted only one. In his annual report for 1893, Olney further disclosed his contempt, and Cleveland's unconcern, for anti-trust action by decreeing that a literal application of the Sherman Law was "out of the question." All ownership of property was "of itself a monopoly," and every business contract or transaction could be viewed as a combination which more or less restrained some kind of trade or commerce.[44]

Cleveland and Olney, in the opinion of orthodox liberal reformers, were stanch defenders of "natural law" and private property. By taking the government out of business affairs, the President had brought the nation back to "that simplicity and economy of its founders." Carl Schurz described Cleveland as "a rock against the powers of evil which menaced the welfare and the honor of the American people." No President had ever done more than Cleveland to defy both the vested interests and the vindictive economic radicals. Insofar as Grover Cleveland allowed businessmen to conduct their own affairs, unhampered by "artificial" interference, and demonstrated his devotion to the principles of classical political economy, he fulfilled admirably his role as the champion of the liberal reformers.[45]

But in 1896 the Cleveland machine lost control of the Democratic party to the "radical" agrarian reformers from the West. Throughout the stolid New Yorker's second term, the more adamantine liberals became increasingly disturbed by the incessant clamor from farmers and labor for redistribution of the wealth and government intervention to protect or favor the "irresponsible classes." They ridiculed the charge that corporations suppressed individualism. Indeed, one liberal insisted that great corporations would "distinctly favor" the growth of individualism in America. The larger the corporation, the more dependent it was on the favor of individuals. Moreover, he insisted, irresponsible agitators grossly exaggerated the dangers of monopoly capitalism. Taking the American Cotton Oil Company as an example, he argued that here, certainly, was no grasping monopoly. Anyone could buy cottonseed, crush it, refine it, and sell it. And American Cotton Oil could do nothing to stop the competitor—"except by underselling him"! [46]

Near the end of his long career as an editor and publicist, Godkin warned of dire consequences unless the country returned to the "natural laws" of political economy. Legislation enacted under the guise of promoting the general welfare by restricting private enterprise, he contended, actually represented the determination of the "poor and ignorant voter" to find a new means of getting something for nothing. Thank God for the courts, the old editor reflected; they, at least, realized the danger and stoutly resisted the irresponsible schemers. His old friend and frequent contributor to *The Nation,* Arthur G. Sedgwick, agreed that only the courts stood between property and a giant conspiracy led by William Jennings Bryan, John P. Altgeld, and other "anarchists" from the West. Property owners themselves were cowards who had consented to the "whole scheme of criminal legislation" enacted at the demand of agitators. Sedgwick warned the American people that they would destroy their entire civilization if they overturned the trusts, pools, and monopolies in their midst. But Godkin was more optimistic than his friend. True, the country had experienced much heartache and delusion; "but 'that too will pass.' " In the long run, "the fittest will survive, and their morality is sure to rule the world." [47]

7

Moral Money

Financial knowledge is now the demand of the hour, for, if financial quackery is allowed to take its place, national bankruptcy and irretrievable dishonor may be the result.

GEORGE W. JULIAN, 1878

Opportunity for safe, careful, and deliberate reform is now offered; and none of us should be unmindful of a time when an abused and irritated people, heedless of those who have resisted timely and reasonable relief, may insist upon a radical and sweeping rectification of their wrongs.

GROVER CLEVELAND, 1887

NOTHING GROVER CLEVELAND DID DURING HIS TWO TERMS in the White House earned him greater acclaim from the "best men" than his plea for tariff reform in 1887 and his fight for repeal of the Sherman Silver Act in 1893. His tariff message to the Fiftieth Congress climaxed a two-decade campaign by liberal reformers to discredit the principle of protection. Repeal of the Silver Act, for most liberals, signaled the salvation of America from economic collapse, political revolution, and moral perfidy. Liberals considered the two matters crucial to the health of political economy and republican institutions. On only one other issue—civil service reform—did they expend more time, effort, and words; and many liberals believed all other issues, including political reform, depended in the final analysis on the success or failure of the battle for hard money and lower tariffs.

Both issues had roots deep in American history, and both had provoked controversy and conflict on earlier occasions; but it was the Republican party's wartime legislative program that activated them for the postwar generation. In 1861 Congress enacted the Morrill Tariff Act, thereby establishing a policy of high protection that lasted, with minor interruptions, until 1913. By the Legal Tender Act of 1862, Congress authorized the Treasury to issue non-interest-bearing paper currency carrying no definite promise of redemption in specie. As the fighting drew to a close, tariffs were twice as high on the average as they had been before the war, and a total of 431 million dollars in inconvertible paper money—greenbacks—circulated throughout the Union. Most liberals showed absolutely no enthusiasm for this situation, although they accepted it during the wartime emergency as an unavoidable evil. Trouble arose after the war, when elements in both major parties tried to make high tariffs and greenbacks permanent features of the nation's fiscal policy. Two other wartime developments also profoundly disturbed liberals and bore upon the ensuing financial controversy: the income tax and the rise of the public debt to nearly three billion dollars. At the end of the war, Americans faced a financial situation unprecedented in their experience: heavy taxation, both internal and external; a large national debt; and a currency no longer based on specie.

Businessmen, politicians, academicians, and reformers of all breeds lined up in opposing camps to debate the proper policies government and business should adopt in coping with the situation. Manufacturers and politicians from the newer industrial areas joined with a handful of economists, led by Henry C. Carey, to propose an essentially Whiggish policy of permanent high tariffs and indefinite retention of greenbacks. Should the nation accept its recommendations, this group believed, both production and consumption of domestic manufactures would rise markedly, to the benefit of the entire economy; for the tariff would promote an expansion of native industries, while the greenbacks would ensure the circulation of the large sums of cheap money a growing economy required. Another group, led by liberal reformers, campaigned strenuously for currency contraction and retirement of the greenbacks; for low tariffs based on revenue needs only; for strict economy in government; and for a gradual reduction of the national debt. A third voice in the controversy resounded from the West, where farmers and the businessmen who served their interests demanded permanent retention of greenbacks and the abandonment of all specie payments, as protection against the deflationary, tight-money policies of the Eastern banking establishment.[1]

Because all Americans at the time believed financial matters were subject to strong moral, almost religious, qualifications, the controversy over fiscal policy produced an emotional eruption on all sides that persisted until well into the twentieth century.

2

Few artificial devices for disturbing the "natural balance" of the economy exasperated liberals more than the protective tariff. In theory, at least, most liberal reformers viewed high tariffs as the absolute antithesis of orthodox economics, a challenge to liberalism's most sacred canons. High tariffs brought the state into private economic affairs, in violation of laissez-faire doctrine. High tariffs flaunted the "law of supply and demand" by interfering with the free play of wages and prices. High tariffs mocked the "law of competition" by conferring special privileges on some businesses to the disadvantage of others. Unlike free trade, which epitomized ideal relations between the individual and the state, the protective system encouraged the individual to look to government for favors and for public solutions to private problems. Moreover, it deliberately forced capital to flow in unnatural channels, violating Adam Smith's fourth rule of taxation, that taxes should be geared solely to the minimum revenue requirements of the public treasury. William Cullen Bryant, editor of the *Evening Post* until 1878 and an implacable foe of high tariffs, praised free trade as one of man's inherent freedoms. High tariffs, the New York Reform Club resolved, contravened the accepted notion of political economy to the point where they had "no right to exist" in a society grounded on the principles of the Declaration of Independence.[2]

Protection caused much of the corruption in postwar politics and business affairs, liberals were convinced. In effect, the tariff was a handout from the government to those businesses that exerted the most pressure on Congress. The easiest way to exert pressure, liberals knew, was to buy the votes of legislators with campaign contributions and outright bribes. Once the government acknowledged a duty to protect special interests, the door would swing open to endless political intrigue, "legislative corruption, jobbing, and meddling." Free trade, on the other hand, offered "absolutely no field to jobbing." Commenting on the Credit Mobilier scandal, Godkin argued that the remedy for such corruption was a simple one: get the government out of the "protective business," the "subsidy business," the "improvement business," and the "development business." Favoritism had caused the scandal, and protection was the most blatant form of favoritism.[3]

As he watched each new session of Congress struggle with the question, Godkin concluded that protection was the "cancer of popular government." It forced businessmen to compete with each other for higher and higher tariff advantages; it encouraged them to rely on artificial standards for prices and wages. It "debauched and silenced" the press and "deadened the public conscience." No nation with universal suffrage could possibly have pure politics when prices rose and fell at the whim of lawmakers in every session of Congress. "This system would eventually corrupt a community of angels." Moreover, the tariff corrupted the general public as well as politicians. "Once admit the right or duty of a government to levy taxes for other purposes than revenue," he observed, "and you clear the coast for Karl Marx and Jaurès and Bebel and Bellamy and the whole crowd of social dreamers and firebrands." Far more than the fuzzy-minded professors and preachers of the new-fangled economics, the protectionists were responsible for having prepared the American worker for socialism. Without question, the high tariff was the "greatest fountain of corruption" ever to afflict the nation.[4]

Offensive to morality and honest economics, the high tariff was also a danger in everyday, practical life. Like Negro slavery, protection polluted everything it touched. People regarded government as a "grab-bag," full of spoil for anyone smart enough to get his share.[5] So pervasive was the greed of the high tariff advocates, that it accounted for the tax evasion, the general breakdown of law, the over-all contempt for authority that liberals felt was characteristic of postwar America.

Reformers who thought seriously about the problems of the American farmer realized that overproduction was the curse of the agrarian community. David A. Wells, who favored admitting foreign raw materials free of duty, pointed out to farmers the need for a profitable and certain market for their surplus products. Past experiences, he granted, had convinced farmers that American raw materials could not compete in foreign markets with finished goods made from the farmer's raw materials. The only protection of any value to the farmer, in other words, was that which the prosperity of American industry bestowed upon him. And industry could prosper only by exploiting the opportunities a free market offered. To be sure, Wells admitted, foreign raw materials would compete with domestic farm products; but a prosperous domestic economy would absorb the goods from both sources. Thus, liberals urged farmers to fight the tariff as they would a thief or a plague. Why should farmers, who made up half of the American community, tolerate a situation in which the other half derived all the benefits from a system of protection? The farmer's troubles would multiply, Carl Schurz warned, as long as he permitted protection to exploit him.[6]

Although most liberals thought depressions were natural occurrences, beyond the ability of man to prevent, they were convinced that protection increased the frequency and severity of economic crises. Protection wasted capital and stifled sound productive impulses with its harsh system of taxation. Wells contended revenue reform would provide some real protection to the economy from periodic breakdowns. American industry, he noted, produced more than the domestic market could consume; but it was unable to dispose of its surpluses abroad because the protective system created artificial barriers to international trade. At the first sign of economic difficulty, industry lowered its output and retrenched financially. Eventually, domestic manufacturers cut production to the point where industry could not meet even the requirements of the domestic market, and a completely artificial economic situation caused the nation to suffer unnecessary hardship. The opening of foreign markets, through a general reduction of tariffs, would enable industry to find new outlets and lessen appreciably the impact of depressions. Abram Hewitt insisted that the depression of the early 1880's was due chiefly to the imposition during the Civil War of higher duties than were needed for protection. Manufacturers had been making huge profits at a time when profits were already large enough without high duties. The tariff had stimulated speculation and overexpansion in business, and Hewitt warned that other crises would follow from a "blind adherence to *ad valorem* duties" in the existing tariff.[7]

Most liberals subscribed wholly to the theory that protective tariffs bred trusts. As Mark Twain observed, a system of "extraordinary" tariffs had created giant corporations in the interests of the rich, while gulling the masses into believing they were the beneficiaries. By awarding special privileges to favored corporations, protection enabled them to flout the "law of competition" and dominate entire industries under artificial conditions. In themselves, trusts were less objectionable than the tariffs that created them; but the tariff-induced trust was an abomination. "In any industry whose product our Government 'protects' by a tariff," one liberal argued, "it is in the power of home manufacturers to extort from the people the full tariff rate as a bonus for their own pockets." He noted that one of the worst offenders in this respect was the Casket and Burial Goods' Trust, an industry so well protected that the authors of the McKinley Tariff would be right at home when they died.[8]

How should the trust problem be solved? By lowering tariffs, letting in foreign competition, and thus breaking up the monopolies, Carl Schurz asserted. Forced to compete not only with other American producers, but with foreign operators as well, the trusts would soon stop limiting production and manipulating prices. Godkin commented that if individuals in America had been left to themselves in building up industries, perhaps the gross production of the country would be less than it was under the protective system; but certainly American society would be in a healthier condition and American industry would not be involved in political intrigues. No "hothouse legislation," such as tariffs and subsidies, would be necessary to save industry from its own follies. Grover Cleveland agreed with his Mugwump supporters that trusts were the "natural offspring" of an artificially restricted market. He avowed his "unalterable hatred" of both trusts and high tariffs, and promised in 1888 that the "checking of their baleful operations" would be among the good results of his proposed tariff reform.[9]

High tariffs did encourage some businessmen to combine operations and control market conditions. But liberal reformers conveniently dodged the tricky monopoly problem when they attributed it to the influence of the tariff. Trusts developed, especially during the 1880's, less from the effects of the protective system than from the "inexorable operation" of the "law of competition" itself.[10] Intense competition, large-scale production, and centralization of financial control almost invariably followed the opening of a promising new industry. And each step increased the likelihood that monopolistic operations would ultimately prevail in the industry. The tariff may have been a blood relative to the trusts, but it was not their mother.

As for the tariff and American labor, liberals had difficulty countering the protectionist argument that high duties shielded the worker from cheap foreign competition and raised his wages by stimulating domestic production. Wells had the problem put squarely to him in 1885 by a worker who, "having no use for Pro-slavery literature of a past age," returned a "Primer of Tariff Reform" the economist had sent him. As a "son of toil, a greasy mechanic," the professed workingman wanted nothing to do with schemes to "reduce my wages or make me any poorer than I am now." Protectionists, naturally, made the most of labor's fears about the results of tariff reform. Jay Gould once thanked Horace Greeley for the "valuable services" the editor had rendered to "the interests of American labor" in advocating a policy of protection. Greeley, long a champion of the tariff as a boon to labor, once investigated a rumor that the carpets in the two chambers of Congress were not of domestic manufacture. "If a Pennsylvania clerk had bought foreign carpets," he blustered, "I am after his scalp." It was the kind of bluster labor appreciated.[11]

Denying flatly that protection raised wages, liberal economists insisted that high tariffs actually lowered real wages by raising commodity prices. They compared the wages of workers in England and the United States to prove that, when the cost of living in this country was considered, protected American workers were actually worse off than their overseas counterparts—a strange bit of economic juggling. Liberals urged workers to reject the promises of protectionists, to rid themselves of the "legalized robbery" being committed in the name of their welfare. High wages in America, one economist asserted, resulted only from the "great general productiveness of labor" and were in no sense due to protection. Godkin warned workers they must learn a simple truth: manufacturers, regardless of their promises that wages would rise under high tariffs, in the end did what "all sensible men do"—paid their workers exactly what their labor was worth. If protectionists were really interested in shielding labor from cheap foreign competition, they should stop importing ignorant Irish and Chinese workers to compete with American citizens "face to face, on a perfect level, with equal civil rights." Members of the Boston Reform League, on the other hand, pointed up another ambivalence among liberals by arguing that free trade would not only benefit American workers; it would also "elevate the oppressed of other nations, and civilize the barbarian" here and abroad.[12]

Some liberals despaired of ever educating the American worker to the advantages of tariff reform. As Sumner complained, only a "great and prolonged effort" by the enlightened few would bring the benighted many to an understanding of what the protective system did to "morals, education, culture, civilization, and national greatness." In *A Connecticut Yankee,* Mark Twain satirized labor's gullibility:

> What these people valued was *high wages* [the Boss noted of his Arthurian hosts]; it didn't seem to be a matter of any consequence to them whether the high wages would buy anything or not. They stood for "protection," and swore by it, which was reasonable enough, because interested parties had gulled them into the notion that it was protection that had created their high wages. I proved to them that in a quarter of a century their wages had advanced but 30 per cent., while the cost of living had gone up 100; . . . but it didn't do any good. Nothing could unseat their strange beliefs.[13]

Although they used the term "free trade" in advancing their tariff views, few liberal reformers were really free-traders themselves. Rather, it was an ideal many of them clung to long after they had abandoned it as a feasible alternative to protectionism. Probably the disastrous defeat of free trade in the Liberal Republican convention convinced most reformers that protection, in some form, was to be a permanent feature of the economy. Thereafter, "moderate protection" or "judicious reform" replaced free trade as the goal of most orthodox liberals.

True to the doctrines of his liberal tutors in England, how-

ever, Godkin never abandoned the free trade ideal. Free trade was
the "natural law of human intercourse," he insisted, even as he
supported the more moderate reforms of Atkinson and Wells. Accused by his enemies of taking "English gold" in return for his attacks on the protectionists, he lashed out at high tariff propagan-
dists who tried to equate advocacy of free trade with disloyalty to
the country. It was high time, he protested, that protectionists drop
their "epithets and insinuations, the talk of 'British gold' and
'British free trade,' and addressed themselves pluckily to the facts
and logic of the matter." Godkin claimed that manufacturers who
demanded tariff protection from the government actually suffered
from bad management. He pointed to the "wonderful success" of
free trade among the states of the Union, and challenged Congress
to affirm its faith in American principles by adopting a similar
policy for the Federal government. Yet Godkin permitted advocates of mild tariff reforms to use his magazine's columns. Probably
he realized that his own extreme views would never gain popular
acceptance in his day.[14]

As late as 1876 Boston still boasted a "free-trade club" composed
of stubborn liberals who believed anything less than absolute free
trade was villainy of a sort. Samuel Bowles dismissed the organization as a naïve collection of ill-advised dreamers whose demands
were "vituperation and rubbish." Tariff reform, the Springfield
editor noted, was "obviously to be a slow and progressive history."
Any rash blow at the existing tariff structure would bring on economic disaster, for many important industries depended upon the
protective system that had developed during and after the war.[15]

Not all men of liberal inclination saw the tariff issue as a matter
of life or death for the economy. Pragmatic political considerations
persuaded young, ambitious liberals to move into the mainstream
of business thinking on the matter. Before he went to Congress,
Henry Cabot Lodge thought a "thorough revision, reduction and
simplification of the tariff" was perhaps the most important means
of ensuring the economic welfare of the country. That was in 1882.
Six years and a bitter national campaign later, Lodge viewed the
tariff issue "simply as a question of expediency." His friend Theodore Roosevelt kept pace with him on this matter, as on so many
issues. Republicans were correct in advocating protection, he told

his fellow members of the Union League Club in New York; but "we certainly should not declare that the maintenance of the present tariff unchanged with all its anomalies was a point to which every other interest and issue should be subordinated." Having made that bold statement in favor of tariff reform, the young politician proceeded to denounce the moderate Morrison Bill and to ridicule Cleveland's tariff views—"for I did not wish the mugwump papers to regard my attitude as in any way one of alliance with them." [16]

Yearning to play the American roles of the British Cobden and Bright, Edward Atkinson and David A. Wells were doubtless the most effective liberal reformers in the fight for tariff revision.[17] Both men had been stanch protectionists before the Civil War; and, although they later became nominal free-traders, neither man ever completely shucked off his protectionism. Rather, both advocated moderate reforms that would ensure the continuing growth of American industry, bring sizable revenues into the Treasury, and correct the more flagrant abuses of extreme protectionism. A man with important ties to New England's processors of raw cotton and manufacturers of finished textiles, Atkinson was no doubt sincere in his belief that lower tariffs benefited the country as a whole. But his reform position nicely complemented his pocketbook interests, too, for Atkinson feared that high duties on imported raw materials would jeopardize the overseas textile markets upon which his business fortunes depended. As for Wells, he became a tariff reformer only after studying the question at first hand as a member of the United States Revenue Commission in 1865 and 1866, and through his close association with Atkinson .According to one tariff historian, Wells exerted more "potent influence" on American tariff thought in the late nineteenth century than any politician or academic economist of his time. Wells and Atkinson certainly enjoyed the respect of all liberal reformers, even those who considered themselves doctrinaire free-traders.[18]

In 1867 Atkinson called for a "gradual and judicious" reduction of import duties to ensure a more stable and reliable condition in the textile industry than had been the case in recent years. Although he called himself a free-trader at the time, he proposed a cut in duties to no lower than 25 per cent. "We must have a large tariff revenue," he explained. Congress should act to admit raw materials free of duty and impose 25 per cent duties on manufactured goods; for, *"you can't get your revenue any other way."* If all theoretical free-traders would admit this factual necessity, he asserted, the antagonism between tariff reformers and manufacturers would disappear.[19]

As the years passed, Atkinson became less and less eager for precipitate tariff reform and more confident that businessmen would eventually see the logic of lower tariffs. During the 1880's he often criticized those reformers who persisted in advocating free trade. "I think Sumner and Perry are doing mischief in exaggerating the burden of protection," he told Wells. Precipitate action would alienate men who were "just ready to lie down," and might, by "unnecessary animosity and exasperation," risk the prospect for judicious reform. Moreover, the currency question was far more crucial than the tariff issue. Atkinson was ready, indeed, to vote for a strong protectionist, provided the man was sound on the question of legal tender. Although he praised Cleveland's tariff message in 1887, he feared and distrusted the Democratic politicians in Congress on just this matter. "There is a great danger now of an ignorant rush to change existing conditions," he warned after the Democrats had won a decisive victory in the off-year elections of 1890. Apparently, he put little credence in the very moderate statements on tariff reform and the settled "hard money" attitudes among such leading Democratic reform politicians as John G. Carlisle and William L. Wilson.[20]

Precisely what kind of tariff policy did Atkinson favor? On numerous occasions he called for reductions in duties to the 25 per cent level; yet in 1884, he opposed a bill to reduce duties generally by 20 per cent. Admittedly, the reduction would have left duties at an average of approximately 38 per cent; but surely a realistic tariff reformer would have welcomed a reduction in any degree from the prevailing high rates. On other occasions, Atkinson warned that the prosperity of American business depended on judicious handling of the tariff issue, with due regard for young industries in need of temporary protection. Yet, although he disliked the McKinley Tariff in general, he opposed most vehemently its provision for high duties on tin-plate, an industry just getting under way in this country. Atkinson thought the provision unwise, for the tin-plate industry involved "nasty, unwholesome work" better suited to "foreign paupers" than to American workingmen. Seemingly, he wanted Congress to adopt a tariff policy in strict conformity with his own amateurishly conceived estimates of the requirements of American industry. But, although the self-confident Bostonian was an expert on cotton and other textile products, he had no real knowledge of the new industries (metals and petroleum, in particular) that had developed since the war.[21]

Atkinson's business experiences introduced him to the study of political economy. David A. Wells stumbled on the subject by chance. In 1857 he lived for a few months in Philadelphia, where he came under the influence of Henry C. Carey, one of the country's leading economists. At the time, Wells was a natural scientist of considerable repute with a number of successful books on chemistry and geology to his credit. He had shown no interest whatsoever in political economy, even as an undergraduate at Williams College, a stronghold of economic orthodoxy, from which he graduated first in the class of 1847. But at Philadelphia he became an admiring disciple of Carey's economic nationalism; and during the early years of the Civil War he published several tracts on political economy, reflecting clearly the protectionist-nationalist view. In 1865, Secretary of the Treasury McCulloch invited him to become a member of the newly established United States Revenue Commission. Wells accepted the position, and thenceforth political economy displaced natural science as the major interest in his life.[22]

Wells served next as Special Commissioner of the Revenue under Presidents Johnson and Grant from 1866 to 1870. By then completely fascinated with the study of political economy, he undertook an intensive examination of fiscal policies. Before Johnson left the White House, Wells had become a leading authority on financial problems and had abandoned Carey's protectionism for the cause of tariff reform. He moved slowly on the tariff question and even approved the Wool and Woolens Tariff Act of 1867, hoping the measure would satisfy the protectionists in Congress. But Wells increasingly invited the hostility of Republican leaders in the legislature by boldly criticizing their protectionism. In 1870, Congress, with the connivance of the Grant administration, neatly abolished the office of Special Commissioner of the Revenue by cutting off its funds. Wells thereupon became a leading publicist for revenue reform and, after the Liberal Republican debacle, a member of the Democratic party. Doubtless his views on the revenue problem had much to do with Cleveland's decision in 1887 to make tariff reform a major political issue in the next presidential election.[23]

Wells often referred to himself as a free-trader; but, like his friend Atkinson, he knew that free trade, however desirable, was an impossible goal in post-Civil War America. Indeed, he often advised against rash cuts in import duties that might cause loss of business confidence and invite economic disaster. The protective system, he recognized, was too deeply rooted to be destroyed overnight. Patience, education, and slow reform might eventually convince the American people that lower tariffs were economically constructive and morally sound. Unlike Atkinson, he welcomed every attempt by low tariff men in Congress to effect moderate, carefully considered reductions. For a reformer, he was a remarkably restrained advocate; yet many times he despaired of ever seeing the enactment of effective tariff reform. At the end of the century, still an orthodox liberal, he attributed most of the world's political and economic troubles to protection of home industries and restrictions on international commerce.[24]

3

If liberal reformers had carried laissez-faire to its logical conclusion, they might have opposed all efforts by the state to extract revenue from the individual by any form of taxation. Indeed, a few doctrinaires had no use for any of the revenue-raising schemes politicians and economists advanced in the late nineteenth century. All taxation throughout history, Godkin decided, was simply the attempt by one class to make other classes pay the expenses of government. Many liberals recognized the need for some method of raising public revenues; yet, in considering specific proposals, they offered only negative criticism without constructive suggestions for possible alternatives. Others studied the problem carefully and sought fair and equitable means of taxation that would harmonize, as closely as possible, with orthodox economic theory.[25]

During the war, the revenue problem had consisted chiefly of finding money for carrying on the conflict. After Appomattox, it became one of reducing the heavy burden of wartime taxation. Congress considered three methods of attacking the problem: removal of the numerous excise taxes, repeal of the income tax law, and reduction of the tariff. All liberals, of course, favored reducing the tariff. In his reports as Revenue Commissioner, Wells recommended gradual but certain removal of most excise taxes. Although he considered the income tax "obnoxious," he favored retaining it for an indefinite period inasmuch as it would probably be less detrimental to the country than any other form of taxation, "the excise on spiritous and fermented liquors and tobaccos excepted." Congress followed the general outline of Wells's recommendations and pared down internal taxes considerably during the immediate postwar years. When certain politicians later attempted to repeal the remaining taxes on whiskey, beer, and tobacco, Horace White accused them of acting on behalf of the protectionists. They were afraid, he charged, that a rapid retirement of the public debt would lead to the reduction of import duties.[26]

Liberals divided sharply on the question of the income tax. Those who opposed it thought it an instrument designed to foist communism, or anarchy, or worse, on the nation. Those who favored it considered it the ideal tax, the one method of raising revenue that promised justice to all taxpayers. Although Wells reluctantly approved its retention in the early postwar period, he later attacked it in the bitterest language. He thought the progressive feature of the tax equivalent to "unmasked confiscation." Any government that taxed one man for holding more property than another was a despotism. Godkin, pleased when Congress repealed the wartime income tax in 1872, carried on a vitriolic campaign in *The Nation* against later attempts to revive the measure. The notion that people of substance had interests different from those of the rest of the community was a "deplorable hallucination," spread by "knavish or demented" silver agitators. When the Supreme Court saved the country from what he called "European communism" in 1895, by declaring the income tax provision of the Wilson-Gorman Tariff Act unconstitutional, Godkin rejoiced that the tribunal had arrested the "downward progress" of the nation. But he denounced the Court's lone dissenter, Mr. Justice Harlan, for having "expounded the Marx gospel from the bench." [27]

Curtis branded the income tax class legislation of the worst kind, repugnant to "the most precious traditions of the English-speaking people." Another liberal reformer warned that the tax would cut off all future support of hospitals, libraries, colleges, and churches, by confiscating the money of the "philanthropic rich." After experiencing mixed feelings about the income tax, Edward Atkinson concluded finally that it was an "economic blunder" and an invitation to fraud and abuse.[28]

Yet several leading academicians in the liberal ranks praised the tax. Arthur Latham Perry and Amasa Walker, two stalwarts among orthodox economists, thought it the fairest of all possible revenue-raising devices. (Ironically, Henry C. Carey, a bitter opponent of the orthodox economists on most issues, denounced the tax and urged that it be abolished forever.) Liberals, generally, followed the patterns of public opinion on the question; and the income tax did not become an issue between the two major parties until 1896. Prominent Democratic spokesmen denounced it as vociferously as did many Republican leaders. Only the discontented agrarian elements in the West and South strongly supported proposals for a national progressive income tax law during the postwar period.[29]

4

At the heart of the financial controversy in the late nineteenth century was the problem of money itself. What was money? Where did it come from and what purposes did it serve? Liberal reformers offered the public some dogmatic answers to these questions; and, by embellishing their economic arguments with strong moral overtones, they heightened the bitterness of the whole postwar debate on the question of national finances. For most liberals insisted that money was the product and slave of "natural laws," that the "honest dollar" had intrinsic, fixed value beyond the power of man

to impair or alter. Moreover, the dollar of the liberals rested firmly
on gold, and gold alone. Liberals did not object to silver coins or
paper money as such; but they demanded that each coin, each
piece of negotiable paper, have behind it for payment on demand
full value in gold. Any nation that disregarded these "natural
laws" affecting money would suffer dire consequences.[30]

Liberals belittled the notion that a government could issue inconvertible paper currency on anything other than a very temporary, emergency basis. During the war they acceded to the idea
fearfully and reluctantly and only because Treasury officials persuaded them that paper money was an absolute necessity in the
wartime emergency. Grudgingly accepting the scheme, they regretted their weakness ever after. Godkin later called the Legal
Tender Act of 1862 "one of the greatest calamities" ever to smite a
commercial society. At the time the Act went into effect, most people assumed the Treasury would withdraw the greenbacks once
hostilities ceased, returning the nation to specie payments and a
"sound money" policy. But after 1865, agrarian inflationists and
businessmen interested in retaining a flexible currency wanted the
inconvertible paper kept in circulation as a permanent part of the
money supply. Liberals roared in protest and opened a desperate
attack on the whole concept of an artificially regulated currency.
"We have never been in any scrape like this before," Godkin
warned his readers, as he rallied the "responsible" men in society
to defend the natural order of things.[31]

Godkin found it difficult to believe the American people would
seriously consider tampering with the currency. In 1867, confident
the people would come to their senses soon, he predicted the "hard
lessons of experience" would teach Americans that "the possession
of long rivers, great mountains, vast prairies and free institutions"
did not liberate them from the laws of political economy. But the
people did not learn the lesson quickly enough to suit the opin-
ionated editor. "Quacks, schemers, and cloudy rhetoricians" tricked
them into supporting nefarious proposals to flood the country first
with cheap paper, then with silver. Indeed, Godkin had never met
an advocate of paper money "who had not a queer look about his
eyes." Behind all these schemes, Godkin saw a great conspiracy to
dishonor the nation by forcing it to repudiate its debts. In 1878,

thoroughly disgusted with the ignorant silverites and "cowardly"
Congress that had passed the Bland-Allison Act, the editor wearily
reminded the lawmakers that they might as well "bow to the popular will about the properties of the circle" as give in to public
opinion in the matter of monetary standards.[32]

Other liberals were equally convinced about the immutable
nature of money. George W. Julian insisted that "real money" had
to be dug from the earth; certainly it could never be manufactured
by legislative fiat. Irredeemable paper money, Curtis observed, was
an evil that emanated from the radical West; and he appealed to
the "natural conservatism" of workers to resist the money schemers.
Americans had only two choices, he asserted: a return with sound
money policies to a state of "solidity, integrity, and safety," or a
plunge with greenbacks into "failure, dishonesty, and ruin." John
Murray Forbes, speaking for New England businessmen, referred
to greenbacks as "the 'legal tender' mongrel, a cross between a
fraud and a folly." Repudiation, he warned, would be the country's "financial Bull Run." [33]

In 1875, Carl Schurz waved the financial "bloody shirt" at the
German-American voters of Ohio. Unless Ohioans elected Hayes
governor over the inflationist Democratic candidate, he warned,
they would see their state topple into a "vortex of profligacy and
corruption." Victory for the currency radicals would discredit republican government throughout the world and expose the American people to the ridicule and contempt of civilized mankind.
Warming up to his subject, Schurz pictured the United States
wallowing in the depths of moral and material bankruptcy—conditions which, as history proved, "never NEVER fail to follow a course
so utterly demented in its wickedness." Ohio voters averted the
catastrophe by electing Hayes. But twenty years later Schurz was
still reciting his moral injunctions against "dishonest" money to
the voters. Edward Atkinson completely echoed Schurz's extreme
views: the retention of paper money in the economy would be
"folly, fraud, treachery, dishonor, theft, stupidity, and everything
else that is weak, miserably and cowardly combined." A sweeping
indictment, but Atkinson meant every word and was as sure of his
opinion "as that two and two make four." [34]

Because liberal reformers considered the money problem a question of "natural laws" and moral precepts, they refused to concede merit, reason, or intelligence to any proposal for expanding the currency. Financial reform, in their view, meant simply immediate contraction of the currency, prompt resumption of specie payments, eventual withdrawal of all irredeemable paper money, and unequivocal adherence to the gold standard. During the immediate postwar years, their greatest fears were that greenbacks would become a permanent part of the currency and that the government would repudiate the national debt. They saw the two threats linked together in a terrible menace to national honor and prosperity. As long as the people considered greenbacks as money, as legal tender for the final discharge of debts, the danger existed that all debts might be repudiated.[35]

But what constituted repudiation? Liberals insisted that each bond issued during the war, regardless of the currency originally exchanged for it, should be redeemed in gold. A promise was a promise; a contract was a sacred agreement. According to Secretary McCulloch in 1867, the wartime bonds carried a "distinct understanding" that they would be paid in gold.[36] Opponents of specie redemption asked by whose "understanding." They argued that most bondholders had exchanged depreciated greenbacks for the government issues. To pay off the bonds at face value in gold would mean that investors would receive a wholly unwarranted margin of profit on their original investments. Inflationists thus demanded that the principal and interest of the obligations be paid in the current paper currency, irredeemable greenbacks. To liberal reformers, this proposal constituted outright repudiation. To forestall the threat, they advocated immediate currency contraction and resumption of specie payments.

David A. Wells proposed probably the most spectacular scheme for ridding the nation of the obnoxious greenbacks. Burn them, he said. Take $500,000 in greenbacks each week and destroy them in the Treasury's furnaces, while upstairs, the department's officers resume specie payments. Other liberals asked Congress to repeal the Legal Tender Act simultaneously with the resumption of specie payments. After abandoning his "cremation theory," Wells advised Samuel J. Tilden to come out in his political speeches merely for "contraction." Avoid details, he told the Democratic leader in

1875. "The masses won't comprehend, and the doctrinaires will fight you." [37]

For several years after the war, Edward Atkinson concentrated on prodding Senator Charles Sumner into taking the lead in Congress in the fight for "honest money." But he suggested no specific method of contraction and resumption. As usual, Atkinson feared precipitate action by politicians who lacked his own deep insight into financial matters. Much as he detested flexible, inconvertible paper money, he did not know precisely how to dispose of it without dangerously disturbing the economy. Yet, Congress should make clear its intention to contract and resume, without indicating the specific date.[38]

Sumner took up the cause with more enthusiasm than Atkinson thought quite necessary. He knew nothing about financial matters, as he told John Bright; but, having decided the money problem was a moral issue, he determined to give it his immediate attention. Relying almost entirely on Atkinson's views, he spoke in the Senate for the orthodox approach to the money problem. In "financial reconstruction," he said, "we must follow Nature, and restore by removing the disturbing cause." As long as a dollar of irredeemable currency remained in circulation, "the Rebellion still lives, in its spurious progeny." Atkinson congratulated the senator on his forthright stand; but Sumner, perhaps carried away by his newly won reputation as a financial expert, then went a step further and thoroughly disconcerted his Boston adviser. In 1868, without consulting Atkinson, he shocked the business community by calling for the resumption of specie payments in eight months. Boston businessmen immediately informed their senator that he had overstepped the bounds: contraction must precede resumption. Sumner thereafter confined himself to generalities about the money problem and regained the confidence of Atkinson and the business community in general.[39]

Liberals hailed the first legal tender decision of the Supreme Court, which declared unconstitutional the original paper money act, and they deplored the attempts of certain legislators to obtain a reconsideration of the issue. "Of all the countries in the world," Godkin grumbled, "America is the last where law can be safely divorced from common sense, and where politicians can with safety intrigue to bring about such results." In the interest of good faith and financial sense, why not act on the maxim that " 'sufficient for the day is the evil thereof?' " A year later, doubtless in response to the business community's insistence upon a policy of gradual contraction and resumption, the Court reversed itself and pronounced greenbacks constitutional as legal tender. "Whenever the politico-economical history of the past thirty years in America comes to be written," the exasperated editor of *The Nation* observed, nearly a quarter of a century after the decision, "the cause and origin of the socialistic phenomena which have marked it assuredly will be found in the legal-tender decision of 1871." The Court had opened the door to all the dishonest schemes—greenbackism, free silver, the income tax—that plagued the nation to the end of the century.[40]

Most liberal reformers had no use for President Grant after his first two years in office, and in 1872 they tried desperately to unseat him. But two years after the Grant-Greeley contest, when the President vetoed Congress's attempt to add $18,000,000 of new legal tender currency to the permanent money supply, liberals praised him as a courageous savior of the nation's honor. John Murray Forbes considered the veto, "next to his military success, the crowning glory of Grant's life," while Horace White thought the action gave Grant a reputation that would outlast all the scandals in his administration. Garfield decided that Grant was "one of the luckiest men that ever sat in the Presidential chair," because of his opportunity to do the country such a vital service with his veto message.[41]

But liberals were wary of the Specie Resumption Act that Grant signed the following year. Drafted by senators Sherman and Edmunds, the measure provided for resumption of specie payments in 1879, and reduction of greenbacks to 300 million dollars, but it made no mention of further contraction of the currency. Liberals blamed Sherman more than Edmunds for the faults of the measure, for the Ohioan, in defending the bill, took an equivocal stand on currency contraction. One liberal organ charged Sherman with preserving the "discreet silence of a conspirator" when questioned about the intent of the Act. Godkin called the measure a "mockery and delusion and a snare" designed to "humbug the public." Only a few weeks earlier, Congress had enacted a high tariff measure, and liberals saw a direct connection between the two measures. Yet Garfield thought the Resumption Act a step in the right direction. He disliked parts of the Act, but at least it was better than nothing.[42]

Liberals disliked silver no less than paper currency, and they considered the "free silver" movement a fraud from the moment it came rampaging out of the West in the 1870's. Warned by friends in the West to avoid attacking the question on moral grounds and to concentrate instead on stressing the "unprofitableness" of silver, Godkin ignored the advice. "Free silver," he insisted, was a dishonest scheme; and the "unprofitableness of cheating can never be made entirely clear to a man bent on cheating." He warned his readers that the Bland-Allison Act (passed in 1878) would never satisfy the "silver fanatics." On the contrary, he predicted—with considerable accuracy—it would persuade them to ask for more. When would legislators learn that inflationists of all breeds were "metaphysicians and dialecticians?" Any compromise with such people was out of the question, for their money was not real money, but "money of the mind." [43]

For men who railed against the tyranny of party discipline and condemned party politicians for supporting automatically the dictates of party, liberal reformers behaved oddly toward legislators who dared to vote for inflationary financial legislation. Godkin flatly labeled the inflationists in Congress, regardless of party, "traitors in the camp." Most liberals dismissed Western and Southern spokesmen for inflationary currency as "rank communists." Grangers, for example, masqueraded as reformers only for the purpose "of making a living at their neighbors' expense." True, a few liberals in the West sympathized with the demands of the farmers; but they exerted little influence on the dominant "best men" in the East who controlled the important liberal organs. Such reformers as Godkin, Schurz, Curtis, Atkinson, Wells, and Norton knew almost nothing about conditions in the agricultural hinterlands. Schurz thought farmers were "well-meaning people" who misread the economic facts of life and thus became easy prey to dishonest financial demagogues. As Wells complained to Atkinson, "How can you hope to get any worth-while reform measures through Congress when the people at home show such little sense?" [44]

5

Clearly, the "people at home," the legislators in Congress, and the public in general needed some sound financial education. As Garfield put it, people needed to be "converted to sound finance" about every six months.[45] Liberal reformers who accepted "free trade," taxation for revenue only, and "honest money" as integral parts of the Nature of Things, thus undertook to guide their less enlightened fellow Americans along the path of financial righteousness. In countering the West's "radical" solutions to its money problems, they always insisted that any compromises on the principles of currency contraction, specie resumption, and "free trade" would undermine the nation's financial integrity. Actually, however, they compromised their own position appreciably when they considered the problem from the standpoint of Eastern big business. For, in testimony before Congress and in their consideration of business's practical requirements, liberals permitted "free trade" to become moderate tariff reform and "immediate contraction and resumption" to become gradual currency reform. Yet, they worked hard to rally public support to the two attenuated positions.

No liberal devoted more time to educating the public on finances than David A. Wells. During the Johnson administration, Wells worked in perfect harmony with his immediate superior, Secretary McCulloch; and after the election of 1868, Wells deluded himself for a time with the thought that he might become McCulloch's successor. But the Radical leaders who put Grant in the White House had other plans. George S. Boutwell, an outright protectionist, became the new Secretary of the Treasury, and the appointment all but assured the failure of Wells's program of revenue reform. As Grant's Special Commissioner of the Revenue, Wells represented a lonely liberal outlook in an administration that grew increasingly antagonistic to any tampering with the financial status quo. But his annual reports and frequent appearances before congressional committees kept the issues before the public, and his office served as a clearinghouse for liberal ideas on finance.[46]

Wells would have been a greater success as Revenue Commissioner had he understood better a few elementary principles of practical politics. In 1867 he went to England and consulted openly with members of the Cobden Club, the leading organization of English Liberals. For some time, Wells had been questioning the wisdom of protectionism; doubtless the contacts in England strengthened his decision to come out in favor of "free trade." At any rate, his annual reports for 1868 and 1869 reflected strongly his new attitude toward the tariff. Led by Secretary Boutwell, his critics charged that "English gold" had effected the change in the Commissioner's views, and they accused Wells of favoring foreign producers over American workingmen. The charges were patently false, but Horace Greeley, Henry C. Carey, and the protectionists in the administration weakened Wells's position and destroyed his usefulness as a government officer. When Congress abolished the office of Revenue Commissioner and retired Wells to private life, Godkin complained bitterly that unscrupulous politicians had sacrificed an outstanding public servant to the requirements of greedy special interests. "Mr. Wells can afford to go, we may be sure, a great deal better than we can afford to lose him." [47]

To many liberals, Wells's dismissal seemed to coincide with Benjamin F. Butler's rise to a position of influence in the administration. Liberals detested Butler as much for his heretical views on finance as for his intense partisanship in the impeachment crisis. The colorful soldier-politician had no use for "free trade" and "honest money," and boldly advocated a high protective tariff and an expanded flexible currency as policies to best serve the interests of Massachusetts workingmen. In 1868, Massachusetts liberals tried desperately to unseat Butler, but their candidate, Richard Henry Dana, Jr., fared miserably in the contest. Both Atkinson and Wells participated in the campaign from behind the scenes, and some liberals thought Wells's dismissal from the administration was Butler's revenge. But, while Butler welcomed and perhaps influenced the decision to oust Wells, many other regular Republicans shared his dislike of the Revenue Commissioner. Wells simply did not belong in the Whiggish councils of the Grant administration.[48]

In national politics liberal reformers interested in revenue and currency readjustments proved no match for the Stalwart and Half-Breed leaders who dominated the Republican party and wrote its platforms. Their problem, as one disillusioned liberal acknowledged at the end of the century, was simply that "old Whiggery" dominated the party. Republican leaders had fought hard and long for the Whiggish economic measures enacted during the Civil War, and they put up fierce resistance to the small group of "impractical idealists" who tried to overturn the program and return the nation to economic policies of an earlier era. Thus, Republican platforms every four years called for high tariffs (to "protect American labor") and for "continuous and steady progress" toward specie payments, rather than for immediate resumption.[49] And the Democrats, much as they professed their devotion to "free trade" and immediate "honest money," had no opportunity to demonstrate their ability to effect these reforms until 1885. Moreover, liberals distrusted the strong inflationist element in the party and noted uneasily the tendency of individual Democratic legislators to disregard the party's platform promises on financial questions.[50]

It was all very discouraging to liberal reformers. The Republicans offered them relatively sound money policies, but absolutely no chance for tariff reform. The Democrats tempted them with probable tariff reform, but only at the risk of inflationary money policies. For added proof that the two great issues bore very little relation to party lines, the Liberal Republican debacle in 1872 drove home the futility of attempting to form a separate party to advance specific reforms. Politics in the postwar period taught William Cullen Bryant the folly of expecting parties to do anything about revenue reform. Political parties were "ignoramuses and imbeciles," incapable of thinking or learning anything, he commented acidly in his last days.[51]

Ironically, a machine politician offered liberals their best opportunity to secure tariff reform before 1885. At the behest of Atkinson, Wells, and the low tariff men in Congress, President Chester A. Arthur in 1882 established a Tariff Commission to study the revenue problem and propose new policies. Strangely enough, when the President attempted to find men to serve on the Commission, some liberals backed away from the responsibility. At least two professed tariff reformers (Hugh McCulloch and A. A. Low) declined the chairmanship; and Edward Atkinson dismissed lightly the suggestion of several prominent businessmen that he offer his services to the President. Arthur, at length, found a chairman in the person of the chief lobbyist at Washington for the National Association of Wool Manufacturers, and he named protectionists to most of the other vacancies on the Commission. But the Commissioners took their work seriously and, although they did not advocate anything faintly resembling a free trade policy, they called for reduced duties on many items in order to cut tariff revenues. Liberal reformers, perversely unhappy that the Commission did not recommend broader changes, declined to support the recommendations or to rally public opinion to the proposed modest revisions. Protectionists in Congress had their own way with the report and wrote a bill that reformed nothing. Even the chairman of the Tariff Commission, suddenly recalling his duties as lobbyist for the wool interests, testified in favor of woolen tariffs higher than those he had recommended in his report. Undaunted, Atkinson observed to Wells: "It simply proves that the tax reformers in Congress are incapable and inefficient; and that you, and I, and the rest of us are the only power to compel reform." [52]

Liberals achieved more success in educating the public through reform organizations than through political action. Scores of reform clubs and "free trade" leagues flourished throughout the period, although only a few organizations made significant contributions to the reform effort. Soon after the war Atkinson and Charles Francis Adams talked of establishing an agency to disseminate "correct financial knowledge among the people." Already busy issuing pamphlets on financial questions under the masthead of the Loyal Publication Society, Atkinson in 1869 helped establish the Boston Reform League, for a time the most influential reform organization in New England. The League's statement of principles reflected clearly the influence of Atkinson and other Massachusetts businessmen who wanted financial reform to come—but not too quickly. It urged "careful abatement" of the "most onerous taxes" and resumption of specie payments "so far as it can be done by legislation." [53]

Two years later, Horace White, Atkinson, and Wells organized the Taxpayers' Union at the nation's capital. With William Grosvenor of Missouri, a zealous financial reformer, as its secretary, the Union issued pamphlets and furnished speakers on revenue questions; but its primary function was to lobby for revenue reform in Congress. For a few years the Union enjoyed some success and became a rallying point for the reformers who organized the Liberal Republican movement. But sharp differences between Eastern and Western reformers in the organization eventually brought about its collapse and, incidentally, demonstrated the futility of attempting to organize a movement for revenue reform on a national scale. Tariff reformers in the East wanted duties removed or lowered only on raw materials; their counterparts in the West asked for free raw and finished imports. Obviously Eastern manufacturers, represented in the reform movement by such men as Atkinson, Wells, and Forbes, would not hear of lower tariffs on goods in competition with their own products. The Taxpayers' Union soon followed the Liberal Republican party into oblivion.[54]

By far the most important revenue reform organization in the postwar period was the American Free Trade League. Organized in 1867 to co-ordinate the efforts of numerous local tariff reform clubs, the League ostensibly championed "free trade." In actual practice, it worked only for moderate tariff revisions. Together with its subsidiary organizations, the Young Men's Free Trade Clubs and the Society for Political Education, the League published pamphlets and books on revenue questions and attempted valiantly to rouse public indignation over the prevailing high tariffs. It grew steadily in strength during the 1870's, flourished during the Cleveland era, and persisted as a significant reform agency into the early years of the twentieth century. Its publication, the "Free Trader," furnished intelligent rebuttals to the high tariff arguments of the "American Protectionist" and the "Iron and Steel Bulletin" of the opposition.[55]

In New York, during the late 1880's, the City Club's successes in the field of municipal reform stimulated the older Reform Club to new activities on behalf of revenue and currency reforms. The Reform Club's committee on tariffs published semi-monthly an aggressive little newsletter filled with statistics and detailed analyses of late tariff news. "Tariff Reform" had few readers among ordinary citizens in New York, but the newsletter furnished facts and figures to editors and lecturers throughout the East. Like most other revenue reform organizations, the Club represented the interests of manufacturers; thus it advocated lower tariffs on raw materials only. Moreover, its committee on sound money espoused the Wells-Atkinson cautious approach to monetary reform, while denouncing the "silver heretics" as rogues and scoundrels. New York businessmen found the Reform Club an attractive association, for the club, asserting that each worthy reform was an efficient ally to every other, promoted "honest currency" and "the business administration" of the city as well as revenue reform.[56]

During Cleveland's first term, Atkinson organized several "Questions Clubs" in Massachusetts. These ambitious little groups sought to pry out of cautious legislators opinions favorable to the Atkinson brand of tariff reform. Few congressmen paid attention to queries from the "Questions Clubs," although several Massachusetts representatives, mindful of political fences at home, responded with the answers Atkinson wanted to hear. A favorite "Questions Club" query asked legislators if they thought Congress should tax "salt fish, smoked herring, frozen fish, potatoes, coal, iron ore, limestone, and iron." Unless smoked herring is a manufactured product, all of these commodities except smelted iron were raw materials.[57]

6

In December 1886, a few weeks after the congressional elections had resulted in a resurgence of Republicanism, Grover Cleveland decided he and the country needed an issue for the next presidential campaign. In his second annual message, the President asked Congress to reduce tariffs "fairly and cautiously" and to suspend silver coinage. Alarmed by the expanding Treasury surplus and by the threat of a critical contraction of the currency which might endanger the stability of the entire economy, Cleveland concluded that revenue reductions would best extricate the administration from its financial and political predicament. The worst aspect of the existing situation, he declared, was the fact that the surplus resulted from "a perversion of the relations between the people and

their government," for tariffs encouraged businessmen to seek special favors and the surplus tempted ordinarily honest citizens to
ask their government for paternalistic legislation. If Congress refused to reduce the surplus by lowering tariffs, the President
warned, the country would be drawn into an orgy of wasteful extravagance, corruption, and national demoralization.[58]

Clearly, liberal reformers had a champion in the White House.
Not only had the President attacked "forthrightly" the revenue
and currency problems; equally important, he had defended the
principle of laissez-faire, had delineated the proper relations between the people and the government, and had placed the fight for
financial reform on a high moral plane. Liberals could not have
asked for a more succinct official expression of their philosophy.

But by late 1886, Grover Cleveland had demonstrated to his
Mugwump supporters that he was, after all, an ordinary human
being and a rather conventional politician. During his first year in
office the President had tried to hold the line against the insistent
demands of Democratic partisans for government jobs. Owing his
election less to the Mugwumps than to his party's loyal supporters,
however, he had been forced eventually to retreat from civil service reform. Badgered by the Mugwumps for his increasingly
equivocal stand on the issue, the President in the same message in
which he called for tariff and revenue reforms referred with fine
impartiality to the "misguided zeal" of the "impracticable friends"
of political reform as well as to its willful enemies.[59]

Liberal reformers, of course, deserved the slap. They had been
thoroughly unrealistic in expecting Cleveland to wipe out the
spoils system, and they had totally ignored the fact that their man
was also the leader of the Democratic party. On the other hand,
Cleveland had exposed himself to criticism from the liberals and
was as much to blame as they for the misunderstanding, for he had
posed as a thoroughgoing reformer during the campaign of 1884.
After the President delivered his message, Carl Schurz, as usual,
was on hand to give him unsolicited advice. He accused Cleveland
of having sacrificed the Democratic party to its "worst element."
He warned the Chief Executive that unless he took immediate and
"heroic" action to save the party from the spoilsmen, he would be
in danger of losing not only the party but his own honor as well.

Schurz said not a word about the President's plea for tariff and revenue reforms.[60] Nor did many other leading liberal reformers. Piqued by Cleveland's retreat on civil service reform, they distrusted his intentions on the financial question and thought he would do nothing to push the reforms through a recalcitrant Democratic Congress.

His third annual message, devoted entirely to the tariff question, changed their minds. Godkin thought the message "the most courageous document" sent to Congress since the Civil War. Schurz admitted that the plea for tariff reform had "profoundly stirred" the country. Liberals generally praised the President for having given the nation an issue for the coming presidential campaign. The "gun that has been fired" by the message would be heard in "every corner and hamlet of the country." It would become the subject of "village debate and neighborhood meditation"; and in the end, a "self-reliant and free people" would give a ringing answer in favor of the President's bold position. Responding to the President's leadership, the Democrats proclaimed in their platform in 1888 that all "unnecessary taxation is unjust taxation," that the Democratic remedy for financial ills was "to enforce frugality in public expense and abolish needless taxation." To which the Republicans responded that they were uncompromisingly in favor of the "American system of protection," and opposed to its destruction by the President and his party.[61]

Cleveland drew the issue in the campaign, but the election resulted in a victory for Benjamin Harrison and the protectionist Republicans. Clearly, Godkin concluded, Cleveland had sacrificed himself to a principle. Yet, he had secured at last an audience for that principle, and "nobody who took part in this first skirmish will lay down his arms till victory is won." In the campaign, few Mugwumps had been able to work up much enthusiasm, however, possibly because they had at last awakened to the realization that no President—however well-intentioned—could give them all they wanted in the way of reform. Moreover, many liberals by 1888 were aware that Grover Cleveland needed the professional politicians within his party much more than he needed the Mugwumps. The liberal journals supported the President in the election and probably most liberal reformers voted for him. But they did so with none of the crusading zeal that had marked their efforts four years earlier.[62]

Four years of Republican rule, under the "caretaker in the White House," as Godkin called Harrison, revived the indignation and spirits of the Mugwumps. Indiscriminate pension raids on the Treasury surplus, the McKinley Tariff, and the Sherman Silver Purchase Act persuaded many liberal reformers that Cleveland, regardless of his shortcomings, was preferable to anything the Republicans had to offer. Moreover, during his enforced absence from the White House, Cleveland successfully convinced many businessmen and most Mugwumps that he really would work for revenue reforms if they would give him back his old job. Revenue reforms, he insisted, were linked inextricably with the "destiny of our country," for they attacked directly the "strongholds of selfishness and greed" that exerted a pernicious influence on patriotism and national virtue. Nor did he ignore the farmers and workers of the country. More than once in the past he had hinted that individual shiftlessness was the main cause of farm failures and unemployment. In 1891 he announced that it was the "tribute" farmers and workers had to pay to the "favorites of governmental care" that caused all their ills.[63]

Cleveland was the "safe" candidate in the campaign of 1892. Tutored in financial matters by such politically minded businessmen as Francis Lynde Stetson and Henry Villard, the Democratic leader had become thoroughly sympathetic to the business community's views on "sound money" and moderate tariff revisions. Carl Schurz wrote to congratulate him on his nomination *by the people over the heads of the politicians*"; but Cleveland received the honor from the hands of the financial backers of the Democratic party rather than from "the people." His victory in the election, according to Godkin, was a triumph of "splendid courage," a vindication of his wisdom and boldness in advocating intelligent reforms. Certainly the victory seemed to indicate that Cleveland had been farsighted and eminently wise on financial questions. But the Republican party had ruined its own chances in the election by choosing first to enact and then to defend the McKinley Tariff. With the possible exception of the Smoot-Hawley Tariff of 1931, no other revenue measure in American fiscal history was so poorly timed or so contemptuous of existing economic conditions. Not only did the measure raise the high protective barriers that already over-protected many industries, but it actually reduced the revenue in-take of the Treasury at a time when the surplus was by no means as perplexing and threatening a problem as it had been a few years earlier. That practical old politician James G. Blaine, keenly aware of the probable effects of the measure, called it "injudicious from beginning to end" and predicted the tariff would defeat the Republican party in 1892. Moreover, the administration forces had wooed the votes of Western representatives for the tariff bill by allowing the Sherman Silver Purchase Act to pass Congress. To businessmen and Mugwumps this bit of political shenanigans endangered the financial integrity of the nation. Money poured into Democratic campaign coffers once businessmen and financiers had satisfied themselves that Grover Cleveland would take immediate steps to remedy the existing dangerous monetary situation.[64]

Elected by a comfortable margin, Cleveland at once honored his indebtedness to the financial community. Ignoring for the moment tariff reform, he called Congress into special session in the summer of 1893 and instructed the legislators to repeal the Sherman Silver Act. Repeal, he promised, would stem the flow of gold from the Treasury and halt the business panic, which even then was blossoming into a full-blown depression. Wielding the weapon of patronage as though he had never heard of civil service reform, the President whipped his party into line, lashed out at his critics, and completely enthralled the Mugwump editors with his display of "courage." When Blaine complained of the President's "pressure" tactics in the House and Senate, Godkin assured his readers that the pressure was only the "public opinion of the United States." When silverites in the Senate conducted a filibuster against repeal, Godkin huffed and puffed against them for lacking the "common decency" to admit defeat. But when at last the repeal bill passed Congress, the editor marveled at the totality of the triumph for responsible finance and acclaimed Cleveland for the speed with which he had achieved the victory. Silver is dead, he proclaimed; the specter of depression is dissipated. David A. Wells, who advised the President and Secretary of the Treasury Carlisle throughout the fight, was somewhat less certain of the results of repeal. The depression, he confided to a friend, would last "sometime longer." [65]

Wells was correct. Unemployment continued to mount after the demise of the Sherman Silver Act, gold continued to pour out of the reserve, and Cleveland continued to look to the financial community for guidance in coping with the situation. Early in 1895, with the gold reserve standing at 41 million dollars, the President invited J. P. Morgan to Washington and arranged for the House of Morgan to save the United States Treasury with a loan of 62 million dollars—in return for an extortionate commission of seven million. Immediately the anti-Cleveland forces in Congress protested. But Godkin assured the nation that Cleveland was master of the situation, and that "all the howlings of the jackals" could not deter him from maintaining the government's "plighted faith." He railed at the "brutish Congress" and "blatherskite press" that dared to suggest the President might have arranged better terms for the government.[66]

Having secured repeal of the Silver Purchase Act, Cleveland next turned to the tariff. Liberal reformers hopefully awaited the President's firm action, for they had viewed tariff reform as the outstanding issue in the campaign of 1892. The Democratic party had received a mandate from the people; the election of Cleveland meant, said one liberal journal, that the principle of high protection had been "finally condemned" by clear and emphatic popular disapproval. But although a moderate tariff reform measure worked its way slowly through the House in the winter of 1893–94, it received little encouragement from the President and active opposition from some of his closest advisers. Indeed, Cleveland acted forcefully only after the bill had been emasculated in the Senate. On July 2, 1894, months after Congress had first taken up the measure, he denounced it in a letter to Congressman William L. Wilson. In doing so, he intimated clearly that the leaders of his own party in the Senate (and especially Senator Gorman) had betrayed their trust and dishonored the Democratic organization. If repeal of the Silver Purchase Act had alienated Democrats in the West and South from Cleveland, the tariff letter finished him with many powerful Eastern Democrats in Congress. The Wilson-Gorman Tariff passed Congress late in July and became law without the President's signature. It effected no reforms of con-

sequence in the tariff structure and succeeded only in laying the
Democratic party open to charges of hypocrisy. Liberals were
stunned; but they blamed "irresponsible" elements in the party,
not Cleveland, for the fiasco. Congress had acted in a "simply
brutal" manner, Godkin concluded; the Democratic party well deserved the censure heaped upon it by the President.[67]

Cleveland saved the gold reserve and shattered the Democratic
party in the process. He failed to effect tariff reform and crippled
the party still more in that process. Acceding completely to the
wishes of his financial backers and advisers in the East, he alienated most Democrats in the West and South. By 1896 he had lost
control of his party and had paved the way for that "pitiful climax" to the history of the Democracy, the nomination of William
Jennings Bryan. Liberal reformers had placed their trust in him as
a champion of revenue reform, however, and by 1897 he had satisfied them to the point where they proclaimed him, as he left office,
one of the greatest Presidents in history.

Liberals really gained very little in the way of revenue reforms
from Cleveland during his two terms. To be sure, the Democratic
leader struck down the bugbear of silver and put an end to the
forced coinage of the inflationary metal. But this action did not
solve the problem of contracted currency, and it intensified, rather
than quieted, the uproar for monetary relief in the agrarian areas.
Moreover, it precipitated the struggle within the party that ended
with the victory of the inflationists at the Democratic convention
in 1896. And if Cleveland was the champion of tariff reform, he
held the title by a most tenuous claim. In the campaigns of 1888
and 1892 he used the issue for political advantage; in office, however, he exerted little of his influence to effect real reform. His tariff messages, in the final analysis, aroused the hopes of reformers,
but they did not bring about tariff reform.

For four decades liberal reformers had fought for financial principles they considered essential to the integrity and honor of any
responsible nation. They had fought well, but they had struggled
increasingly in vain against economic conditions brought on by the
growth of industry and high finance that they simply did not
understand. In 1896 they sacrificed tariff reform to "sound money"
by supporting McKinley against Bryan. But it must have been evi-

dent to them at the time that neither party really offered them the slightest assurance that it would respect the old natural laws governing currency and revenues. With the approach of the new century, the old economic canons became hopelessly outdated; the decade of the 1890's marked the last stand of old-fashioned laissez-faire. It marked the end, too, of whatever power and influence the old-fashioned liberals had ever exerted in politics.

8

The Dangerous Classes

It is a great pity that we cannot shut up the mouths of the Anarchists by love. But as we cannot shut them up by love, we must do it by fear, that is, by inflicting on them the penalties which they most dread; and the one most appropriate to their case when they kill people, is death. The frantic exertions they are making just now to escape the gallows, and the joy with which they would welcome a "life sentence," shows clearly that the gallows is the punishment the case calls for.

E. L. GODKIN, November 1887

The last two months have been full of heartache and horror for me, on account of the civil murder committed last Friday at Chicago. . . . It's all been an atrocious piece of frenzy and cruelty, for which we must stand ashamed forever before history. But it's no use. I can't write about it. Some day I hope to do justice to these irreparably wronged men.

WILLIAM DEAN HOWELLS, November 1887

IF LIBERAL REFORMERS DETESTED CORRUPT POLITICS, PRO-
tective tariffs, and paper currency, they frankly feared the encroachment in society and politics of the "dangerous classes." Any
individual or group that seemed to threaten by word or deed the
existing social and economic order fell into this category. Most
union members and practically all labor leaders belonged to the
"dangerous classes." Farmers who betrayed their tradition of
"rugged independence" to advocate inflationary currency and government regulation of business automatically became members of
the "dangerous classes." At various times throughout the postwar
period liberals relegated a marvelous array to membership in the
iniquitous cabal: Irish immigrants in New York; "alien agitators"
of unspecified national origins; Benjamin F. Butler; anarchists,
communists, and socialists; drunkards and home-wreckers; Governor
Altgeld of Illinois; the "rabble" that participated in strikes and
demonstrations against the Nature of Things; the social reformers
who told the "rabble" that the Nature of Things was unnatural.
Several Eastern editors, terrified by the railroad riots of 1877, furnished their readers with vivid descriptions of the "dangerous
classes." Their inventories included howling mobs, suspicious-
looking individuals, rough elements, loafers, nonproducers, bullies,
reckless agitators, white-livered demagogues, roaming bands of

worthless fellows, incendiaries, loud-mouthed orators, rapscallions, terrible tramps, riffraff, habitual law-breakers, drunken section-men, frenzied roughs, communistic Bohemians, belligerent Poles, deadbeats, blacklegs, Paris Communists, wretched people, brigands, enemies of society, cowardly mobs, felons, idiots, and motley gangs.[1]

These misguided or deliberately vicious people belonged to a great conspiracy against property, traditional moral principles, laws of nature, and capital. According to liberal theory, the owners of capital had a natural right to use their capital as they saw fit, free from governmental or other artificial limitations. Workingmen had a natural right to offer their services freely and to make the best terms possible with anyone who bid for their services. These transactions were strictly private in nature, subject to no restrictions save those imposed by certain immutable "natural laws." Left to themselves, labor and capital would adjust to each other's requirements in any given situation; for, so long as both relied solely upon their "natural rights," neither could take advantage of the other. Every artificial limitation, however slight, on the free interplay of capital and labor altered the natural relations of the various elements in the economy and weakened the moral foundations of society.[2]

In the deterministic world of the orthodox liberals no individual suffered economic hardship except as a result of his own short-comings. When the farmer failed or became bankrupt, Grover Cleveland once observed, "we may, I think, confidently look for shiftlessness." Only the "industrious, intelligent, and contented farmer" became a "safe and profitable citizen." Arthur Latham Perry saw no sense or reason in the "common jealousy" of workers toward their employers. After all, they were partners in the same business; their interests were identical. Workers who were "intelligent, prudent, skilful," inevitably received their just rewards. Those who failed at their jobs or suffered hardships had nobody to blame but themselves.[3]

As a rationale for the acquisitive spirit, social Darwinism blended perfectly with these dogmas of orthodox liberalism and reinforced the deterministic view of society. Godkin concluded that the only plausible solution to the labor problem was to make the manual laborers of the world content with their lot. Any other approach would fail, for Nature had decreed by law that "the more intelligent and thoughtful of the race shall inherit the earth and have the best time," while all others must content themselves with a life "on the whole dull and unprofitable." Socialism, which Godkin interpreted to mean any effort by government to ameliorate the "dull and unprofitable" life of the poor, was an attempt to contravene the law and "ensure a good time to everybody." [4]

As defenders of individualism, liberal reformers insisted that artificial interference in the labor problem demoralized workers and destroyed their self-confidence and self-respect. Only rarely did they acknowledge the possibility that the industrial order itself undermined individualism and that great masses of workers could not possibly negotiate with their employers on an individual basis. Edward Atkinson argued that workers must retain the liberty to make their own contracts, for if the American worker was "unfit" to bargain for himself, democracy surely was a failure and American institutions were no better than those of Europe. Workers who looked to government for help in solving their problems, Godkin warned, subverted a doctrine which was the cornerstone of democracy. [5]

Some liberal reformers urged workers and employers to settle their differences in an atmosphere of brotherhood, and a few even went so far as to suggest that government might manufacture a little brotherhood by enacting arbitration laws. Godkin dismissed their suggestions as ridiculous efforts to change human nature. "The energetic, industrious, sagacious, and frugal," he commented, had an "unbrotherly way of getting rich faster than the slothful, the lazy, the stupid, ignorant, and drunken." Moreover, they had an "odious fondness" for keeping the fruits of their labor for themselves and their heirs. He deplored the growing tendency of politicians and public figures to treat the worker as a "peculiar being," deaf to the hearing of unpleasant truths and deluded into thinking that the laws of the universe always acted favorably to his interests. Henry Ward Beecher told his congregation that all persons have the right to work "when or where they please, as long as

208 THE BEST MEN

they please, and for what they please." Any attempt to infringe on
this right or to put "good workmen" on a level with "poor workmen" was a preposterous effort to regiment labor.[6]

Yet even the most orthodox liberals admitted grudgingly that relations between labor and capital constituted a serious problem. As
workers became steadily more militant in demanding a fair share
of the national wealth, liberal reformers sought means of educating
them and of treating their grievances without upsetting the Nature
of Things.

2

"When a man goes on the wrong road himself," Theodore Roosevelt once remarked, "he can do very little to guide others aright,
even though these others are also on the wrong road." [7] Observing
the activities of labor unions and assessing the platforms of labor
reform conventions during the postwar period, liberal reformers
concluded that labor leaders were indeed taking workers down the
wrong road. To be sure, workers had grievances that required attention. But their leaders, instead of teaching them the basic identity of interests between capital and labor, harangued them with
wild charges against employers and whipped up dangerous class
hatreds. Instead of advising workers to wait patiently for "natural
laws" to rectify temporary imbalances in the economy, agitators
urged their ignorant charges to demand "unnatural" concessions
from businessmen. Moreover, these labor leaders destroyed the traditional individualism of the American worker by teaching him
that government should provide him special favors and privileges.
According to Godkin, the typical labor leader wanted only to put
all workers, regardless of capacity or ambition, on the "same dead
level" in wages and hours, and to halt the "very growth of civilization" by denying to people of refinement and culture the means of
"gratifying their tastes or following their favorite pursuits." [8]

When workers complained of low wages or asked for increases
based on the high profits of their employers, liberals urged them to
have faith in the great law of supply and demand. When labor was
scarce and capital plentiful, wages would rise; when capital retrenched and labor became plentiful, wages would fall. There was

no mystery to the operation of the law, for it was all as simple and mechanical as any process known to science. "The facts stare us plainly in the face, if we will only look at them," Sumner insisted. Wages had nothing whatsoever to do with prices and profits. Indeed, one political economist argued that workers did not even have a just claim to the minimum wage necessary to keep a man and his family from starvation. To be sure, employers ought to acknowledge that there was a right and a wrong way in dealing with workers; yet, "every man's labor is worth what some other man will do it equally well for, and no more." Liberals pointed to the "wage-fund" theory as proof that strikes for higher pay could not possibly succeed. Because only so much money was available in the economy for the payment of labor, wages at any given time for an individual worker could be determined simply by dividing the "wage-fund" of that particular time by the number of laborers available.[9]

Shortly after the war, several liberals expressed great concern about the "unnatural" wages servants were receiving from masters and mistresses. Charles Loring Brace deplored the tendency of servants to "flit about" from household to household, subjecting mistresses to "great humiliation" and discomfort and driving wages to unnaturally high levels. According to Godkin, servants in only a very few cities in America received the "political economist's market price" for their labor. The situation was serious. "Impudent" servants and irresponsible men of wealth were forcing the middle classes into a plainer style of living. "Mr. Corner, of the Stock Exchange, or Mr. Putemthrough, of the Great Gammon and Spinach Company," gave "John, or Thomas, or Bridget" not what they deserved in wages, but what they asked.

Why did the matter upset Godkin? Was this not a classic example of the law of supply and demand in "inexorable operation?" Servants were scarce, capital was plentiful; according to liberal theory wages had to rise in such a situation. Perhaps Godkin relied on the "wage-fund" theory to conclude that servants were receiving more than they deserved. More likely he decided that servants, because they were an essential means of gratifying the tastes of people of refinement and culture, did not labor under the natural laws of political economy. At any rate, he noted optimistically that the spread of education and taste, doubtless, would gradually correct the evil. In the meantime, mistresses could console themselves with the knowledge that they were performing a valuable philanthropic service:

> Each lady must remember that for a considerable portion of her life she is at the head of a "Philanthropic Servants-Training School," where one rough and ignorant peasant woman after another is taught cleanliness, order, good taste, and good cooking, and is fitted to be the wife of some laborer, or policeman, or mechanic, or upper servant by-and-bye. Thousands of nice laboring men's homes over the country are the fruits of the long and apparently useless torments of our mistresses. Our very evils come from our blessings.[10]

In a rare moment of economic heresy, Godkin once admitted that the law of supply and demand was a hard taskmaster, that he could understand the reluctance of many workers to await its operation. The worker's "poverty, ignorance, and social position" prevented him from being what economists assumed him to be—a free agent. Often the natural working of the laws of economics was a slow process; workers became impatient and sometimes resorted to strikes and other unnatural devices to collect their rightful wages. Too often the victims of the "arbitrary rule of individuals," workers proved by striking that they were eager to live under the rule of natural law. Until employers willingly obeyed the law of supply and demand, Godkin conceded for the moment, strikes and peaceful demonstrations might be useful means of "testing the market" and of determining the prevailing "wage-fund" quotient. But workers should not abuse the strike privilege or attempt to evoke legislative interference in their contractual relations with employers.[11]

Like wages, working conditions depended solely on the operation of "natural laws" in the orthodox liberal's deterministic society. In 1867 a convention of labor reformers in New York proposed to amend the state constitution to prohibit the employment in factories of children under ten years of age. Quick to see the dangers in such a scheme, Godkin warned workers that they were asking for the impossible. Even the most "conscientious employer," he argued, could refuse to employ children only at the risk of losing the services of the parents. There might well be something to be said for controlling child labor; nonetheless, a constitutional amendment to that effect would open the door to further regimentation. In the end, the constitution would contain a complete code to regulate all political, moral, and "sanitary" conditions—to "tell us what to eat, drink, avoid, hope, fear, and believe." [12]

At every opportunity liberal reformers attacked the movement for state and Federal eight-hour day laws. Reflecting clearly the middle-class outlook of organized labor, the eight-hour movement was an attempt by union leaders to alleviate mildly the plight of exploited workers without challenging anything basic in the capitalistic system. It was a reform liberals might have approved on the same humanitarian grounds that had moved many of them earlier to champion the abolition of slavery. Refusing to compromise their rigid dogmas, however, they attacked the eight-hour proposal as though it threatened the very foundations of civilization. One critic admitted that the nation might benefit if the work day was reduced. As the "true middle class," he noted, labor deserved every consideration—moral, intellectual, and recreational—for it served as the "fountain of physical vigor" for the nation. Yet, "if we work too little, we thereby impoverish the country, and all grow poor together." Moreover, workers already misused their leisure hours by drinking, fighting, and stirring up trouble; doubtless, under an eight-hour system they would use their extra time in similar fashion. [13]

And what would the eight-hour day do to the nation's industries? Many liberals decided that the reform would upset production schedules, disorganize factory discipline, and bring many industries down in ruin. James Russell Lowell admired Wendell Phillips for his courage and vigor in championing the rights of labor. But Phillips's plan for an eight-hour work day, if adopted, would create a "material and unideal" world that Lowell, for one, "would not care to live in." Expressing a typical Mugwump opinion during the campaign of 1884, Horace White accused the Republican party of furthering "one of the most arrant communistic delusions of the day" by including an eight-hour plank in its platform. "Six dollars per day of eight hours' labor!" The mere idea of such a scheme shocked George William Curtis. Half the business-

men in the country, he argued, would welcome the guarantee of
such a profit. Godkin dismissed the proposal as "cheap clap-trap."
Like legislation to prohibit liquor consumption, the eight-hour
proposal was an attempt to do what could only be done by a total
change in human nature. As Wendell P. Garrison advised workers,
the hours of labor could be commended only to "the humane revision of employers." [14]

Basil March, the middle-class protagonist in William Dean
Howells's novel of protest, *A Hazard of New Fortunes,* learned
that society operated less under the beneficent protection of "natural laws" than on the principle of chance. The discovery induced
him to revise his opinions about the "laws" and the integrity of the
individual. "It ought to be law as inflexible in human affairs as
the order of day and night in the physical world," he observed,
"that if a man will work he shall both rest and eat, and shall not
be harassed with any question as to how his repose and his provision shall come." Unlike many liberal reformers, Howells viewed
the individual as a flesh and blood being, not as a helpless tool of
some economist's laws. Other reformers often urged workers to
improve their minds, to seek out culture during their leisure hours,
and to help elevate the general "tone" of society. But when workers appealed for higher standards of living and shorter work hours,
liberals accused them of seeking money to waste on drink and
extra time to associate with "agitators." Apparently, workers were
"free agents" only at the moment they sold their services to employers.[15]

As much to counter the influence of "labor agitators" as to improve the lot of the workingman, liberal reformers proposed a
variety of solutions to the problems of American labor. Probably
most believed labor would be best served by better living conditions, as at the "model" town of Pullman, and by better education,
as practiced at Cooper Union. Some called for the rich and the
well-born to lead a moral crusade against the hedonism of all social
classes. Charles Dudley Warner thought workers behaved in a
"mischievous" manner because wealthy members of society, with
their "bacchanalian revel and prodigality of expense," set ruinous
examples for them. Moreover, he insisted that responsibility for
correcting this deplorable condition lay with the rich, not with the

workers. William Lloyd Garrison, who agreed that "sensual indulgence" and "licentious perversion of liberty" endangered the
republic, also considered workers the villains. Even Henry George
acknowledged the innate viciousness of man, though he thought
this made the duty of reformers only more clear. Much of the "dis-
sipation" in American society, he observed, resulted from impulses
for which workers found no wholesome outlets. Among the "more
cultured and comfortable" people, these impulses sought satisfaction in higher social and intellectual pleasure.[16]

Probably most liberals believed that the businessman's cavalier
disregard for "natural laws" bore a direct relation to the workingman's reliance upon artificial assistance. Tariffs, subsidies, charters
of privilege, and other special legislation for businessmen created
in the labor force a desire to get while the getting was good. Liberals based many of their arguments for lower tariffs, sound money,
and laissez-faire on the assumption that these reforms would do
much to remove the inequalities between capital and labor. Everyone, capitalist and worker alike, needed more education in political economy. "Let education send into our society a body of
laborers educated and intelligent," Rutherford B. Hayes remarked.
Henry James thought both businessmen and laborers expected
their problems to have easy solutions. Tariffs and strikes were of
the same stripe, for both subverted the "natural laws." Professional
champions of labor, like professional politicians and unscrupulous
businessmen, misled the average American worker; and liberal reformers, therefore, ought to do everything possible to inculcate
among the rank and file of labor a healthy respect for sound principles of political economy.[17]

No man could ever be "dragooned" into showing respect for
morality, Godkin contended. In order to make men more moral,
"you must not legislate, but *teach;*" and the sooner people learned
that simple truth, the sooner labor would become more tranquil.
Perhaps the most important lesson labor had to learn concerned
the true nature of capital. As it was, Godkin argued, labor's conception of capital was utterly at variance with that of all sound
economists. Indeed, it would be hard to find a more striking example of "mischief" brought on by the misuse of words. Workers the
world over imagined the capitalist to be a "very odious but ficti-

tious person, wallowing in luxury and self-indulgence, absolutely indifferent to the sorrows of those who have little money." During times of labor unrest he became an ogre, who "summons the militia to his aid and shoots Labor down." Ridiculous! Godkin snorted. Laborers must learn that the capitalist was their partner in operating the economy. No sane employer would deliberately mistreat his workers. Capitalists worked hard, saved their money, and contributed to the well-being of the workingman by using their superior intelligence and ability.[18]

Determined to prove to workers that capitalists had their interests at heart, Horace White in 1885 described in glowing terms the "model town" of Pullman, Illinois. "The idea at the bottom of the enterprise was neither philanthropy nor avarice," he asserted, "but an intelligent conception that the highest rate of profit for capital was consistent with the highest state of comfort for labor." George M. Pullman had attracted to the town a class of men capable of forming their own opinions as to the "state of the markets." No trade unions, professional labor reformers, or "socialist spouters" cluttered up the town to deceive the men. Nor did the company corrupt the workers by giving them something for nothing. "Mr. Pullman has secured himself the first and most important factor in the successful conduct of any business." So much had been done for the workers, White concluded, that the future could be trusted to take care of itself. Other businessmen would do well to follow the Pullman example and thereby win the loyalty of their workers.[19]

Some liberals put their faith in thrift as the solution to the labor problem. William Graham Sumner advised workers to solve their own problems by accumulating capital and investing it in savings banks. By thus developing a vital interest in the protection of property, they would become happy, well-adjusted citizens, deaf to the siren calls of "agitators." Sumner offered no suggestions as to how workers were to accumulate capital after they had fed, clothed, and housed their families and attended to medical and other expenses. He was less concerned with the "how" of the solution than with the "why," and it was enough for him that the savings panacea would undercut the "agitators." One of his favorite anecdotes concerned the "agitator" who admitted that he could get along with any audience except

> "these measly, mean-spirited workingmen, who have saved a few hundred dollars and built a cottage, with a savings bank mortgage, of which they rent the second story and live in the first. They," said he [the "agitator"], "will get up and go out, a benchful at a time, when I begin to talk about rent." [20]

Practical Christianity and temperance, some liberals asserted, would help solve the labor problem. William E. Dodge, a businessman and philanthropist known to his friends as the "Christian Merchant," thought social unrest had no place in God's divine scheme. Dodge preached the doctrine of the stewardship of wealth and used much of his fortune to further the "Christian education" of workers. Because he thought drink caused most of the worker's problems, he located his factories only in villages that banned all alcoholic beverages. As a result, he boasted, his workers were frugal men who, in many cases, owned their own homes. Godkin, too, thought that intemperance was probably the greatest of the evils from which the working poor suffered. It made little sense, he insisted, to cut the worker's day to eight hours, to provide him with extra holidays, or to "hand over all the property in the world" to him, when the property and the free time would be squandered in a "rum-hole." [21]

Moral rejuvenation, indeed, appealed to almost all nineteenth-century reformers as a panacea for the problems of industrialism. From Sumner to Ely, orthodox and "ethical" liberals taught Christian morality as a prequisite to all other solutions for the problems of the poor. Sumner wrote that mankind's only hope of a better and happier life lay in "the enhancement of the industrial virtues and of the moral forces which thence arise." Industry, self-denial, and temperance were the "laws of prosperity for men and states." Ely, who sympathized strongly with labor unions and other efforts of workers to better their own conditions, advised workingmen to avoid liquor, demagogues, and unsound politics, and to seek guidance from the Christian church; for, "Christ and all Christly people are with you for the right." [22]

Philanthropy and charity, tied closely to the concepts of Christian reform and moral rejuvenation, appealed to some liberals as solutions. Roeliff Brinkerhoff participated actively in the Liberal Republican movement; but after the demise of that reform effort, he traded political activity for a "higher and better mission" in philanthropic work, in which he saw concrete evidence of his reform efforts and helped directly to alleviate the plight of underprivileged workers. Writing in *The Nation*, Samuel Eliot asserted that "If it has not charity, a nation, like a man, is nothing." Yet, *The Nation*'s editors had little sympathy for the philanthropic approach. Doubtless, philanthropy had its place and was a necessary, if unfortunate, service the rich owed to the poor. But all philanthropic and charitable enterprises, Godkin and his disciples believed, ought to rest on "sound business principles," lest the recipients of gifts lose their self-respect and sense of self-reliance.[23]

Probably the most ambitious proposal for alleviating the plight of low-income workers and the unemployed poor came from Edward Atkinson. In 1892 the indefatigable businessman-reformer from Boston came up with a wondrous compound of philanthropic concern for the poor, dietetics, and amateur economics, in a treatise entitled *The Science of Nutrition, also The Art of Cooking in the Aladdin Oven with Directions and Many Recipes.*[24] Profoundly disturbed by the pessimistic implications of Malthusian theory, Atkinson for years had studied the science of nutrition and the culinary art in an attempt to discover cheaper and more efficient methods for utilizing and preparing food. Eventually he discovered a method of cooking, not new but long forgotten, based on the use of the Aladdin Oven, a fireless cooker designed to conserve heat and improve the flavor of common or relatively unpalatable foods. The method was simple, inexpensive, and efficient—three characteristics that commended it, in Atkinson's opinion, to laboring men and others who had to live on limited means. Had the ambitious Bostonian publicized his discovery solely on its merits as an aid to better nutrition, he might have attracted the interest of workers. But Atkinson decided that his stove should be used to counter the pernicious influences of unions and workers' cooperatives, so he advertised his scheme as a remedy for socialism. Aware of Atkinson's stubborn anti-union views, workers naturally scoffed at the Aladdin Oven and looked upon it only as another slick contrivance designed to reduce their costs of living and, thus, their wages. Atkinson asserted that the oven and the new method of food preparation would afford a savings of five cents a day for each member of an average lower class family. Could starry-eyed advocates of the eight-hour day match this? Or "the anarchist, the communist, the socialist, the protectionist, the free-trader, the co-operator, the paper-money man, the knight of labor, or the sentimentalists"? [25]

Much to Atkinson's disappointment, no one rushed to accept his stove as a substitute for higher wages and shorter hours. As Eugene V. Debs noted, the Boston business leader was trying to teach a "science of the shinbone diet." Debs insisted that American workingmen were determined not to live as "Huns," and he predicted correctly that Atkinson's dietary mission would be a miserable failure. Undaunted, Atkinson was sure his epitaph would read: "He taught the American people how to stew." [26]

From lower tariffs to Aladdin Ovens, liberals proposed solutions to the labor problem that evaded the basic issues. Workers wanted decent wages, shorter hours, and better working conditions. But they wanted, as well, something less tangible—some acknowledgment by their employers that they were self-respecting human beings. Unwilling to consider themselves members of a proletariat, American workers wanted desperately to believe in the middle-class myth of the self-made man. Liberal reformers occasionally recognized the middle-sized aspirations of labor, and their panaceas purportedly were designed to elevate workers from the lower classes to higher stations in society. But few liberals did very much to put the ideal into practice.

Instead, they relied on the old copybook maxims of "Christian morality" and Poor Richard. Andrew Carnegie's views on the labor problem probably reflected the sentiments of most liberal reformers. The ironmaster told workers that life in the "humble cottages" of the poor was greatly to be preferred to life in the palaces of the rich. Rest content with what you have, he preached; wealth brings to its owners burdensome responsibilities which the poor should be happy to avoid. For workers who did not wish to rest content with what they had, Carnegie and his friends could propose only the competitive struggle in the world of chance. Ambitious men knew that the only escape from poverty was the moral route, strewn with opportunities for those who would recognize them. Let a man live wisely, inculcate upon his children good habits and sound notions, and capitalize on whatever chances he could find or make. Only thus could he hope to better his position.[27]

3

Liberals had mixed feelings about trade unionism in America. They saw nothing basically wrong in the idea of workers banding together for mutual benefits or for resisting the practices of unscrupulous employers. Yet they viewed the typical trade union as a device tending to the destruction or weakening of traditional American individualism. And they abhorred—indeed, they positively dreaded—the tactics some unions used in dealing with employers. In spite of their occasional pronouncements of sympathy with the principle of trade unionism, most liberals thoroughly disapproved the activities of any union that attempted to provide anything more than a social outlet or some harmless rudimentary education for its members.

Even their expressions of sympathy did not go very far. After analyzing the trade union movement and its leaders, Charles Dudley Warner concluded that most labor organizers were troublemakers, who made a business of "agitation" and prospered at the expense of the ordinary workingmen. But Warner damned some employers as well, charging that many businessmen were guilty of cruel and inhumane labor practices. In considering workers only in the cold, mechanistic logic of the law of supply and demand, employers offered labor little choice but to organize against the established system. Warner's Nook Farm friend, Mark Twain, predicted that labor unions would flourish naturally in America as the only economic protection available to workers, though he seems to have paid little attention to their development or problems. No one disliked the anti-individualist implications of unionism more than William Dean Howells. But he saw, too, that workers had to organize if they were to combat the combined strength of employer associations and trusts. He and a handful of other liberals actively supported the union movement, for they felt that the "inherent citizenship" of workers should be exercised as a "corrective" in the state of politics and the laws of economics.[28]

But the trouble with labor unions, most liberals believed, was that they were under the control of men who represented the worst characteristics of American society. Not only did labor leaders deliberately mislead their followers with muddle-headed ideas about the nature of capital; even worse, they themselves were completely unfit to exercise the power which leadership of a union gave them. John Hay's description of a labor leader in *The Breadwinners* (perhaps the most graphic anti-union novel in American literature) doubtless reflected the views of many liberal reformers:

> It was a face whose whole expression was oleaginous. It was surrounded by a low and shining forehead covered with reeking black hair, worn rather long, the ends being turned under by the brush. The mustache was long and drooping, dyed black and profusely oiled, the dye and the grease forming an inharmonious compound. The parted lips, which were coarse and thin, displayed a perfect set of teeth, much discolored with tobacco. The eyes were light green, with the space which should have been white suffused with yellow and red. It was one of those gifted countenances which could change in a moment from a dog-like fawning to a snaky venomousness.

Hay claimed the labor leader was the only character in the novel drawn from real life.[29]

Most liberals considered active trade unions a menace to industrial stability as well as to individualism. Alarmed at the power of the Knights of Labor, Atkinson urged employers to band together as "Squires of Work." He thought the term "scab" eventually would become an epithet any "independent worker" would be proud to bear. Unions existed only to advance wages and shorten hours of work, and to encourage other such "subtle restrictions of individual liberty." One of Atkinson's protégés, William Mason Grosvenor, like most other orthodox liberals considered labor merely a commodity on the market. But he asserted publicly that his primary objection to trade unions was their threat to individualism. In no other relation in life did a man "surrender so much of his freedom" as when he joined a union. Relating an imaginary conversation between a union leader and an unorganized worker, Grosvenor rang the changes on motherhood, fatherhood, and patriotism. Labor, said Grosvenor's ruggedly independent worker, cannot ask of any man that he shall "cease to be free." It could not ask that he shall "cease to be a good citizen, a good worker, a good father, or a good husband." Think of the women, he advised the union man; "be larger and broader," and admit that the union "is not the cause of the wife, whose maternity should make her sacred to you, and whose faithful work all these years at home needs to be protected far more than the labor of the men in your shops." [30]

Samuel Bowles likened trade union members to a sect of "Adullamites in political economy." Unions embraced as leaders and members "repudiators, proscriptionists, conspirators against the laborers who will not join a trade's union, men who believe in strikes, who hate the negro and the Chinaman, who clamor for a division of property and the abolition of money." More than anything else in the union movement, George William Curtis deplored its tendency to promote class divisions and hatreds in American society. Labor leaders who declared it the "imperative duty" of every worker to join a union were attempting to create a "special class" in classless America. As unions grew in strength and influence, Curtis became increasingly concerned with the effects of organization on the worker's rugged independence. Perhaps workers had the right to associate with others in asking for terms of employment suited to their needs. But the "correlative rights" were equally clear: the right of each man to decide how much money he should pay for labor; the right of employers to unite in refusing to pay more than they thought advantageous to their own interests; and the absolute right of property owners to control the disposition of their property. Whether composed of workers or employers, any association of individuals that attempted to interfere "unlawfully or unnaturally" with the rights or property of others deserved society's condemnation. Obviously, Curtis did not consider the property—the labor—of the workingman worthy of as much protection as the more tangible property of the landowner or industrialist.[31]

Conceding reluctantly the right of workers to organize in defense of their legitimate interest, *The Nation's* Godkin nonetheless thought trade unions "hostile to civilization" and "drags on the wheels of both moral and material progress." Stupid businessmen sometimes left workers no alternative but to organize; but the intelligent employer, Godkin asserted, obviated the necessity for unions by infusing into his relations with labor something more than the "spirit of contract or patronage merely." He paid his workers the best wages the market allowed, protected them from arbitrary or hasty dismissal, assured them kindly and considerate treatment—in short, made them feel that the union was not a necessity to them. Yet, this kind of intelligence was rare among employers in American industry, and Godkin foresaw the continuance and growth of unions. Properly managed, organizations of workers might become useful appurtenances in certain industries. But only unions of "sober, rational, and business-like" temper, only unions that respected the "rules of morality," deserved the public's approval. Godkin refused absolutely to countenance the existence of unions that prevented men who wanted to work from "exercising that freedom." Let a worker join a union and strike to his heart's content, if that was his foolish inclination. But let him refrain, on pain of losing his job and of receiving actual physical punishment, from interfering with the right of other workers to bargain independently with their employers.[32]

In 1883 the printers and pressmen of every major metropolitan newspaper in New York walked out on strike and provided Godkin with an opportunity to assess firsthand the tactics of labor's leaders. As editor of the *Evening Post*, he negotiated with the unions and struggled manfully to hold together a united front of editors and publishers in resisting the demands of the strikers. The experience taught him a "terrible lesson" about trade union morality. In the long preliminary negotiations with the unions, Godkin thought he had been bargaining with honorable men on honorable terms. Although the talks had settled nothing, they had ended with "expressions of mutual respect and good will." The workers had given notice that in all probability they would strike his presses at some time in the future, and Godkin had assumed that the strike would be simply a "friendly trial of strength." Suddenly, and without definite notice of intent, the newspaper's entire staff of printers and compositors had walked out. "Dishonorable,"

Godkin cried. Clearly, the union bosses had taken over the matter from the "honorable" workers with whom he had negotiated earlier. Reacting swiftly to the union action, Godkin hired non-union men to fill the empty jobs; but the union immediately made the entire matter even more dishonorable by insidiously infiltrating the ranks of these "scabs" and by completely disrupting the operation of the paper. The "friendly trial of strength" with "respectable, intelligent, and self-respecting men" degenerated into a "series of tricks usually resorted to only by criminals." For weeks Godkin fumed editorially in *The Nation* about the "absurdities" of the union's demands. One by one, however, the *Evening Post*'s competitors settled with the strikers, and ultimately Godkin resumed negotiations. It was all such a waste, he concluded. The city's newspapers granted only a few minimum demands of the workers. Yet everyone had suffered from the strike, and the public had been given another glimpse into the "intolerable" conditions that prevailed within the unions.[33]

One answer to unionism, liberals thought, was for employers to imitate the workers—to organize in order to resist strikes and other "unnatural" attacks. Associations of employers could take "corrective action" against the "meddling activities" of unions. Moreover, liberals who deplored governmental interference in the affairs of business called, after 1890, for government prosecution of unions as monopolies under the Sherman Act. David M. Means, an amateur economist who frequently contributed to *The Nation*, insisted that the anti-trust law "stands squarely across the path" of striking union members who tried to force employers to accept their unreasonable demands. No writer for *The Nation* under Godkin's editorship ever called for anti-trust prosecution of an employers' association or an industrial monopoly. But the journal called frequently, especially during the 1890's, for government action against trade unions.[34]

Almost alone among liberal reformers in the business world, Abram Hewitt sought some satisfactory compromise with workers on the union issue. Perhaps because he owned great factories himself, Hewitt was determined to bring labor and capital together in mutual harmony. Workers ought to organize in unions, he asserted. Employers ought to recognize unions and work closely with union representatives in the interest of industrial efficiency. If labor and management once acknowledged their community of interests, business would prosper, workers would be happy, and labor strife would come to a welcome end. Moreover, Hewitt declared, businessmen ought to consider seriously a plan to share profits with their workers. The iron magnate actually wanted to see a conservative labor movement develop—a network of unions that would associate itself inextricably with the capitalistic system and spurn the appeals of socialism. His prediction in 1878 that labor would become a conservative force in the economy came true in the 1890's with the rise of the American Federation of Labor. But during the intervening years, Hewitt displayed a rather ambivalent attitude toward unions in his own ironworks. Indeed, no union of any sort ever achieved much success in organizing his plants. At one time the Knights of Labor managed to establish a fair-sized local in one Hewitt plant; but Hewitt, who hated the "one big union" idea, harassed the unit and succeeded with little trouble in driving it from the premises. He preferred the trade or craft union principle of the American Federation of Labor and insisted that employers must always control the hiring and firing of personnel in their businesses. Though more enlightened in many ways than most of his fellow liberals, Hewitt agreed with them that union militancy should be resisted at every opportunity.[35]

Nor was militant labor their only target. Most liberal reformers considered farm organizations no better than trade unions. Especially after it developed an interest in politics, the Grange impressed liberals as a tragic symbol of the American farmer's surrender to pernicious, imported doctrines. Once the farmer had been the symbol of rugged independence in American society; now, with the rise of the Grange, he had succumbed to the philosophy that the government owed him a living. Moreover, liberals disliked the fact that agrarian organizations multiplied the already numerous and dangerous economic and social divisions in society. They were ready to tolerate such organizations as inevitable counterparts to other special interest divisions, but only so long as farmers operated them on sound, businesslike principles. Like unions, however, the Grange and the Alliances seemed habitually to exceed the bounds of responsible action: they attempted to sub-

vert "natural laws" and they obstructed the efficient operation of
the entire economy with their demands for cheap money and railroad regulation. The whole process of divide and grab distressed
Godkin. Farming in the West, he concluded, had become little
more than a branch of speculative commerce. Its "business union,"
the Grange, was merely one of a countless number of similar
unions all over the country, each of them tearing apart the once
homogeneous elements of American society.[36]

The real trouble with these "business unions" of farmers, was
that they entertained some strange beliefs as to the nature of political economy. Much as liberals disliked certain undesirable practices of the railroads, they shrank from the "radical" antidotes
proposed by the Grange and the Alliances. Railroad managers
often engaged in corrupt and unscrupulous attempts to alter the
natural operations of the economy, but farmers took unreasonable
revenge against them by clamoring for "communistic" money and
government regulation beyond all limits of good sense. Godkin
compared the demands of the farmers with those of the old Know-
Nothings and charged that the Grange existed only to promote
confusion. Charles Francis Adams, Jr., ridiculed the farmer's notions of political economy. Doubtless, he observed, the "late Dr.
Adam Smith," were he alive in 1873, would be astonished to learn
that ignorant American farmers were disputing so many points of
his economic philosophy. Even when farmers met the reformers on
their own ground, many liberals were incapable of viewing the
problem rationally. In 1874 the president of the Illinois State
Farmers' Association addressed a meeting of the American Social
Science Association, setting forth a scholarly, reasonable exposition
of the agrarian position. It was a performance entirely in accord
with the association's insistence that social science should be considered in a calm, rational manner. But in the discussion following
the address, the "social scientists" present showed complete ignorance of the speaker's position and kept referring to the iniquitous
monetary policy of the agrarian community. Some embarrassment
may have followed the secretary's announcement, as the meeting
ended, that the speaker was a hard-money man who was "continually urging that question upon the attention of the farmers of
Illinois." [37]

Once again liberal reformers blinded themselves to the middle-class aspirations of an important segment of American society. Because agrarian organizations demanded certain concessions from the dominant economic interests in the nation, liberals assumed that they wanted to destroy capitalism and blindly upset the Nature of Things. Honest as well as dishonest people, they were persuaded, fell victims to crackpot schemes and demagogues, simply because they did not know what went on in the world of economics. Nothing would change unless Nature willed the change, and neither workingmen nor farmers had any control over Nature's whim. Thus, liberal reformers dismissed agrarian and labor reformers as members of the "dangerous classes" or as weaklings unfit to survive in a competitive society.[38]

4

Violence and threats of violence seared much of the history of post-Civil War America. The period was marked by bloody rioting, prolonged and disorderly strikes, and ominous breakdowns of civil order. Every instance of violence, no matter how petty, was exaggerated in the public press—by the reporters for the great metropolitan newspapers, by columnists in the influential weekly journals, by cartoonists such as Thomas Nast. As farmers pressed their demands, people in the Eastern states often became hysterical about the threat of revolution in the West. As labor became more militant, liberal reformers grew more hysterical about the threat of anarchy in the industrial East. Doubtless the violence of the Civil War and Reconstruction periods had much to do with the general sensitivity to civil turbulence later in the century. But by reacting irrationally to outbursts of violence, liberal reformers showed too that they lacked faith in the ability of the American people and republican government to solve the problems of industrialism. Godkin and his disciples, for example, were morbidly preoccupied with violence, with the threat of anarchy and communism they saw hanging over the nation throughout the period. They seemed always to sense revolution breathing down their necks, to smell the blood of martyrs, indeed, to anticipate the sharp edge of the guillotine. Everything that seemed to challenge their own dogmatic opinions they treated as a national peril. Everyone who questioned their economic views they considered a villain intent on destroying American institutions.

Perhaps there was some excuse for Godkin's irrational behavior. After all, he came to this country at the age of twenty-five, strongly imbued with English Liberalism. A product of the Anglo-Irish middle class, he had come to admire and emulate the English upper classes with whom he had been in contact during his early years. As an educated, cultured, fluent Englishman in America (never as an Irishman), he sought to establish himself as an oracle of gentility, of "tone," of taste. Godkin seldom ventured west of the Hudson River, confining his contacts for the most part to the moneyed aristocracy of the eastern seaboard and the latter-day Brahmins of Boston and Cambridge. He knew little of his adopted country, of the hopes and fears of the average American, or of the conditions here that made people markedly different from their English cousins. His criticisms were more often destructive than constructive. Moreover, he was a thoroughgoing social snob. The son of an Irish Presbyterian minister of modest means, he considered himself in America a member of the cultured aristocracy.

Most of Godkin's fellow liberal reformers, on the other hand, were native-born Americans who knew well their country and its traditions.[39] Why did they follow Godkin's lead in viewing with alarm every sign of discontent among their underprivileged countrymen? Why did they, too, react to violence with violence—with demands that strikers be shot, that anarchists be hanged, that aliens either stay at home or leave at home their pernicious doctrines? Why did they fear their fellow Americans? Perhaps because, in reality, they lacked faith in their precious "natural laws" of political economy. As long as those laws operated for the benefit of capital and property, liberals loudly proclaimed their inviolability and denounced all attempts to interfere in the economy. But when "natural laws" broke down under the impact of the factory system, liberals panicked and sought to defend them by calling for "unnatural" interference on the side of capital in labor disputes. As the old liberalism began to die, a new liberalism arose to take its place —a liberalism that accepted the industrial system and strove to balance its deficiencies with positive action by government. Orthodox liberals stubbornly insisted that their way was the only way; they resisted bitterly every proposed change in economic theory and practice; they fought each new idea as though its acceptance would bring on a major catastrophe. The old laws could not sanction the provision of "artificial" aids to the poor, the unemployed, and the other unfortunates in society. Yet industrialism, while it created great national wealth and ultimately raised the standard of living of the average American, also created poverty for hordes of people and subjected millions of workers and farmers to severe social and economic traumas—depressions, financial panics, unemployment, and loss of personal identity and dignity in society. Liberal reformers became deathly afraid of the poor and the unfortunate, afraid that the underprivileged masses would rise up and strike down property and all that was decent and respectable in life.

Their vaunted respect for the law blinded them to its iniquities. Garfield declared that "against all comers I am for the reign of law in this republic and for an army large enough to make it sure." To him, as to other liberals, the law existed primarily to protect private property. "Hands off," Henry Ward Beecher warned the Federal government from his pulpit; "see to it that we are protected in our rights and in our individuality. No more than that." But when Beecher spoke of rights, he meant property rights—"no more than that." [40] Liberals claimed to detest the crude businessmen who ran most of the giant corporations in postwar America. Yet they ultimately became stanch supporters of these same men; for, no matter how corrupt or unscrupulous or cruel a businessman was in his daily affairs, he stood for property. In showdowns between capital and labor, or between the business interests of the East and the agrarian forces of the West, most liberals unhesitatingly aligned with the representatives of industrial capitalism. Their fears and shortsighted view of these conflicts in American society prevented them from realizing that they need not have taken sides at all, that their self-proclaimed role as independent reformers fitted them best to serve as impartial arbiters between the extremes.

To the end, Godkin insisted that he did not object to the *principle* of the strike. His own experience with the strike against the *Evening Post,* however, confirmed his opinion that strikes brought out the dishonest and downright villainous elements in society.

Moreover, he condemned in the strongest terms any strike that seemed to impede the performance of public services; for the law ought not to tolerate any "loss, inconvenience, and annoyance" to the public. Curtis treated *every* strike as a threat to public safety and good order. And Samuel Bowles, after the failure of a telegraphers' strike in 1870, expressed satisfaction at the "discomfiture" of the strikers and congratulated Western Union for having resisted successfully the "impudent demands" of its workers.[41]

A few liberals probed more deeply than Godkin or Curtis into the problem of strikes. After he left the White House, Rutherford B. Hayes concluded that strikes and boycotts were "akin to war." Neither could be justified except on grounds analogous to those that justified armed conflict among nations—intolerable injustice and oppression. After the violence of the Molly Maguire strikes subsided late in the 1870's, Bowles softened a bit and called upon his readers to examine thoughtfully the conditions which had bred that terrible outburst. In 1878 Congress debated a bill to increase the size of the standing army, ostensibly to cope with the "Indian problem," actually to prevent a recurrence of the bloody riots of the previous year. As a Democratic representative from New York, Abram Hewitt argued against the measure, asserting that the right to strike was a just right which government should not restrain. Admitting that the wisdom of strikes was quite another matter, Hewitt insisted nonetheless that no man could coerce another to work against his will.[42]

That was precisely the point, James A. Garfield replied in debate. No one denied the right of any man to refuse to work. "I have never heard of an American anywhere," he argued, "who denied the right of a thousand or ten thousand men to refuse to work unless their wages were increased, or to refuse to work if their wages were diminished." But it was a criminal act, the Ohio congressman added, reflecting his narrow view of the strike as a weapon in industrial disputes, for a man engaged in a strike to deny work to other men. The real mischief in a strike was created when a man, eager to work, was "coerced, menaced, driven, overpowered, forbidden to work." Ironically, Hewitt eventually took precisely the same position. During a strike in 1902 he asserted that it would be better to shut down businesses than to permit strikers to "deny the right of employment and of labor upon which the whole structure of free government is founded." But this particular strike involved his own factories; the strikes of 1877 had affected only the railroads.[43]

This question of "right to work" was the strongest objection raised by liberals to the strike weapon. Godkin insisted that a striker forfeited all rights once he left the job. If the worker had a right to quit work, the employer had an equal right to refuse re-employment later—especially in cases where the worker injured the employer's interests by walking out on strike. Curtis declared that strikers, by denying work to others, invited "anarchy" and became "enemies of civilized society." The whole concept of the closed shop was alien to nineteenth-century American liberals, and they viewed labor's attempts to achieve solidarity in strikes as unwarranted infringements on the freedom of the individual. They proposed no "right to work" legislation, however, for they regarded *any* law regulating the relations between labor and capital as dangerous government interference in the economy.[44]

Perhaps even more than strikes, all the new "isms" of the time badly frightened most liberal reformers. Lacking the broad humanitarian and libertarian outlook of the antebellum crusades, liberal reform was insulated against the new ideas and new reforms of the postwar period. With their doctrinaire view of the world and its problems, the adherents to orthodoxy rejected the efforts of the new social reformers and ethical economists to reintroduce the element of humanitarianism in middle-class reform. Indeed, they labeled such efforts to aid the underprivileged as "socialism." But if it was socialism, it was less the variety offered by Karl Marx than that of the experimenters at Brook Farm. Orthodox liberals refused to make the distinction. They criticized Richard T. Ely for his refusal, as they saw it, to make impartial judgments in social and economic questions. Ely picked and chose his way carefully to avoid being accused of "heading directly for the camp of the socialist and anarchist," but that was precisely where he was heading, they charged. Godkin was sure that "labor legislation" and the demands of the new reformers for a more equitable distribution of wealth constituted definite preparations for communism in America. In 1876 he observed that a proposal to put the unemployed to work on government-sponsored public works projects stimulated in the minds of

the poor the "vague hopes and the confusions" from which communism sprang.[45]

Naturally, liberal reformers had nothing good to say for Marxian
socialism. Few of them really knew what it was or bothered to
distinguish between it and the agitation for higher standards of
living and better working conditions. It was enough for them that a
man agitated for anything, for agitation alone reflected the influence of communism, socialism, and anarchism. "I call all of the
lawless agitators and their followers anarchists," Hayes once observed. "They train under the red flag," a banned American workingmen ought to abhor as they rallied to the "old flag—the Stars
and Stripes—the emblem of liberty regulated by law." Theodore
Roosevelt expressed well the view of liberal reformers when he
condemned all foes of that "orderly liberty" without which the
republic must "speedily perish." They were the worst enemies of
America, and the most dangerous of them was the "reckless labor
agitator who arouses the mob to riot and bloodshed." [46]

Godkin asserted baldly in 1880 that the Democratic party was full
of "communists." By communists, of course, he meant advocates of
inflationary currency, those "sworn enemies of public and private
credit." Guilty of advocating foolish monetary schemes and of attempting to undermine the national honor, these radicals also despised intelligence and persons "with marks of mental superiority to
the simple Democrat who carries the hod up to the bricklayer." Any
nation that allowed itself to be governed by such men would
"speedily disappear" from the community of civilized states.[47]

Most orthodox liberals were not intolerant nativists. They welcomed immigrants who settled down to become good, substantial
citizens and who obeyed the laws, both man-made and "natural."
Liberal businessmen welcomed immigrants who came over to enter
the army of cheap labor for American factories. But they balked at
admitting immigrants who came for the "sole purpose" of poisoning
the minds of sturdy, native-born American workers and farmers
with pernicious alien doctrines. They saw direct connections between the Paris Commune and the Molly Maguires, between the
rise of socialist political parties in Europe and the spread of radicalism in the American West. Clearly, they concluded, European
immigrant "agitators" were behind most of the violence and dis-
affection among American workers and farmers.

Congressman Garfield, apparently forgetting the Sons of Liberty and the Boston Tea Party, observed that the spirit of mob violence and misrule was "not born on our soil, nor in harmony with our traditions." Rather, it was the "red fool-fury of the Seine" transplanted here, "taking root in our disasters, and drawing its life only from our misfortunes." Garfield could offer only army rifles as an efficient, cheap method of dealing with the "disasters" and "misfortunes" that fertilized the alien growth. Communistic European notions were ruining America, Henry Ward Beecher was sure. "The theories of Europe," he warned alien agitators, "we reject because they are against natural law and will never be practicable." Charles Eliot Norton returned in 1870 from a protracted visit abroad to announce that the European masses needed only a strong man to lead them in a revolution which would alter the face of society. His friend Curtis, convinced that it was the "natural view" of ignorant foreigners to curse the rich and expect alms from government, feared that the revolution would quickly spread to America. "Bloated bondholders" in this country would take the place held elsewhere by "bloated aristocrats." [48]

There was a certain irony in Godkin's efforts to blame the foreign-born for America's problems. Perhaps he felt compelled to live down his own alien birthright. At any rate, he insulted and ridiculed Irish immigrants at every opportunity. They swarmed to this country in great hordes for the express purpose of advancing their "wild desires and wilder dreams." They ought to be shown promptly that American society, based on individual freedom, was "impregnable" and immune to their schemes. Indeed, it would be "cruel" to the newcomers to let them suppose that they could impose their vicious ideas here. Immigrants, he charged, had caused the great railroad riots of 1877. No government could tolerate conditions in which a few thousand "day-laborers of the lowest class" could suspend, even for a day, the commerce and industry of the nation, merely because they wanted to extort ten or twenty cents a day more in wages from their employers.[49]

Even the eight-hour day movement, Godkin argued, was a European importation, brought over by men who believed in the "odious despotism of a secret, oath-bound 'union.'" Immigrants as a group displayed a remarkable lack of intelligence, evidence of which any responsible citizen could see in every labor dispute, every radical agrarian proposal. After troops broke a strike at the Milwaukee works of McCormick Harvester in 1886, Godkin savagely berated a Polish-born alderman of that city who had had the temerity to protest the use of force in labor disputes. Such behavior, the editor commented, was changing the opinions of thoughtful people about the recent partition of Poland. Where Americans once had viewed the partition as a "monstrous crime," recent events at Milwaukee were leading many to "condemn the Powers for not having gone further and partitioned the individual Poles as well as Poland." [50]

On May 3, 1886, an unknown person threw a bomb at a force of policemen in Chicago's Haymarket Square and set off a nationwide outburst of hysteria. The terrible incident occurred during an outdoor meeting of striking workers, called by a small group of anarchists. No police force in the country had a worse reputation for brutality than Chicago's, and the uniformed men who attempted to break up the Haymarket meeting were led by a sadistic inspector with a long record of indiscriminate head-smashing. As a result of the bombing and subsequent riot, eight suspected anarchists were arrested and subsequently convicted of murder. The identity of the actual bomb-thrower was never learned, but the mere fact that anarchists had been involved in the meeting was enough to convince most people that the accused men were guilty of the crime. "It is no time for half measures," the editor of the *Springfield Republican* wrote, insisting that the authorities should frankly make an example of the orators at the meeting. "The red flag has been waved once too often in Chicago." George William Curtis, ordinarily the most gentle of souls, praised the "heroic fidelity and bravery" of the Chicago police in their battle with "brutal ruffians, all of whom seem to have been foreigners." The affair was an "outburst of anarchy—the deliberate crime of men who openly advocate massacre and the overthrow of intelligent and orderly society." The only "merciful" thing to do was to throw the full weight of society against the offenders, to bring to bear the "most complete and summary methods of repression." [51]

In crying for vengeance, *Harper's Weekly* was no match for *The Nation*. "The truth is," Godkin informed his readers, "there is no 'grit' about our American variety of anarchist." Apparently the more determined members of the sect stayed at home in Europe; either that, or after coming to America they turned "chicken-hearted" in the environment here. How else explain the "disgusting spectacle" of the accused Chicago anarchists' attempts to save themselves from the gallows? These ruffians had left "no stone un-turned" to postpone being hanged, proving that, for all their tirades against America, they preferred to continue living here.

As the appeals dragged on, Godkin became impatient to see blood flow. Much could be said in favor of the slow thoroughness of the judicial process, he conceded, but unhappily it also afforded people an opportunity to forget the atrocity and to "lash themselves into sympathy" with the doomed criminals. Look at the present case, he said. All sorts of people—clergymen, philanthropists, and other soft-headed individuals—were circulating petitions for, of all things, clemency. These misguided sentimentalists should remember that all but one of the criminals were foreigners, men with infected minds, whose release or escape from the hangman would bring every malcontent and scoundrel in Europe swarming to our shores. Moreover, Godkin scoffed at the argument that it was "bad policy" to punish men for their opinions. In the first place, these men were not being punished for their opinions; but even if they were, the state certainly had every right to protect itself from their doctrines. The notion that any nation must tolerate speech which induced people to attack private property was "historically absurd." [52]

When at last, on November 11, 1887, the state of Illinois avenged itself and soothed Godkin's impatience by hanging four of the Hay-market anarchists, other liberal spokesmen hastened to assure the public that the criminals had died for murder, not for their opin-ions. But often their words betrayed them, for their words suggested that they realized full well how strongly the opinions of the anar-chists had figured in the case. Although he insisted that the execu-tions were not an act of vengeance upon opinions and their advo-cates, Curtis announced that the hangings constituted a "solemn declaration" by the nation that it would not tolerate the violent overthrow of "every precious right of civilized man." He went on to castigate all ignorant foreigners who came to America for the pur-pose of denouncing the law as "organized tyranny," prosperous and successful men as "capitalistic demons," and officers of the law as "slaves of despotism." As "enemies of the human race," agitators henceforth would be held responsible for any acts of violence their doctrines inspired.

In the *Springfield Republican,* Samuel Bowles, Jr., lamented that one of the condemned men had managed to escape the gallows by committing suicide in his cell. As for Godkin, the execution provided him with a new opportunity to attack the "sentimentalists" who had sought clemency for the anarchists. In doing so, he drew an extremely thin line between opinions and criminal acts. All "social philosophers," including "philanthropic clergymen and college professors, and labor speculators," ought to ponder diligently the great lesson of the hangings. "Some of them—we say it advisedly—have gone and are going far to share in the bloodguiltiness of this diabolical Anarchist agitation." After all, it was these "social philosophers," with their harebrained ideas about society and political economy, who encouraged the notion that the owners of property were a "band of robbers" and who, by clear implication, were morally responsible for such acts of violence as the Haymarket Massacre. The great conspiracy against property was indeed a far-reaching plot.[53]

In sharp contrast to Godkin's vengeful reaction to the Haymarket affair, William Dean Howells viewed the actions of the authorities as a disgrace to the country. Warning that the state was creating martyrs to an unworthy cause, he worked hard to obtain a commutation of the death sentence for the condemned men. "All over the world people must be asking themselves, What cause is this really, for which men die so gladly, so inexorably?" When the victims went to the gallows, Howells remarked bitterly that "this free Republic has killed five men for their opinions." The entire affair had a marked effect on his political and economic views, for it persuaded him to turn his back at last on the old orthodox political economy of the liberals and to seek a new, more humane public philosophy. "I don't know yet what is best," he admitted to Hamlin Garland; "but I am reading and thinking about questions that carry me beyond myself and my miserable literary idolatries of the past." Still a "slave of selfishness," he was no longer content to be so. But Howells was an exception among liberals. Most of those who bothered to speak out at all on the Haymarket affair followed the lead of Godkin and Curtis.[54]

5

No issue in late-nineteenth-century America more vividly exposed the ambivalence in the liberal attitude toward laissez-faire than the labor problem. The most coercive power of any government is its military arm, and liberal reformers approved and often demanded the full use of that power against American workers. They deplored the presence of the Federal army in the South during the 1870's and clamored for its removal. Race riots and the protection of Southern Negroes in their basic civil rights were matters for local government. But strikes were matters for the United States Army, for strikes threatened property rights rather than human rights. For all their vaunted concern for the individual, liberal reformers readily and repeatedly set aside human rights whenever the rights of property came under attack. Much as they deplored outbursts of human passion and pleaded for reasoned solutions to human problems, most liberals agreed that the only sure method for dealing with violence among strikers was to shoot the offenders. After all, as Godkin insisted, "common sense" did not allow any "parleying" over the fallacy that people had the right to seize other people's property. Rather, such actions must be refuted "with gunpowder and ball." [55]

When the Milwaukee strike failed in 1886, Godkin announced almost gleefully that "a single volley at long range" had showed the mob that the troops meant business, and had broken the backbone of an insurrection. To Curtis, labor riots offered proof that the nation needed bigger and better militias. "It is henceforth no holiday business to serve in the militia," he observed in 1877. Every citizen must be made a possible soldier and minuteman, and Congress should immediately reinforce the standing army. State and local officials who refused to put down disturbances by the use of sufficient military or police force for the protection of property were almost as bad as the "communists" themselves. As a good American, Godkin deplored the sight of cowardly mayors and sheriffs and

governors, who stood by while strikers pursued "poor men with
brickbats, bludgeons, and pistols." But Godkin had faith in the
strength of property. Ultimately the "communists" would learn that
property, when really alarmed, was a terrible antagonist—that its
strength was tremendous and that it had "no bowels of compassion." Property, as Godkin interpreted it, indeed had no compassion; for he asserted that nothing would clear the brains of the
"agitator" or "elevate his moral nature" so much as to assure him
that if he attempted to carry out his theories he would be killed.[56]

Godkin's anti-labor attitude was too vicious for Carl Schurz to
accept. After Henry Villard purchased the New York *Evening Post*
in 1881, Godkin, Schurz, and Horace White for a time shared editorial direction of the newspaper. It was an association fraught with
trouble, for Godkin always chafed in editorial situations that denied him full control. And Schurz was as unhappy with the editorial misalliance as Godkin. From the beginning Godkin ran the
Evening Post as though it were his personal organ. During a telegraphers' strike in 1883, he announced imperiously that all men
employed in telegraphic and railroad services should be governed
"on the same principles as an army." Schurz exploded. "No man has
to be 'governed' on army principles except those who enlist in the
army," he reminded his impetuous partner. With other liberals,
Schurz shared a distaste for many of labor's practices, particularly
strikes. But Godkin's hysterical fear of the American workingman
shocked him. In reply to Schurz's reminder, Godkin drafted a
haughty note that, fortunately for their friendship, he never sent.
Instead, he told his distressed partner to his face that he considered
himself responsible for the paper's editorial policy and boasted that
he was not afraid of being called "the organ of a corporation."
Schurz immediately resigned from the paper, leaving Godkin free to
continue his tirades against labor. The triumvirate's third member,
Horace White, fully shared Godkin's extreme sentiments and
bowed willingly to his editorial dictates.[57]

A few other liberals like Schurz kept relatively cool heads. Abram
Hewitt told his colleagues in Congress who wanted to increase the
standing army in 1878 that they should not, in their panic over
labor's militancy, ignore certain elemental facts. Responsibility for
checking disorders, he reminded them, rested first with the local

police, then with the local sheriff, then with the governor of a state. The Constitution provided for the intervention of Federal troops only as a last resort, and only after a state had done "its full duty in maintaining a police and a citizen soldiery, and had found itself overpowered." Even Hayes, who as President in 1877 ordered Federal troops into ten states to quell strike disorders, understood this basic constitutional provision. Moreover, he knew that the mere presence of troops would break a strike, and he disliked the idea of intervening in this "unnatural" manner in the struggle between labor and capital. "The strikes have been put down by *force*," he noted, after the riots had ended; "but now for the *real* remedy." What was wrong in American society? he asked himself. Why did railroad men who, as a rule, were "good men, sober, intelligent, and industrious," suddenly become strikers? Could not something be done both to educate the strikers and to control the capitalists, in order to end or diminish the evil? But although he had good intentions and was moved by humanitarian impulses, Hayes lacked the vigor as Chief Executive to do anything constructive about the condition he recognized and deplored.[58]

Grover Cleveland, too, wanted to bring about a reconciliation between capital and labor. "Our workingmen are not asking unreasonable indulgence," he observed in his letter of acceptance in 1884; as intelligent and manly citizens, they sought only the same considerations that other interests gained. A year after taking office he asked Congress to establish a permanent labor commission, consisting of three appointed members, charged with "the consideration and settlement, when possible," of all controversies between labor and capital. The establishment of such a body would be a sign to labor that it had a right to be represented in government. He conceded the commission would lack enforcement powers, but he thought it would exercise a salutary influence by focusing the force of public opinion on any party that refused to take advantage of its facilities. It was a reasonable proposal, one which would have made the government an interested party, but not a coercive force, in labor-management disputes. Had it been adopted in 1886 it might have prevented, or at least meliorated, the disastrous strikes at Homestead and Pullman in the following decade. But the proposal, like so many of Cleveland's other requests to Congress, received no further backing from the White House and languished in committee until it was forgotten. Probably *The Nation* spoke the sentiments of many liberals when it censured the President for having proposed an unwarranted scheme to increase the power of the Federal government. As Horace White observed, the only concern of the Federal authorities in strikes was to suppress public disorder in the individual states.[59]

The Homestead Strike of 1892 opened a period of labor and agrarian unrest that thoroughly frightened liberal reformers and caused the more pessimistic of them to question seriously the future of law and order in America. "Society and civilization are at bay," *Harper's Weekly* warned, commenting on the Pennsylvania steel dispute. "An armed mob has overthrown the rule of law, usurped the possession and control of property, superseded the guardians of the peace, and proclaimed its own will as supreme." As usual, *The Nation* issued a call for Federal troops. Homestead workers would pay dearly for their brutal treatment of the Pinkerton men who had tried "lawfully" to protect property and had fired on the strikers "only in self-defence." Following Homestead came the march of Coxey's Army, a demonstration of the unemployed during the depression of the mid-1890's against the negative attitude of the Cleveland administration. Some liberals regarded it as a negligible affair, characterized by few supporters and a total lack of "respectability, moral, intellectual, or material." Others saw it as a prelude to rebellion. "We have, in fact, come dangerously near the condition of things at the time of the French Revolution," Godkin warned, as he contemplated fearfully the advance of the American *sans-culottes*. Fortunately, the "revolution" died harmlessly on the grass at the nation's captial.[60]

But on May 11, 1894, a strike began at the Pullman Palace Car Company in Illinois, and by mid-June it had developed into a nation-wide test of strength between the American Railway Union, led by Eugene V. Debs, and the entire railroad industry. It was a strike calling for the most judicious handling by the authorities at all levels of government; for not only did it involve an industry vital to the nation's welfare, but it concerned as well a flagrant case of labor exploitation by an imperiously arbitrary employer. According to liberal theory, the situation called for government to provide police protection to private property and individuals and to refrain from interfering in the dispute on either side. At Chicago, the center of the strike, Mayor John P. Hopkins and Governor John P. Altgeld maintained law and order and resolved to let the two disputants settle their conflict free from outside interference. But to the leaders of the railroad industry, the Pullman strike was no ordinary labor dispute. On the contrary, they viewed it as an opportunity to crush unionism in railroading once and for all. And they were determined to exert all the power at their disposal against the strikers.[61]

The power they relied on ultimately was that of the United States government. Management in this dispute had a powerful ally in Richard Olney, the former railroad lawyer whom Grover Cleveland had made Attorney General at the start of his second administration. Together, Olney and the railroad managers created a situation that not only broke the strike, but ultimately brought the strike leaders into court as well. By persuading an abysmally uninformed President that strikers were interfering with the transport of the mails and that local authorities in Illinois were taking no action to halt the practice, Olney obtained the dispatch of fourteen thousand Federal troops to Chicago, and, even more important, a court order enjoining the strike leaders from prolonging the dispute. It was not, of course, the first time that troops had been used against labor. But Cleveland's forceful actions in this strike marked a new departure in the policy of the Federal government toward labor disputes. This was massive use of Federal military and judicial power, massive interference by the government in the affairs of private industry. Moreover, the interference came over the indignant protests of Governor Altgeld, who challenged in vain Cleveland's authority under the Constitution to send troops into a state without the permission of the local officials. Here, if ever, was a magnificent opportunity for orthodox liberals to defend the principles of laissez-faire and the rights of the individual states against Federal encroachment.[62]

By 1894, however, orthodox liberals were no more interested than Grover Cleveland in defending genuine laissez-faire. They praised Cleveland as a courageous champion of law and order, consigned the striking Pullman and railroad workers to the ranks of the "dangerous classes," and vilified John P. Altgeld as an insidious "communist" and irresponsible demagogue. Even before Cleveland ordered out troops, they had surmised that the remedy for the strike would have to be "sending the militia to shoot [strikers] down and drive Debs into the seclusion of some liquor saloon." The time had come to use "bayonet and the bullet" in railroad affairs.[63] Labor's insolence had become intolerable, Rollo Ogden charged. "While crying to heaven against the oppression of employers, it subjects delicate women and helpless and innocent children to discomforts and dangers in a way to bring a blush to the cheek of a Zulu." He praised Cleveland's troop order as an "encouraging demonstration" that American patriotism could still be counted upon in times of national peril. The President's prompt and resolute action overrode all partisan distinctions and stemmed entirely from the "purest love of country." Godkin called the Executive Order the "voice of the nation" demanding that the law be maintained. Anyone defying that voice would be swept out of the way, and "out of existence if need be." [64]

After the strike collapsed, one liberal found it in his heart to ask mercy for the strikers whom Federal marshals had arrested under the court injunction. But he was concerned less with the welfare of the indicted men than with his own fears that misguided citizens might interpret the punishment as an act of judicial vengeance. Even the poorest member of the community should possess "unshaken confidence" in the integrity of judges and the impartiality of justice. But it seemed that many common people were beginning to think that the courts had allied themselves with the great corporate interests, and it was imperative that they be disabused. Late in July, Cleveland appointed a special commission to investigate the Pullman strike—an agency similar to the one he had asked Congress to establish eight years earlier. For thirteen days the commission took testimony and examined the claims and actions of both labor and management. In its official report to the President, it recommended that employers recognize and deal with labor unions and that the government provide the machinery for compulsory arbitration of all labor disputes in the railroad industry. Neither business nor Congress paid much attention to the recommendations, but orthodox liberals felt obliged to attack the commission for proposing such "radical" remedies to the labor problem. Rollo Ogden accused the commission of "coddling labor," of overstepping the bounds of "propriety and prudence." The investigators, he charged, had ignored acts of vandalism committed by the strikers and had tried to put the blame for violence on the railroad managers. Moreover, they had sullied the reputation of George M. Pullman, that firm rock against which the idea of lawless unionism had crushed itself. Americans owed Pullman a great debt, "whether he is a likable and kindly man or not." Providence had never showed more "tender care" for the country than in having this "unpleasant man" ready for that emergency.[65]

Spokesmen for orthodox liberalism dismissed Altgeld's protest against Cleveland's troop order as the work of a "champion of disorder." They had cordially detested the Illinois governor since 1893, when he had pardoned the two Haymarket victims who were still in prison. At that time, Godkin had denounced Altgeld as an anarchist. The editor's old political enemy, Theodore Roosevelt, agreed completely with him on this point. In pardoning the anarchists, Altgeld had proved that he was the "foe of the law-abiding and the friend of the lawless classes," and his defiance of Cleveland was precisely what might be expected of such a man. One liberal journal called Altgeld's arguments against the Executive Order mere "constitutional pedantries" and predicted that the President's statements on the matter would become "political classics." *The New York Times* denounced Altgeld as "thickhided and anarchistic," while Godkin thought he was simply a "professional blatherskite." Genuinely fearful of the rising radicalism of the West, Roosevelt leveled probably the most abusive diatribe of all at the unfortunate Illinoisan. Altgeld's "blatant demagogism," he charged, "jeopardizes the existence of free institutions." If the Federal government ever got into the hands of such a man, the Republic would "go to pieces" in a year. In *The Nation,* Edward P. Clark, Rollo Ogden, and Horace White kept up a running attack on the governor and made dire predictions as to what would happen to the country if he and his "populist" cohorts ever acquired real power. Happily, however, as Clark noted, the President possessed the necessary power not only to suppress mobs, but to overcome "anarchist Governors" as well.[66]

At the end of the century, orthodox liberals still clung to the

fiction that military interference in labor disputes was a defense of
the laissez-faire principle. Never did they acknowledge that the
mere presence of armed soldiers was enough to break the back of
any strike, nor did they even consider the possibility that employers
might be guilty of provocative acts designed to invite government
intervention in strikes. Overwhelmed by phantasmal fears of the
"dangerous classes," they sanctioned and encouraged actions which
amounted to brutal, indiscriminate suppressions of individual
rights. Libertarian in intent, they became Draconian dogmatists in
practice, insisting that all who disagreed with their own approaches
to the labor problem were charlatans or worse.

"Intolerance would never have permitted the immense growth of
foolish opinion in the world which has been fostered by our days of
toleration," Rollo Ogden observed in 1891.[67] Perhaps this was what
was wrong with the world—this ridiculous notion of tolerance that
plagued nineteenth-century-America. There had been a time, liberals thought, when "monstrosities went to the wall, freaks got no
foothold; the brains once out, the man died." But now, instead of
mercifully killing absurd ideas out of hand, men cherished convictions of every conceivable stripe and hue. Striking out pitilessly at
such notions and their preachers was the duty of all rational men,
for a little persecution now and then would quickly show what
convictions were worth suffering for. As Ogden bluntly put it, a
man would take the trouble to "verify his guesses" if he found them
"leading him to the rack."

Perhaps orthodox liberalism in America could have survived attacks by businessmen on laissez-faire, or a cynical disregard of reform among politicians, or even the relentless growth of centralized
power in government and economic affairs. But it could not survive
the loss of its most essential ingredient—a broad and tolerant view
of human affairs. Once fear dissolved that ingredient, orthodox liberalism had little to offer modern America. Once well-intentioned
men of good will permitted unreasoning fear to turn them into
hysterical defenders of the status quo, all that remained was a
shabby dogma, unworthy of the name liberalism.

9

The Heart of the Matter

Is this the country that we dreamed in youth,
Where wisdom and not numbers should have weight,
Seed-field of simpler manners, braver truth,
Where shams should cease to dominate
In Household, church, and state?

JAMES RUSSELL LOWELL, 1876

For my own part I really think the civil service reformers or
Mugwumps come nearer to being lineal descendants of the abo-
litionists than any other existing manifestation of the national
conscience—reviled if not persecuted and mobbed. So I regard
the Nation, *begun in 1865, a true continuation of the* Liberator,
ended in 1865.

WENDELL P. GARRISON, 1893

SHORTLY BEFORE HE RETIRED FROM *The Nation*, GODKIN considered the "unforeseen tendencies of democracy" he had discerned during his long career as an American editor. Never one to shirk generalizations, he noted especially the ascendancy of the "boss" over the statesman; rule by a coalition of ignorant legislators and credulous voters; a corrupting preoccupation with money-making at all levels of society; and a creeping, unhealthy influence in public affairs of the great metropolitan centers. Clearly, democracy had deviated from the path its early advocates had hoped it would follow. Clearly, too, Godkin's experiences with democracy had changed him from a hopeful pundit at the end of the Civil War to a disillusioned censor at the turn of the century.[1]

Godkin's associates in the "party of the centre" shared his gloomy view, in one degree or another; and throughout the period they sought political remedies for the ailments that afflicted American democracy. Good government was their Holy Grail, and to gain it they threw themselves awkwardly into national politics, struggled to organize grass roots movements in the cities, on occasion played the game of the bosses themselves, and flirted with a variety of schemes to diminish the influence of the "dangerous classes" in politics. Civil service reform was the one issue they all agreed to; and ultimately it became the totem of their clan, the symbol of political purity and independence.

What did liberal reformers mean by good government? Some thought it meant nothing more than strict adherence to the "natural laws" of political economy. Others viewed it as government by the enlightened few for the ignorant many. Still others considered it government operated on "businesslike" principles. All of them insisted it meant government free from graft, bribery, lobbying, and other forms of actual or potential corruption. Beyond that, doubtless, no two liberals knew precisely what to demand. Perhaps Wendell P. Garrison expressed the view of all civil service reformers when he defined good government as "government in accordance with the principles which lie or are supposed to lie at the basis of our republic," and bad government as "such a perversion of those principles as tends to overthrow the system." [2] All reformers—liberal, radical, social, ethical—could agree with that definition. But who was to say what principles lay at the basis of the republic or what constituted perversion of the system? Henry George, Edward Bellamy, Richard T. Ely, and Terence V. Powderly all believed in good government and civil service reform. Yet, Godkin, Garrison, and other liberals believed these men were utter scoundrels—participants in the great conspiracy against property and order.

In the last analysis, good government meant government responsive to the demands of those who clamored for it. And liberal reformers in the age of enterprise had some very specific demands: laissez-faire in economic matters, protection of property, minimal taxation, strict public economy, and suppression of the "dangerous classes." Moreover, they clamored for good government more persistently and more noisily than any other group of reformers in postwar America. Occasionally they achieved some success; more often, they met frustrating defeat at the hands of the "bad government" forces. Frequently they wasted time and effort in spirited assaults against windmills.

2

What caused the open corruption in American politics during the era? Liberals studied the phenomenon closely and assigned responsibility to several factors. For one thing, government interfered too much in private economic affairs. For another, legislators squandered public funds on benefits to favored corporations or on useless public projects, oblivious of their responsibilities to the taxpayers. Businessmen who had learned to lobby and bribe their way into lucrative contracts during the war carried on the same sharp practices during peacetime in a wild scramble for franchises and subsidies. Corporations demanded privileges in the form of high tariffs and set an example of greed and dishonesty. Moreover, paper money stimulated the corrupt influences into action. Because liberals believed the circulation of greenbacks meant eventual repudiation of the national debt, they considered the irredeemable paper an impossible substitute for real money and a major stimulus to fraud.[3]

Greed seemed to infect the entire community. "When we the people learn (among other things) to consider wealth basely acquired and ignobly enjoyed a reproach and not a glory," one disturbed liberal observed, "we shall have a right to hope for honest rulers." The pursuit of wealth for its own sake and by any means available became an accepted part of the American creed, or so liberals thought. "Get money. Get it quickly. Get it in abundance. Get it in prodigious abundance. Get it dishonestly if you can, honestly if you must." That was Jay Gould's philosophy, Mark Twain said, and it was doing "giant work" everywhere. Liberal reformers feared that too many Americans applauded this cynical philosophy if they did not actually practice it. Somewhere in the past, probably during the war, something had gone wrong in politics; some wrong principle had become an accepted way of doing things. Unnoticed by the public at the time, it had grown to become a vast, entrenched political power, supported by an army of lackeys and defying both public opinion and the public conscience. What had been the mischief? Legal tender? The high wartime tariff? Radical "extremism" during Reconstruction? As the war and Reconstruction years receded into the past, liberals tended to blame all of these "mischiefs" for the sickness which seemed to afflict democracy. Yet, typically, they considered corruption more a symptom of individual immorality than a manifestation of social or economic maladjustment.[4]

Corruption fed upon itself. It tore down decent institutions. As

George W. Julian lamented, it "inundated the whole land" with its "desolating effects," spreading from the Reconstruction governments of the South to the cities of the North, from the cities to the statehouses, from the states to Washington. More damning, it debilitated the moral strength of the decent citizens who sought to check its growth. The Citizens Committee, a reform group flourishing briefly in New York after the war, saw corruption as a "foul and monstrous conspiracy," swelling in magnitude and influence every day. One contemporary authority on municipal government indicted corruption as the spawner of a fearsome array of evils: "the adulation of power and man-worship, the craven, fawning temper, the spirit of intrigue, suspicion, and calumny, the suppression of individual freedom, and the insolence of place." Asked to explain why good men tolerated such conditions, Seth Low asserted that corruption so demoralized intelligent citizens that they often voted to continue "ring rule" in their cities merely to advance the fortunes of their chosen political party at the state and national levels. Godkin feared that corruption might even undermine the judicial system, which he saw as the great citadel of orthodox liberalism in America. To liberal reformers, then, the moral deterioration brought on by corruption made political reform not simply a desirable goal. It was a matter of life or death. A corrupt monarchy might endure by rule of force; a corrupt republic must perish.[5]

Convinced as they were that rich men ought naturally to be "best men," liberals for a time hoped that the entry of successful businessmen into politics would provide a healthy influence to help in routing the spoilsmen. It seemed axiomatic to such men of high principle as George William Curtis that a nation should manage its affairs with the same efficiency and economy that prevailed in private enterprise. Francis Parkman was more pejorative than many of his friends on the matter, insisting that only the services in politics of experienced businessmen could possibly counter the "evil" of universal suffrage. When New York "independents" gathered at Cooper Union in 1888 to honor their businessman-mayor, Abram Hewitt, *The Nation* claimed that the gathering of businessmen and reformers brought together more "intelligence and character" than the city had seen in one spot for years. Because the modern city was essentially a corporation engaged in the management of property

for "the general comfort and convenience," Godkin argued, it followed naturally that businessmen should be in charge of its
operation.[6]

In the wake of the Tweed Ring scandal, Samuel J. Tilden realized that the Republicans would make political capital out of the
charge that the Democrats in New York were coddling a gang of
machine politicians. He knew, of course, that the opposition had its
own "bosses" and that Republicans as well as Democrats had supported Tweed; nonetheless, he was too much the practical politician not to realize that his own party was particularly vulnerable on
the point. To counteract the charge, he encouraged his aides to
recruit "hostile or neutral captives" from the business community to
act as fronts for his party. Show off the businessmen in the Democratic party, he told them in effect.[7]

Actually, most of the leading politicians in the United States
during these years were either businessmen themselves or the sons
and grandsons of businessmen. And they were far better educated,
as a group, than the vast majority of Americans. They required no
prodding from liberal reformers to enter politics, nor did they feel
obliged, while in office, to cater to the reform element in the electorate. Directly or indirectly, they followed the policies of other
businessmen who remained out of the political limelight, and they
brought, wherever possible, the current practices of business to the
offices of government. It took most liberals a long time to realize
that these businessmen-politicians were as little interested in reform
as the so-called professional politicians. They had assumed that the
average man of wealth was an Edward Atkinson or a John Murray
Forbes, dedicated to clean government, tariff revisions, and other
liberal reforms. But gradually they came to resent the "parading of
great business interests" in public offices. By 1886, Carl Schurz had
concluded that the millionaire businessman in politics was not necessarily a blessing to the cause of good government. Too many men
of great wealth purchased political power and intimidated opponents by flaunting their economic influence. Schurz noted with
some alarm that "one seat after another" in the Senate was falling
into their hands. Late in life, after a long career in municipal
affairs, another reformer discovered a disquieting truth about political corruption: absolute honesty in public affairs was highly un-

likely in view of the general cupidity in American society, and "while every business firm, trade, profession, and calling is in constant conspiracy against the public." Businessmen themselves, he added, brought these virulent influences directly into the chambers of government.[8]

Charles Dudley Warner observed that a society which permitted any man to become a millionaire by "manipulating railways" and "cheating stockholders" must expect corruption in its politics. But the "un-American" relationship between business and politics, he reasoned, was an unnatural condition created by the immorality of individual politicians and businessmen. Like other liberals, he remembered—or thought he remembered—a better day, when businessmen left politics to the statesmen and did not ask favors of government. Old-fashioned liberals conceded reluctantly that standards of public morality had changed and that politicians expected to be the handymen of big businessmen. They could not admit that the change reflected anything more serious than personal immorality in the individuals involved. Once again, the terrible ambiguity that beset them in all their relations with the business community during the Gilded Age dulled their perception and blunted their attack on political corruption. Not until early in the next century did the muckrakers assess more fully the nature of the relationship between politics and business in an undisciplined capitalistic economy. As Lincoln Steffens learned, the political condition of every big city in the land pointed to the conclusion that "business and politics must be one; that it was natural, inevitable, and—possibly—right that business should—by bribery, corruption, or—somehow get and be the government." [9]

Nor did liberal reformers recognize that the character and function of the political "boss" changed with the times. Both William M. Tweed and Marcus A. Hanna were "bosses"; but Tweed was an amateur from another era compared with the Ohio industrialist-politician. After all, Tweed went to jail; Mark Hanna begot a President. Liberal reformers treated Hanna, Thomas C. Platt, and the other new-style "bosses" as reincarnations of Tweed. But Tweed only dispensed the spoils to petty ward-heelers and only corrupted one city. Hanna and company, through their officeholding minions, controlled a nation's political, economic, and diplomatic destinies.

Their business was business; politics for them was only a means of advancing the interests of the business community. The moral attack of liberal reformers made little impression on them.[10]

3

Immoral politicians, most liberals conceded, persuaded the ignorant mob to support their machines and the foolish legislation they sponsored. But the mob itself was also a source of political corruption. Too often frustrated by professional politicians in their attempts to purify government, many liberals steadily lost faith in popular government after 1872. They made few attempts, moreover, to learn the grievances or examine the actual living conditions of the "dangerous classes." To be sure, all liberal reformers agreed that the masses needed more education. As Godkin noted, an ignorant citizen was "but one degree removed from a traitor or alien enemy." If the majority of the American people ever became "vicious, degraded, cowardly, and ignorant," the days of the republic were numbered. But neither Godkin nor many of his friends proposed positive measures for expanding educational opportunities for the masses, and they fought bitterly against all attempts to provide Federal assistance to public education, even for Negroes in the South.[11]

While most liberals frowned on the indiscriminate bigotry of Know-Nothingism, increasingly during the postwar period their political frustrations led them to question the wisdom of unrestricted immigration. Ignorant Europeans swarmed into the cities to become the pliant tools of unscrupulous "bosses." Unfit to play an intelligent role in American politics, they seemed to overpower the respectable citizenry by sheer force of numbers, and their presence was a formidable roadblock in the path of political reform. Irish Catholics, one liberal observed in 1876, imposed such an "unusually heavy strain upon our political institutions," that only Providence could be trusted to permit the American system of government to endure the trial. Ironically enough, Godkin also blamed Irish immigrants for most of the trouble in politics. They lacked the "self-restraint and instinctive discrimination of men bred to the responsibilities of citizenship." German immigration he welcomed as a

means of offsetting the "effervescing" influence of his own countrymen. Another liberal characterized Irish-Americans as "notoriously
the most active, elbowing, pushing, grasping politicians in our
country." [12]

Corruption worked two ways with ignorant people, liberals believed. Foreigners and indigents brought an unhealthy influence
into politics, and the brand of politics practiced in the large cities
corrupted the masses by deluding them into thinking they were
getting something for nothing. Moreover, corrupt politicians encouraged businessmen to bring boatloads of penniless, illiterate foreigners to America. It was all well and good to supply American
factories with cheap, imported labor; but employers ought to consider the unfortunate political effects of bringing in workers by the
boatloads. When Massachusetts shoe manufacturers imported Chinese laborers to work at cheap wages in their factories, Godkin
warned that the influx of this type of foreigner made it imperative
that "stringent measures" be adopted against such practices. Otherwise it would do no good to "wave the flag" and "read the Bible" to
the newcomers, for eventually they would overpower the intelligent
element in politics. Abram Hewitt, irked by Pennsylvania steel
manufacturers who imported cheap labor for their mills and under-
sold Hewitt's own works, declared in 1888 that the time had come
for the United States to be "the country for Americans." The
"horde of European workers" that poured in annually threatened
the welfare of American workingmen and presented a real danger
to good government. [13]

Doubtless the most ironic display of political nativism among
liberals came from Edward P. Clark, one of Godkin's assistants on
the *Evening Post*. Profoundly disturbed by the rumblings of Populist discontent in the West during the late 1880's, Clark charged
that the People's party was the tool of iniquitous foreigners. In
Milwaukee the party had put up an election ticket selected by a
convention, "not more than six or eight of whose members were
born in this country." In the list of delegates, Clark spotted such
"sample" names as "Schilling, Blatz, Rudzinski, Czerwinski, Hani-
zeski, Andrzejerski, Neuka, Esche, Schleifer, Klefisch, Vogt, Lamm,
Billerbeck." Fortunately, the "friends of good government" in Wisconsin had united to defeat this un-American crowd. At the time

Clark wrote his piece of nativist nonsense, he owed his job to a German immigrant (Carl Schurz), his employer was another German immigrant (Henry Villard), and his immediate superior was an Irish immigrant (Godkin).[14]

Perhaps because they looked upon the suffragettes as eccentrics, liberal reformers had little good to say about the crusade to give women the vote. Thomas Wentworth Higginson, to be sure, participated actively in the movement; but he failed to interest his friends in the cause. Voluble, demonstrative, and impulsive, women would dilute what little of calmness and reason remained in politics, Charles Francis Adams, Jr., was sure. Out of respect for the women themselves, his friend Parkman urged, "let us pray for deliverance from female suffrage." Curtis conceded that the subject was no longer "ridiculous" in politics, though all he would offer was some occasional advice for Higginson to pass along to the women. As for Godkin, he positively distrusted the ladies. Too often, Susan B. Anthony and her cohorts were caught flirting with such heretical schemes as the greenback movement and the agitation for an eight-hour day—clear evidence that she and her "fellow-laborers" were "wild visionaries." Another *Nation* man predicted that the "worst and most ignorant women" would all vote at once, under universal suffrage, while ladies of gentility would "hold aloof for some years." Still, he conceded, in the long run the respectable women surely would not want to see election after election carried "by the votes of their servants," while they stayed at home.[15]

But there was another aspect of this question that deeply troubled E. L. Godkin. Was it not probable that sex would rear its ugly head if women received the vote? With men and women thrown together in politics, to play a game "that even men find debauching," was it not altogether likely that the influence of sex would breed a "deeper, and darker corruption," the like of which no free country had ever experienced? Godkin must have considered congressmen a ruttish lot, for he envisioned bacchanalian orgies in the legislative anterooms if women ever entered politics actively. Legislation would come under the influence of "what are called 'female charms,' but which, for the purposes of this discussion—which requires exceedingly plain speaking—we shall call by its proper name, the sexual passion." The time might well come when a "liaison" between "Mr. Smith and Miss Brown" would result in both miscreants voting next day for the duty on—pig iron! High tariffs and low necklines obviously made a dangerous combination.[16]

How did liberal reformers propose to nullify the influence in politics of ignorant and poor men, if not of excitable and promiscuous women? As their distrust of the masses transformed itself into a settled hostility, their talk turned more and more to proposals for restricting the suffrage. Genuinely fearful that the old, discredited doctrine of the divine right of kings was being supplanted by the equally absurd doctrine of the divine right of the people, they suffered a political disorientation that sometimes brought them to the edges of panic. Not that the majority of liberals gave up their devotion to the possibilities of democracy. On the contrary, in setting themselves the task of salvaging intelligence and integrity in politics, they conceived their role as that of aristocratic guardians, protecting popular government over the long run from its supposed friends. Perhaps after a period of "ignorant fermentation," during which the "barbarians" would have their way, American politics would one day accept the enlightened leadership they offered.[17]

For Godkin, it was a matter of the decent, intelligent people maintaining civilization; and he saw hope only in reform that would markedly change the composition and character of the electorate. "If a spring be muddy," he mused, "the water which flows from it will be muddy, no matter what the arrangements of pipes or hydrants you may make." The sensible way to clean out the muddy spring of American politics was to restrict the suffrage, and Godkin was ready with specific proposals. In city politics, he suggested, allow only the taxpaying householders to vote on important civic measures and give them veto power over all appropriations of money. At a higher level, let Congress establish forthwith a national literacy test for all potential voters. Apply it first to all new immigrants and all Southern Negroes; later, broaden it to include all new registrants and (after a year in which they should learn English) all other voters. Because the average immigrant's ignorance shielded him from all civilizing instrumentalities in America, he remained a foreigner "in spite of himself." A literacy test thus would serve two admirable purposes: it would force the immigrants to learn about their new country, and it would raise the general tone of politics. Civilization would survive.[18]

Most liberals heartily approved the idea of a literacy test, even if they did not share Godkin's morbid concern for the fate of civilization. Norton mourned that the founding fathers had lacked foresight in failing to write a literacy requirement into the Constitution. Terming the influence of Southern Negroes in politics "The New Ordeal," Samuel Bowles called for "impartial but educated suffrage." Going even further than Godkin, Abram Hewitt proposed a fourteen-year residence requirement, as well as a literacy test, for aliens who desired to become citizens. For a time, Congressman James A. Garfield toyed with the idea of proposing a property qualification for voters, although he finally concluded that the matter was best forgotten. It bothered him to realize that the vote of a single naturalized foreigner could neutralize the vote of an A. T. Stewart; two men without a dollar, it meant, could "dispose of the pecuniary interests of a man worth many millions." Doubtless the most imaginative proposal for squelching the influence of illiterate voters came from Mark Twain. In his ideal "Republic of Gondour," a true aristocracy of intelligence and substance reigned, based primarily on the level of education attained by the citizenry. Universal suffrage was guaranteed, for each person, however poor or ignorant, had one vote. But the man with a common school education and no property had two votes; and the man with a high school diploma and no property, four votes. If the graduate had property "to the value of three thousand *sacos*," he cast an additional vote; and for every "fifty thousand *sacos*" more in property he received still another vote. Finally, the man with a university education cast nine votes, regardless of his material wealth.[19]

Precisely what political rights *any* person was entitled to was a bothersome question in some liberal quarters. Few reformers were as jaundiced as Francis Parkman, who had no use for universal suffrage in any guise. But others pondered the extent to which the doctrine of natural rights had warped the common sense of Americans in the matter of granting the franchise. Could the voter retain any sense of individual responsibility at the polling place, given the popular notion that he had a natural right to be there?

Godkin was dubious: the whole idea of natural rights, he thought, had been preached in America to the point where people had lost sight of the "fiduciary character" of the voting privilege. Government in any country was a product of expedience, he noted, which was to say that any state had the power, "deducible from the right of self-preservation," to say absolutely which of its citizens should vote. With a firmer grasp on the realities of American politics, his friend Charles Eliot Norton reminded him that few people were really concerned about the "natural right" to vote; it was the pragmatic political right that counted. And subject only to a literacy qualification, that right was a "sound and wholesome doctrine." Doubtless, Norton understood that any serious effort to discredit the *principle* of universal suffrage in America would be a sterile undertaking indeed. Godkin, on the other hand, suffered from a chronic inability or unwillingness to differentiate between the state and "civilization"; unrestricted suffrage might open the way to a tyranny, from which only the state could rescue civilization. Fear for the survival of decency and intelligence led him to espouse a lame and static theory of democracy. In this case, at least, the cloistered Brahmin had a clearer understanding of the American experience than did the worldly New York editor.[20]

Other liberals had difficulty in balancing equality with political rights. Charles Dudley Warner thought the ballot in the hands of all was perhaps the only safeguard against a tyranny of wealth in the hands of the few. At least, it was the nearest thing to a guarantee against socialism and other unwise economic doctrines. Democracy, he noted, offered men a means of eradicating abuses and of improving life, for under universal suffrage men could vote both for protection and for improvement. At the same time, Warner believed that "all men are created unequal." The whole notion of equality in the United States had led to the dangerous theory of a totally unrestricted suffrage, a condition he thought unwise. "No matter what the majority is in intellect and morals," he complained, "fifty-one ignorant men have a natural right to legislate for the one hundred, as against forty-nine intelligent men."[21] Warner's attitude toward suffrage was an ambiguous one; for his distrust of equalitarianism ultimately forced him to question the notion that all men had a natural right to vote. Like Norton, however, he

understood better than Godkin the meaning of political rights in
America. Education would provide a check on equalitarianism, as
well as on the natural rights theory. In the hands of an informed
electorate, universal suffrage was a safeguard in a democracy; it
became a danger only when truly ignorant men formed the majority. To prevent it from becoming a danger, it should be broadened
as people became more literate. Arbitrary restriction would do no
good.

Big city politicians, including a few liberal reformers, easily resolved the dilemma. They agreed that the franchise in the hands of
poor, illiterate voters was potentially a dangerous instrument. Conceivably, they admitted, "radicals" or demagogues could capture it
and turn it against the very foundations of property and order. But
controlled by a strong, well-run political machine, it was rendered
harmless and, at times, beneficial. In New York, Horatio Seymour
and Samuel J. Tilden welcomed the support of "adopted citizens"
and worked with Tammany's sachems to get the newcomers naturalized as quickly as possible. John Kelly of Tammany once notified Tilden that he needed at least eight thousand dollars for "nat-
uralization alone" in preparing for an upcoming election. He
promptly received a generous check to supplement the one thousand dollars Tilden already had contributed to the cause.[22]

Tilden displayed far more political acumen than most other political reformers; he understood that many Irish immigrants went
into politics from a natural desire to better themselves and rise
above poverty. He reminded his critics that the great influx of
immigrants had built the railroads of the country, produced most of
the goods in the businessmen's factories, and provided the North
with the manpower it had needed to break the rebellion. To be
sure, Tilden spoke in 1872 as a practicing politician ambitious for
office and as a leader of a party that drew much of its support from
the big city populations. But he noted bluntly and as a matter of
proven fact that critics of the immigrant element in politics were for
the most part men of "pecuniary independence and leisure" who
had selfishly abdicated their power of leadership in the affairs of the
city. They had scarcely any right to demand the disfranchisement of
other voters or to complain because foreign-born citizens took an
interest in practical politics. Moreover, he reminded New Yorkers

that they lived in a cosmopolitan city where more than three-fifths of the voters were naturalized citizens. "This is the state of things. Who could alter it if he would? Who dare say that, on the whole, he would alter if he could?" The only sensible approach to the problem of self-government in a society based on equal and universal suffrage was for all Americans to work together as best they could. "We can only do so," he warned, "on the large liberal statesmanship on which we began, and never by going back toward the dark night of proscription and bigotry." [23]

Fourteen years later, the wisdom of Tilden's approach to the problem should have impressed itself clearly in the minds of all liberal reformers who feared the power in politics of the "dangerous classes." For in the mayoralty election of 1886, Tammany Hall, with the votes of the ignorant, the poor, and the foreign-born, delivered the city of New York and the civilization of the "best men" from the "radicalism" of Henry George. The voters gave the election to Abram Hewitt, a man who wanted to restrict the suffrage.

4

Increasingly in the postwar period, liberal reformers turned to civil service reform as a panacea for all the ills of the nation—economic, social, moral, as well as political. It was the issue that naturally succeeded the abolitionist crusade, they thought, and if it lacked the drama of the earlier movement, it was a cause "no whit inferior in dignity or worth." Indeed, like the crusade to emancipate the slaves, the battle for political reform struck at a condition that threatened to destroy the foundations of republican government.[24]

Before the war the malignancy had been the tyranny of chattel slavery; now it was the tyranny of the spoils system. Liberals saw political patronage as the root and source of bribery and corruption, a symbol of national shame and demoralization. In the hands of irresponsible party leaders the spoils system became a dangerous weapon, for it enabled the politicians to regiment great masses of voters and to create, in effect, an army of mercenaries always ready at a command to overpower decent citizens. Patronage destroyed the confidence of ordinary people in popular government and saddled the nation, as Curtis expressed it, with "an oligarchy of stipendiaries, a bureaucracy of the worst kind," which exercised a despotic control over the parties. Those who dispensed patronage, at all levels of government, were "vampires who suck the moral life-blood of the nation," despots who commanded the loyalties of "the rings, the demagogues, the Swartwouts,[25] the pretorian guards, all the minions of prejudice, passion, and selfish interest." One liberal cursed them as "powers of darkness" who deliberately fostered ignorance and viciousness among the voters. "They are the common enemies of all who war against sin and suffering." [26]

Ahead of all other arguments for civil service reform stood the moral appeal. Without morality in government all talk of other reforms was futile, liberals argued, and only the adoption of the merit system for political appointments would restore morality to government. Charles J. Bonaparte of Baltimore, an outstanding leader in the crusade, acknowledged freely that the basic principle of civil service reform was the simple one of "high morality." Another reformer warned that legislation and "all human contrivances" would avail nothing unless the people restored "Christian character" to public affairs. The "moral rottenness" that patronage spawned in politics, Godkin declared, threatened not only governmental efficiency, but the "fundamental virtues of our civilization" as well. If the United States was to preserve its dignity and respectability in the eyes of the world, it could do so only by cleaning out the "Augean stables" of its politics.[27]

Civil service reform, as such, was not a real issue between the two major parties at any time during the postwar period, and it did not become important enough for the politicians to give it much attention until about 1870. Lincoln, of course, had made brilliant use of the patronage in the campaign and election of 1864, and Johnson had done his futile best to use it in the congressional elections of 1866. Subsequent Republican Presidents and Democratic candidates all pronounced themselves in favor of good government and political purity and denounced the spoils system in stock phrases. General Grant deemed the matter important enough to ask Congress in 1870 for legislation aimed at the "elevation and purification" of the civil service. Two years later the Democratic platform denounced the existing system as "a mere instrument of partisan tyranny and personal ambition," and asked that the public service once again be made an honorable calling. Similar statements came from both parties in succeeding campaigns and from Hayes, Garfield, and Arthur at the White House. Hayes especially made civil service reform a major theme of his annual addresses to Congress.[28]

An early indication that liberal reformers took an unrealistic view of the issue appeared in the election of 1872. All parties in that canvass favored civil service reform. But while the Republican platform called for a reform to abolish the "evils of patronage" and to establish standards of honesty and efficiency for public officials, the Liberal Republicans and their Democratic allies demanded a sweeping "thorough reform" of the civil service as the *sine qua non* of good government.[29] In effect, Republicans argued that the evils of the system could be eliminated without wrecking the political system itself; whereas their opponents, reflecting the adamancy of the liberals, gave the impression that they wanted to destroy the entire system—a position that clearly asked too much, too soon.

To be sure, the movement for civil service reform was in large measure a rather conventional case of political "outs" attempting to displace the "ins." [30] Certainly the careers of such reformers as George W. Julian, George William Curtis, and Carl Schurz reflect the usual political struggle among competing groups. But, as a group, civil service reformers argued from a strong philosophical position as well. After all, the political situation at the close of the Civil War was not one that necessarily precluded the rise of the "best men" to positions of influence and power. Indeed, it was a leading spokesman *in* the Senate for the "best men," Charles Sumner, who precipitated the wartime debate—brief and anemic as it was—on the issue, by introducing, in April 1864, a bill to provide competitive examinations for admission to the civil service. As early in the postwar period as the summer of 1866, B. Gratz Brown of Missouri issued an appeal for civil service reform, at a time, certainly, when his political future was by no means foreclosed by the spoilsmen who later became the favorite targets of reformers.[31] Like all great political issues, civil service reform reflected a multitude of motives among a variety of reformers and disgruntled politicians. Among liberal intellectuals, at least, it was a philosophical question cast in a political mould: ought not the best minds, the fittest individuals, the responsible body of men in society, be in a position to counter the rising influence of ignorance and sheer numbers in American politics?

In spite of the real differences among advocates of the merit system, all were agreed on the necessity for reform of some kind. Yet the movement for a civil service law made little headway prior to 1880. It lacked organization, it had no central direction to speak of, and it failed to excite popular support. As the reformers themselves admitted, it was a rather prosaic crusade when compared with the recent exciting, dramatic struggle for emancipation. Moreover, the trials of Reconstruction, the disputed election of 1876, and the preoccupation of lawmakers with currency and tariff matters made it difficult for the reform to get a public hearing.

As a Radical Republican, Charles Sumner was perhaps more conscious than many of his colleagues that a favorable climate for change would characterize the immediate postwar period, and he thought the time was right in 1864 to start Congress thinking about political reform. "Our whole system is like molten wax, ready to receive an impression," he noted. As it turned out, Sumner's timing was off. Congress had no time (or inclination, for that matter) to consider civil service reform while the war still raged. Nothing more was heard of the proposal until December 20, 1865, when Congressman Thomas A. Jenckes of Rhode Island introduced a bill to establish an independent agency within the government to pass on the qualifications of candidates for public position. A serious student of public administration, Jenckes had investigated the civil service practices of Prussia, England, France, and China before introducing his measure; and his carefully drafted bill, although it failed to pass Congress, became a model for all later proposals. He reintroduced his bill each year until 1871, but the measure never got past the House committees. It brought the reform to the attention of his colleagues, however, and it inspired liberal reformers generally to intensify their activities on its behalf.[32]

In the Senate, Carl Schurz, Henry Wilson, and Lyman Trumbull failed to get a similar hearing for civil service reform measures; but in 1871 Trumbull attached a rider to an appropriations bill authorizing the President to establish a Civil Service Advisory Board. The measure passed, and Grant immediately called in George William

Curtis to become chairman of the new Board. On December 18, 1871, Curtis and his colleagues * presented their first report to the executive—a document that rang all the changes on the evils of the spoils system. It recommended, as its most important proposals, the classification of all government positions and the adoption of competitive examinations. Grant made an honest attempt to carry out the board's recommendations, but the reforms faced too much opposition in Congress. From the beginning the board and the President met resistance and failed to procure enough money to make more than a token attempt at reform.

Curtis's loyalty to the President and his confidence in Grant's sincerity earned him much petulant and undeserved criticism from some of his fellow liberal reformers. Seeing only Grant's weaknesses and horrified by the scandals in the administration and the "excesses" of Radical Reconstruction, they went off in righteous indignation to that chimera of 1872, the Liberal Republican party. In effect they left Curtis alone on the real battlefield of reform to carry on the fight without allies. Had they supported the efforts of Grant and Curtis to implement the Civil Service Advisory Board's recommendations, they might have gained some slight but real political reform during the 1870's. Lacking any visible public support, Grant gave in to the spoilsmen in his party. Curtis resigned his post in 1873, and that too was a blunder, for he could easily have remained in the administration to take advantage of Grant's undoubted desire to effect some kind of reform. The President appointed Dorman B. Eaton to replace Curtis, but the resignation of the first chairman of the board fatally undermined the already weak congressional support for reform. In 1875 Grant abandoned the entire business, and the board went out of existence, a victim as much of the petty bickering and impatience of liberal reformers as of the blows of the spoilsmen.[33]

In Scotland several years later, happily enjoying temporary exile from the political battlefield, Grant watched bemused as Hayes struggled to cope with the reformers' demands. The new President would soon learn, he predicted, that he had two "humbugs" to deal

---

* Alexander G. Cattell, Joseph Medill, Dawson A. Walker, E. B. Elliott, Joseph H. Blackfan, and David C. Cox.

with—civil service reform itself and the reformers.[34] It was the
passing judgment of a man disillusioned by his rasping contact with
the political perfectionists.

There is a certain irony in the fact that the most vigorous civil
service reformer to gain high political office before Theodore Roosevelt's time reached his position through the spoils system. For Carl
Schurz, a thoroughgoing reformer who wielded the reform broom
vigorously as Secretary of the Interior under Hayes, received his
appointment as a reward for his services during the campaign of
1876. Hayes went into office under the cloud of the disputed election; and, although he was pledged to work for civil service reform
and did so, he lacked support in Congress and accomplished little in
the way of permanent reform. Too many Republican legislators
and party chieftains resented Schurz's ruthless suppression of the
spoils system within the Interior Department. Moreover, like Curtis,
Hayes suffered from the zeal of his friends. Impatient for results and
willing to settle for nothing less than a complete overhaul of the
civil service system, Godkin badgered the President throughout his
term in office. He accused him of hypocrisy on the subject of reform,
charging that Hayes had come out for good government during his
campaign only to win the "indispensable" support of the "Independents." No matter that Hayes had been a political reformer in
Ohio, or that he gave Schurz a free hand in the Interior Department, or that he defied the spoilsmen in his own party by removing
several henchmen of the powerful Senator Conkling from lucrative
posts. The President had failed to put a new civil service law on the
books, and that was enough to condemn him as a "mystery" where
reform was concerned. Typically, Hayes answered the criticism by
commenting in his diary: "I would like to make it clear to all
friends of reform, that public opinion and Congress must be right
on the question before we can have a thorough and complete reform." It was wise advice, but it reached "all friends of reform"
only when the diary was published in 1924, somewhat too late to do
any good.[35]

By 1877 it had become clear to most civil service reformers that
some sort of organized campaign to educate Congress and the public
was an absolute necessity. Prior to that time, local reform groups,
such as the Citizens Association and the Reform Club of New York,

had provided the only organized agitation for political reform. They had rallied the support of prominent businessmen to the cause of good government and, although they had achieved only limited and temporary successes in municipal reform, they had inspired enough desire for clean politics to give later reform groups a fair chance to make good on a larger scale. In 1877 liberal reformers and a number of businessmen organized the New York Civil Service Reform Association. The Reverend Henry W. Bellows became its first president and Dorman B. Eaton headed the executive committee. Torn by a factional struggle between the "all or nothing" reformers and the less ambitious but more realistic moderates, the association fell apart within a year. But it was the base from which the National Civil Service Reform League later grew. In 1880 the New York organization came to life again under the guiding hand of George William Curtis. Dominated now by practical reformers and businessmen, it settled down to the unspectacular chore of preparing a measure that would have some chance of acceptance in Congress. Within three months it achieved notable success. Drafted by Eaton, with the assistance of Curtis and Silas Burt, a bill to reform the appointive functions of the President and legislators went to Congress by way of Senator Pendleton of Ohio. By then the association claimed 583 members in thirty-three states, and its example inspired reformers in other major cities across the land to organize similar groups. Baltimore, Boston, Philadelphia, Indianapolis, Milwaukee, and San Francisco soon made the crusade for political reform a national movement.[36]

Representatives from these local groups met at Newport in 1881 to organize the National Civil Service Reform League. Curtis had called the meeting, and he became the league's first president. Its executive committee immediately issued a public statement outlining a four-point program for practical reform: a campaign of publicity and education; work within Congress, state legislatures, and city councils for favorable laws; exposure of spoilsmen everywhere; and election of a President pledged to honest enforcement of civil service reform.

Doubtless, the secret of the league's success was its strict adherence to its main objectives. It did not dabble in peripheral reforms, nor did it ask for legislation it knew it had no chance of getting. Its leaders remained firmly committed to the idea of practical reform, based on realistic appraisal of the existing political situation. Not that the National League abandoned the moral attack on the spoils system. On the contrary, it used every argument its leaders could lay their hands on to convince the public that there was something rotten in the existing system. But in proposing a plan to replace the spoils system the leaders kept their feet firmly on solid ground. Curtis and Eaton guided the new organization during its early years and moulded it in the pattern of the successful and still active New York Association. In striking contrast to the success of the national and New York groups, the Cambridge Civil Service Reform Society accomplished almost nothing—probably because its leaders spent too much time trying to attract only men of "high character and repute." [37]

Like other liberal reform organizations, the National Civil Service Reform League functioned chiefly as an educational agency. Among its members were talented orators and publicists—such men as Schurz, Bonaparte, Burt, Storey, Lucius B. Swift, William Dudley Foulke, Everett P. Wheeler, and Theodore Roosevelt. Their participation in the crusade enabled the league to become an effective propaganda outlet. The organization established its own magazine (the *Civil Service Record*, which later became *Good Government*), and it offered prizes to school children for essays on political reform. It lobbied in Congress and other legislative bodies; it endorsed candidates friendly to its cause; it attacked unsparingly the worst spoilsmen in Congress. In 1882 it claimed credit, probably deserved, for the election of a sizable contingent of new congressmen pledged to vote for the Pendleton bill. All in all, it was the most effective organization concerned with liberal reform in the late nineteenth century, and its influence became even greater in the twentieth.[38]

Nonetheless, it was the assassination of Garfield that opened the way for passage of the Pendleton bill. The single rash act of a disgruntled petty spoilsman did as much for the cause of political reform as all the speech-making and writing of the liberal reformers. To be sure, the reformers were on the ground and ready with a well-considered measure. They knew exactly what they wanted, and they were prepared to press the attack immediately. On January 16, 1883, Senator Pendleton's bill became law. It established an independent commission within the government with authority to classify Federal jobs and administer competitive examinations to applicants. Moreover, it removed classified employees from the direct control of party bosses by prohibiting campaign assessments and indiscriminate removals from office for political reasons. Only about fourteen thousand government workers came under the classification provision of the Act; but good government men were satisfied that the law was a healthy start in the right direction. After 1883 they concentrated their efforts on persuading Presidents to extend the coverage and administer the Act faithfully and forcefully.

The liberal reformers expected miracles from Cleveland. "The great contest for the final establishment of Civil Service Reform is now at hand," Curtis exulted immediately after the Democratic victory in 1884. If the President-elect did what Curtis trusted he would do, no future Executive would dare undo his work. Godkin assured his readers that Cleveland would not disturb any officer in the Federal government "on account of his political opinions." Of course, the editor added, he might find some "incompetents" to dismiss. Yet Cleveland knew that the Mugwumps not only had "dictated" his nomination, but had elected him as well. He would listen to them and represent their point of view; indeed, he would be their representative in the cabinet. Six months after the inaugural, Godkin congratulated Cleveland for his conduct of public affairs "upon business principles." Already the President had vindicated the wisdom of the Mugwump revolt, by overhauling the government, suppressing wasteful methods, abolishing sinecures, and reforming abuses.[39]

Just what Godkin saw in Cleveland's performance to justify his exultant tribute to the President is a mystery. Forced to play the game of politics according to the established rules (as modified only slightly by the Pendleton Act), Cleveland all but ignored the spirit of the merit system and awarded jobs almost solely on the basis of service to the Democratic party. And he found a strikingly large number of "incompetents" in the Federal service—"incompetent" Republicans, that is. By July 1886, he had decided that 90 per cent of the government officers under his direct control were "incompetent." In the Interior Department alone he cleared out 68 per cent of the workers whose jobs could be filled by new appointments under the Pendleton Act; and he made almost a clean sweep of fourth-class postmasters. To be sure, Cleveland always paid lip service to civil service reform. A few months after taking office he admitted to a close friend that the reform had come to stay and that those who opposed it would "leave their corpses on the field." At the same time, however, he wondered how many Democrats he could appoint to the Civil Service Commission without raising a storm among the Mugwumps. Perhaps he wanted to be a civil service reformer; if so, the party gave him no opportunity to prove it. He impressed David A. Wells, who had intimate contact with the administration, as a man who wanted to follow the spirit as well as the letter of the Pendleton Act, but who faced immense political obstacles he simply could not overcome. Actually, he did nothing more substantial for political reform than to proclaim repeatedly his devotion to it. But as he pointed out to the president of the Civil Service Commission, Dorman B. Eaton, he could do little more than refrain from taking a "backward step" as long as public opinion did not yet fully support the principle of the Act. Public opinion, in this case, clearly meant Democratic party opinion.[40]

Cleveland learned quickly after taking office that his Mugwump friends could be as bothersome as office-seekers. For liberals showered him with unsolicited and often unwanted advice. (To the dismay of Carl Schurz, some Mugwumps also presented him with requests for government jobs!) True to form, Schurz appointed himself a one-man "kitchen cabinet" to advise and instruct the new President. Whenever he thought the administration was straying from its mission to represent the "moral force in politics," he badgered Cleveland with stern warnings and implied reprimands. When it became clear that the President was suspending employees for purely political reasons, the old reformer formally rebuked him: "It is of the highest consequence to the American people that the public pledge of a President should be regarded as a moral obligation of the first order." Cleveland was in danger of making people wonder whether he was a "conspicuous example of the strictest fidelity in this respect." Understandably, Cleveland bristled under this kind of criticism. He complained that it would take him three or four hours to answer one particularly lengthy disquisition from Schurz. (Informed of the President's remark, Schurz commented:

"Might I not say that he could possibly find those three or four hours where I found three or four months to advocate his election?") Publicly Cleveland remained on good terms with the Mugwumps; privately he lashed out at the professed friends of civil service reform who "yet mischievously and with supercilious self-righteousness" discredited every reform attempt not in exact accord with their own "attenuated ideas." Demanding complete and immediate perfection, they crippled with their "carping criticism" the work carried on by actual workers in the field of reform.[41]

Friends of the administration found it necessary to speak bluntly to impatient liberals who wanted Cleveland to throw over the Democratic organization and give the reformers everything they demanded. What was the use of pitching into Cleveland and the Democrats? Wells asked his friend Atkinson. The President was "sound as a nut" on reform; give him time to show his hand. An old politician gave Godkin some practical advice about politics in general. "A President may march well in advance of his party if he be sustained by a community," he told the impatient editor, "but he cannot keep far in advance of the community." Reformers expected too much of Cleveland, for *If the President stands by reformers where there are reformers it is about all he can do.*" [42]

But Cleveland's best was not good enough for most liberal reformers. Disappointed in his performance, they withheld from him in 1888 the enthusiastic support they had given him four years earlier. Some of them went so far as to vote for Harrison in order to punish Cleveland for his less than perfect administration of the Pendleton Act. Others remained indifferent throughout the campaign and voted for him only as the lesser of two evils. As Schurz observed, the Democratic leader had missed an opportunity to perform a great service to the cause of clean politics and good government in America. But the misgivings liberals had in 1888 about their quondam champion disappeared quickly during Harrison's first two years in office. Appalled by the open scramble for offices, the displays of "insolence" by Republican bosses, and the President's haphazard administration of the civil service law, liberals began to look back on Cleveland's four years as a period of great progress. Harrison's presidency, according to Garrison, was "a very humiliating phase of political profligacy." [43]

Harrison's one redeeming act, in the opinion of liberal reformers, was his naming of Theodore Roosevelt to the Civil Service Commission in 1889. Even that resulted from the party's appreciation of Roosevelt's service during the presidential campaign. Moreover, as Civil Service Commissioner, the young Republican continued to work for his party. He went to great lengths to dissociate himself from any identification with the Mugwumps, and he campaigned actively against Cleveland in 1892. In his work he did less than his fellow members on the Commission and seemed most interested in advancing his own political fortunes. Yet his characteristic flair for publicity and energetic public display of support for the Pendleton Act aided materially the cause of civil service reform. Cleveland was happy to keep him on as Commissioner until 1895.[44]

When Cleveland returned to the White House in 1893, most liberals were much more worried about silver than about the spoils system. They considered repeal of the Sherman Silver Purchase Act and a return to "sound money" absolutely essential to the economic and moral safety of the country. Cleveland thus had a relatively free hand in dispensing patronage, and he used it to good advantage. True, Schurz kept close watch on him and continued to remind him of his "moral duty." It would have been constitutionally impossible for the old reformer to have behaved otherwise. Godkin, on the other hand, was so impressed by Cleveland's "courage" in pressing for currency and tariff reforms that he blandly excused some of the President's most blatant political expedients. Shortly after the election, the editor asserted that Cleveland's tariff and silver views gave him "a priori protection of the strongest kind against all accusations of bargain-making in order to obtain the Presidency." During the fight for repeal of the Sherman Act, Cleveland used patronage as his strongest weapon against Democratic legislators who opposed his policy. Liberal critics directed none of their sharp barbs at him for exploiting the spoils system, however. Rather, they flung them indiscriminately at the obstinate opponents of the President who dared to defend the heretical silver idea.[45]

Cleveland took the plaudits of liberal reformers with him when he retired in 1897. During his second term he had extended the provisions of the Pendleton Act to cover about 85,000 of the 205,000 government employees, and liberals considered this enough to give him his laurels as a reform President.[46]

5

Proponents of the merit system argued that the reform would elevate the tone of public affairs by making fitness the sole qualification for public employment. Under the spoils system, they complained, good men had no chance to serve the people. Party managers passed over educated, qualified candidates and distributed offices to "hacks" and ward-heelers who had done their bidding during campaigns and would continue to serve them in government. Once in office, the beneficiaries of the system viewed their positions chiefly as opportunities to fatten their own purses at the public expense. Economy and efficiency, as well as morality, suffered grievous blows in city, state, and Federal offices, staffed with rascals and incompetents who knew nothing and cared nothing about their duties and responsibilities as servants of the taxpayers. Eliminate the motive of private gain in politics, liberals demanded, and make all applicants for government jobs take competitive examinations. Then the higher types of men would come forward to serve their country with decency and honor—the college-educated men, the bright young men of breeding, in short, the "best men."

Liberals acknowledged frankly that civil service reform, by assuming that some men were more fit than others for public office, would attract the "best men" to government work. They overlooked the fact that some of the "fittest" and best educated men in the country already held many positions in government. Indeed, Congress throughout the late nineteenth century was replete with "fit," educated men who opposed civil service reform at every turn and despised the liberal reformers and their objectives. Neither education, nor means, nor "fitness" alone guaranteed honest, efficient public service, as the performances of Senators Ingalls and Conkling, Vice-President Colfax, Congressman Oakes Ames, and scores of other politicians attest.[47]

Not, at least, the kind of honest, efficient service some liberals had in mind. Such reformers as Dorman B. Eaton, William Dudley

Foulke, George H. Pendleton, and, after 1884, Theodore Roosevelt, always viewed civil service reform as a practical necessity. They fought for it because they thought it would curb the excesses of the spoils system and promote greater efficiency in government. Never did they expect it to solve economic problems, effect a revolution in political morality, eliminate the spoils system entirely, or perform other miracles. To be sure, they expected to receive more from it than the Pendleton Act and its application ultimately gave them. But their arguments for the most part stressed the need for practical, reasonable reform, based on thorough study of the problem and on an intelligent assessment of the reform's probable results. Curtis and Schurz, in their public pronouncements, at least, also often recognized the impossibility of reforming the system to their liking with a few sweeps of the broom. Curtis in particular sometimes combined the idealism of the reformer with the practicality of the professional politician, and, notwithstanding his mistake in deserting Grant in 1873, no man deserves more credit for the ultimate legislative success of civil service reform.[48]

Yet both Curtis and Schurz often struck a note of pique in their arguments that inspired their opponents to call them "snivil-service" reformers. Schurz treated Presidents as errant children, scolding, rebuking, and lecturing them on their duties and moral obligations. Occasionally Curtis's enthusiasm got the better of him and caused him to picture the wholly dire consequences of a continuation of the spoils system. But the "snivil-service" epithet best described Godkin, Norton, the Adamses, W. P. Garrison, Horace White, and the rest of the "*Nation* crowd." These were the reformers to whom "fitness" for public office meant something more than mere competence, or even excellence. For what they meant by "honest, efficient public service" was government by an elite class of men like themselves. Distrustful of democracy and contemptuous of the brash, rich businessmen-politicians in government, they pictured themselves as ideal public servants. Well-bred, financially comfortable, "disinterested" in such sordid matters as party politics, and supremely confident that they alone understood the meaning of virtue in society, they resented bitterly the power and authority that "lesser men" than they exercised. They were the "best men," and they knew it; yet they never could have won high office in a democracy, for they flaunted their distaste for democracy. A carping, pedantic, often sniveling quality permeated their remarks on political reform. They displayed toward their opponents not mere political disapproval, but a scornful vindictiveness sadly devoid of compassion or understanding of human nature.

All of the liberal proposals for reforming politics, including civil service reform, rested essentially on the proposition that the American people as a whole were unworthy of self-government. Restriction, not reform, was the basic ingredient in their view of democracy. Had they been the dominant leaders in the crusade for the merit system, doubtless Senator Pendleton's bill would have remained for many years only a proposal and not a statute. In the campaign for "good government," fortunately, their patent distrust of the masses, together with their contempt for professional politicians and their cloistered outlook on politics, circumscribed the impact of their dogmatism and restricted their influence.

10

The Politics of Nostalgia

Since I gave up trying to make a rope of sand—an independent party composed exclusively of good men—I have been in the school of party politics and the lesson I have learned there practically at least is to show some liberality toward those who differ from me.

HENRY CABOT LODGE, 1890

"A rayformer thries to get into office on a flyin' machine. He succeeds now an' thin, but th' odds are a hundherd to wan on th' la-ad that tunnels through."

MR. DOOLEY

W E ALL EXPECTED FAR TOO MUCH OF THE HUMAN race," Godkin acknowledged tardily in 1898. "What stuff we used to talk." [1] Reformers generally tend to expect too much of their fellow men, which may explain why so many erstwhile crusaders end their days in apathy or despair. To most reformers, moreover, the past has an almost irresistible attraction. Much of the history of dissent in America concerns the efforts of men and women to revive the "good old days," and often the inability to recapture the past adds to the frustrations with the present. So it was with liberal reformers in the Gilded Age: they asked too much of mankind, and they struggled futilely to escape the consequences of time.

Perhaps there never was, in actual fact, a typical liberal reformer. Some very real differences in character, temperament, and intellect, not to say in specific attitudes toward issues, among the "best men" make it difficult to generalize about them with certainty. Like most movements, the crusade for liberal reform drew votaries of kaleidoscopic motives and aims. Moreover, it was far too loose a confederation ever to count more than a handful of full-time, permanent partisans. Men signed on and backed off at will, joining perhaps only for a national presidential campaign, or to press for a single pet reform, or to express an indistinct but felt sense of frustration or outrage. Doubtless, Godkin was the pre-eminent spokesman for lib-

eral reform, functioning as an oracle to his own generation of reformers and as something of a fashionable pundit to their young
gentlemen sons in the colleges and universities of the day. Certainly
his imprint on the movement was massive and commanding, giving
it a distinctive flavor it definitely would have lacked without his
presence. Yet Godkin was also an exotic in his adopted land, always
just on the periphery of American life. Too testy, too patently
aristocratic in manner, too downright distrustful of democracy, he
was less representative of the average liberal reformer than, say,
Curtis or Schurz or Storey or Atkinson. Each reformer contributed
or withheld from the movement according to his individual pre-
dilections and whims; yet certain qualities set liberal reform off
from other political and social phenomena of the Gilded Age and
gave to all liberal reformers a generalized identity which makes it
possible to distinguish them as a group. Turned and shaken, then,
the kaleidoscope reveals a pattern of moods, attitudes, and responses, characteristic of a figurative liberal reformer.

Unable to come to terms with his age, the liberal reformer exaggerated its defects and overrated the past. Plunging impulsively into
the logical fallacy of *post hoc, ergo propter hoc,* he imagined that a
simple temporal relationship linked everything he despised in the
Gilded Age to the war or to an unprecedented deterioration of the
average American's moral sensibilities. The war had spawned a new
politician—the wily and resourceful scoundrel who lacked all sense
of civic decency. It had bred a system of high tariffs that turned
honest businessmen into money-grubbers and encouraged all classes
to look to government for special privileges and favors. War had
sapped the worker of his sturdy independence and filled his head
with nonsense about unions and the right to strike against his bene-
factors. It had robbed voters of their common sense, turning them
against the reasoned appeals of the "better element" in politics and
moulding them into the cat's-paws of party bosses. Worst of all, the
government's wartime policy of issuing unbacked paper currency in
lieu of hard money had given many people the ridiculous notion
that greenbacks had become a permanent part of the nation's
money supply. To the liberal, it was obvious that an insidious
blight had swept across the country, leaving its victims dangerously

receptive to the ruinous nostrums of political and economic quacks.

Viewing postwar America as a series of little morality plays, he instinctively stepped forward to play the role of Virtue. Certainly he seemed eminently qualified for the part. He possessed a wonderful confidence in his own power to distinguish between right and wrong. As a member of the "better classes," he boasted a courageous independence and integrity of purpose that ordinary men lacked. He presented himself as one who, unshackled by obligations to parties or politicians, would bring a firm, prosaic sense of duty to public affairs. There was no sophistry in his argument that he alone represented political and economic wisdom in a society riddled with absurd theories and shallow ideals. He trusted his own good sense completely. If irresponsible reformers experimented with unsound financial practices or beguiled simple workingmen and farmers into supporting prodigal schemes for improving their lot, the liberal would approach economic problems with a reverential respect for the "Nature of Things." If professional politicians cynically deceived the voters with promises they could not keep, the liberal would reject such charlatanry and offer himself as a realist who knew that man could not defy certain immutable laws of political economy. Moreover, he would never be a passionate bystander, carping from the sidelines as the nation went to perdition. As guardian of the right, he proposed to broadcast his influence for decency throughout society. No economic, political, or social evil would escape his attention.

Everything considered, his campaign to reform postwar society was a pathetic failure. As an economic reformer, the liberal fell far short of his goals and subverted his own principles. As a political reformer, he achieved only a modest, somewhat illusory success. As a social reformer, he exerted a negative influence on the efforts of other reformers to cope with the human problems raised by the Industrial Revolution. At the end of the nineteenth century, the only enduring monument to his efforts was the Pendleton Act—and his work was only partially responsible for passage of that mild reform measure.

Liberal reform championed orthodox liberalism, yet prostituted its creed to suit the pragmatic needs of big business. It demanded universal respect for the "natural laws" of political economy, yet manifested a shallow regard for those laws in its disingenuous approach to labor's grievances. Pledged to campaign for "safe, careful, and deliberate" correction, achieved without resort to extremism of any sort, liberals often discarded moderation for malice, deliberation for impetuosity. They taught that a decent respect for tested moral precepts promoted material well-being as well as spiritual satisfaction. But liberal reformers arbitrarily selected the moral criteria by which they judged the problems of an industrial society, and they were quick to condemn as immoral anyone who disagreed with them. By their equivocal behavior, they exposed their cause to warranted charges of bigotry and hypocrisy.

Spurning the thought of becoming professional party men, liberals glorified the "independent man" in politics. Independence, they decided, offered them the most feasible means of attaining their goals, while assuring them a comfortable immunity from the pernicious influence of party politics. But if their independence insulated them from the professionalism of the party men, it also shielded the party men from liberalism and muffled the voice of reform in high political circles. Their "party of the centre" carried no important elections, and the few representatives it placed in public office were forlorn dissenters whom loyal party men overwhelmed by sheer force of numbers. Yet liberals always expected regular Democrats and Republicans to drop whatever else they were doing and yield to their wishes. Each presidential nominating convention saw them step daintily into the stream of party politics and impatiently command all other swimmers to quit the water.

Moreover, liberals unmercifully pilloried the true political independents of the time—the rebels who cut loose from the established party system and worked in such causes as Populism, the single-tax movement, socialism, and the labor reform parties. Ben Butler, whatever else he may have been, certainly was the outstanding political rebel of his day. Liberals only reluctantly conceded Butler's membership in the human race, and they reacted as irrationally to the political restlessness of Wendell Phillips.

Mr. Dooley's "la-ad that tunnels through"—the party worker who made a vocation of politics—knew the value of votes and where to find voters. So did the liberal reformer. But the party man knew also how to attract the voters and what bargains to make for their support. The typical liberal reformer possessed neither the inclination to "get down" among the masses of voters nor the proper equipment for reaching them from afar. His "independent" journals, for all their energetic and often trenchant comments on important issues, reached only a handful of substantial citizens, most of whom already agreed with his views. He chose to exclude the average voter from his "party of the centre" and from most of his reform organizations, preferring instead the safe company of his fellow "best men." His speeches overflowed with turgid language and meaningless abstractions about good government, irresponsible finances, and ad valorem duties. Perhaps they made heady listening for his friends, but doubtless they drove many ordinary citizens in his audiences to seek relief at the nearest saloon or ward club.

On rare occasions the liberal reformer ventured down to the level of the voting masses on philanthropic missions to spread the gospel of civic decency or to entice the people away from the bosses. Usually he returned from these excursions more appalled by the bad manners and intemperate habits of the lower classes than by the indifference of the voters to his appeals. Education and cultural refinement, he often observed, would emancipate the people from their enslavement to the bosses and would drown out the siren songs of labor agitators and other "radicals." But, with dogged consistency, he opposed meaningful proposals to provide workers and their families with the means, the opportunity, and the incentive to acquire good taste and enlightenment.

At heart, the typical liberal reformer believed in government by an elite—in rule by men whose breeding, education, and "natural proclivities" set them far above the masses and endowed them with the wisdom and restraint essential to the proper functioning of government. Such men were constitutionally incapable of governing badly, of acting in a manner detrimental to the country's good name and honor. History proved, he insisted, that antebellum America had produced in each generation a crop of model statesmen—leaders of intellectual and moral stature whose splendid tutelage had enabled the nation to prosper and become great. Politics in those days had been an honorable profession; politicians had been virtuous men who had sought only to create and preserve an ideal republic.

With a conceit tempered only by patent sincerity, the liberal reformer offered postwar America his services as the natural and logical successor to the Nestors of the earlier day. Throughout most of the postwar period he practiced the politics of nostalgia. Not until the last years of the century, after he had become painfully aware that no one had accepted his offer, could he bring himself to admit that the past had vanished forever. And he was never quite capable of conceding that the "golden age" had existed, for the most part, in a corner of his own imagination. He never really understood why the people rejected his services.

2

Nostalgia is a powerful magnet; it attracts the historian today as it did the liberal reformer in the past. Perhaps antebellum America *was* a better place to live in than the turbulent Union that emerged from a long and bloody sectional conflict. Perhaps liberals once actually knew a world fashioned to endure, a halcyon society in which ordinary citizens deferred to the judgments of well-bred, intelligent gentlemen. Perhaps, too, people in those days listened attentively when learned critics and statesmen discoursed on politics and morality. Relegating most postwar politicians to a gallery of monsters, Henry Adams and Vernon L. Parrington in their histories overpraised the antebellum leaders, and their hastily sketched caricatures are no substitute for more lifelike portraits. Still, while conceding that history has sometimes been uncritical when comparing the Clays, Websters, Bentons, and Lincolns with politicians of succeeding generations, we can appreciate the liberal's esteem for the giants of his youth.

We can appreciate, too, the liberal's evident distress about his position in postwar society. After all, he was a worthy representative of a way of life ambitious men had once aspired to emulate. At a time when standards seemed almost to have disappeared, at least he attempted to maintain settled rules of conduct. An expensive education had refined his native intelligence; extensive travel and study abroad had imbued him with a worldly outlook that contrasted sharply with the provincialism of his countrymen. Although many of his reformist ideals suffered from his pedantic addiction to economic orthodoxy, some were as sound as his background. There was no cant in his scornful attitude toward business immoralities and tainted politics; and his mistrust of centralized power stemmed from his strong, Jeffersonian conviction that power breeds tyranny. Postwar America desperately needed someone of ability and intelligence to discipline its reckless drive into the industrial era, and the liberal reformer might well have been the man to handle the reins.

His inability to do so resulted, in part, from the weaknesses in his program. An archaic economic philosophy chained him to the past and predetermined the unhappy fate of his crusade to defend his precious "natural laws." Classical liberalism had, from the start, contained the seeds of its own destruction in its attempt to make an absolute of economic individualism. As the English Liberals had learned, absolute individualism clashed disastrously with the collective behavior of individuals in societal existence. Liberalism had no appeal to the masses, because it could not demonstrate, except in theory, that its benefits would ever spread beyond a narrow circle of propertied men.

Moreover, the liberal attempted to carry out his reforms in a decidedly hostile environment. His pleas for restraint in business affairs, coming at a time when the dollar symbolized success, rarely penetrated a wall of public indifference. Under the best conditions, the business of reform brings few rewards and a profusion of frustrations to its proponents. During the Gilded Age, when few Americans had yet acquired a taste for self-criticism, it seemed a hopeless task. Little wonder that Henry Adams, nursing his bruised ego and expressing the bewilderment of most liberals, complained that postwar America had rejected him.

Neither Adams nor his fellow "best men" in the "party of the centre" would concede that they had first rejected postwar America before it cast them aside. For all its sordid reek and blackness, industrialism had not yet brought the deadness of purpose, the paucity of meaningful nonconformity, the amiable hollowness, that blight its years of maturity. Much abused by critics at the time and by historians later, the Gilded Age was a period of exciting social change. It laid down a revolutionary challenge to responsible men, a challenge to harness the industrial giant and make it work for the benefit of all, rather than for the comfort of a privileged few. For all his intellectual endowment, the liberal reformer closed his mind to the challenge. He fancied himself a realist, but he never grasped the realities of the Industrial Revolution. Rather, he was an abstract philosopher who allowed his dreams of an ordered society to prevent him from understanding that order in human affairs proceeds as much from adaptation to new conditions and absorption of new ideas as from constancy to established patterns. He turned away from his age not only because it refused his advice, but also because it insisted that he live in it. If society would not change to suit his high standards, he would escape it or stubbornly resist its claims to his services.

Ultimately, the liberal's intellectual arrogance and unreasoning fear destroyed his good influence. His confidence in his own moral excellence deteriorated into a brass-bolted certitude that denied any sense of rightness in other men. Intemperate and intolerant in his relations with his obvious enemies, he managed to alienate his own best allies as well—the moderates in both parties whose support was essential to the success of his program. Often he frankly acknowledged his fear of democratic averages; they were responsible, he said, for the low state of human nature. But he had a poor opinion of human nature, anyway; and, as the age wore on, he displayed more fear of people in general than of democratic averages. His reforms reflect his indifference to the everyday problems of people, and his methods suggest that he thought the average citizen deserved little voice in the consideration of weighty political and economic questions. In his entire approach to the business of reform he adopted an attitude considerably less patrician than magisterial.

Gradually his petulant animosity gave way to a pervasive and ill-concealed dread. Each rumble of discontent from the people sent him into a panic. Too often he displayed an ugly streak of authoritarianism, and he came increasingly to look upon force as the only effective weapon against dissent. Moreover, he was strangely reluctant to extend compassion to the victims of force and other misfortunes. Above all, the liberal reformer lacked the humility that comes with true intellectual and moral superiority. He was incapable of giving to lesser men than he even a measure of the respect he demanded from them.

Doubtless, most liberal reformers suffered from a melancholy feeling of social displacement. In a society that flaunted contempt for established standards, they knew the bitterness and frustration that tear at the sensibilities of outraged moralists. They once fancied themselves capable of persuading society to defer to their judgment and obey their injunctions. When their goal proved to be a chimera, they concluded that they and their age were incompatible. To paraphrase Lionel Trilling's judgment on another group of liberals, they clung to earlier attitudes with a stubborn, increasingly satisfied tenacity, and allowed their own virtuous political and social opinions to do duty for percipience.[2] Ultimately, their failure of perception opened the way for a self-fulfilling prophecy of national ruin and corruption. Torn between nostalgia and hope, they gave way to a remembrance of things past; but because they could not really escape the present, the pharisaic, self-righteous spirit that had always been within them surfaced and became the prism through which they viewed the world around them. In the end, they were reduced to playing the role of querulous aristocrats in a nation that had long since become infatuated with democracy.

Notes

CHAPTER 1 THE NATURE OF LIBERAL REFORM

1. Kirk, *The Conservative Mind: From Burke to Eliot* (Chicago, 1953; 3rd rev. ed., 1960), 38off. See also Clinton Rossiter, *Conservatism in America: The Thankless Persuasion* (New York, 1955; 2nd ed., rev., 1962), ch. IV, for a provocative discussion of liberalism and conservatism.

2. Eric F. Goldman, *Rendezvous with Destiny: A History of Modern American Reform* (New York, 1953), 317–18; ch. II, *passim*.

3. To Charles Francis Adams, Jr., November 2, 1864, in Worthington C. Ford (ed.), *A Cycle of Adams Letters, 1861–1865* (2 vols., Boston and New York, 1920), I, 211–12.

4. To Charles Francis Adams, Jr., November 21, 1862, in Ford (ed.), *A Cycle of Adams Letters,* I, 195–7.

5. Note esp. William Cullen Bryant, James A. Garfield, David Ames Wells, Bliss Perry, John Bascom, David Dudley Field, Paul A. Chadbourne, Alfred Clark Chapin, John Boyd Thacher, Horace E. Scudder, Rollo Ogden, Francis Lynde Stetson, and Hamilton W. Mabie. See Frederick Rudolph, *Mark Hopkins and the Log: Williams College, 1836–1872* (New Haven, Conn., 1956); and *The Centennial Anniversary of the Founding of Williams College* (Cambridge, Mass., 1894).

6. *The Nation,* LXXXI (July 13, 1905), 30.

7. Adams to Charles Milnes Gaskell, May 24, 1875, in Harold D. Cater (ed.), *Henry Adams and His Friends: A Collection of His Unpublished Letters* (Boston, 1947), 67.

8. James D. Richardson (ed.), *A Compilation of the Messages and Papers of the Presidents, 1789–1897* (10 vols., Washington, D.C., 1913), VII, 5174.

9. *Nation,* VIII (January 21, 1869), 46.

CHAPTER 2   RETREAT TO REFORM

1. *Political Recollections, 1840–1872* (Chicago, 1884), 331.

2. Two first-rate biographies, Irving H. Bartlett, *Wendell Phillips: Brahmin Radical* (Boston, 1961), 276–92, and John L. Thomas, *The Liberator, William Lloyd Garrison: A Biography* (Boston, 1963), 420–35, recount the agony of the split between the two reformers. James M. McPherson, *The Struggle for Equality: Abolitionists and the Negro in the Civil War and Reconstruction* (Princeton, N.J., 1964), 287–307, places the schism in the larger context of the whole antislavery movement.

3. Wendell Phillips Garrison to William Everett, October 24, 1887, Garrison Family Papers (Houghton Library, Harvard University); Curtis, "The Duty of the American Scholar," August 5, 1856, in Charles Eliot Norton (ed.), *Orations and Addresses of George William Curtis* (3 vols., New York, 1894), I, 15–16; William Lloyd Garrison to Charles Eliot Norton, January 13, 1865, Charles Eliot Norton Papers (Houghton Library, Harvard University).

4. *The American Political Tradition and the Men Who Made It* (New York, 1948), 142–4.

5. For a detailed description and analysis of the commission's work, see John G. Sproat, "Blueprint for Radical Reconstruction," *Journal of Southern History,* XXIII (1957), 25–44. The commission's preliminary and final reports are in *War of the Rebellion: A Compilation of the Official Records of the Union and Confederate Armies* (128 vols., Washington, D.C., 1880–1901), Series 3, III, 430–54, and Series 3, IV, 289–382. The Papers of Charles Sumner (Houghton Library, Harvard University) contain numerous letters from the commission's members. McPherson, *The Struggle for Equality,* 178–91, discusses the AFIC's links with the antislavery movement. McPherson's book is an excellent study of the relationships among politics, abolitionism, and Reconstruction, as is LaWanda and John H. Cox, *Politics, Principle,*

and Prejudice, 1865–1866: Dilemma of Reconstruction America (New York, 1963). Willie Lee Rose, *Rehearsal for Reconstruction: The Port Royal Experiment* (New York, 1964), is a superb examination of reformist ideas in actual application. The most lucid and sophisticated overview of the period is Kenneth M. Stampp, *The Era of Reconstruction, 1865–1877* (New York, 1965).

6. Norton, "The Advantages of Defeat," *Atlantic Monthly*, VIII (1861), 360–65; Norton to Frederick Law Olmsted, September 16, 1866, Norton Papers. See also Kermit Vanderbilt, *Charles Eliot Norton, Apostle of Culture in a Democracy* (Cambridge, Mass., 1959), an excellent biography; and George M. Frederickson, *The Inner Civil War: Northern Intellectuals and the Crisis of the Union* (New York, 1965), in which the apocalyptic views of Norton and others are discussed.

7. Harold F. Williamson, *Edward Atkinson, the Biography of an American Liberal, 1827–1905* (Boston, 1934), 85.

8. "I want to try the experiment fully and fairly and see whether the best writers in America cannot get a fair hearing from the American public on questions of politics, art and literature through a newspaper." Godkin to Frederick Law Olmsted, May 5, 1865, in Rollo Ogden, *Life and Letters of Edwin Lawrence Godkin* (2 vols., New York, 1907), I, 235–6.

9. William M. Armstrong, "The Freedmen's Movement and the Founding of the *Nation*," *Journal of American History*, LIII (1967), 708–26, is a definitive account of the journal's birth.

10. Wendell P. Garrison to Francis J. Garrison, November 9, 1868, Garrison Family Papers.

11. Godkin has been treated with kid gloves in many general accounts of the period; and some historians have been so taken with his brilliance as a journalist as to overlook his incredibly obtuse views on some aspects of American life and his downright ignorance of others. The only biography is Ogden, *Life of Godkin*, friendly and uncritical. Alan Pendleton Grimes, *The Political Liberalism of the New York Nation, 1865–1932* (James Sprunt *Studies* in History and Political Science, vol. 34, Chapel Hill, N.C., 1953), is a valuable estimate of Godkin as well as of the journal. Louis Filler, "The Early Godkin," *The Historian*, XVII (1954), 43–66, and Edward C. Kirkland, *Business in the Gilded Age: The Conservative Balance Sheet* (Madison, 1952), 21–40, are discerning essays. *The Nation* itself, from 1865 to 1900, should be consulted to appreciate fully the significance of Godkin's editorship.

12. *Nation*, I (July 6, 1865), 39.

13. *Nation,* II (May 4, 1866), 568.

14. "Broadside," announcing publication of *The Nation,* 1865; and *Nation,* I (November 9, 1865), 581–2.

15. *Nation,* I (December 28, 1865), 806–7.

16. *Nation,* I (August 17, 1865), 198–9; (December 21, 1865), 744; III (November 18, 1866), 370–71; also W. F. Allen, *Nation,* I (September 28, 1865), 393.

17. *Nation,* IV (February 21, 1867), 150–51; II (April 5, 1866), 423–4.

18. George S. Merriam, *Life and Times of Samuel Bowles* (2 vols., New York, 1885), II, 31–2; Norton to Olmsted, September 16, 1866, Norton Papers.

19. Storey to his father, December 4, 1867, May 17, 1868, in M. A. De-Wolfe Howe, *Portrait of an Independent: Moorfield Storey, 1845–1929* (Boston, 1932), 47–8, 113.

20. Schurz to his wife, August 27, 1865, and speech, "The Road to Peace," September 19, 1868, in Frederic Bancroft (ed.), *Speeches, Correspondence, and Political Papers of Carl Schurz* (6 vols., New York, 1913), I, 268–9, 471. (Hereafter cited as Bancroft (ed.), *Schurz.*) Schurz's report to the President is in *Senate Executive Documents,* 39 Cong., 1 Sess., No. 2.

21. *Nation,* III (October 18, 1866), 310–11.

22. Eric L. McKitrick, *Andrew Johnson and Reconstruction* (Chicago, 1960), is by far the best assessment of Johnson's difficulties with the Radicals, but see also Benjamin P. Thomas and Harold M. Hyman, *Stanton: The Life and Times of Lincoln's Secretary of War* (New York, 1962), and John G. Sproat, "Edwin M. Stanton and Reconstruction," Unpublished Master's Thesis, University of California, Berkeley, 1952. W. R. Brock, *An American Crisis: Congress and Reconstruction, 1865–1867* (New York, 1963), is a discerning study of the problem prior to the impeachment crisis. *Trial of Johnson, President of the United States* (3 vols., Washington, 1868), is the official record of the proceedings, while David M. Dewitt, *The Impeachment and Trial of Andrew Johnson* (New York, 1903), is the standard account of the trial.

23. Norton to Godkin, March 1, 7, 1868, Edwin Lawrence Godkin Papers (Houghton Library, Harvard University); *Nation,* VI (March 5, 1868), 184–5.

24. *Nation,* VI (March 5, 1868), 185; Storey to his father, March 3, 1868, in Howe, *Storey,* 75–6; Curtis to Richard Henry Dana, November 24, 1868, Richard Henry Dana Papers (Massachusetts Historical Society);

Curtis, "The Public Duty of Educated Men," June 27, 1877, in Norton (ed.), *Curtis Orations*, I, 276–7.

25. Atkinson to Sumner, June 22, 1868, Sumner Papers; *Harper's Weekly*, XII (June 6, 1868), 354; Storey to Helen Appleton, May 17, 1868, in Howe, *Storey*, 109. Doubtless the most famous account of the impeachment affair and treatment of the seven dissenters is John F. Kennedy, *Profiles in Courage* (New York, 1955), ch. 6. In a dramatic and factually accurate account the late President assumed that impeachment must be equated with a criminal indictment. But the Radical leaders in 1868 did not rule out the possibility that impeachment can be a purely political proceeding, nor do some historians today.

26. Dana to Godkin, November 7, 1868, Godkin Papers.

27. George W. Julian, *Speeches on Political Questions* (New York, 1872), 217–18. See also Patrick W. Riddleberger, *George Washington Julian, Radical Republican: A Study in Nineteenth-Century Politics and Reform* (Indianapolis, Ind., 1966), 187–95. This is a discerning study of a significant figure in Radical and Liberal Republicanism. On Stevens, see Fawn M. Brodie, *Thaddeus Stevens: Scourge of the South* (New York, 1959), 232–3; Richard Current, *Old Thad Stevens, A Story of Ambition* (Madison, Wis., 1942); and Ralph Korngold, *Thaddeus Stevens, A Being Darkly Wise and Rudely Great* (New York, 1955).

28. *Nation*, IV (March 21, 1867), 225–6, (May 16, 1867), 394–5; Godkin to Norton, quoting Curtis, May 9, 1867, in Ogden, *Godkin*, I, 301–2.

29. *Nation*, VIII (1869), 125; Grimes, *Political Liberalism of the Nation*, 9.

30. Vincent P. De Santis, *Republicans Face the Southern Question: The New Departure Years, 1877–1897* (Baltimore, 1959), traces in illuminating detail the political trail Republicans followed in attempting to cope with the problem of the freedmen, while striving desperately to maintain their power base in the South. Stanley P. Hirshson, *Farewell to the Bloody Shirt: Northern Republicans and the Southern Negro, 1877–1893* (Bloomington, Ind., 1962), further documents the story. Patrick W. Riddleberger, "The Break in the Radical Ranks: Liberals vs Stalwarts in the Election of 1872," *Journal of Negro History*, XLIV (1959), 136–57, and "The Radicals' Abandonment of the Negro During Reconstruction," ibid. XLV (1960), 88–102, are careful, suggestive evaluations of the manner in which certain select "Liberal Radicals" rationalized their change of views on the Negro question. I am indebted to Riddleberger for suggesting, in these articles and in conversations with me, some of the generalizations herein ad-

vanced about the transition of some Republicans from Radicalism to Liberalism.

31. The best analysis of race concepts in America is still Gunnar Myrdal, *An American Dilemma: The Negro Problem and Modern Democracy* (New York and London, 1944), part II.

32. Charles Francis Adams, Jr., to Charles Francis Adams, November 2, 1865, in Ford (ed.), *A Cycle of Adams Letters*, II, 216; in *Harper's Weekly* see, e.g., XVII (February 22, 1873), 160, and XX (October 28, 1876), 872, for contrasting caricatures of Negroes.

33. Samuel L. Clemens, *Mark Twain's Sketches, New and Old* (Hartford, 1875), 202–7; note also the characters of Jim in *Huckleberry Finn* and Roxana in *Pudd'nhead Wilson*. Sympathetic if somewhat over-dramatized conceptions of Negroes appear in the writings of John De Forest, Albion W. Tourgee, and George Washington Cable.

34. James Bryce, *The American Commonwealth* (2 vols., New York, 1888), II, 496–7.

35. *Nation*, I (August 17, 1865), 198; V (August 1, 1867), 90–91.

36. Bliss Perry, *Life and Letters of Henry Lee Higginson* (Boston, 1921), 259; Adams to his father, November 2, 1865, in Ford (ed.), *Cycle of Adams Letters*, II, 219.

37. *Nation*, II (January 25, 1866), 97; (February 1, 1866), 129.

38. *Springfield Republican*, March 8, 1865; *Harper's Weekly*, XI (March 9, 1867), 146; *Nation*, III (November 29, 1866), 430–31; Godkin to Norton, February 28, 1865, Norton Papers; Greeley to Colfax, February 25, 1866, Greeley-Colfax Correspondence, 1842–71 (New York Public Library).

39. March 24, 1866, Sumner Papers.

40. Godkin to Norton, May 9, August 1, 1867, Norton Papers; *Nation*, X (January 6, 1870), 2; (February 10, 1870), 83; XIX (October 22, 1874), 262–3; Greeley to O. Johnson, July 23, 1868, Letters of Horace Greeley, 1836–73 (New York Public Library); Seymour to Tilden, October 3, 1872, Samuel Jones Tilden Papers (New York Public Library).

41. George E. Woodberry to Charles H. Barrows, December 8, 1877, Charles Henry Barrows Papers (Houghton Library, Harvard University); Merriam, *Bowles*, II, 238–40; *Nation*, XII (March 23, 1871), 192–3; XIX (October 29, 1874), 278–9; A. G. Sedgwick, *Nation*, XIX (September 17, 1874), 180–81; Schurz to Godkin, March 31, 1871, and speech at St. Louis, September 24, 1874, in Bancroft (ed.), *Schurz*, II, 254; III, 90–91; Forbes to Sumner, August 10, 1872, Sumner

Papers; *Harper's Weekly,* XVIII (April 11, 1874), 310; *Springfield Republican,* January 29, 1872; *Chicago Tribune,* March 16, 1871.

42. *Nation,* x (May 19, 1870), 314; XIV (November 14, 1872), 308; Garrison to Francis J. Garrison, December 31, 1874, Garrison Family Papers. See also speech by Schurz, September 24, 1874, in Bancroft (ed.), *Schurz,* III, 88–9, 93–4.

43. New York *Tribune,* March 5, 1872; Pike, *The Prostrate State: South Carolina Under Negro Government* (New York, 1874), esp. pp. 9–71. Robert F. Durden, *James Shepherd Pike: Republicanism and the American Negro, 1850–1882* (Durham, N.C., 1957), esp. chs. 2, 7, and 8, is an excellent analysis of Pike's racism and its results. Durden compares the published book with Pike's private journal and shows the dearth of Pike's evidence and the manner in which he twisted material from the journal for publication in the book.

44. *An American Dilemma,* 445. Stampp, *Era of Reconstruction,* ch. I, analyzes the Reconstruction myth as historians have contributed to it in the past. See also Rayford W. Logan, *The Negro in American Life and Thought: The Nadir, 1877–1901* (New York, 1954), 10ff., and Bertram Schrieke, *Alien Americans: A Study of Race Relations* (New York, 1936), 110–42.

45. "The Advantages of Defeat," *Atlantic Monthly,* VIII (1861), 361.

46. H. S. Foote, Jr., to Schurz, November 6, 1871, Schurz to J. D. Cox, November 22, 1871 (copy), Greeley to Schurz and the "National Convention of the Liberal Republicans of the United States," May 20, 1872, Carl Schurz Papers (Manuscript Division, Library of Congress); Bancroft (ed.), *Schurz,* III, 329–32; Schurz to Godkin, June 23, 1872, ibid. II, 382–5.

47. *Nation,* x (May 12, 1870), 280; (May 19, 1870), 314.

48. Garrison to William Lloyd Garrison, November 1, 1877, Garrison Family Papers; Williamson, *Atkinson,* 98, quoting a letter to Gustav Herrmann, April 11, 1877; *Nation,* XXIII (November 9, 1876), 280–81. Even before the compromise was reached, while the election was still in dispute, liberals showed little concern about the outcome. They were confident that reconciliation between the sections was imminent no matter who was declared President. Their great fear, prior to Hayes's inauguration, was that certain Democratic "hotheads" might resort to violence as a means of installing Tilden in the White House.

49. *Springfield Republican,* December 5, 1876; February 20, 26, 1877. For insights into the nature of the compromise and its implications, see C. Vann Woodward's brilliant studies of reconciliation and re-

demption: *Reunion and Reaction: The Compromise of 1877 and the End of Reconstruction* (Boston, 1951), and *Origins of the New South, 1877–1913* (Baton Rouge, La., 1951).

50. *Nation,* XVIII (May 21, 1874), 326–7; speeches by Schurz, e.g. December 15, 1870, January 30, 1872, September 24, 1876, in Bancroft (ed.), *Schurz,* II, 6–7, 322–3, III, 93–4; Woodward, *Reunion and Reaction,* 25. For an awestricken account of Radical state government in action, see Andrew Dickson White, *Autobiography* (2 vols., New York, 1914), I, 175–6.

51. *Nation,* XVIII (April 16, 1874), 247–8.

52. *Springfield Republican,* February 14, 1876, March 15, 1877; Wendell P. Garrison to William Lloyd Garrison, February 7, 1875, Wendell P. Garrison to Francis J. Garrison, November 7, 1876, Garrison Family Papers; *Nation,* XIX (October 29, 1874), 278–9; Riddleberger, *Julian,* 283–4. Bliss Perry, *Richard Henry Dana, 1851–1931* (Boston, 1933), 142, quotes the elder Dana advising his young son that civil service reform was "something more profound" than the question of civil rights.

53. *Nation,* XX (June 3, 1875), 372.

54. Riddleberger, *Julian,* 288–91. Conservative Southern whites used such terms as "Africanization," "barbarism," "black menace," and "carpetbag scoundrelism," to describe the Republican governments in the South. In the North, Pike wrote of "the overshadowing mass of black barbarism at the South," and described Negroes as "ignorant, narrowminded, vicious, worthless animals," in *The Prostrate State,* 48, 67.

55. "The New South," in Edwin D. Shurter (ed.), *The Complete Orations and Speeches of Henry W. Grady* (Norwood, Mass., 1910), 1–22. See also James Parton, "Antipathy to the Negro," *North American Review,* CXXVII (1878), 476–91; *Harper's Weekly,* XXXII (January 21, 1888), 38–9; *Nation,* XXXVII (October 18, 1883), 326; XLII (January 21, 1886), 51–2.

56. Pamphlet, Massachusetts Reform Club, 1890.

57. *Congressional Record,* 51 Cong., 1 Sess., 6543. See John A. Garraty, *Henry Cabot Lodge, A Biography* (New York, 1953), 117–22, for the story of the bill and its defeat. De Santis, *Republicans Face the Southern Question,* 196–215, is a perceptive analysis of Republican motives in casting aside the measure. Liberal reformers and "independents" shared many of these motives, and in some cases displayed more prejudice against the bill than did the party leaders.

58. *Nation,* L (January 23, 1890), 64; Schurz, October 20, 1890, in Ban-

croft (ed.), *Schurz*, V, 71–3; Cameron, August 9, 1890, interview with the Associated Press, quoted in James Ford Rhodes, *History of the United States from Hayes to McKinley, 1877–1896* (New York, 1919), 361.

59. Journal of Henry Cabot Lodge, January 5, 1891. I am indebted to Professor John A. Garraty of Columbia University for permission to examine the typescript copy of the Lodge Journal in his possession.

60. E. P. Clark, *Nation*, LV (August 25, 1892), 130–40.

61. Claude G. Bowers, *The Tragic Era: The Revolution After Lincoln* (Cambridge, Mass., 1929). As recently as 1961 a national news magazine, *U. S. News and World Report,* could present a feature story on integration in the South and its roots in history, under the headline "Another Tragic Era?"

CHAPTER 3   RELUCTANT REFORMERS

1. Tweed's story is best related in Alexander B. Callow, Jr., *The Tweed Ring* (New York, 1966), a perceptive study of machine politics. See also Seymour J. Mandelbaum, *Boss Tweed's New York* (New York, 1965), for insights into the changing nature of urban problems in the mid nineteenth century. Revealing analyses of politics as business in the period are found in Russel B. Nye, *Midwestern Progressive Politics* (East Lansing, Mich., 1951), ch. 1, and Thomas G. Cochran and William Miller, *The Age of Enterprise: A Social History of Industrial America* (New York, 1942), 154–63.

2. *Nation*, XVIII (April 9, 1874), 231.

3. Alexander Mackay-Smith to Godkin, April 21, 1890, Godkin Papers; entry, October 14, 1882, in vol. I of the "Minutes, etc., 1882–1892" [in manuscript] of the New York City Reform Club (New York Public Library). (Hereafter cited as New York Reform Club Minutes.)

4. John R. Young, *Around the World with General Grant* (2 vols., New York, 1879), II, 304.

5. Hans L. Trefousse, *Ben Butler: The South Called Him "Beast"* (New York, 1957), and Robert S. Holzman, *Stormy Ben Butler* (New York, 1954), are recent re-evaluations of Butler's role in war and politics. Butler's own account is *Autobiography and Personal Reminiscences of Major-General Benj. F. Butler: Butler's Book* (Boston, 1892).

6. XVIII (April 9, 1874), 230–31.

7. For example, Emerson appealed to George William Curtis to speak in Massachusetts and "save our district from the ignominy and mis-

chief of Butler"; Emerson to Curtis, November 7, 1868, George William Curtis Papers (Houghton Library, Harvard University); Samuel Shapiro, *Richard Henry Dana, Jr., 1815–1882* (East Lansing, Mich., 1961), 141–53, recounts the pitiful efforts of reformers to deal with Butler in a political campaign.

8. Bryce, *American Commonwealth,* II, 166–8, 583–4; Tilden to A. E. Burr, March 13, 1867 (copy), Tilden Papers.

9. "Phases of State Legislation," *Century,* VII (April 1885), 820–31; entry, December 6, 1886, vol. I, New York Reform Club Minutes.

10. "The Public Duty of Educated Men," June 27, 1877, in Norton (ed.), *Curtis Orations,* I, 266–9; similar sentiments were expressed by Godkin, *Nation,* II (April 19, 1866), 491–2.

11. *American Commonwealth,* II, 63–5.

12. Speech by Abram Hewitt, *Congressional Record,* 44 Cong., 1 Sess., 3338; Eric Goldman, *Charles J. Bonaparte, Patrician Reformer* (Baltimore, 1943), 29–30.

13. Norton to Godkin, July 26, 1872, Godkin Papers; A. G. Sedgwick, "Standards of Manners," *Nation,* XXXVII (July 5, 1883), 7–8.

14. Godkin to *London Daily News,* September 7, 1867, in Ogden, *Life of Godkin,* I, 313–22.

15. *Nation,* XXXVIII (May 1, 1884), 380–81; James C. Malin, "Roosevelt and the Elections of 1884 and 1888," *Mississippi Valley Historical Review,* XIV (1927), 23–38 (esp. 33); Theodore Roosevelt, *An Autobiography* (New York, 1913), 221–2; William Dudley Foulke, *A Hoosier Autobiography* (New York, 1922), 133–4.

16. *Springfield Republican,* November 1, 1872; Norton (ed.), *Curtis Orations,* I, 32; Lodge Diary, September 23, 1874, Henry Cabot Lodge Papers and Diary (Massachusetts Historical Society).

17. Moorfield Storey, *Politics as a Duty and as a Career* (New York, 1889), 6–7, 14–15; Howe, *Storey,* 34.

18. "The Unemployed Rich," *Nation,* XXVI (May 30, 1878), 354–5; *Nation,* II (April 19, 1866), 491–2.

19. Storey, *Politics as a Duty,* 28–9.

20. Curtis to Daniel Ricketson, December 21, 1869, Curtis Papers; Adams to Storey, quoted in Howe, *Storey,* 7; Roeliff Brinkerhoff, *Recollections of a Lifetime* (Cincinnati, 1904), 227; Cleveland to Wilson S. Bissell, November 13, 1884, in Allan Nevins (ed.), *Letters of Grover Cleveland* (Boston, 1933), 48; H. H. Haight to Horatio Seymour, July 31, 1868, Tilden Papers. See also Hayes to K. Rogers, January 17, 1872, in Rutherford B. Hayes Papers (Library of Congress).

21. Storey's autobiography (manuscript), quoted in Howe, *Storey,* 144;

entries, October 14, 27, 1882, vol. I, New York Reform Club Minutes; Circular, August 20, 1888, New York Reform Club.

22. New York Reform Club, *Officers and Committees, Members, Constitution, By-Laws, Rules* (New York, 1888–1913) ; entry, November 4, 1889, vol. II, New York Reform Club Minutes.

23. Mrs. John T. Sargent (ed.), *Sketches and Reminiscences of the Radical Club of Chestnut Street, Boston* (Boston, 1880) ; pamphlets on the Society for Political Education, David A. Wells Papers (New York Public Library) ; Fred B. Joyner, *David Ames Wells, Champion of Free Trade* (Cedar Rapids, Iowa, 1939), 147–50.

24. "Introductory Note" and Henry Villard, "Historical Sketch of Social Science," *Journal of Social Science,* I (1869), 1–10; "Officers and Members of the Association," ibid. 195–200; III (1871), 202–5; VI (1874), 3–11; Luther Lee Bernard and Jessie Bernard, *Origins of Sociology: The Social Science Movement in the United States* (New York, 1943), 527–607.

25. Irwin Unger, *The Greenback Era: A Social and Political History of American Finance, 1865–1879* (Princeton, 1964), 135–9, is an illuminating discussion of the "scientific" orientation of the association's founders.

26. New York *World,* April 15, 1883; New York *Tribune,* June 17, 1879.

27. In 1881 a group of "gentlemen from all over the country" met at fashionable Newport, of all places, to confer on reform matters. George W. Curtis to John D. Long, August 8, 1881, John D. Long Papers (Massachusetts Historical Society).

28. "Minutes, etc.," *Publication No. 1* (n.d.), City Club of New York, 10–14.

29. *Publication No. 1,* City Club of New York, 15–16; Allan Nevins, *The Evening Post: A Century of Journalism* (New York, 1922), 485–6; *Nation,* XLIV (April 21, 1892), 296–7; pamphlet, "What the City Club Has Done," (n.d.), City Club of New York.

30. Pamphlet, "What the City Club Has Done," City Club of New York; Nevins, *Evening Post,* 485–6.

31. *Monthly Bulletin No. 9,* July 1896, and *Annual Report, 1894–1895,* City Club of New York.

32. Curtis, "New York and Its Press," speech, June 8, 1881, in Norton (ed.), *Curtis Orations,* I, 309; Bancroft (ed.), *Schurz,* II, 55–6; Albert Bigelow Paine (ed.), *Mark Twain's Notebook* (New York, 1935), 202–3.

33. "The Public Duty of Educated Men," June 27, 1877, in Norton (ed.), *Curtis Orations,* I, 276.

34. "New York and Its Press," June 8, 1881; "The Public Duty of Educated Men," June 27, 1877, in Norton (ed.), *Curtis Orations*, I, 274–309.

35. Cyril Clemens (ed.), *Washington in 1868* (Webster Groves, Mo., 1943), 33–4; William Dean Howells (ed.), *Mark Twain's Speeches* (New York, 1923), "Taxes and Morals," 276–7; Albert Bigelow Paine (ed.), *Mark Twain's Autobiography* (2 vols., New York, 1924), II, 10–11.

36. "George William Curtis," an obituary essay, September 1, 1892, *Springfield Republican;* George L. Prentiss, *Our National Bane; or, The Dry Rot in American Politics* (New York, 1877), 62–3.

37. Sherman S. Rogers, "George William Curtis and Civil Service Reform," *Atlantic Monthly*, LXXI (1893), 15–25; Schurz, "Curtis," 622; Curtis, "Public Duty of Educated Men," *passim*, and "The Duty of the American Scholar," *passim*, in Norton (ed.), *Curtis Orations*, I; *Brooklyn Daily Eagle*, September 26, 1877.

38. Storey, *Politics as a Duty*, 7–8 et passim; Howe, *Storey*, 178 et passim.

39. Howe, *Storey*, 1–3.

40. Lodge Diary, January 16, 1878.

41. *Nation*, XVI (March 6, 1874), 160–61; Schurz to Godkin, March 31, 1871, in Bancroft (ed.), *Schurz*, II, 252–3; Charles Nordhoff to Schurz, April 17, 1872, Schurz Papers (MSS.); Greeley to Colfax, November 6, 1870, Greeley-Colfax Correspondence; Kenneth R. Andrews, *Nook Farm: Mark Twain's Hartford Circle* (Cambridge, Mass., 1950), 110–11.

42. *Nation*, IV (March 7, 1867), 191–2; VII (July 9, 1868), 24–5; John Bigelow to Sumner, November 2, 1870, Sumner Papers; Lodge Diary, April 22, 1876.

43. *Nation*, XIV (April 11, 1872), 236–7; XIX (November 19, 26, 1874), 328–9.

44. *Springfield Republican*, December 15, 1876.

45. *Nation*, L (May 22, 1890), 406; *The New York Times*, August 15, 1855.

46. Rollo Ogden, *Nation*, LIV (April 14, 1892), 278; Godkin, "Popular Government," in his *Problems of Modern Democracy* (New York, 1896), 72; *Nation*, XI (December 8, 1870), 380–81; Thomas F. Devlin, *Municipal Reform in the United States* (New York, 1896), 174.

47. Adams to David A. Wells, December 1, 1874, David Ames Wells Papers (Library of Congress); Henry H. Curran, *City Club of New York* (New York, 1906), 4–5; Curtis, "Machine Politics and the Remedy," May 20, 1880, in Norton (ed.), *Curtis Orations*, II, 157–60; Til-

den to ———, August 12, 1871, Tilden Papers; Bryce, *American Commonwealth,* II, 168–9.

48. Paine (ed.), *Mark Twain's Notebook,* 210; *Nation,* III (September 6, 1866), 188–9; VI (January 23, 1868), 68–9; Frederick J. Brown to Godkin, n.d., Godkin Papers; Wendell P. Garrison to William Lloyd Garrison, January 11, 1866, Garrison Family Papers.

49. Henry W. Bellows, *Civil Service Reform* (New York, 1877), 16; *Nation,* V (October 17, 1867), 314–15; Samuel J. Barrows, *Municipal Reform* (New York, 1888), 17; Wendell P. Garrison to William Lloyd Garrison, September 12, 1868, Garrison Family Papers; Schurz, *Reminiscences,* II, 101–4.

50. Schurz, "Curtis," 615; Lodge Diary, January 11, 1878; *Nation,* III (November 1, 1866), 341; XXII (May 11, 1876), 302–3; XXXII (June 9, 1881), 400–401; Norton (ed.), *Curtis Orations,* I, 340–41; Howe, *Storey,* 5.

CHAPTER 4   "SADLY HONEST-LOOKING GENTLEMEN"

1. *Nation,* L (May 22, 1890), 406. Bryce commented on the paucity of issues in American politics on which parties would take a stand. See *American Commonwealth,* II, 27–9.

2. Schurz, "The Road to Peace," September 19, 1868, in Bancroft (ed.), *Schurz,* I, 464–8; *Springfield Republican,* July 8, 1868.

3. Numerous expressions of fear about tampering with the currency are found in the papers of public men in this period. See, e.g., Charles Eliot Norton to Sumner, February 7, 1868, Edward Atkinson to Sumner, June 22, 1868, Sumner Papers; Greeley to Colfax, February 25, 1866, Greeley-Colfax Correspondence; Norton to Godkin, February 6, 1868, Godkin Correspondence.

4. *Nation,* III (October 11, 1866), 291–2. Godkin modified his aversion to "military men" in politics after hearing General James A. Garfield defend sound currency. *Nation,* VI (June 4, 1868), 445–6.

5. Storey to his mother, November 25, 1867, quoted in Howe, *Storey,* 42–3; *Springfield Republican,* May 22, 1868; Norton to Godkin, March 6, 1869, Godkin Correspondence; Atkinson to Nordhoff, June 20, 1868 (copy), Edward Atkinson Papers (New York Public Library).

6. Norton to Godkin, May 30, 1868, Godkin Papers.

7. Curtis to Norton, March 13, 1869, Curtis Papers.

8. *Harper's Weekly,* XV (March 25, 1871), 258; Curtis to Higginson, December 29, 1871, Thomas Wentworth Higginson Papers (Houghton

Library, Harvard University); *Springfield Republican*, January 1, 1872.

9. *Nation*, XI (April 28, 1870), 266. Accounts of the Grant administration are Allan Nevins, *Hamilton Fish: The Inner History of the Grant Administration* (New York, 1936); William B. Hesseltine, *Ulysses S. Grant, Politician* (New York, 1935); and Josephson, *The Politicos*, 61–213.

10. *Nation*, XI (November 17, 1870), 322; Curtis to Norton, June 26, 1870, Curtis Papers; White, *Trumbull*, 341; *New York Standard*, April 1, 1872; Greeley to Colfax, November 6, 1870, Greeley-Colfax Correspondence; *Springfield Republican*, January 2, 1872.

11. *Springfield Republican*, July 23, November 25, 1870; May 5, 1871.

12. Schurz to Godkin, March 31, 1871, Godkin Papers; Curtis to Norton, June 30, 1872, Norton Papers; *Springfield Republican*, December 1, 1870

13. John Bigelow to Sumner, November 2, 1870, Justin S. Morrill to Sumner, September 10, 1870, Sumner Papers; Curtis to Norton, June 26, 1870, Curtis Papers; Curtis to David A. Wells, August 31, 1871, Wells Papers; *Nation*, XIV (March 7, 1872), 148–9; *Springfield Republican*, January 21, 1870.

14. Norma L. Peterson, *Freedom and Franchise: The Political Career of B. Gratz Brown* (Columbia, Mo., 1965), is a fresh look at the intricacies of Missouri politics. See also Thomas S. Barclay, *Liberal Republican Movement in Missouri, 1865–1871* (Columbia, Mo., 1926). The only study of Liberal Republicanism as a national movement is Earle D. Ross, *The Liberal Republican Movement* (New York, 1919). Though an excellent descriptive account, this work does not probe the motives of Liberal leaders, nor does it examine critically the non-reform elements in the party. Very valuable in this respect is Matthew T. Downey, "Horace Greeley and the Politicians; The Liberal Republican Convention in 1872," *Journal of American History*, LIII (March 1967), 727–50.

15. New York *Tribune*, December 13, 1870.

16. Joyner, *Wells*, 117–18; Nevins, *Evening Post*, 394–5; Ross, *Liberal Republican Movement*, 14–15.

17. See also Ross, *Liberal Republican Movement*, 17–28.

18. *Springfield Republican*, November 17, 1871; *Cincinnati Commercial*, May 3, 1871; Schurz, "Address to the People of Missouri," September 11, 1870, in Bancroft (ed.), *Schurz*, I, 511; Schurz, Senate speech, December 15, 1870, *Congressional Globe*, 41 Cong., 3 Sess., 127–8; Schurz to J. D. Cox, November 14, 1871 (copy), Schurz Papers; Schurz to Godkin, March 3, 1871, Godkin Papers.

19. *Springfield Republican,* April 20, 1872; Col. A. K. McClure, ibid. January 24, 1872.

20. Nordhoff to Schurz, April 17, 1872, Schurz Papers; Julian, *Recollections,* 337; Riddleberger, *Julian,* 262–73; White to Sumner, Edward Atkinson to Sumner, both April 13, 1872, Sumner Papers.

21. Curtis to Norton, June 30, 1872, Norton Papers; *Harper's Weekly,* xvi (November 2, 1872), 843.

22. Nevins, *Evening Post,* 395; *Nation,* xiv (March 7, 1872), 148–9, and throughout the ensuing campaign.

23. Atkinson to Sumner, April 3, 8, 1874, Sumner Papers; *Springfield Republican,* March 16, 1872; *Chicago Tribune,* April 27, 1872.

24. Speech, May 2, 1872, in Bancroft (ed.), *Schurz,* ii, 354–61; Kirk H. Porter (comp.), *National Party Platforms* (New York, 1924), 77–8. Ross, *Liberal Republican Movement,* ch. 3, reviews the proceedings, as do Claude M. Fuess, *Carl Schurz, Reformer* (New York, 1932), and Josephson, *The Politicos,* 158–64; but the best account of the reformers' defeat is Downey, "Greeley and the Politicians." The official record is *Proceedings of the Liberal Republican Convention in Cincinnati* (New York, 1872).

25. Godkin to M. A. DeWolfe Howe, November 28, 1899, Godkin Papers; Greeley to Colfax, November 6, 1870, Greeley-Colfax Correspondence; Curtis to Higginson, December 30, 1871, Higginson Papers. Biographies of Greeley, none outstanding, include Henry L. Stoddard, *Horace Greeley, Printer, Editor, Crusader* (New York, 1946), and William H. Hale, *Horace Greeley, Voice of the People* (New York, 1950). Greeley's own *Recollections of a Busy Life* (New York, 1868) provides insight into the man's background and personality.

26. Norton to Godkin, July 26, 1872, Godkin Papers; Garrison to Francis J. Garrison, May 6, 1872, Garrison Family Papers; Julian, *Recollections,* 337–52; Riddleberger, *Julian,* 271–3; Nordhoff to Gordon L. Ford, May 7, 1872, Charles Nordhoff Papers (New York Public Library); Merriam, *Bowles,* 187–8; Atkinson to Schurz, June 1, 1872, Schurz Papers; *Springfield Republican,* November 4, 1872; *Chicago Tribune,* May 6, 1872; White to Trumbull, May 4, 1872, Trumbull Papers.

27. Schurz to Bowles, May 11, 1872, in Bancroft (ed.), *Schurz,* ii, 396. The correspondence between Schurz and Greeley is in Bancroft (ed.), *Schurz,* ii, 370–77, and is further elaborated upon in Schurz, *Reminiscences,* iii, 350–51.

28. Ross, *Liberal Republican Movement,* ch. 4; New York *Tribune,* May 27, 31, 1872; *Springfield Republican,* June 14, 1872; *Nation,* xiv (June 27, 1872), 413; Schurz to Godkin, May 20, June 23, November 23,

1872, Godkin to Schurz, June 28, 1872, Godkin Papers; Godkin to Schurz, May 19, 1872, Schurz Papers.

29. Grant to Conkling, July 9, July 15, 1872, Roscoe Conkling Papers (Manuscript Division, Library of Congress).

30. Curtis to Dana, September 2, 1872, Dana Papers; *Nation*, xv (July 18, August 15, 1872), 36–7, 100–101; Atkinson to Sumner, April 8, 1872, Sumner Papers; Forbes to Sumner, August 10, 1872, in Hughes (ed.), *Forbes Letters*, ii, 178–83; Curtis to Norton, June 30, September 6, 1872, Curtis Papers; *Harper's Weekly*, xvi (May 18, 1872), 386; *Springfield Republican*, May 11, August 24, September 3, October 22, November 4, 18, 1872.

31. McPherson, "Grant or Greeley? The Abolitionist Dilemma in the Election of 1872," *American Historical Review*, lxxi (1965), 43–61; Trumbull to Horace White, April 24, 1872 (copy), Trumbull Papers. Ross, *Liberal Republican Movement*, 184–8, notes the overwhelming financial advantage of the Republicans.

32. Riddleberger, "The Break in the Radical Ranks," 148, suggests that many "Liberal Radicals" were really Democrats at heart and would have been Democrats in name in the 1840's and 1850's if the anti-slavery crusade had not absorbed them.

33. John Murray Forbes to Bristow, January 15, 1876, Schurz to Bristow, February 15, 1876, Benjamin H. Bristow Papers (Manuscript Division, Library of Congress).

34. "The Issues of 1874, Especially in Missouri," September 24, 1874, in Bancroft (ed.), *Schurz*, iii, 93–4.

35. Adams to David A. Wells, November 13, 1873, Wells Papers.

36. Cater (ed.), *Adams and His Friends*, 67.

37. Brooks Adams, "The Platform of the New Party," *North American Review*, cxix (July 1874), 33–60; New York *Tribune*, January 31, 1875; Lawrence Shaw Mayo (ed.), *America of Yesterday, as Reflected in the Journal of John Davis Long* (Boston, 1923), 134.

38. Lodge Diary, June 23, 1875, February 24, March 5, 1876; New York *Tribune*, January 31, 1875; Lodge to Schurz, December 13, 1875, Schurz Papers; Garraty, *Lodge*, 41–2. Garraty notes that the Lodge Diary is not always a reliable indication of the Massachusetts politician's feelings, for Lodge tampered with some of the original entries in his later years.

39. Schurz to W. M. Grosvenor, July 16, 1875, Schurz to Samuel Bowles, January 4, 16, 1876, Schurz to Bristow, February 15, 1876, Bristow to Schurz, February 18, 1876, in Bancroft (ed.), *Schurz*, iii, 156, 218–22; *Nation*, xxii (June 1, 1876), 344.

40. Schurz to Francis A. Walker, April 6, 1876, Schurz to "a Republican,"

April 22, 1876, in Bancroft (ed.), *Schurz,* III, 228–9, 233–9; Dorman B. Eaton to Curtis, May 13, 1876, Curtis Papers. Associated with Schurz in issuing the call were Horace White, William Cullen Bryant, Henry Cabot Lodge, Theodore D. Woolsey, and Alexander Bullock.

41. *Nation,* XXII (May 18, 1876), 313; *New York Commercial Advertiser,* May 17, 1876.

42. May 16, 1878, in Bancroft (ed.), *Schurz,* III, 240–48.

43. *Nation,* XXII (June 22, 1876), 393; Josephson, *Politicos,* 213–16; Paul L. Haworth, *The Hayes-Tilden Disputed Election of 1876* (Cleveland, 1906), 17–25; Porter (comp.), *Platforms,* 94–8.

44. Harry Barnard, *Rutherford B. Hayes and His America* (Indianapolis, Ind., and New York, 1954), 270–74, 311, *et passim;* Vincent P. De Santis, "President Hayes's Southern Policy," *Journal of Southern History,* XXI (1955), 476–94.

45. Nevins, *Hewitt,* 304; Haworth, *Hayes-Tilden Election,* 26–35; Porter (comp.), *Platforms,* 86–91; Tilden note, probably to Kelly, 1873, in John Bigelow (ed.), *The Letters and Literary Memorials of Samuel J. Tilden* (2 vols., New York, 1908), I, 320; Josephson, *Politicos,* 216–20.

46. *Springfield Republican,* February 9, 1876; *Nation,* XXI (October 7, 1875), 224–5; Merriam, *Bowles,* 247–8; Nevins, *Evening Post,* 400–405.

47. *Harper's Weekly,* XX (July 15, 1876), 570, my italics; Curtis to Hayes, June 30, 1876, Hayes Papers (Library of Congress); Gordon Milne, *George William Curtis and the Genteel Tradition* (Bloomington, Ind., 1956), 151–2; Richard Lowitt, *A Merchant Prince of the Nineteenth Century: William E. Dodge* (New York, 1954), 323–4. Milne's excellent study of Curtis's literary career is of limited use to the political historian, although it provides fruitful insights into the man's character and personality.

48. Norton to Curtis, November 3, 1876, Norton Papers; *Springfield Republican,* November 6, 1876; Nevins, *Evening Post,* 400–405; Storey's Autobiography (in manuscript), quoted in Howe, *Storey,* 146; Nordhoff to Gordon L. Ford, September [?], 1876, Nordhoff Papers.

49. Howells, *Sketch of the Life and Character of Rutherford B. Hayes (etc.)* (Boston, 1876); Mark Twain to Howells, August 9, September 14, 1876, in Paine (ed.), *Mark Twain's Letters,* I, 281, 286; Paine (ed.), *Mark Twain's Notebook,* 130; Andrews, *Nook Farm,* 110–14 *et passim;* Howells to Charles Dudley Warner, August 23, 1876, in Mildred Howells (ed.), *Life in Letters of William Dean Howells* (2 vols., New York, 1928), I, 226.

50. *Nation,* XXIII (July 6, 1876), 4–5; Godkin to Norton, July 14, 1876, Norton Papers.

51. *Nation,* XXIII (August 10, 1876), 84–5.

52. *Nation,* XXIII (October 19, 1876), 242–3.

53. Schurz to Hayes, June 21, 1876, Schurz to Adams, July 9, 1876, in Bancroft (ed.), *Schurz,* III, 248–52, 258–9.

54. July 22, 1876, in Bancroft (ed.), *Schurz,* III, 261–80.

55. The extensive pre-election correspondence between Hayes and Schurz is published, in part, in Bancroft (ed.), *Schurz,* III, 248–339.

56. See correspondence between Schurz and Charles Francis Adams, Jr., Alphonso Taft, and A. T. Wickoff, July–November, 1875, in Bancroft (ed.), *Schurz,* III, 156–217; Schurz, *Reminiscences,* III, 362–3, 368.

57. Schurz to Murat Halstead, February 19, 1877, Halstead to Schurz, February 20, 1877, Hayes to Schurz, February 25, 1877, Schurz to Hayes, February 26, 1877, in Bancroft (ed.), *Schurz,* III, 397–9, 402–5; Schurz, *Reminiscences,* III, 373–5. John Bigelow, in his edition of the *Tilden Letters,* II, 430–32, makes the cabinet appointment part of a great conspiracy between Hayes and Schurz.

58. Peterson, *Freedom and Franchise,* views Schurz with a keen, skeptical eye.

59. Garraty, *Lodge,* 44–8; Charles Francis Adams, Jr., to Schurz, July 11, 1876, Schurz Papers.

60. Adams to Charles Milnes Gaskell, June 14, 1876; Adams to Lodge, June 19, 24, August 5, 31, September 4, 1876, in Worthington C. Ford (ed.), *Letters of Henry Adams (1858–1891)* (2 vols., Boston and New York, 1930), I, 288–90, 295–9.

61. "The 'Independents' in the Canvass," *North American Review,* CXXIII (October 1876), 426–67. On p. 426 the publisher announced a change of editors because of "differences" in political views.

62. Schurz, "Address to the People," May 16, 1878, in Bancroft (ed.), *Schurz,* III, 240–48.

63. *Nation,* XXII (May 25, 1876), 327.

64. Hayes's letter of acceptance, July 8, 1876, in Charles Richard Williams, *The Life of Rutherford Birchard Hayes* (2 vols., Boston and New York, 1914), I, 460–62; Hayes to Schurz, June 27, 1876, Schurz to Hayes, July 5, 1876, in Bancroft (ed.), *Schurz,* III, 253–8.

65. Edward Sparks, *National Development, 1877–1885* (New York, 1907), 117.

66. Barnard, *Hayes,* 474–8; Flick, *Tilden,* 429–38.

67. *Springfield Republican,* April 16, 1880; Lea to Godkin, January 8, 1880, Godkin Papers.

68. George F. Hoar, in his *Autobiography of Seventy Years* (2 vols., New York, 1903), I, 388, recalled that he had countered Edmunds's disclaimer of presidential ambitions by reminding the Vermonter of "the

fun you would have vetoing bills." Edmunds "smiled, and his countenance beamed all over with satisfaction at the idea, and he replied, with great feeling: 'Well, that would be good fun.'"

69. Schurz to Curtis, December 29, 1879, Schurz to Lodge, January 3, May 23, 1880, in Bancroft (ed.), *Schurz*, III, 454–96, 506–7; *Nation*, XXIX (August 21, September 11, 25, 1879), 122–3, 175–6, 206.

70. *Nation*, XXX (June 17, 1880), 448–50; Theodore Clarke Smith, *The Life and Letters of James Abram Garfield* (2 vols., New Haven, 1925), II, 943ff.; Charles R. Williams (ed.), *Diary and Letters of Rutherford Birchard Hayes* (5 vols., Columbus, Ohio, 1922–26), III, 600–601; Josephson, *Politicos*, 277–87.

71. Bellows to Hancock, June 25, 1880, Henry W. Bellows Papers (Massachusetts Historical Society).

72. Porter (comp.), *Platforms*, 99–101, 108–12; *Springfield Republican*, June 7, 1880; Garfield to George F. Hoar and the Republican National Convention, July 12, 1880, in Burke A. Hinsdale (ed.), *The Works of James Abram Garfield* (2 vols., Boston, 1883), II, 782–7.

73. John Sherman, *Recollections of Forty Years* (2 vols., Chicago, 1895), II, 779; Curtis to Henry W. Bellows, July 14, 1880, Bellows Papers.

74. Schurz to Lodge, June 22, 1880, Schurz to Garfield, July 20, 1880; in Bancroft (ed.), *Schurz*, III, 507–8, IV, 1–4.

75. Garfield to Schurz, July 22, 1880, quoted in Smith, *Garfield*, II, 1004–5.

76. *Nation*, VI (June 4, 1868), 445–6; XXX (June 10, 17, 24, 1880), 427, 449, 467–8; XXXI (July 1, 15, 22, 1880), 4–6, 36, 54; Smith, *Garfield*, II, 720.

77. Garfield to Hinsdale, July 25, 1880, in Mary L. Hinsdale (ed.), *Garfield-Hinsdale Letters: Correspondence Between James Abram Garfield and Burke Aaron Hinsdale* (Ann Arbor, Mich., 1949), 454–6.

78. Smith, *Garfield*, II, 718–19, 721–2; Garfield to Hinsdale, May 20, 1879, in Hinsdale (ed.), *Garfield-Hinsdale Letters*, 416–17.

79. Albert Bigelow Paine, *Mark Twain, A Biography: The Personal and Literary Life of Samuel Langhorne Clemens* (3 vols., New York, 1912), II, 391; Henry Adams to Lodge, October 30, 1880, in Ford (ed.), *Adams Letters*, I, 327–8; Schurz to Garfield, November 3, 1880, in Bancroft (ed.), *Schurz*, IV, 50.

80. Schurz to Garfield, January 2, 16, February 22, 1881, in Bancroft (ed.), *Schurz*, IV, 78–88, 115; *Nation*, XXXI (November 18, 1880), 352–4; Norton to Richard Henry Dana, February 27, 1881, Dana Papers; Blaine to Garfield, December 10, 1880, Garfield to Blaine, December 19, 1880, in Gail Hamilton (Mary Abigail Dodge), *Biography of James G. Blaine* (Norwich, Conn., 1895), 491–3.

CHAPTER 5   THE MYOPIC MUGWUMPS

1. The events and personalities of this period are treated in detail in the biographies cited here, as well as in such interpretive studies as Josephson, *The Politicos,* and Hofstadter, *American Political Tradition* and *The Age of Reform* (New York, 1955) . Geoffrey Blodgett, *The Gentle Reformers: Massachusetts Democrats in the Cleveland Era* (Cambridge, Mass., 1966) , though concentrating on Massachusetts Mugwumps, gives insight into the entire period. The only comprehensive study of the election of 1884 is Harrison C. Thomas, *The Return of the Democratic Party to Power in 1884* (New York, 1919) , a work valuable for its many facts, even though they are not always entirely accurate. See also J. Rogers Hollingsworth, *The Whirligig of Politics: The Democracy of Cleveland and Bryan* (Chicago, 1963) , chs. 1 and 2.
2. Carl Schurz to J. W. Hoag, June 29, 1884, in Bancroft (ed.) , *Schurz,* IV, 210–12.
3. Blaine was one of the few who ever successfully challenged the floor leadership of Thaddeus Stevens during the immediate postwar years. Edward Stanwood, *James Gillespie Blaine* (Boston and New York, 1905) , overestimates Blaine's radicalism during Reconstruction. David S. Muzzey, *James G. Blaine: A Political Idol of Other Days* (New York, 1934) , more accurately assesses Blaine's role. Blaine's autobiography (or, more correctly, his personal commentary on postwar politics) , *Twenty Years of Congress: From Lincoln to Garfield* (2 vols., Norwich, Conn., 1884–86) , was written after he had been dismissed as Arthur's Secretary of State and while he was preparing for the election of 1884. Nevertheless, the book is a valuable document on men and events of the period.
4. Blaine was the first man in Congress to attack the inflationary proposals of Butler and Pendleton in 1867. Moreover, his equivocal stand on tariff reform prevented either the extreme protectionists or the "free-traders" from foisting their views on a Republican party which, in the 1870's and early 1880's at least, steered a middle course on the question. See Muzzey, *Blaine,* 54–7; Stanwood, *Blaine,* 121–2, 130–31. Blaine set forth his views on civil service reform in *Twenty Years of Congress,* II, 644–51, and in correspondence with Garfield. Richard Hofstadter's brief sketch of Blaine in *American Political Tradition,* 172–4, is considerably less perceptive than Hofstadter's assessments of

other American politicians. Blaine certainly was evasive on many political issues, but he was not a facile, dishonest bounder. He was an
ambitious politician rather well attuned to the political temper of
postwar Americans—probably a majority of them.

5. Adams to Godkin, February 13, [1884], Godkin Papers.
6. Charles Nordhoff to Worthington C. Ford, April 17, 1884, Nordhoff
   Papers.
7. There is no satisfactory full-length biography of Cleveland. Allan
   Nevins, *Grover Cleveland: A Study in Courage* (New York, 1932),
   could have been written by a nineteenth-century liberal reformer. The
   author rationalizes questionable incidents in Cleveland's career and
   describes some of his subject's most obtuse actions as examples of
   courage. Robert McElroy, *Grover Cleveland: The Man and the Statesman* (2 vols., New York, 1923) is valuable chiefly because it contains
   excerpts from Cleveland's correspondence. Horace S. Merrill, *Bourbon
   Leader: Grover Cleveland and the Democratic Party* (Boston, 1957),
   although lacking detail, is a reasonable, brief evaluation.
8. Mark D. Hirsch, *William C. Whitney, Modern Warwick* (New York,
   1948), 180–87; Merrill, *Bourbon Leader*, 19–21.
9. Merrill, *Bourbon Leader*, 17.
10. Roosevelt to Walter Sage Hubbell, August 14, 1884, in Elting E. Mor-
    ison (ed.), *The Letters of Theodore Roosevelt* (8 vols., Cambridge,
    Mass., 1951–54), I, 77–9; Merrill, *Bourbon Leader*, 41–2.
11. Cleveland to Edgar K. Apgar, August 29, 1884, Cleveland to Wilson
    S. Bissell, April 22, 1883, Cleveland to Charles S. Fairchild, March 17,
    1884, Cleveland to Daniel Manning, June 30, 1884, in Allan Nevins
    (ed.), *Letters of Grover Cleveland, 1850–1908* (Boston and New York,
    1933), 15–16, 21, 30–31, 35–6.
12. *Appletons' Annual Cyclopaedia, 1884*, 766–7; *The New York Times*,
    February 23, 24, 1884.
13. *Nation*, XXXVII (November 29, 1883), 439; XXXVIII (April 24, 1884),
    118; *Harper's Weekly*, XXVIII (February 23, 1884), 118; Schurz to
    P. B. Plumb, May 12, 1884, in Bancroft (ed.), *Schurz*, IV, 201–202;
    The New York Times, April 15, 1884. Blodgett, *The Gentle Reform-
    ers*, ch. 1, is a thorough examination of the New England reformers'
    role in the election of Cleveland.
14. *Harper's Weekly*, XXVIII (March 15, 1884), 166; *Nation*, XXXVIII
    (March 6, 1884), 201.
15. Roosevelt to Lodge, May 26, 1884, in Morison (ed.), *Roosevelt Let-
    ters*, I, 70; Henry Cabot Lodge (ed.), *Selections from the Correspon-
    dence of Theodore Roosevelt and Henry Cabot Lodge, 1884–1918* (2

vols., New York, 1925), I, 11–12; Claude M. Fuess, "Carl Schurz, Henry Cabot Lodge, and the Campaign of 1884," *New England Quarterly*, V (1932), 467–8; Howe, *Storey*, 148–9; *Harper's Weekly*, XXVIII (February 2, 1884), 70; *The New York Times*, May 9, 1884.

16. Wells to Richard Rogers Bowker, May 7, 1883, January 13, 1884, Richard Rogers Bowker Papers (New York Public Library).

17. *Official Proceedings of the Republican National Convention, 1884* (Minneapolis, 1903), 126–8 *et passim; Appletons' Annual Cyclopaedia, 1884,* 768–9.

18. Quoted in Joseph B. Foraker, *Notes of a Busy Life* (2 vols., Cincinnati, 1916–17), I, 167–8.

19. Roosevelt to Anna Roosevelt, June 8, 1884, in Morison (ed.), *Roosevelt Letters,* I, 70–72; Foraker, *Notes,* I, 168.

20. Porter (comp.), *Platforms,* 132–6.

21. *Nation,* XXXVIII (June 12, 1884), 495; *The New York Times,* June 13, 1884; *Appletons' Annual Cyclopaedia, 1884,* 770; *Harper's Weekly,* XXVIII (June 14, 1884), 374.

22. Schurz to J. W. Hoag, June 29, 1884, Schurz to G. W. M. Pittman, June 15, 1884, in Bancroft (ed.), *Schurz,* IV, 204–5, 210–12; *Harper's Weekly,* XXVIII (June 21, 1884), 390.

23. *The New York Times,* June 13, 1884; Eliot, quoted in *The New York Times,* June 14, 1884; Storey, quoted in *Harper's Weekly,* XXVIII (June 28, 1884), 406.

24. *Official Proceedings of the National Democratic Convention, 1884* (New York, 1884), 203–6; *Appletons' Annual Cyclopaedia, 1884,* 770–73.

25. Porter (comp.), *Platforms,* 116–23.

26. *Official Proceedings . . . Democratic Convention, 1884,* 203–6; *Nation,* XXXIX (July 17, August 7, 1884), 44, 102.

27. *Official Proceedings . . . Democratic Convention, 1884,* 285–6; *Springfield Republican,* July 21, 1884.

28. *Official Proceedings . . . Democratic Convention, 1884,* 293–6.

29. *The New York Times,* August 20, 1884.

30. When Barnum went to the Senate in 1876, Godkin charged that he had "bought up" and owned the state of Connecticut. *Nation,* XXII (May 18, 1876), 314.

31. Carleton Putnam, *Theodore Roosevelt: The Formative Years, 1858–1886* (New York, 1958), 379–80, 491; Roosevelt to Lodge, August 12, 1884, in Lodge (ed.), *Roosevelt-Lodge Correspondence,* I, 5–7; Morison (ed.), *Roosevelt Letters,* I, 76n; DeAlva S. Alexander, *The Political History of the State of New York, 1774–1905* (4 vols., New York,

1906–23), IV, 7, 16–19; Everett P. Wheeler, *Sixty Years of American Life* (New York, 1917), 415; *Harper's Weekly*, XXVIII (July 19, 1884), 458.

32. *Appletons' Annual Cyclopaedia, 1884*, 773; *The New York Times*, July 22, July 23, 1884; *Harper's Weekly*, XXVIII (August 2, 1884), 494; Rhodes, *United States, 1877–1896*, 217n.

33. Roosevelt to Richard Rogers Bowker, October 31, 1884, in Morison (ed.), *Roosevelt Letters*, I, 85; "The Record of the Democratic Party," speech, in Theodore Roosevelt, *Works* (24 vols., New York, 1923–26), XIV, 52.

34. July 22, 1884.

35. Atkinson to William Fowler, December 15, 1884, Atkinson Papers; Adams to John Hay, July 3, 1884, Adams to Charles Milnes Gaskell, September 21, 1884, in Ford (ed.), *Henry Adams Letters*, I, 359–60; Goldman, *Bonaparte*, 22.

36. Twain to Thomas Bailey Aldrich, November 29, 1884, Thomas Bailey Aldrich Papers (Houghton Library, Harvard University); Albert Bigelow Paine (ed.), *Mark Twain's Speeches* (New York, 1910), 120–30; Andrews, *Nook Farm*, 114–16; Twain to Howells, September 17, 1884, in Paine (ed.), *Mark Twain's Letters*, II, 445.

37. Paine (ed.), *Mark Twain's Speeches*, 120–30.

38. *Nation*, XXXIX (July 17, August 14, October 23, 1884), 46, 126, 346–7; New York *Evening Post*, July 31, October 11, 13, November 4, 1884.

39. *Nation*, XXXIX (October 2, 1884), 281; McElroy, *Cleveland*, I, 98; Hirsch, *Whitney*, 227–8, 238–9, 244; Herbert L. Satterlee, *J. Pierpont Morgan: An Intimate Portrait* (New York, 1939), 191, 218; Frederick Lewis Allen, *The Great Pierpont Morgan* (New York, 1949), 75–6; Joseph G. Pyle, *The Life of James J. Hill* (2 vols., New York, 1926), I, 425–7; William C. Hudson, *Random Recollections of an Old Political Reporter* (New York, 1911), 240–41. Actually, the Whitney-Manning machine was the successor to Tilden's earlier machine.

40. *Harper's Weekly*, XXVIII (June 14, 1884), 374; "Cleveland and Honesty" (press clipping, October 17, 1884), and "Address" (press clipping, July 23, 1884), George William Curtis Papers and Scrapbooks (Houghton Library, Harvard University); Carl Schurz, "George William Curtis, Friend of the Republic," *McClure's Magazine*, XXIII (1904), 614–23.

41. *Harper's Weekly*, XXVIII (July 19, 1884), 458; "Address," Curtis Papers and Scrapbooks.

42. Roosevelt to Bowker, October 31, 1884, in Morison (ed.), *Roosevelt Letters*, I, 85–6; Howells to Twain [n.d.], quoted in Paine (ed.),

Mark Twain's Letters, II, 444–5; *Nation,* XXXIX (August 7, October 23, 1884) , 106–7, 346–7.

43. *Nation,* XXXIX (September 18, 1884) , 238; Foraker, *Notes of a Busy Life,* I, 171–2; Perry, *Dana,* 128–9.

44. White, *Autobiography,* I, 208; *Nation,* XXIII (July 6, 1876) , 1.

45. *Nation,* XXXIX (July 24, September 4, 1884) , 61, 68, 185; *The New York Times,* August 19, 1884; Garrison to Samuel May, August 12, 1884, Garrison Family Papers; Hoar, quoted in Frederick H. Gillett, *George Frisbie Hoar* (Boston and New York, 1934) , 289–91.

46. Hoar, *Autobiography,* I, 408.

47. Roosevelt to Lodge, June 18, 1884, in Morison (ed.) , *Roosevelt Letters,* I, 74–5; Lodge Diary, March 20, May 30, 1885.

48. Schurz to Lodge, July 12, 1884, in Bancroft (ed.) , *Schurz,* IV, 215–18.

49. Lodge to Schurz, July 14, 1884, Schurz to Lodge, July 16, 1884, in Bancroft (ed.) , *Schurz,* IV, 218–22.

50. *The New York Times,* August 19, 1884; New York *Herald,* July 16, 1884; *Nation,* XXXIX (July 14, August 21, 28, October 16, 1884) , 62, 150, 165, 320; see also Howe, *Storey,* 155–6.

51. Roosevelt to Lodge, June 18, July 28, August 24, 1884, Roosevelt to Anna Roosevelt, September 20, 1884, in Morison (ed.) , *Roosevelt Letters,* I, 74–6, 79–80, 81–2.

52. Roosevelt to Bowker, October 31, 1884, in Morison (ed.) , *Roosevelt Letters,* I, 85–6; "The Independents Who Would Not Bolt," "The National Issues of 1884," and "The Record of the Democratic Party," speeches, in Roosevelt, *Works,* XIV, 41–57; Malin, "Roosevelt and the Elections of 1884 and 1888," 33.

53. *Nation,* XXXIX (November 2, 20, 1884) , 386, 387, 408.

54. Lodge Diary, December 23, 1890, January 1, April 4, 1891; Lodge to Smalley [?], February 9, 1893, John T. Morse to Lodge, February 26, 1903, Lodge to Morse, February 28, 1903, Lodge Papers; *Congressional Record,* 53 Cong., 2 Sess., 4528.

55. Lodge to Barrett Wendell, December 26, 1906, Lodge to James Ford Rhodes, January 18, 1909, Lodge Papers; Roosevelt to Lodge, May 15, 1885, in Morison (ed.) , *Roosevelt Letters,* I, 90; Roosevelt to William Dudley Foulke, January 4, 1907, quoted in Foulke, *Hoosier Autobiography,* 133–4.

56. *Nation,* XXXIX (November 13, 1884) , 406, 413–14; *Harper's Weekly,* XXVIII (November 15, 1884) , 748–9; Curtis to Arthur Hobart, November 18, 1884, Henry H. Edes Papers (Massachusetts Historical Society) ; Howe, *Storey,* 159–60; Schurz to George Fred. Williams, November 16, 1884, in Bancroft (ed.) , *Schurz,* IV, 290.

57. *Appletons' Annual Cyclopaedia, 1884,* 774–5; *Nation,* XXXIX (November 13, 1884), 411; Norton to James Russell Lowell, November 16, 1884, in Sara Norton and M. A. DeWolfe Howe (eds.), *Letters of Charles Eliot Norton* (2 vols., Boston and New York, 1913), II, 165–6.
58. New York *Herald,* November 14, 1884.
59. Williams (ed.), *Hayes Diary,* IV, 172–4; Sherman, *Recollections,* I, 888; Hoar, *Autobiography,* I, 408; Thomas, *Return of the Democratic Party,* 228–31; Edward Stanwood, "Election Superstitions and Fallacies," *Atlantic Monthly,* CX (1912), 553–62, esp. 559; Stanwood, *Blaine,* 291; William G. Rice and Francis Lynde Stetson, "Was New York's Vote Stolen?" *North American Review,* CXCIX (1914), 79–92.
60. Blaine to Stephen B. Elkins, July 27, 1884, quoted in Stanwood, *Blaine,* 285; Donald B. Chidsey, *The Gentleman from New York: A Life of Roscoe Conkling* (New Haven, 1935), 373–7; Louis J. Lang (ed.), *The Autobiography of Thomas Collier Platt* (New York, 1910), 180–84.

CHAPTER 6   THE NATURE OF THINGS

1. Godkin, "The Labor Crisis," *North American Review,* CV (1867), 177–213; Tilden to the Democratic State Committee of New York, August, 1873, Tilden Papers.
2. Sidney Fine, *Laissez-Faire and the General-Welfare State: A Study of Conflict in American Thought, 1865–1901* (Ann Arbor, Mich., 1956), is a distinguished study of the impact of industrialism on laissez-faire. See esp. chs. I and III. Insights into the businessman's mind and estimates of industrialism's influence on postwar society are provided in Thomas G. Cochran and William Miller, *The Age of Enterprise: A Social History of Industrial America* (New York, 1942), chs. 7–11; and by Edward C. Kirkland, *Business in the Gilded Age,* and *Dream and Thought in the Business Community, 1860–1900* (Ithaca, N.Y., 1956). Still immensely valuable, too, is Charles A. and Mary R. Beard, *The Rise of American Civilization* (2 vols., New York, 1927; rev. edn., 2 vols. in 1, New York, 1946), II, ch. 20. Robert G. McCloskey, *American Conservatism in the Age of Enterprise: A Study of William Graham Sumner, Stephen J. Field, and Andrew Carnegie* (Cambridge, Mass., 1951), is a realistic appraisal of American conservatism as it relates to American business.
3. Ogden, *Godkin,* I, 11–12, quoting Godkin's notebooks. See also Kirkland, *Business in the Gilded Age,* 27–9.

4. *Nation,* II (June 12, 1866), 745–6; XXXVII (November 15, 1883), 409–10; Godkin, "Aristocratic Opinions of Democracy," *North American Review,* C (1865), 194–232. See also Grimes, *Political Liberalism of . . . Nation,* 13–15.

5. *Nation,* II (April 5, 1866), 417; III (August 30, 1866), 173–4; IV (May 16, 1867), 394–5.

6. Atkinson to Wells, April 11, 1866, quoted in Williamson, *Atkinson,* 59–60.

7. Cooper, quoted in Nevins, *Hewitt,* 288; Lowitt, *Dodge,* 349–50.

8. Cochran and Miller, *Age of Enterprise,* 67–72; David P. Edgell, *William Ellery Channing, an Intellectual Portrait* (Boston, 1955), 186–7.

9. Norton, "Waste," *Nation,* II (March 8, 1866), 201–2; Curtis, "The Duty of the American Scholar," in Norton (ed.), *Curtis Orations,* I, 8–10; *Nation,* XLII (June 8, 1886), 419; Godkin, *Unforeseen Tendencies of Democracy* (Boston, 1898), v–vi.

10. Roosevelt, *American Ideals and Other Essays, Social and Political* (New York, 1897), 9–10; Nevins, *Hewitt,* 295.

11. Lieber, quoted in Edward Atkinson, *Industrial Exhibitions* (Boston, 1882), and cited in Irvin G. Wyllie, *The Self-Made Man in America: The Myth of Rags to Riches* (New Brunswick, N.J., 1954), 142 (see also 140–41, 151–5); Godkin, "Aristocratic Opinions of Democracy," 218–19.

12. Ogden, *Godkin,* II, 131; Godkin, "Social Classes in the Republic," *Atlantic Monthly,* LXXVIII (1896), 724.

13. Roosevelt, *American Ideals,* 344; Charles Francis Adams, Jr., *An Autobiography, 1835–1915* (Boston and New York, 1916), 160; Godkin, "The Expenditures of Rich Men," *Scribner's Magazine,* XX (1896), 499.

14. Godkin, "Expenditures of Rich Men," 500; and "Idleness and Immorality," in *Problems of Modern Democracy,* 193–4; entry (undated) and entries, December 10, 1887, March 22, 1889, in Williams (ed.), *Hayes Diary,* IV, 355–6, 367, 457; Roosevelt, *American Ideals,* 5–6; Schurz to Winslow Warren, October 16, 1886, in Bancroft (ed.), *Schurz,* IV, 457–60; *Nation,* LI (November 20, 1890), 395.

15. Sumner, "The Forgotten Man," in Albert G. Keller and Maurice R. Davie (eds.), *Essays of William Graham Sumner* (2 vols., New Haven, Conn., 1934), I, 488; *Nation,* XXVII (August 8, 1878), 78–9.

16. Paine (ed.), *Mark Twain's Autobiography,* I, 250ff; Andrews, *Nook Farm,* 114, 118, 122–3, 185; Bernard De Voto (ed.), *Mark Twain in Eruption* (New York, 1940), xxiii–xxvii, 2–4, 14–17, 77, 97–106; Theodore Dreiser, "Mark the Double Twain," *English Journal,* XXIV

(1935), 615–27; Walter F. Taylor, *The Economic Novel in America* (Chapel Hill, N.C., 1942), 128–33.

17. Entries, January 22, 1886, December 4, 1887, February 6, 1891, in Williams (ed.), *Hayes Diary,* IV, 261, 354–5, 637.

18. Entries, May 28, 29, 1887, September 5, 1888, January 13, 1889, in Williams (ed.), *Hayes Diary,* IV, 327, 404–5, 434–5. Howells to James, October 10, 1888, Howells to Edward Everett Hale, October 28, 1888, in Mildred Howells (ed.), *Howells Letters,* I, 417–19.

19. Howells to Hamlin Garland, November 6, 1888, in Mildred Howells (ed.), *Howells Letters,* I, 419; entry, January 13, 1889, in Williams (ed.), *Hayes Diary,* IV, 434–5; Howells, "Are We a Plutocracy?" *North American Review,* CLVIII (1894), 185–96; Howells, "The Nature of Liberty," *Forum,* XX (1895), 401–9; Louis J. Budd, "Howells' 'Blistering and Cauterizing,'" *Ohio State Archaeological and Historical Quarterly,* LXII (1953), 334–47. Robert L. Hough, *The Quiet Rebel: William Dean Howells as Social Commentator* (Lincoln, Neb., 1959), is a valuable study of the novelist's metamorphosis from orthodox liberal to social democrat.

20. *Nation,* X (February 10, 1870), 89–90; Richard T. Ely, *Ground Under Our Feet: An Autobiography* (New York, 1938), 125.

21. Ely, *Ground Under Our Feet,* 136.

22. Perry, *Principles of Political Economy* (New York, 1891), xi; Newcomb, *Nation,* XLII (April 8, 1886), 292–3, XLIII (October 7, 1886), 293–4.

23. Williamson, *Atkinson,* 54, 176, 242–60; Godkin, "'The Economic Man,'" first published in *North American Review* (1891), reprinted in Godkin, *Problems of Modern Democracy* (New York, 1903), 156–79; *Nation,* XXVI (May 16, 1878), 318–19. Joseph Dorfman, *The Economic Mind in American Civilization, 1606–1918* (3 vols., New York, 1946–49), III, ch. VII, is a penetrating examination of liberal economics in conflict with the changing times.

24. Ely, *Ground Under Our Feet,* 139–45; Ely, *The Past and Present of Political Economy* (Baltimore, 1884), 64; Lloyd to William M. Salter, October 30, 1885 (copy), Henry Demarest Lloyd Papers (State Historical Society of Wisconsin); Hans B. Thorelli, *The Federal Antitrust Policy: Origination of an American Tradition* (Stockholm, 1954), 119; Dorfman, *Economic Mind,* III, 161–74.

25. Thorelli, *Antitrust Policy,* 111–12. Thorelli, Fine, *Laissez Faire,* and Dorfman, *Economic Mind,* III, all are reliable, scholarly treatments of the monopoly problem and its ramifications.

26. Entries, March 18, 20, 26, 1886, March 11, 1888, in Williams (ed.),

Hayes Diary, IV, 277–8, 374; Barnard, *Hayes*, 246–67; Curtis W. Garrison (ed.), "Conversation with Hayes: A Biographer's Notes," *Mississippi Valley Historical Review*, XXV (1938), 369–80.

27. *Harper's Weekly*, XXXII (1888), 998; *Chicago Tribune*, March 17, September 2, 1883.

28. J. G. Hodgskin, *Nation*, XII (April 6, 1871), 232–3; White, *Nation*, XLIV (May 5, 1887), 380–81; also *Nation*, XLIII (July 8, 1886), 66.

29. *Nation*, II (March 15, 1866), 329; XXXVII (September 6, 1883), 201.

30. *Springfield Republican*, January 18, 1870.

31. Thorelli, *Antitrust Policy*, 123–5; Ely, *Ground Under Our Feet*, 265–9; Ely, "The Nature and Significance of Monopolies and Trusts," *International Journal of Ethics*, X (1900), 273–88; Dorfman, *Economic Mind*, III, 257–8.

32. Lloyd to Ely, March 30, 1898 (copy), Richard T. Ely Papers (State Historical Society of Wisconsin, Madison); Ely, *Problems of Today: A Discussion of Protective Tariffs, Taxation, and Monopolies* (New York, 1890), 253; Fine, *Laissez Faire*, 230–31; Allan Nevins, *Study in Power: John D. Rockefeller, Industrialist and Philanthropist* (2 vols., New York, 1953), II, 140–44.

33. "Americans and the English" [1872], in Paine (ed.), *Mark Twain's Speeches*, 35–6.

34. Nevins (ed.), *Strong Diary*, IV, 203.

35. *Nation*, I (September 14, November 16, 1865), 328–9, 616–17; II (January 11, April 19, 1866), 39–40, 482; XVII (July 17, 1873), 36–7.

36. *Nation*, XVII (July 17, 1873), 36–7; XXIV (March 8, 1877), 143–4.

37. The essays appeared originally (1869–71) as articles in the *North American Review*. The most recent collected edition, *Chapters of Erie* (Ithaca, 1956), includes Henry Adams's essay on the gold conspiracy as well as Charles Francis Adams, Jr.'s essays on the Erie war.

38. Adams, *Nation*, XVI (April 10, 1873), 249–50; Adams, "The Granger Movement," *North American Review*, CXX (1875), 394–425; Dorfman, *Economic Mind*, III, 23–6. Kirkland, *Charles Francis Adams, Jr., 1835–1915: The Patrician at Bay* (Cambridge, Mass., 1965), ch. II, analyzes Adams's peculiar dual role as railroad reformer and railroad executive.

39. *Nation*, XXXIV (March 2, 1882), 180–81; White, *Nation*, XL (May 28, 1885), 437–8; Villard, *Nation*, XLIV (February 3, 1887), 93–4.

40. Atkinson to H. V. Poor, January 15, 1887, Atkinson Papers; Nathaniel W. Stephenson, *Nelson W. Aldrich: A Leader in American Politics* (New York, 1930), 68; Ingalls, quoted in *Harper's Weekly*, XXXI

(1887), 70; *Nation,* LXVI (March 24, 1898), 219–20; Thorelli, *Antitrust Policy,* 197, 231–2, *et passim;* Schurz, "The Tariff Question," October 20, 1890, in Bancroft (ed.), *Schurz,* V, 61–2.

41. Bryce, *American Commonwealth,* II, 27; A. G. Sedgwick, *Nation,* LXVIII (June 1, 1899), 412–13.

42. Porter (comp.), *Platforms,* 120–21; Merrill, *Bourbon Leader,* 72–9, 84–6; Cleveland to the House of Representatives, February 16, 1887, in Richardson (ed.), *Messages and Papers of the Presidents,* VII, 5142–3.

43. Olney to Charles E. Perkins, December 28, 1892, quoted in Josephson, *Politicos,* 526; Henry James, *Richard Olney and His Public Service* (Boston and New York, 1923), 28–30.

44. Albert H. Walker, *History of the Sherman Law* (New York, 1910), 87–123; "Annual Report of the Attorney General of the United States for the Year 1893," *House Executive Documents,* 53 Cong., 2 Sess., No. 7 (Ser. No. 3218), xxvi–xxviii.

45. *Nation,* XLIV (March 10, 1887), 202; XLVII (July 5, 1888), 4; LV (December 15, 1892), 444; Schurz, "Grover Cleveland's Second Administration," May 1897, in Bancroft (ed.), *Schurz,* V, 359, 369–70.

46. *Nation,* LVIII (March 1, 1894), 149–50; T. L. Greene, *Nation,* LXI (July 25, 1896), 58–9.

47. *Nation,* LX (May 23, 1895), 394; LXI (October 10, 1895), 251–2; Sedgwick, *Nation,* LXIV (April 8, 1897), 257–8; LXV (July 15, 1897), 44–5; LXVI (March 24, 1898), 219–20.

CHAPTER 7   MORAL MONEY

1. Robert P. Sharkey, *Money, Class, and Party: An Economic Study of the Civil War and Reconstruction* (Baltimore, 1959), and Irwin Unger, *The Greenback Era: A Social and Political History of American Finance, 1865–1879* (Princeton, N.J., 1964), are indispensable guides to the incredibly complex problem of money during the period. Sharkey's political economy is more persuasive to me than Unger's, and his over-all conclusions are eminently satisfactory. On the other hand, Unger weaves intellectual history into the picture in such a way as to provide the larger canvass Sharkey lacks. Unger's analysis of the "soft money" and "hard money" schools is especially clear and valuable.

2. *Nation,* VIII (January 21, 1869), 44; X (April 28, 1870), 263; XV (December 12, 1872), 374; Godkin, "Some Political and Social Aspects of

the Tariff," *New Princeton Review,* III (1887), 164–76; New York *Evening Post,* March 25, 1872; New York Reform Club, "The Logic of Protection," pamphlet, n.d., 10–11.

3. *Nation,* III (July 5, 1866), 10; IV (May 30, 1867), 436; X (February 10, 1870), 81; XVI (January 30, 1873), 68.

4. *Nation,* X (March 30, 1870), 132; LIII (July 2, 1891), 4–5; LVIII (March 15, 1894), 189–90; Schurz, "The Tariff Question," October 20, 1890, in Bancroft (ed.), *Schurz,* V, 67–70, 76–7; Wells to Atkinson, July 14, 1866, Atkinson Papers; A. L. Earle, *Our Revenue System and The Civil Service* (New York, 1872), 38–9; Van Buren Denslow, *Freedom in Trade* (Cambridge, 1882), 26.

5. Wendell P. Garrison, *Nation,* LIV (May 16, 1892), 478.

6. Wells, "Report of the Special Commissioner . . . 1866," 34–6; John Bascom, "The Interests of the Farmer Indefinitely Postponed," in H. W. Furber (ed.), *Both Protection and Free Trade* (Boston, 1888), 502–3; John L. Hayes, "The Farmers' Question," ibid. 477–501; Schurz, "The Tariff Question," in Bancroft (ed), *Schurz,* V, 66–7.

7. William Graham Sumner, *Protection and Revenue in 1877* (New York, 1878), 6–8; Wells, "Necessity and Benefits of the Speedy Reduction of Tariff Taxation," in Furber (ed.), *Both Protection and Free Trade,* 401–27; Hewitt, "Business Depression and Revenue Reform," *Albany Argus,* December 26, 1883.

8. De Voto (ed.), *Mark Twain in Eruption,* 2–4, 97–106; John DeWitt Warner, in *Tariff Reform* (the semimonthly publication of the New York Reform Club's committee on tariff reform), V (June 30, 1892), 704–5, 710.

9. Schurz, "The Tariff Question," 61–2; Godkin, "Aspects of the Tariff," 169–70; Cleveland to the Democratic National Convention, September 8, 1888, in George F. Parker (ed.), *The Writings and Speeches of Grover Cleveland* (New York, 1892), 24.

10. See Chapter 6.

11. William Wallace Lee to Wells, February 7, 1885, quoted in Joyner, *Wells,* 146–7; Gould to Greeley, February 2, 1870, Greeley Papers; Greeley to Colfax, January 19, 1870, Greeley-Colfax Correspondence.

12. Arthur Latham Perry, "Does Protection Raise Prices," in Furber (ed.), *Both Protection and Free Trade,* 516; Frederick W. Taussig, "Tariffs and Wages," ibid. 455–6; J. Schoenhof, "Comparing American Wages with English Wages . . . ," ibid. 521–8; Amasa Walker, "The Fallacies of the Protective Theory," ibid. 146–7; John DeWitt Warner, "Labor, Wages, and Tariffs," *Tariff Reform,* II (January 15, 1890), 154–9; Godkin, "Aspects of the Tariff," 172; "Broadside No. 1," June

1, 1869, Boston Reform League; *Nation,* XLVI (May 24, 1888), 420; Schurz, *Nation,* XXXVI (February 8, 1883), 118.

13. Sumner, *Protection and Revenue in 1877,* 2–4; Mark Twain, *A Connecticut Yankee in King Arthur's Court* (New York, 1889), 299–300; Tom L. Johnson, "Free Wool," speech, March 31, 1892, copy in Tom L. Johnson Papers (Western Reserve Historical Society, Cleveland). In 1919, after years of struggling against the protectionists, Henry Watterson concluded that the whole question of the tariff was bound up in the "ancient, everlasting scheme—'The good old role—the simple plan,/ That they should take who have the Power/ And they should keep who can.'" Watterson, *Marse Henry,* II, 255–6.

14. *Nation,* IV (February 7, May 30, 1867), 101, 436; VIII (January 21, 1869), 44; X (March 3, 1870), 132; XXIX (November 20, 1879), 338–9; Rollo Ogden, *Nation,* XLVII (September 13, 1888), 204–5.

15. *Springfield Republican,* January 15, 1872, February 2, 1876.

16. Lodge Diary, April 28, 1882; Lodge, quoted in Garraty, *Lodge,* 114; Roosevelt to Lodge, January 17, 1888, in Morison (ed.), *Roosevelt Letters,* I, 137.

17. "Why can't I get free of the necessity of earning a living. You and I could become the Cobden and Bright of this country." Atkinson to Wells, November 8, 1884, Wells Papers.

18. Edward Stanwood, *American Tariff Controversies in the Nineteenth Century* (2 vols., Boston and New York, 1903), II, 158.

19. "On the Collection of Revenue," quoted in Williamson, *Atkinson,* 73–8; Atkinson to Wells, November 11, 1875, Atkinson Papers.

20. Atkinson to Wells, September 21, 1882, Atkinson to Worthington C. Ford, September 21, 1882, Atkinson to Wells, October 4, 1882, Atkinson to Benjamin Butterworth, November 8, 1890, Atkinson Papers; Williamson, *Atkinson,* 147–9; James A. Barnes, *John G. Carlisle, Financial Statesman* (New York, 1931), 69, 124–5, *et passim;* Festus P. Summers, *William L. Wilson and Tariff Reform* (New Brunswick, N.J., 1953), 58–9 *et passim.*

21. David A. Wells to Richard R. Bowker, n.d., Bowker Papers; Williamson, *Atkinson,* 134–5, 151–2.

22. Joyner, *Wells,* 10–24; Herbert R. Ferleger, *David A. Wells and the American Revenue System, 1865–1870* (New York, 1942), 1–21.

23. Ferleger, *Wells,* examines in detail the duties and experiences of the Revenue Commissioner; Joyner, *Wells,* 164–72.

24. Wells, "Necessity and Benefit of the Speedy Reduction of Tariff Taxation," in Furber (ed.), *Both Protection and Free Trade,* 401–27; Wells, "The Meaning of Revenue Reform," *North American Review,*

CCXXXII (1871), 104–53; Wells to Atkinson, December 19 [1880?], Atkinson Papers; Wells, *Recent Economic Changes* (New York, 1890), 260; Wells to Bowker, n.d., Bowker Papers.

25. *Nation,* LX (April 11, 1895), 272; Sumner, "Protectionism," in Keller and Davie (eds.), *Sumner Essays,* II, 388–9.

26. Ferleger, *Wells,* 56–8, 63; White, *Nation,* XXXIII (November 17, 1881), 389–99. Elmer Ellis, "Public Opinion and the Income Tax, 1860–1900," *Mississippi Valley Historical Review,* XXVII (1940), 225–42, is a valuable analysis of the controversy waged by opposing elements of the press on the income tax question.

27. Wells, "The Communism of a Discriminating Income Tax," *North American Review,* CXXX (1880), 236–46; Wells to Atkinson, March 23, 1894, Atkinson Papers; *Nation,* X (June 30, 1870), 411; XXVI (March 7, May 7, 1878), 162–3, 287; LX (May 23, 30, 1895), 394, 427.

28. *Harper's Weekly,* XXII (1878), 107, 146–7; Rollo Ogden, *Nation,* LVIII (January 11, 1894), 24–5; Atkinson to W. D. Bynum, January 3, 1894, Atkinson Papers; Williamson, *Atkinson,* 188–9; Perry Belmont, *An American Democrat* (New York, 1940), 452; Pierce, *Sumner Memoir,* IV, 418.

29. Ellis, "Income Tax," 230–31; Dorfman, *Economic Mind,* III, 7.

30. Unger, *Greenback Era,* 41–162, and James A. Barnes, "Myths of the Bryan Campaign," *Mississippi Valley Historical Review,* XXXIV (1947), 367–404, are discussions of the various concepts of money in the late nineteenth century.

31. *Nation,* XXVI (February 14, 1878), 106–7.

32. *Nation,* IV (June 27, 1867), 518–19; X (February 17, 1870), 100; XVI (February 27, 1873), 144–5; XVII (September 25, 1873), 201; XIX (December 7, 1874), 392; XXIII (November 9, 1876), 280–81; XXVI (February 14, 1878), 107.

33. Julian, "Is the Reformer Any Longer Needed?" *North American Review,* CXXVII (1878), 249–50; *Harper's Weekly,* IX (1865), 675; XIV (1870), 66–7; Forbes to John H. Clifford, January 27, 1862, Forbes to William Pitt Fessenden, January 13, 1862, in Hughes (ed.), *Forbes Letters,* I, 280, 288. See also Horace White, *Nation,* I (August 17, 1865), 187; and Charles C. Norvell, *Nation,* XXVI (February 28, 1878), 146–7.

34. Schurz to Sumner, June 5, 1865, "Honest Money," speech, September 27, 1875, "Honest Money and Honesty," speech, September 5, 1896, in Bancroft (ed.), *Schurz,* I, 259, III, 163–4, 181–2, V, 326–7; Atkinson to Henry Ward Beecher, October 10, 1867; Atkinson to William B. Allison, December 13, 1867, Atkinson Papers.

35. See *Nation*, VI (June 4, 1868), 446–8, for a typical expression of these fears.

36. "Annual Report of the Secretary of the Treasury for the Year 1867," *House Executive Documents*, 40 Cong., 2 Sess., No. 2 (Ser. No. 1328).

37. Wells, *New York Herald*, February 13, 1875; Joyner, *Wells*, 179–80; John A. Dix to Tilden, May 15, 1868, George Ticknor Curtis to Tilden, July 10, 1875, Wells to Tilden, November 9, 1875, in Bigelow (ed.), *Tilden Letters*, I, 225–7, 391–2, II, 439–40; Nevins, *Hewitt*, 405; Norton to Godkin, February 6, 1868, Godkin Papers; Charles Nordhoff to Wells, n.d., Nordhoff Papers.

38. Atkinson to Sumner, December 3, 1867, February 19, 1868, July 3, 1868, Sumner Papers; Wendell P. Garrison to Francis J. Garrison, August 2, 1868, Garrison Family Papers.

39. Atkinson to Sumner, February 3, April 21, 1868; Sumner to Bright, February 4, 1868, Sumner Papers; Charles Sumner, *Works* (15 vols., Boston, 1870–83), XII, 447–50; Pierce, *Sumner Memoir*, IV, 353–6, 418–19.

40. *Nation*, x (March 24, April 7, 1870), 188–9, 218–19; LX (May 23, 1895), 394.

41. Forbes, quoted in Hughes (ed.), *Forbes Letters*, II, 185; White, *Trumbull*, 362; Garfield to Hinsdale, April 23, 1874, in Hinsdale (ed.), *Garfield-Hinsdale Letters*, 286; entry, April 21, 1874, in Williams (ed.), *Hayes Diary*, III, 255; *Springfield Republican*, April 23, 1874; Cary, *Curtis*, 235.

42. Sherman, *Recollections*, I, 509–18; *Springfield Republican*, January 12, 1875, February 14, 1876; *Nation*, XIX (December 24, 31, 1874), 411, 429; Garfield to Hinsdale, January 11, 1875, in Hinsdale (ed.), *Garfield-Hinsdale Letters*, 310; *Harper's Weekly*, XIX (1875), 26; Royal Cortissoz, *Life of Whitelaw Reid* (2 vols., New York, 1921), I, 381.

43. *Nation*, XIX (December 10, 1874), 376; XXVI (January 24, February 28, 1878), 52–3, 145.

44. *Nation*, VII (July 9, 1868), 24–5; XII (January 27, 1876), 57–8; Wells to Atkinson, June[?] 1876, Atkinson Papers; Schurz, "Honest Money and Honesty," 286–7. Horace White, in his biography of Lyman Trumbull, devoted only a few brief sentences to his subject's participation in the Populist movement.

45. Garfield to A. G. Riddle, September 3, 1877, in Smith, *Garfield*, II, 655.

46. Joyner, *Wells*, 89–90.

47. Ferleger, *Wells*, 300–303; Joyner, *Wells*, 76–84, 139–40; *Nation*, x

(June 23, 30, 1870), 359, 398; *Springfield Republican,* July 10, 1870.

48. Atkinson to Sumner, July 25, 1868, Sumner Papers; Atkinson to Lester S. Taylor, November 7, 1868, Atkinson Papers; *Springfield Republican,* October 24, 1868; Merriam, *Bowles,* 91–3.

49. Porter (comp.), *Platforms,* 83–4, 95–6, 110, 132–3, 147–8, 173–4, 202–3.

50. Brinkerhoff, *Recollections,* 193–4, 205–11; Schurz to Parke Godwin, May 28, 1872, Miscellaneous Letters of Carl Schurz (New York Public Library); *Springfield Republican,* March 18, 26, May 10, 1872; *Nation,* XXXI (September 30, 1880), 232–3; Roosevelt to Bowker, October 31, 1884, in Morison (ed.), *Roosevelt Letters,* I, 86.

51. Bryant to John H. Gourlie, June 17, 1875, in Parke Godwin, *A Biography of William Cullen Bryant* (2 vols., New York, 1883), II, 365; Frederick F. Cook to Godkin, October 2, 1870, Atkinson to Norton, July 19 (copy), August 2, 1865, Godkin to Atkinson, July 17, 1865 (copy), Godkin Papers; Henry G. Philpott to Wells, November 13, 1882, Wells to Philpott, June 16, 1884, David Ames Wells Papers (New York Public Library).

52. Atkinson to Wells, May 29, July 11, 1882, Atkinson Papers; Howe, *Arthur,* 220–26; Stanwood, *Tariff Controversies,* 203–7.

53. Adams to Norton, December 10, 1867, Norton Papers; Atkinson to Haskell[?], January 11, 1869, Atkinson Papers; Boston Reform League, "Broadside No. 1," June 1, 1869.

54. Williamson, *Atkinson,* 87–8; *Springfield Republican,* June 11, 1872.

55. Joyner, *Wells,* 117–18, 136–7; Ferleger, *Wells,* 281–3; R. G. McClelland to Wells, June 18, 1875, Emerson W. Judd to Wells, July 18, 1882, Wells Papers; Schurz to Godkin, March 31, 1871, in Bancroft (ed.), *Schurz,* II, 252–3; *Nation,* X (April 28, 1870), 263.

56. New York Reform Club, "Circular," August 10, 1888; Seth Low, *Tariff Reform in the Present Canvass* (New York Reform Club Series, No. 8, 1888); Howe, *Storey,* 146–7.

57. Samuel W. Mendum, "The Questions Clubs and the Tariff," *North American Review,* CL (1890), 301–9.

58. Richardson (ed.), *Messages and Papers,* VII, 5082–5114 (esp. 5093–8). Blodgett, *The Gentle Reformers,* 70–99, discusses in illuminating detail the tariff issue among New England Mugwumps.

59. Richardson (ed.), *Messages and Papers,* VII, 5112–13.

60. Schurz to Cleveland, December 15, 1886, in Bancroft (ed.), *Schurz,* IV, 463–70.

61. Richardson (ed.), *Messages and Papers,* VII, 5165–76; Schurz to Oscar S. Strauss, February 7, 1888, in Bancroft (ed.), *Schurz,* IV, 492; *Nation,*

XLV (December 8, 1887), 447; Porter (comp.), *Platforms*, 142–3, 147.

62. *Nation*, XLVI (June 14, 1888), 481–2; XLVII (October 25, November 8, 1888), 326–7, 406; Schurz to Thaddeus C. Pound, September 15, 1888, in Bancroft (ed.), *Schurz*, IV, 510–28; Howe, *Storey*, 180–81.

63. *Nation*, XLVII (August 2, 16, November 8, 1888), 85, 124, 365; XLVIII (April 18, May 2, 30, 1889), 315, 355, 436; Cleveland to Sherman Hoar, December 24, 1888, Cleveland to J. A. Hill, March 24, 1890, in Nevins (ed.), *Cleveland Letters*, 194, 220–21; "The Principles of True Democracy," speech, January 8, 1891, in Parker (ed.), *Cleveland Writings*, 267; Josephson, *Politicos*, 488–92.

64. Schurz to Moorfield Storey, November 1, 1891, Schurz to Cleveland, June 1892, in Bancroft (ed.), *Schurz*, V, 82–3, 85–6; *Nation*, LV (November 10, 1892), 346; H. T. Peck, "Mr. Godkin and His Book," *The Bookman*, II (1896), 480–88; Muzzey, *Blaine*, 444–7; Josephson, *Politicos*, 512–17.

65. "Proclamation," June 30, 1893, and "Special Session Message," August 8, 1893, in Richardson (ed.), *Messages and Papers*, VIII, 5828, 5833–7; *Nation*, LVII (August 3, 10, 31, September 28, October 5, November 2, 1893), 76, 91, 145, 148, 219, 240, 258, 322; Wells to Thomas F. Bayard, September, 1893, quoted in Joyner, *Wells*, 198.

66. *Nation*, LX (February 21, 28, 1895), 137, 158; Merrill, *Bourbon Leader*, 182–5.

67. *Harper's Weekly*, XXXVI (1892), 1106; XXXVIII (1894), 506; Atkinson to Nordhoff, June 4, 1890, Wells to Atkinson, February 10, 1891, Atkinson Papers; *Nation*, LIX (August 16, 23, 1894), 111, 129. See Josephson, *Politicos*, 542–54, for a good account of the tariff fight.

CHAPTER 8 · THE DANGEROUS CLASSES

1. *The New York Times*, July 25, 26, 27, 1877; *Springfield Republican*, July 24, 26, 1877; see also Samuel Yellen, *American Labor Struggles* (New York, 1936), 21–2.

2. Perry, *Elements of Political Economy* (13th edn., New York, 1875), 149, 166–7; Sumner, "The Challenge of Facts," in Keller and Davie (eds.), *Sumner Essays*, II, 97; *Harper's Weekly*, XXXIV (1890), 134.

3. Address, September 8, 1884, in Parker (ed.), *Cleveland Writings*, 137–8; Perry, *Political Economy*, 154, 163.

4. Godkin, "Idleness and Immorality," and "The Duty of Educated Men in a Democracy," *Problems of Modern Democracy*, 193–4, 207–8.

5. Atkinson, *Nation,* III (August 30, 1866), 161–2; Atkinson to Samuel Gompers, August 27, 1889, Atkinson Papers; *Nation,* IV (May 23, 1867), 405–6.

6. Entry, March 11, 1888, in Williams (ed.), *Hayes Diary,* IV, 374; *Springfield Republican,* January 6, 1872, February 15, 1876; David A. Wasson, in Sargent (ed.), *Radical Club,* 222; Aaron M. Powell, *Annual Report of the Reform League* (New York, 1871), 13–14; *Nation,* IV (June 27, 1867), 510–11, XIV (January 4, 1876), 5–7; Beecher, quoted in *The New York Times,* July 30, 1877.

7. Roosevelt, "How Not to Help Our Poorer Brothers," *American Ideals,* 223.

8. *Nation,* VIII (February 4, 1869), 85–6; John S. Hittell, *Reform or Revolution?* (San Francisco, 1900), 30; Perry, *Political Economy,* 166; Atkinson, *Labor and Capital: Allies Not Enemies* (New York, 1879), 15–17, *et passim.*

9. Sumner, "The Philosophy of Strikes," and "Strikes and the Industrial Organization," in Keller and Davie (eds.), *Sumner Essays,* II, 31–2, 39–43; Frederick W. Taussig, *Nation,* XL (January 29, 1885), 91; White, *Nation,* XLVII (September 5, 1888), 165–6; also Godkin, *Nation,* II (April 26, 1866), 380; XXXVII (July 19, August 23, 1883), 46–7, 156.

10. *Nation,* II (May 29, 1866), 681; Brace, *Nation,* I (October 26, 1865), 527–8.

11. Godkin to Norton, 1867, quoted in Ogden, *Godkin,* II, 44–5; *Nation,* IV (April 25, 1867), 334–6; V (October 3, 1867), 275–6.

12. *Nation,* I (August 17, 1865), 198–9; V (July 4, 1867), 3; VIII (February 4, 1869), 85–6.

13. F. J. Kingsbury, in *Nation,* III (November 22, 1866), 412–13; S. G. Fisher, *Nation,* I (October 26, 1865), 517–18.

14. Lowell and White, *Nation,* III (October 4, 1866), 272–3, and XXXVIII (June 16, 1884), 540; also *Nation,* I (November 16, December 21, 1865), 615–16, 775–6; IV (June 27, 1867), 518–19; XXXIX (July 17, 1884), 46; Garrison, *Nation,* II (March 22, 1866), 360; *Harper's Weekly,* XII (1868), 51; Perry, *Political Economy,* 167.

15. William Dean Howells, *A Hazard of New Fortunes,* 2 vols. (New York, 1889), II, 252–3; Atkinson, "The Hours of Labor," *North American Review,* CXLII (1886), 507–15; *Nation,* VII (July 2, 1868), 6–7.

16. Warner, "Some Causes of the Prevailing Discontent," *The Complete Writings of Charles Dudley Warner* (15 vols., Hartford, 1904), XIV, 366–70; Garrison, quoted in Ralph Korngold, *Two Friends of Man* (Boston, 1950), 364–5; E. H. Rogers to John D. Long, January 26,

1888, John D. Long Papers (Massachusetts Historical Society); Henry George to Charles H. Barrows, April 26, 1880, Barrows Papers.

17. Entry, February 6, 1891, in Williams (ed.), *Hayes Diary,* IV, 637; James, *Nation,* XI (September 1, 1870), 132–3; *Nation,* V (October 3, 1867), 275–6.

18. *Nation,* V (October 3, 1867), 275–6; VIII (February 4, 1869), 85–6; XLIII (July 29, 1886), 90; (September 2, 1886), 191.

19. Atkinson, *The Industrial Progress of the Nation* (New York, 1890), 207; White, *Nation,* XL (May 7, 1885), 378; *Harper's Weekly,* XXI (1877), 638. The great Pullman strike occurred nine years after White wrote his tribute to the company. Stanley Buder, *Pullman: An Experiment in Industrial Order and Community Planning, 1880–1930* (New York, 1967), is an estimable analysis of an experiment liberal reformers viewed as significant.

20. Sumner, "The Power and Beneficence of Capital," and "Reply to a Socialist," in Keller and Davie (eds.), *Sumner Essays,* II, 14–30, 123–30; *Nation,* XLIII (July 29, 1886), 90.

21. Lowitt, *Dodge,* 285–7, 335; *Nation,* XLIV (February 24, 1887), 158–9.

22. Sumner, "The Challenge of Facts," in Keller and Davie (eds.), *Sumner Essays,* II, 118, 121; Samuel Rezneck, "Patterns of Thought and Action in an American Depression, 1882–1886," *American Historical Review,* LXI (1956), 284–307.

23. Brinkerhoff, *Recollections,* 425; *Nation,* I (October 26, 1865), 519–20; *Harper's Weekly,* I (October 17, 1857), 658.

24. (Boston, 1892.)

25. Atkinson, *Science of Nutrition,* 4–7 et passim; Atkinson, *Industrial Progress,* 347–8; Williamson, *Atkinson,* 269–72.

26. Debs, quoted in Williamson, *Atkinson,* 272; Atkinson to Albert Shaw, June 6, 1891, Atkinson Papers.

27. Carnegie, *Gospel of Wealth,* xi–xiii; Sumner, "The Philosophy of Strikes," in Keller and Davie (eds.), *Sumner Essays,* II, 31–8; Nevins, *Hewitt,* 412–13.

28. Warner, "Some Causes of the Prevailing Discontent," *Works,* XIV, 355–62; Mark Twain, *Connecticut Yankee,* 303; Philip S. Foner, *Mark Twain: Social Critic* (New York, 1958), 166–76; Howells, *A Hazard of New Fortunes,* II, 252ff; George Mayberry, "Industrialism and the Industrial Worker in the American Novel, 1814–1890," Unpublished Ph.D. Dissertation, Harvard University, 1942, 182–7; Robert W. Hume, "Labor Reform," *The Standard,* I (1870), 27–8; Powell, *Annual Report, 1871* (Reform League), 13; Edward Wenning to Richard T. Ely, August 15, 1888, Ely Papers.

29. Hay, letter to the editor of *Century*, XXVII (1883–84), 795; *The Bread-Winners* (1884; biog. edn., New York, 1899), 74–5.

30. Williamson, *Atkinson*, 267–8; Wendell P. Garrison to William Lloyd Garrison, August 12, 1877, Garrison Family Papers; Grosvenor, *Trades Unions* (n.p., 1885), 4, 38–9, *et passim*.

31. *Springfield Republican*, October 24, 1870; *Harper's Weekly*, x (1866), 578; xxx (1886), 210, 226, 338.

32. *Nation*, XLIII (May 6, 1886), 376–7. See also Henry Ward Beecher, *The New York Times*, July 30, 1877.

33. *Nation*, XXXVII (November 22, 29, December 6, 1883), 428, 463–4, 486. References to similar conditions are in *Nation*, XLII (April 22, 1886), 334; XLIII (December 9, 1886), 469–70; XLIV (January 13, 1887), 28–9.

34. Edmund Quincy, *Nation*, II (June 19, 1866), 777; Means, *Nation*, LXV (July 22, 1897), 63–4.

35. Nevins, *Hewitt*, 413–17, 427–31, 510, 573–5.

36. *Nation*, XVII (July 17, 1873), 36; XVIII (January 22, April 23, 1874), 55–6, 262–3; XXI (July 8, 1875), 18; Fred A. Shannon, *The Farmer's Last Frontier: Agriculture, 1860–1897* (New York, 1945), 176, 303–5.

37. *Nation*, XXI (July 22, 1875), 52–3; XXII (January 27, 1876), 57–8; LIII (November 26, 1891), 403; Adams, *Nation*, XVI (April 10, 1873), 249–50; Willard C. Flagg, "The Farmers' Movement in the Western United States," *Journal of Social Science*, VI (1874), 100–115.

38. Atkinson to Charles Nordhoff, November 1892, quoted in Williamson, *Atkinson*, 178–9; Schurz, "Honest Money and Honesty," in Bancroft (ed.), *Schurz*, V, 286–7; Benton H. Wilcox, "An Historical Definition of Northwestern Radicalism," *Mississippi Valley Historical Review*, XXVI (1939), 377–94.

39. See, e.g., *Harper's Weekly*, XXI (1877), 618; entry, May 12, 1886, in Williams (ed.), *Hayes Diary*, IV, 286.

40. Hinsdale (ed.), *Garfield Works*, II, 549–50; Beecher, *The New York Times*, July 30, 1877.

41. *Nation*, XXXVII (July 26, 1883), 70–71; *Harper's Weekly*, XXX (1886), 179, 274, 663; *Springfield Republican*, January 18, 1870.

42. Entry, April 6, 1886, in Williams (ed.), *Hayes Diary*, IV, 280; *Springfield Republican*, February 7, 1876; *Congressional Record*, 45 Cong., 2 Sess., 3538. See also Ely, *The Labor Movement in America* (New York, 1886), 295–8.

43. *Congressional Record*, 45 Cong., 2 Sess., 3636; Nevins, *Hewitt*, 595–6.

44. *Nation*, II (May 11, 1866), 594; *Harper's Weekly*, XXI (1877), 618, 638–9.

45. Sumner, "The Challenge of Facts," in Keller and Davie (eds.), *Sumner Essays*, II, 118; *Nation*, XXVI (May 9, 1878), 302; LIX (July 19, 1894), 41–2; Simon Newcomb, *Nation*, XLIII (October 7, 1886), 293–4; Lodge Diary, December 20, 1890; Cochran and Miller, *Age of Enterprise*, 236–7.

46. Entry, May 12, 1886, in Williams (ed.), *Hayes Diary*, IV, 285; Roosevelt, *American Ideals*, 6–7.

47. *Nation*, XXVI (May 9, 1878), 302–3; XXXI (September 9, 1880), 181–2.

48. Garfield, *Congressional Record*, 45 Cong., 2 Sess., 3636; Beecher, *The New York Times*, July 30, 1877; Norton to Godkin, January 16, 1870, Godkin Papers; *Harper's Weekly*, XXII (1878), 667.

49. *Nation*, XXV (August 2, 1877), 68–9; XLIII (July 8, 1886), 26.

50. *Nation*, XLII (May 13, 1886), 391; XLIII (July 8, 1886), 26; XLIV (January 27, 1887), 70; Brace, *Dangerous Classes*, 29–30.

51. *Springfield Republican*, May 5, 1886; *Harper's Weekly*, XXX (1886), 306; Yellen, *Labor Struggles*, ch. 2.

52. *Nation*, XLV (October 27, November 10, 1887), 326–7, 366–7.

53. *Harper's Weekly*, XXXI (1887), 850–51; *Springfield Republican*, September 15, November 11, 12, 1887; *Nation*, XLV (November 10, 17, 1887), 366–7, 388; *The New York Times*, November 12, 1887; Williams (ed.), *Hayes Diary*, IV, 282, 285–6, 288.

54. Howells to Curtis, August 8, 1887, Curtis Papers; Howells to Judge Roger A. Pryor, September 25, 1887, Howells to the New York *Tribune*, November 4, 1887, Howells to Francis P. Browne, November 11, 1887, Howells to William Cooper Howells, November 13, 1887, Howells to Mrs. Achille Frechette, November 18, 1887, Howells to Hamlin Garland, January 15, 1888, Howells to Samuel L. Clemens, April 5, 1888, in Mildred Howells (ed.), *Howells Letters*, I, 401–11.

55. *Nation*, XXV (August 9, 1877), 85–6.

56. *Nation*, XXXI (September 9, 1880), 181–2; XLII (May 13, 1886), 391; XLIV (January 27, 1887), 70; Rollo Ogden, *Nation*, LX (January 3, 1895), 4–5; *Harper's Weekly*, XXI (1877), 618.

57. Nevins, *Evening Post*, 455–7; Schurz to Godkin, August 9, 1883, Schurz Papers; Godkin to Schurz, draft letter, August 11, 1883, Schurz to Godkin, October 3, 1883, Godkin Papers.

58. *Congressional Record*, 45 Cong., 2 Sess., 3538; entry, August 5, 1877, in Williams (ed.), *Hayes Diary*, III, 440–41; Howe (ed.), "Notes of Four Cabinet Meetings," 288–9; Barnard, *Hayes*, 445–7.

59. Parker (ed.), *Cleveland's Writings*, 11; McElroy, *Cleveland*, II, 138–9; Cleveland to Congress, April 22, 1886, in Richardson (ed.), *Messages and Papers*, VII, 4979–82; White, *Nation*, XLII (April 29, 1886), 354.

60. *Harper's Weekly,* XXXVI (1892), 674–6; XXXVIII (1894), 411; Means, *Nation,* LV (July 14, 1892), 22, LV (August 25, 1892), 138–9, LVIII (May 10, 1894), 340; A. G. Sedgwick, *Nation,* LXIV (April 8, 1897), 257–8.

61. Yellen, *Labor Struggles,* ch. 4, gives an excellent account of the strike and an analysis of Cleveland's actions. See also Almont Lindsey, *The Pullman Strike* (Chicago, 1942), and Josephson, *Politicos,* 568–83.

62. Nevins, *Cleveland,* 614–18, 627–68; McElroy, *Cleveland,* II, 156–7.

63. *Nation,* LIX (July 5, 1894), 1; *Harper's Weekly,* XXXVIII (1894), 650.

64. *Nation,* LIX (July 12, 1894), 19; Ogden, *Nation,* LIX (July 12, 19, 1894), 22, 40; Godkin to Laurence Godkin, July 12, 1894, Godkin Papers.

65. Means, *Nation,* LIX (September 13, 1894), 190–91; Ogden, *Nation,* LIX (November 22, 1894), 376; United States Strike Commission, "Report and Testimony on the Chicago Strike of 1894," in *Senate Executive Documents,* 53 Cong., 3 Sess., No. 7, xlvii–liv, *et passim.*

66. *Nation,* LVI (June 29, 1893), 464; LIX (July 12, 1894), 19; Clark, *Nation,* 22–3; Ogden, *Nation* (November 29, 1894), 376; White, *Nation* (December 27, 1894), 456; *Harper's Weekly,* XXXVIII (1894), 674–5; *The New York Times,* July 7, 1894; Roosevelt, *American Ideals,* 7–9; Nevins, *Cleveland,* 624–7; Harvey Wish, "Altgeld and the Progressive Tradition," *American Historical Review,* XLVI (1941), 813–31. For the exchange of telegrams between Altgeld and Cleveland, see Nevins (ed.), *Cleveland Letters,* 360–62.

67. *Nation,* LII (May 28, 1891), 434–5.

CHAPTER 9   THE HEART OF THE MATTER

1. *Unforeseen Tendencies of Democracy* (Boston, 1898), iii–vii.

2. To his father, February 7, 1875, in Garrison Family Papers.

3. Curtis to Norton, May 3, 1870, Curtis Papers; Executive Committee of Citizens and Taxpayers, *Appeal for Financial Reform* (New York, n.d.), 10–11.

4. Entry, September 22, 1871, in Nevins (ed.), *Strong Diary,* IV, 386; De Voto (ed.), *Mark Twain in Eruption,* 77; Prentiss, *Our National Bane,* 3–4; *Nation,* IV (April 18, 1867), 315–16.

5. Julian, "Is the Reformer Any Longer Needed," 258; Citizens Association, *Appeal Against Abuses* (New York, 1866), 24–5; Prentiss, *Our National Bane,* 7–8; Low, "Why We Must Solve the Municipal Problem," (pamphlet, New York Reform Club, n.d.); *Nation,* X (March

10, May 19, 1870), 153–4, 314; XVII (October 23, 1873), 268–9; Schurz, *Nation*, XXXIV (May 25, 1882), 438–49; *Springfield Republican*, March 15, 1877.

6. Curtis, "Civil Service Reform," 20–22; Parkman, "The Failure of Universal Suffrage," *North American Review*, CXXVII (1878), 1–20; *Nation*, X (March 10, 1870), 153–4; XV (December 19, 1872), 400–401; XLVII (October 11, 1888), 428; Samuel Bowles to Godkin, June 22, 1870, Godkin Papers; Hamilton A. Hill, "The Relation of Business Men to National Legislation," *Journal of Social Science*, III (1868), 148–68; Nevins, *Hewitt*, 437–8.

7. Tilden to W. Cassidy, 1871, Tilden Papers; Barrows, *Municipal Reform*, 10–11; entry, April 14, 1883, in New York Reform Club Minutes, I; Patton, *Municipal Reform*, 14–15, 32–3. Tammany Hall's active supporters in 1866 included such businessmen-liberal reformers as Tilden, August Belmont, Oswald Ottendorfer, and Edwards Pierrepont; "Broadside," 1866, Tilden Papers.

8. Miller, "American Historians and the Business Elite," 184–208; *Springfield Republican*, October 20, 1880; Schurz to Winslow Warren, October 16, 1886, in Bancroft (ed.), *Schurz*, IV, 457–60; Thomas F. Devlin, *Municipal Reform in the United States* (New York, 1896), 162–3.

9. Warner, *Works*, XIV, 331; Lincoln Steffens, *Autobiography* (New York, 1931), 606.

10. *Nation*, LXII (February 27, 1896), 172; Barrows, *Municipal Patriotism* (New York, 1890), 4–5; Josephson, *Politicos*, 410–11, 425–6; Cochran and Miller, *Age of Enterprise*, 154–5.

11. Emerson, in Sargent (ed.), *Radical Club*, 28; Godkin to Henry W. Bellows, February 4, 1869[?], Henry W. Bellows Papers (Massachusetts Historical Society); *Nation*, IV (May 30, 1867), 434–6; XXVI (April 18, 1878), 275; Wendell P. Garrison to William Lloyd Garrison, February 7, 1875, Garrison Family Papers; Hofstadter, *Age of Reform*, 142–3; Nye, *Midwestern Progressive Politics*, 25–6.

12. John Taylor Hall to William Ward, December 30, 1876, Hall Papers; Nevins, *Evening Post*, 479–81; *Nation*, III (October 18, 1866), 312–13; VI (January 23, 1868), 63; XV (December 19, 1872), 400–401; "Power of the Irish in American Cities," *Littell's Living Age*, CLXXI (1886), 382–4. Vanderbilt, *Norton*, 42, notes that Norton sympathized with the Know-Nothings in the 1850's.

13. *Nation*, XI (July 14, 1870), 20; Nevins, *Hewitt*, 515–16.

14. *Nation*, XLIV (March 31, 1887), 264–5.

15. Adams, "The Protection of the Ballot in National Elections," *Journal of Social Science*, I (1869), 91–111; Parkman, "The Woman Question,"

North American Review, CXXIX (1879), 321; Curtis to Higginson, June 13, 1867, November 11, 1871, Higginson Papers; *Nation,* III (November 29, 1866), 421; Thomas G. Shearman, *Nation,* III (November 20, 1866), 498–9; Sargent (ed.), *Radical Club,* 28.

16. *Nation,* XII (April 20, 1871), 270–72; XVIII (May 14, 1874), 311–13.

17. Godkin to Moorfield Storey, May 23, 1891, Godkin Papers; Godkin, "Legislation and Social Science," *Journal of Social Science,* III (1871), 115–32; *Nation,* XXIV (April 26, 1871), 245–6; Vanderbilt, *Norton,* 44–6.

18. *Nation,* I (July 20, 1865), 69; III (October 18, 1866), 312–13; IV (May 20, 1867), 434–6; XI (July 14, 1870), 20; LII (April 16, 1891), 312; Norton to Godkin, April 14, November 4, 1865, Godkin Papers.

19. *Springfield Republican,* August 7, 1867; Norton to Godkin, March 6, 1869, Godkin Papers; Nevins, *Hewitt,* 515–16; Garfield to Hinsdale, January 21, 1875, in Hinsdale (ed.), *Garfield-Hinsdale Letters,* 314; Samuel L. Clemens, *The Curious Republic of Gondour and Other Whimsical Sketches* (New York, 1919), 3 *et passim.* See also *Annual Report of the Personal Representation Society* (New York, 1867), 10, 39.

20. Parkman, "The Failure of Universal Suffrage," *passim;* Godkin to Norton, February 28, April 13, 1865, Norton Papers; Norton to Godkin, February 26, March 5, 1865, Godkin Papers. See also Vanderbilt, *Norton,* 44–6.

21. Warner, *Works,* XIV, 348–55; XV, 108–12, 201; Paul J. Carter, "The Social and Political Ideas of Mark Twain," Unpublished Ph.D. Dissertation University of Cincinnati, 1939, 114–19.

22. John Kelley to Tilden, R. P. Flower to Tilden, both October 22, 1866, Tilden Papers. See also Cochran and Miller, *Age of Enterprise,* 267.

23. Interview with a New York *World* reporter, November 3, 1872, in Bigelow (ed.), *Tilden Letters,* I, 311–16.

24. Wendell P. Garrison to William Lloyd Garrison, November 1, 1877, Wendell P. Garrison to William Everett, May 2, 1893, Garrison Family Papers. Ogden, *Godkin,* II, 40–41. The fight for a merit system has a history extending back to the establishment of the Federal government under the Constitution. No attempt is made here to relate that story, or to delve into the important but peripheral subject of the administration of personnel in the government, either before the Pendleton Act or after. Ari Hoogenboom, *Outlawing the Spoils: A History of the Civil Service Reform Movement, 1865–1883* (Urbana, Ill., 1961), is now the standard work on the subject.

25. Samuel Swartwout was a corrupt Collector of the Port of New York

appointed by Andrew Jackson. In 1838 Swartwout fled the country after embezzling a million and a quarter dollars. For a time thereafter in New York, the term "to swartwout" meant to act in the manner of a Tammany chief.

26. Julian, "Is the Reformer Any Longer Needed," 240; Prentiss, *Our National Bane*, 7–8; Curtis, Introduction to Dorman B. Eaton, *Civil Service in Great Britain* (New York, 1880), vi; Curtis, "Civil Service Reform," in Norton (ed.), *Curtis Orations*, II, 27–28; Schurz, Senate speech, 1870, in Bancroft (ed.), *Schurz*, II, 58–9; Warner, *Works*, XIV, 325; Bonaparte, "Phi Beta Kappa Address," Harvard, 1899, quoted in Joseph B. Bishop, *Charles Joseph Bonaparte: His Life and Services* (New York, 1922), 81–2.

27. Barrows, *Municipal Patriotism*, 17; Andrew D. White to David A. Wells, October 31, 1882, Wells Papers; Bonaparte, quoted in Bishop, *Bonaparte*, 61–2; Cary, *Curtis*, 201–2; William D. Foulke, address to the Indiana Civil Service Reform Association, October 8, 1886, in William Dudley Foulke Papers (Manuscript Division, Library of Congress); Perry, *Dana*, 142; *Nation*, XXXII (March 24, 1881), 198–9; speech by Godkin, 1894, quoted in Ogden, *Godkin*, II, 184–5; Watson D. Hinckley to Richard T. Ely, November 18, 1877, Ely Papers.

28. Harry J. Carman and Reinhard H. Luthin, *Lincoln and the Patronage* (New York, 1943), ch. 10; Beale, *Critical Year, passim;* Grant, Hayes, Garfield, and Arthur, in Richardson (ed.), *Messages and Papers*, VI, 4063, 4396, 4513–18, 4555–8, 4601–2, 4647–50.

29. Porter (comp.), *Platforms*, 72, 77, 82.

30. Hoogenboom, *Outlawing the Spoils*, ix.

31. Peterson, *Brown*, 159.

32. Sumner to Francis Lieber, May 15, 1864, in Pierce, *Sumner Memoir*, IV, 190–92; A. Bower Sageser, *The First Two Decades of the Pendleton Act: A Study of Civil Service Reform* (Lincoln, Neb., 1935), 14–20; Schurz to William Grosvenor, March 28, 1869 (copy), Schurz Papers; J. G. Rosengarten, *Nation*, VI (May 28, 1868), 425–6. See also Hoogenboom, *Outlawing the Spoils*, 10–12 *et passim.*

33. *Springfield Republican,* January 1, July 9, 10, 1872; Curtis to Higginson, December 29, 1871, Higginson Papers; *Harper's Weekly*, XV (1871), 258; *Nation*, XVI (March 6, 1873), 160–61; Hoogenboom, *Outlawing the Spoils,* chs. VI and VII; Sageser, *Pendleton Act*, 24–30. Eaton offered a flimsy apology for the Grant-Curtis fiasco in the *Journal of Social Science*, VIII (1876), 54–78.

34. Grant to Gen. E. F. Beale, September 9, 1877 (copy), U. S. Grant Papers, Library of Congress.

35. *Nation,* XXXI (July 8, 1880), 24; Curtis W. Garrison (ed.), "Conversations with Hayes: A Biographer's Notes," *Mississippi Valley Historical Review,* XXV (1938), 369–80, esp. 373–4; entry, July 11, 1880, in Williams (ed.), *Hayes Diary,* III, 609–10.

36. Citizens Association, *Reform in New York City* (New York, n.d.), 5–12; "Minutes, etc.," I, Reform Club; New York Civil Service Reform Association, *Purposes of the Civil Service Reform Association* (New York, 1882); Hoogenboom, *Outlawing the Spoils,* 186ff.; Carl R. Fish, *Civil Service and Patronage* (New York, 1905), 210ff.; Frank M. Stewart, *The National Civil Service Reform League: History, Activities, and Problems* (Austin, Texas, 1929), 23–7.

37. Stewart, *Reform League,* 9–12; Norton to Curtis, January 17, 1881, Norton Papers.

38. Roosevelt to Lodge, December 27, 1888, Roosevelt to Bonaparte, December 21, 1889, in Morison (ed.), *Roosevelt Letters,* I, 151, 207–8; Stewart, *Reform League,* 9–12; Fish, *Civil Service,* 217.

39. Curtis to Arthur Hobart, November 18, 1884, Edes Papers; Curtis to Foulke, January 14, 1885, Foulke Papers; *Nation,* XXXIX (November 13, 20, 27, 1884), 413–14, 432, 452; XLI (September 10, 1885), 252–3; Howe, *Storey,* 178–9.

40. Cleveland to Wilson S. Bissell, September 24, 1885, Cleveland to Easton, September 11, 1885, in Nevins (ed.), *Cleveland Letters,* 74–5, 78–9; Wells to Bowker, 1885, Bowker Papers; Address, September 10, 1892, in William Dudley Foulke Papers, Library of Congress; Fish, *Civil Service,* 222; Merrill, *Bourbon Leader,* 91–101.

41. Schurz to George Fred. Williams, November 23, 1884, Schurz to Cleveland, November 15, December 10, 1884; March 26, June 25, 1885; January 16, December 15, 1886, Charles R. Codman to Schurz, January 31, 1887, Schurz to Codman, February 3, 1887, in Bancroft (ed.), *Schurz,* IV, 288–90, 293, 297–304, 364–6, 401–4, 414–18, 463–77; Storey to Cleveland, 1885, quoted in Howe, *Storey,* 179–80; Norton to Curtis, February 27, 1887, Norton Papers; Cleveland to Eaton, September 11, 1885, Cleveland to Wilson S. Bissell, September 24, 1885, Cleveland to Silas W. Burt, November 8, 1885, in Nevins (ed.), *Cleveland Letters,* 74–5, 78–9, 93–5.

42. Wells to Atkinson, February 10, 1891, Atkinson Papers; Charles C. Nott to Godkin, January 19, 1887, Godkin Papers; Thomas F. Bayard to Schurz, May 8, 1886, in Bancroft (ed.), *Schurz,* IV, 439–42.

43. Garrison to William Roscoe Thayer, January 30, 1892, in J. H. McDaniels (ed.), *Letters and Literary Memorials of Wendell Phillips Garrison* (Boston and New York, 1909), 16; Schurz to Thaddeus C.

Pound, September 18, 1888, in Bancroft (ed.), *Schurz*, IV, 510–28; Lodge Diary, December 20, 1890; *Nation*, LV (November 24, 1892), 384.

44. Roosevelt to Lodge, June 24, 29, July 1, 6, 11, 1889, in Morison (ed.), *Roosevelt Letters*, I, 166–72; Roosevelt, *Autobiography*, 144ff. (in which he refers to civil service reform as "applied idealism"); Malin, "Roosevelt . . . 1884 and 1888," 38; Sageser, *Pendleton Act*, 141–3.

45. Schurz to Cleveland, March 30, April 10, 1893, in Bancroft (ed.), *Schurz*, V, 134–7, 139–42; *Nation*, LV (November 24, 1892), 384; LVII (September 29, 1893), 262.

46. Fish, *Civil Service*, 222; Schurz, "Grover Cleveland's Second Administration," speech, 1897, in Bancroft (ed.), *Schurz*, V, 342–73; *Nation*, LXIV (March 2, 1897), 156–7; Storey to William H. Moody, December 27, 1897, in Howe, *Storey*, 211–13.

47. Curtis, Introduction to Dorman B. Eaton, *Civil Service in Great Britain* (New York, 1880), v–vi; James A. Hamilton, *Nation*, II (April 26, 1866), 522–4; Andrew D. White, "Do the Spoils Belong to the Victor?" *North American Review*, CXXXIV (1882), 111–33; Godkin, "The Civil Service Reform Controversy," ibid. 379–94; Goldman, *Bonaparte*, 21–2; William Dudley Foulke, *Fighting the Spoilsmen* (New York, 1919), 6; Keller and Davie (eds.), *Sumner Essays*, II, 323; Stewart, *Reform League*, 84–5.

48. Roosevelt, in his *Autobiography*, 162–4, lashed out at the petty meanness of many civil service reformers and derided them for their snobbish ways. But in the 1870's and early 1880's, at least, he displayed many of the same characteristics that he deplored later in other reformers.

CHAPTER 10   THE POLITICS OF NOSTALGIA

1. Godkin to Norton, November 29, 1898, Norton Papers.
2. *The Liberal Imagination: Essays on Literature and Society* (New York, 1950), *passim*.

Bibliography

This bibliography is a selective list of manuscript collections, newspapers, periodicals, and contemporary books and pamphlets containing source materials that were most useful to me in studying the liberal reformers and their opponents. Liberals wrote extensively for *Atlantic Monthly, Forum, Harper's Weekly, Independent, Journal of Social Science, Nation,* and *North American Review.* Because almost every issue of these periodicals contains pertinent articles, I have contented myself with listing the periodicals only, rather than specific articles by specific authors. A wealth of secondary works aided me, as did a number of government publications. Because the most important of these are cited in the footnotes, often with comments, I have refrained from listing them again here.

MANUSCRIPT MATERIALS

Thomas Bailey Aldrich Papers. Houghton Library, Harvard University.
Ethan Allen Papers. New York Public Library.
John A. Andrews Papers. Massachusetts Historical Society.
Edward Atkinson Papers. Massachusetts Historical Society.
Edward Atkinson Papers. New York Public Library.
George Bancroft Papers. Massachusetts Historical Society.
Charles Henry Barrows Papers. Houghton Library, Harvard University.
Edward Bellamy Papers. Houghton Library, Harvard University.
Henry W. Bellows Papers. Massachusetts Historical Society.

John Bigelow Diary, 1843–1911. New York Public Library.

Richard Rogers Bowker Diaries and Papers. New York Public Library.

Benjamin H. Bristow Papers. Manuscipts Division, Library of Congress.

Silas W. Burt, Notes and Clippings on Civil Service. New York Public Library.

Roscoe Conkling Papers. Manuscripts Division, Library of Congress.

Peter Cooper Papers. Cooper Union Library, New York.

George William Curtis Papers and Scrapbooks. Houghton Library, Harvard University.

George William Curtis Papers. Staten Island Institute of Arts and Sciences, New York.

Richard Henry Dana Papers. Massachusetts Historical Society.

Henry H. Edes Papers. Massachusetts Historical Society.

Richard T. Ely Papers. State Historical Society of Wisconsin, Madison.

William E. Endicott Papers. Massachusetts Historical Society.

Bishop Samuel Fallows Papers. State Historical Society of Wisconsin, Madison.

Charles James Folger Papers. New York Public Library.

Gordon Lester Ford and Worthington C. Ford Correspondence with David Ames Wells. New York Public Library.

William Dudley Foulke Papers. Manuscripts Division, Library of Congress.

Garrison Family Papers. Houghton Library, Harvard University.

William Lloyd Garrison Papers. Boston Public Library.

William Lloyd Garrison Papers. Massachusetts Historical Society.

Joshua Reed Giddings-George Washington Julian Papers (on microfilm). University of California Library, Berkeley.

Richard Watson Gilder Papers. New York Public Library.

Edwin Lawrence Godkin Papers. Houghton Library, Harvard University.

Edwin Lawrence Godkin Papers. New York Public Library.

Ulysses S. Grant Letterbooks. Manuscripts Division, Library of Congress.

Horace Greeley Papers. New York Public Library.

Horace Greeley-Schuyler Colfax Papers. New York Public Library.

John Taylor Hall Papers. New York Public Library.

Rutherford B. Hayes Papers. Manuscripts Division, Library of Congress.

Rutherford B. Hayes Diaries, Scrapbooks, and Papers. Rutherford B. Hayes Memorial Library and Museum, Fremont, Ohio.

Thomas Wentworth Higginson Papers. Houghton Library, Harvard University.

Tom L. Johnson Papers. Western Reserve Historical Society, Cleveland.

George C. Jones Papers. New York Public Library.

Samuel M. Jones Scrapbook. Toledo Public Library.

George Washington Julian Papers and Diary (on microfilm). University of California Library, Berkeley.

Labor and Liberalism Collection. State Historical Society of Wisconsin, Madison.

Amos A. Lawrence Papers. Massachusetts Historical Society.

Henry Demarest Lloyd Papers. State Historical Society of Wisconsin, Madison.

Henry Cabot Lodge Papers and Diary. Massachusetts Historical Society.

John D. Long Papers. Massachusetts Historical Society.

Joseph P. McDonnell Papers. State Historical Society of Wisconsin, Madison.

Levi Parsons Morton Papers. New York Public Library.

New York City Reform Club Papers. New York Public Library.

Otis Norcross Papers. Massachusetts Historical Society.

Charles Nordhoff Papers. New York Public Library.

Charles Eliot Norton Papers. Houghton Library, Harvard University.

Edward W. Ordway Papers. New York Public Library.

Henry J. Raymond Papers. New York Public Library.

Edward H. Rogers Papers. State Historical Society of Wisconsin, Madison.

James Frances Ruggles Papers. New York Public Library.

Samuel Bulkely Ruggles Papers. New York Public Library.

Carl Schurz Papers. Manuscripts Division, Library of Congress.

Carl Schurz Papers. New York Public Library.

A. T. Stewart Papers. New York Public Library.

Moorfield Storey Papers. Manuscripts Division, Library of Congress.

Charles Sumner Papers. Houghton Library, Harvard University.

Samuel J. Tilden Papers. New York Public Library.

Lyman Trumbull Papers. Manuscripts Division, Library of Congress.

Henry Villard Papers. Houghton Library, Harvard University.

David Ames Wells Papers. Manuscripts Division, Library of Congress.

David Ames Wells Papers. New York Public Library.

NEWSPAPERS

Albany Argus
Boston Evening Transcript
[Boston] *Liberator*
Brooklyn Daily Eagle

Chicago Tribune
Cincinnati Commercial
Cincinnati Inquirer
Cleveland Plain Dealer
Louisville Courier-Journal
[New York] *Commercial Advertiser*
[New York] *Evening Post*
New York Herald
New York Journal
[New York] *Standard*
New York Sun
The New York Times
New York Tribune
New York World
Springfield Republican

CONTEMPORARY PERIODICALS

Andover Review
Appleton's Journal
Arena
Atlantic Monthly
Bookman
Century Magazine
Civil Service Record [1881–1892; Boston Civil Service Reform Association]
Commercial and Financial Chronicle
Dial
Forum
Good Government [1892–present; National Civil Service Reform League]
Harper's Monthly Magazine
Harper's Weekly
Harvard Graduates' Magazine
Independent
International Review
Journal of Social Science
Littell's Living Age
McClure's Magazine
The Nation
New Princeton Review
North American Review

Scribner's Magazine
Scribner's Monthly
Sound Currency [1894–1905; New York Reform Club]
Tariff Reform [1891–1892; New York Reform Club]
Unitarian Review
Williams Quarterly

CONTEMPORARY BOOKS, ARTICLES, AND PAMPHLETS

Adams, Brooks, *The Law of Civilization and Decay.* New York, 1895.
Adams, Charles Francis, Jr., *An Autobiography, 1835–1915.* Boston and New York, 1916.
Adams, Charles Francis, Jr., and Henry Adams, *Chapters of Erie.* Ithaca, N.Y., 1956.
Adams, Charles Kendall, *The Limitations of Reform.* Madison, Wis., 1894.
Adams, Henry, *The Degradation of the Democratic Dogma.* New York, 1919.
——, *The Education of Henry Adams.* Boston and New York, 1918.
Allen, Stephen Merrill, *The Old and New Republican Parties.* Boston, 1880.
Altgeld, John P., *Live Questions.* Chicago, 1899.
American Free Trade League, *Free Trade Almanac.* Boston, 1902–3.
Andrews, Christopher C., *Administrative Reform as an Issue in the Next Presidential Canvass.* Cambridge, Mass., 1888.
Atkinson, Edward, *Industrial Exhibitions.* Boston, 1882.
——, *Labor and Capital, Allies Not Enemies.* New York, 1879.
——, *Revenue Reform.* Boston, 1871.
——, *The Science of Nutrition; also The Art of Cooking in the Aladdin Oven, with Directions and Many Recipes.* Boston, 1892.
——, *Taxation and Work.* New York, 1892.
Bancroft, Frederic (ed.), *Speeches, Correspondence, and Political Papers of Carl Schurz.* 6 vols. New York, 1913.
Barns, William E. (ed.), *The Labor Problem: Plain Questions and Practical Answers.* New York, 1886.
Barrows, Samuel J., *Municipal Reform.* New York, 1888.
Beale, Harriet S. Blaine (ed.), *Letters of Mrs. James G. Blaine.* 2 vols. New York, 1908.
Bellows, Henry W., *Civil Service Reform.* New York, 1877.
Belmont, Perry, *An American Democrat: The Recollections of Perry Belmont.* New York, 1940.

Bernard, George S., *Civil Service Reform versus the Spoils System*. New York, 1885.

Bigelow, John (ed.), *The Letters and Literary Memorials of Samuel J. Tilden*. 2 vols. New York, 1908.

Blaine, James G., *Political Discussions: Legislative, Diplomatic and Popular*. Norwich, Conn., 1887.

———, *Twenty Years of Congress: from Lincoln to Garfield*. 2 vols. Norwich, Conn., 1884–86.

Boston Reform League, *Broadside No. 1*. Boston, 1869.

Boutwell, George S., *Reminiscences of Sixty Years in Public Affairs*. 2 vols. New York, 1902.

Bowen, Francis, *American Political Economy*. New York, 1870.

Brace, Charles Loring, *The Dangerous Classes of New York and Twenty Years' Work Among Them*. New York, 1872.

Breen, Matthew P., *Thirty Years of New York Politics, Up-to-Date*. New York, 1899.

Brinkerhoff, Roeliff, *Recollections of a Lifetime*. Cincinnati, 1904.

Brown, Willard, *Civil Service Reform in the New York Customs House*. New York, 1882.

Bryce, James, *The American Commonwealth*. 2 vols. New York, 1888; 3rd edn., New York, 1906.

Buckman, B. E., *Samuel J. Tilden Unmasked!* New York, 1876.

Bullock, Charles J., *Essays on the Monetary History of the United States*. New York, 1900.

Burns, W. F., *The Pullman Boycott: A Complete History of the Great R.R. Strike*. St. Paul, Minn., 1894.

Butler, Benjamin F., *Autobiography and Personal Reminiscences of Major-General Benj. F. Butler: Butler's Book*. Boston, 1892.

Butts, Isaac, *Protection and Free Trade*. New York, 1875.

Carey, Henry C., *Miscellaneous Works*. Philadelphia, 1875.

———, *Principles of Social Science*. 3 vols. Philadelphia, 1858–59.

Carnegie, Andrew, *Autobiography*. Boston, 1920.

———, *Triumphant Democracy*. New York, 1886.

Carwardine, William H., *The Pullman Strike*. Chicago, 1894.

Cater, Harold D. (ed.), *Henry Adams and His Friends: A Collection of His Unpublished Letters*. Boston, 1947.

Chamberlin, Everett, *The Struggle of '72*. Chicago, 1872.

Choate, Joseph H., *Addresses in Memory of Carl Schurz*. New York, 1906.

Citizens Association of New York, *Appeal Against Abuses*. New York, 1866.

City Club of New York, *Annual Report . . . 1894*. New York, 1894.

City Club of New York, *Annual Report . . . 1895.* New York, 1895.

———, *Monthly Bulletin No. 9.* New York, 1896.

———, *Publication No. 1.* New York, n.d.

———, *What the City Club Has Done.* New York, n.d.

Clarke, Grace Julian (ed.), *Later Speeches of George W. Julian on Political Questions.* Indianapolis, Ind., 1889.

Clarke, William H., *The Civil Service Law: a Defense of Its Principles.* New York, 1888.

Clemens, Cyril (ed.), *Washington in 1868.* Webster Groves, Mo., 1943.

Clemens, Samuel L., *Mark Twain's Sketches, New and Old.* Hartford, Conn., 1875.

Clemens, Samuel L., and Charles Dudley Warner, *The Gilded Age.* Hartford, Conn., 1873.

Cleveland, Grover, *Presidential Problems.* New York, 1904.

———, *The Self-Made Man in American Life.* New York, 1897.

Codman, John, *Shipping Subsidies and Bounties.* New York Reform Club Series, No. 7, 1889.

Commons, John R., *Myself.* New York, 1934.

Cox, Samuel S., *Three Decades of Federal Legislation, 1855 to 1885.* San Francisco, 1885.

Curran, Henry H., *City Club of New York.* New York, 1906.

Curtis, George William, *From the Easy Chair.* 1st series, New York, 1900.

———, *The Life, Character and Writings of William Cullen Bryant.* New York [1879].

———, *Party and Patronage.* New York, 1892.

———, *The Situation.* New York: National Civil Service Reform League, 1886.

———, *Wendell Phillips, A Eulogy.* New York, 1884.

Dacus, Joseph A., *Annals of the Great Strikes in the United States.* Chicago, 1877.

Denslow, Van Buren, *Freedom in Trade.* Cambridge, Mass., 1882.

Depew, Chauncey M., *My Memories of Eighty Years.* New York, 1922.

Devlin, Thomas F., *Municipal Reform in the United States.* New York, 1896.

De Voto, Bernard (ed.), *Mark Twain in Eruption.* New York, 1940.

Dewees, Francis P., *The Molly Maguires.* Philadelphia, 1877.

Earle, A. L., *Our Revenue System and the Civil Service.* New York, 1872.

Eaton, Dorman B., *Civil Service in Great Britain: A History of Abuses and Reforms and Their Bearing upon American Politics.* Introduction by George William Curtis. New York, 1880.

———, *The Government of Municipalities.* New York, 1899.

———, *Secret Sessions of the Senate.* New York, 1886.

———, *The Term and Tenure of Office.* New York, 1881.

Edgar, George P. (comp.), *Gems of the Campaign of 1880. By Generals Grant and Garfield.* Jersey City, N.J., 1881.

Eldridge, Benjamin P., *Our Rival, the Rascal.* Boston, 1897.

Ely, Richard F., *Ground Under Our Feet: An Autobiography.* New York, 1938.

———, *The Labor Movement in America.* New York, 1886.

———, *The Past and Present of Political Economy.* Baltimore, 1884.

———, *Problems of Today.* New York, 1888.

———, *Recent American Socialism.* Baltimore, 1887.

———, *Social Aspects of Christianity.* New York, 1889.

———, *Socialism: An Examination of Its Nature, Its Strength and Its Weakness, With Suggestions for Social Reform.* New York, 1894.

———, *The Social Law of Service.* New York, 1896.

Emerson, Edward Waldo (ed.), *The Early Years of the Saturday Club, 1855–1870.* Boston and New York, 1918.

Executive Committee of Citizens and Taxpayers, *Appeal for Reform.* New York, n.d.

Field, David Dudley, *Some Reprehensible Practices of American Government.* New York Reform Club Series, No. 8, 1890.

Flower, Benjamin O., *Progressive Men, Women and Movements of the Past Twenty-Five Years.* Boston, 1914.

Foraker, Joseph B., *Notes of a Busy Life.* 2 vols. Cincinnati, 1916–17.

[Forbes, John Murray], *Fossils in re Free Ships and Reform of Tariff and Civil Service.* Boston, [1890].

Ford, Worthington C. (ed.), *A Cycle of Adams Letters, 1861–65.* 2 vols. Boston and New York, 1920.

———, *Letters of Henry Adams (1858–1891).* 2 vols. Boston and New York, 1930.

Foster, William E., *The Civil Service Reform Movement.* Boston, 1882.

Foulke, William Dudley, *Fighting the Spoilsmen: Reminiscences of the Civil Service Reform Movement.* New York and London, 1919.

———, *A Hoosier Autobiography.* New York, 1922.

Furber, H. W. (ed.), *Both Protection and Free Trade.* Boston, 1888.

Garrison, Curtis W. (ed.), "Conversations with Hayes: A Biographer's Notes," *Mississippi Valley Historical Review,* XXV (1938), 369–80.

Garrison, Wendell P., and Francis J. Garrison, *William Lloyd Garrison, 1805–1879.* 4 vols. New York, 1885–1889.

George, Henry, *Protection or Free Trade*. New York, 1886.

Gilder, Richard W., *Grover Cleveland: A Record of Friendship*. New York, 1910.

Gladden, Washington, *The Cosmopolis City Club*. New York, 1893.

———, *Recollections*. Boston, 1909.

———, *Ruling Ideas of the Present Age*. Boston, 1895.

Godkin, Edwin L., *Problems of Modern Democracy*. New York, 1896.

———, *Reflections and Comments, 1865–1895*. New York, 1896.

———, *Unforeseen Tendencies of Democracy*. Boston, 1898.

Godwin, Parke, *A Biography of William Cullen Bryant*. 2 vols. New York, 1883.

Grant, Ulysses S., *Personal Memoirs of U. S. Grant*. 2 vols. New York, 1885–86.

Greeley, Horace, *Hints toward Reform*. New York, 1850; 2nd edn., New York, 1857.

———, *Recollections of a Busy Life*. New York, 1868.

Grosvenor, William M., *Does Protection Protect?* New York, 1871.

———, *Trades Unions*. n.p., 1885.

Halloran, Matthew F., *The Romance of the Merit System: Forty-Five Years' Reminiscences of the Civil Service*. 2nd edn., Washington, D.C., 1929.

Hamilton, Gail [Mary Abigail Dodge], *Biography of James G. Blaine*. Norwich, Conn., 1895.

Hauser, Elizabeth J. (ed.), *Tom L. Johnson: My Story*. New York, 1911.

Higginson, Mary Thacker (ed.), *Letters and Journals of Thomas Wentworth Higginson, 1846–1906*. Boston and New York, 1921.

Higginson, Thomas Wentworth, *Common Sense About Women*. Boston, 1882.

———, *Contemporaries*. Boston, 1899.

———, *Part of a Man's Life*. Boston, 1905.

———, *Wendell Phillips*. Boston, 1884.

Hinsdale, Burke A. (ed.), *Works of James Abram Garfield*. 2 vols. Boston, 1882–83.

Hinsdale, Mary L. (ed.), *Garfield-Hinsdale Letters: Correspondence Between James Abram Garfield and Burke Aaron Hinsdale*. Ann Arbor, Mich., 1949.

Hoar, George Frisbie, *Autobiography of Seventy Years*. 2 vols. New York, 1903.

Howe, Frederic C., *Confessions of a Reformer*. New York, 1925.

Howe, George F. (ed.), "President Hayes's Notes of Four Cabinet Meetings," *American Historical Review*, XXXVII (1932), 286–9.

Howe, Julia Ward, *Reminiscences, 1819–1899*. Boston, 1899.

Howe, Mark A. DeWolfe (ed.), *Later Years of the Saturday Club, 1870–1920*. Boston and New York, 1927.

Howells, Mildred (ed.), *The Life in Letters of William Dean Howells*. 2 vols. New York, 1928.

Howells, William Dean, *Impressions and Experiences*. New York, 1896.

———, *Literary Friends and Acquaintances: A Personal Retrospect of American Authorship*. New York, 1900.

———, *My Mark Twain*. New York, 1910.

———, *Sketch of the Life and Character of Rutherford B. Hayes (etc.)*. Boston, 1876.

———, (ed.), *Mark Twain's Speeches*. New York, 1910.

Hudson, William C., *Random Recollections of an Old Political Reporter*. New York, 1911.

Hughes, Sarah Forbes (ed.), *Letters and Recollections of John Murray Forbes*. 2 vols. Boston and New York, 1899.

International Free Trade Alliance, *Our Revenue System and the Civil Service*. New York, n.d.

Jones, Samuel M., *The New Right*. New York, 1899.

Julian, George Washington, *Political Recollections, 1840 to 1872*. Chicago, 1884.

———, *Speeches on Political Questions*. New York, 1872.

Junius [pseudonym], *The Civil Service Sham*. Washington, 1886.

Keller, Albert G. and Maurice R. Davie (eds.), *Essays of William Graham Sumner*. 2 vols. New Haven, Conn., 1934.

Kelley, William D., *Speeches, Addresses and Letters on Industrial and Financial Questions*. Philadelphia, 1872.

Lambert, Henry, *The Progress of Civil Service Reform in the United States*. Boston, 1885.

Lang, Louis J. (ed.), *The Autobiography of Thomas Collier Platt*. New York, 1910.

Lieber, Francis, *Notes on Fallacies Peculiar to American Protectionists*. New York, 1869.

Lodge, Henry Cabot, *Historical and Political Essays*. Boston, 1892.

———, *Speeches and Addresses, 1884–1909*. Boston, 1909.

———, (ed.), *Selections from the Correspondence of Theodore Roosevelt and Henry Cabot Lodge, 1884–1918*. 2 vols. New York, 1925.

Long, John D. (ed.), *The Republican Party: Its History, Principles, and Policies*. Chicago, 1888.

Low, Seth, *Tariff Reform in the Present Canvass*. New York Reform Club Series, No. 4, 1888.

Low, Seth, *Why We Must Solve the Municipal Problem.* New York, n.d.

Lowell, James Russell, *The Independent in Politics.* New York Reform Club Series, No. 1, 1888.

McCabe, James D., *Behind the Scenes in Washington.* New York, 1873.

———, *History of the Great Riots.* Philadelphia, 1877.

McClure, Alexander K., *Recollections of Half a Century.* Salem, Mass., 1902.

McCulloch, Hugh, *Men and Measures of Half a Century.* New York, 1888.

McDaniels, J. H. (ed.), *Letters and Memorials of Wendell Phillips Garrison.* Boston and New York, 1909.

McNeill, George E. (ed.), *The Labor Movement: The Problem of To-Day.* Boston, 1887.

Massachusetts Reform Club, *Reports* and *Pamphlets.* Boston, 1889–90.

Mayo, Lawrence Shaw (ed.), *America of Yesterday, as Reflected in the Journal of John Davis Long.* Boston, 1923.

Merriam, George S., *The Life and Times of Samuel Bowles.* 2 vols. New York, 1885.

Miller, J. B., *The Unconstitutionality of a Tariff for Protection Only.* New York Reform Club Series, No. 5, 1889.

Moore, Joseph S., *The Champion Tariff Swindle of the World.* New York, 1888.

———, *The Parsee Letters; Addressed to Horace Greeley.* New York, 1869.

Morison, Elting E. (ed.), *The Letters of Theodore Roosevelt.* 8 vols. Cambridge, Mass., 1951–54.

National Civil Service Reform League, *Minutes of the Executive Committee.* New York, 1884.

———, *Proceedings.* New York, 1881.

Nevins, Allan (ed.), *The Letters and Journal of Brand Whitlock.* New York, 1936.

———, (ed.), *Letters of Grover Cleveland.* Boston and New York, 1933.

Nevins, Allan, and Milton Halsey Thomas (eds.), *The Diary of George Templeton Strong.* 4 vols. New York, 1952.

New York Civil Service Reform Association, *List of Members of the Civil Service Reform Association.* New York, 1881.

———, *Primer of Civil Service Reform.* New York, n.d.

———, *Purposes of the Civil Service Reform Association.* New York, 1882.

———, *Report of the Executive Committee.* New York, 1881–95.

New York *Evening Post, Mr. Blaine and the Little Rock and Fort Smith Railroad.* New York, 1884.

————, *Mr. Blaine's Railroad Transactions . . . Including All the Mulligan Letters*. New York, 1884.

New York Reform Club, *General Descriptions, etc.* New York, 1889.

————, *The Logic of Protection*. New York, n.d.

————, *Officers and Committees, Members, Constitution, By-Laws, Rules.* New York, 1888–1913.

————, *True or False Finance*. New York Reform Club Series, No. 3, 1888.

Norton, Charles Eliot (ed.), *Letters of James Russell Lowell*. 2 vols. New York, 1894.

————, (ed.), *Orations and Addresses of George William Curtis*. 3 vols. New York, 1894.

Norton, Sara, and M. A. DeWolfe Howe (eds.), *Letters of Charles Eliot Norton*. 2 vols. Boston and New York, 1913.

Noyes, Alexander D., *Thirty Years of American Finance*. New York, 1902.

Ogden, Rollo, *Life and Letters of Edwin Lawrence Godkin*. 2 vols. New York, 1907.

Paine, Albert Bigelow (ed.), *Mark Twain's Autobiography*. 2 vols. New York, 1924.

————, (ed.), *Mark Twain's Letters*. 2 vols. New York, 1917.

————, (ed.), *Mark Twain's Notebook*. New York, 1935.

————, (ed.), *Mark Twain's Speeches*. New York, 1923.

Parker, George F. (ed.), *The Writings and Speeches of Grover Cleveland*. New York, 1892.

Parkhurst, Charles H., *Our Fight With Tammany*. New York, 1895.

Peck, Harry T., *Twenty Years of the Republic, 1885–1905*. London, 1906.

Perry, Arthur Latham, *Elements of Political Economy*. New York, 1865; 13th edn., New York, 1875.

Personal Representation Society, *Annual Report*. New York, 1867.

Pierce, Edward L. (ed.), *Memoir and Letters of Charles Sumner*. 4 vols. Boston, 1878–93.

Poore, Ben Perley, *Reminiscences of Sixty Years in the National Metropolis*. 2 vols. Philadelphia, 1886.

Powell, Aaron M., *Annual Report of The Reform League*. New York, 1871.

Prentiss, George L., *The National Crisis*. New York, 1862.

————, *Our National Bane; or, the Dry Rot in American Politics*. New York, 1877.

The Reform Movement; A National Convention Called to Meet at Cincinnati, May 1, 1872. Washington, D.C., 1872.

Richards, Laura E. (ed.), *Letters and Journals of Samuel Gridley Howe.* 2 vols. Boston, 1909.

Roosevelt, Theodore, *American Ideals, and Other Essays, Social and Political.* New York, 1897.

———, *An Autobiography.* New York, 1913.

———, *Letters to Anna Roosevelt Cowles, 1870–1918.* New York, 1924.

———, *Works.* 24 vols. New York, 1923–26.

Salter, William, *The Life of James W. Grimes.* New York, 1876.

Sanborn, Franklin B., *Recollections of Seventy Years.* Boston, 1909.

Sargent, Mrs. John F. (ed.), *Sketches and Reminiscences of the Radical Club of Chestnut Street, Boston.* Boston, 1880.

Schafer, Joseph (ed.), *Intimate Letters of Carl Schurz, 1841–1869.* Madison, 1928.

Schurz, Carl, *Civil-service Reform and Democracy.* New York, 1893.

———, *Honest Money and Labor.* New York, 1879.

———, *The Necessity and Progress of Civil Service Reform.* New York, 1894.

———, *The Reminiscences of Carl Schurz.* 3 vols. New York, 1907–8.

Seymour, Horatio W., *Government and Co., Limited; An Examination of the Tendencies of Privilege in the U.S.* Chicago, 1895.

Shaw, Albert (ed.), *The National Revenues.* Chicago, 1888.

Sherman, John, *Recollections of Forty Years in the House, Senate and Cabinet.* 2 vols. Chicago, 1895.

Sherman, Porter, *A Tariff Primer.* New York, 1891.

Storey, Moorfield, *Address to the Independent Voters of Massachusetts.* Boston, 1886.

———, *The Democratic Party and Civil-Service Reform.* New York, 1897.

———, *Politics as a Duty and as a Career.* New York, 1889.

———, *The Purposes and Work of the Massachusetts Reform Club.* Boston, 1900.

———, *The Record of Benjamin F. Butler.* Boston, 1883.

Sumner, William Graham, *Lectures on the History of Protection in the United States.* New York, 1881.

———, *Protection and Revenue in 1877.* New York, 1878.

———, *Protectionism: the Ism Which Teaches that Waste Makes Wealth.* New York, 1885.

Taussig, Frank W., *Protection to Young Industries as Applied in the United States.* New York, 1886.

———, (ed.), *State Papers and Speeches on the Tariff.* Cambridge, 1893.

Trumbull, Lyman, "Correspondence," *Mississippi Valley Historical Review,* I (1914), 101–8.

Volwiler, Albert T. (ed.), *The Correspondence Between Benjamin Harrison and James G. Blaine, 1882–1893*. Philadelphia, 1940.

Walker, Amasa, *The Science of Wealth*. Philadelphia, 1872.

Warner, Charles Dudley, *Complete Writings of Charles Dudley Warner*. 15 vols. Hartford, Conn., 1904.

Watterson, Henry, *"Marse Henry": An Autobiography*. 2 vols. New York, 1919.

Welch, F. G., *That Convention; or, Five Days a Politician*. New York, 1872.

Wells, David Ames, *The Creed of Free Trade*. Boston, 1875.

——, *The Decay of Our Ocean Mercantile Marine*. New York Reform Club Series, No. 6, 1889.

——, *Freer Trade Essential to Future National Prosperity and Development*. New York, 1882.

——, *Practical Economics*. New York, 1885.

——, *Recent Economic Changes*. New York, 1890.

Wheeler, Everett P., *Sixty Years of American Life*. New York, 1917.

White, Horace, *The Life of Lyman Trumbull*. Boston and New York, 1913.

Williams, Charles R. (ed.), *Diary and Letters of Rutherford Birchard Hayes*. 5 vols. Columbus, Ohio, 1922–26.

Index